On State Secession from International Law Perspectives

Jing Lu

On State Secession from International Law Perspectives

Springer

Jing Lu
School of Law
Sun Yat-sen University
Guangzhou, China

ISBN 978-3-030-07357-2 ISBN 978-3-319-97448-4 (eBook)
https://doi.org/10.1007/978-3-319-97448-4

Softcover re-print of the Hardcover 1st edition 2018

This Springer imprint is published by the registered company Springer Nature Switzerland AG
The registered company address is: Gewerbestrasse 11, 6330 Cham, Switzerland

Preface

This book entitled *On State Secession from International Law Perspectives* is a dissertation submitted to and accepted by the Faculty of Law of the University of Regensburg for a doctoral degree in the summer term 2018.

The motive for this research can be traced back to the time I saw the NATO bombing of Yugoslavia on TV: although at that time I knew nothing about international law, I was pretty sure that such military action should be considered from the perspective of international law. I feel so blessed that I have completed this research, which deals with the issue of secession from various perspectives of international law, including not only the use of force.

This piece of work is dedicated to my parents, whose constant support has been indispensable for the completion of the dissertation. Besides, I want to express my sincere gratitude to my supervisor, Professor Robert Uerpmann-Wittzack, whose valuable instructions help me greatly in developing my understanding of international law. I am also grateful to Professor Alexander Graser, the second evaluator of my dissertation, whose course is a source of inspiration for me.

During the writing process I have been awarded a scholarship for outstanding self-financed students abroad from China Scholarship Council and a scholarship aimed at promoting gender equality in research and teaching from the University of Regensburg. I need to thank these institutions not only because they have eased my financial burden but also because they have given me strong encouragement by granting scholarships to me.

Any errors and omissions are my responsibility. Special thanks go to those who work on the publication of this dissertation.

Guangzhou, China
June 2018

Jing Lu

Contents

Chapter 1
Introduction

1.1 Secession as a Multi-Dimensional International Legal Problem

In order to effectively settle secessionist conflicts, it is necessary to recognize the nature of secession as a multi-dimensional international legal problem in the first place. Unfortunately, many focus only on some dimensions while, inadvertently or not, ignoring other dimensions of this issue. Needless to say, human rights protection is invariably the most conspicuous dimension of a violent secessionist conflict. To some extent, this is also quite understandable because secessionist conflicts "constituted nearly half of the major violence between states and non-state actors in the 20th century ... they kill more people because they are more frequent and tend to last much longer than interstate wars."[1] In this sense, it is not wrong to say that the settlement of secessionist conflicts should be based on the protection of human rights. The problem is that many fail to realize that human rights protection in a violent secessionist conflict is not one-sided, only protecting secessionists against state violence; human rights protection in a violent secessionist conflict should be unbiased, namely protecting secessionists against state violence and protecting non-secessionists against violence from armed secessionists. Undeniably, if one focuses only on protecting secessionists against state violence but largely ignores the protection of non-secessionists against violence from armed secessionists, one can hardly contribute to the settlement of a secessionist conflict in a positive way.

Closely related to the protection of human rights is the right to self-determination. Similarly, the promotion of self-determination is not one-sided either: if secessionist self-determination is recognized, non-secessionist self-determination should also be recognized. Therefore, any secessionist conflict is, in essence, a conflict of self-determination between secessionists and non-secessionists. Many see a secessionist conflict as a conflict between self-determination and sovereignty instead of

[1] Coggins (2011), p. 35.

J. Lu, *On State Secession from International Law Perspectives*,
https://doi.org/10.1007/978-3-319-97448-4_1

conflicting rights to self-determination. Admittedly, treating a secessionist conflict as a conflict between self-determination and sovereignty is not wrong, but it is not as helpful as treating such a conflict as a conflict between conflicting rights to self-determination: after all, it is quite difficult, if not impossible, to judge which side should take precedence from the perspective of international law, when self-determination and sovereignty seem to be in opposition. However, it is relatively clear that both secessionist self-determination and non-secessionist self-determination should be treated equally. More importantly, when a secessionist conflict is treated as a conflict between self-determination and sovereignty, the dimension of non-secessionist self-determination admittedly tends to be overlooked; this is undoubtedly unfair for non-secessionists from a legal point of view. A secessionist conflict, violent or not, cannot be effectively settled if the right to self-determination of non-secessionists has not been fully respected.

Indeed, the dimension of non-secessionist self-determination is closely associated with the distribution of territorial interests. A secessionist conflict is also a struggle over territorial interests between secessionists and non-secessionists. More specifically, secessionists intend to unilaterally transform co-ownership of a particular piece of territory into exclusive ownership on the basis of self-determination, and non-secessionists aim to maintain co-ownership and oppose the unilateral transformation on the same basis. In this sense, one could say that in a secessionist conflict the respect for the right to self-determination has much to do with the respect for territorial interests; a fair distribution of territorial interests between secessionists and non-secessionists is actually an inherent requirement of respecting the right to self-determination. Unfortunately, compared with the dimension of human rights protection, the territorial dimension has not gained sufficient attention, and this neglect is problematic, as it directly hinders the settlement of a conflict, thus influencing the protection of human rights in a secessionist conflict.

The interplay between human rights protection and distribution of territorial interests is also an important but more often than not overlooked dimension of the issue of secession. For this reason, an attack launched by armed secessionists is usually interpreted as resistance against sovereign repression instead of a violent attempt to unilaterally transform co-ownership of a particular piece of territory into exclusive ownership. In the same vein, military action taken by the authorities against secessionists is usually interpreted as sovereign repression against human rights and self-determination rather than defense of territorial co-ownership and non-secessionist self-determination. Needless to say, such interpretation fails to contribute to a fair distribution of territorial interests between secessionists and non-secessionists as it favors secessionists to the detriment of non-secessionists, thus affecting human rights protection. As long as a fair distribution of territorial interests is absent, the attack and defense of territorial interests will not cease and in this process, violations of human rights of both secessionists and non-secessionists will become inevitable. Therefore, it is certainly ill-advised to overlook the interplay between human rights protection and distribution of territorial interests in the settlement of a secessionist conflict.

When it comes to violence, another important dimension of the issue of secession is revealed. This dimension is fairly complicated, as it concerns more than just internal actors of a secessionist conflict, namely secessionists and non-secessionists. External actors are also involved, and their military involvement might become the determinant in the development of a secessionist conflict. In order to have an overall picture of external military involvement in a secessionist conflict, one must first review the general regulations of international law with regard to the use of force. Equally importantly, one must discern whether the external use of force has made a contribution to conflict settlement in practice rather than in theoretical hypotheses. The interplay between internal violence and external violence is also noteworthy: if external violence or the threat of it can actually encourage the intensification of internal violence, external actors participating in a secessionist conflict need to be more cautious about the use of force, whether it is approved by the UN Security Council or not. The problem is that external actors participating in a secessionist conflict do not only consider the effective settlement of the conflict: history and reality show that they also think a good deal about geopolitical interests. External actors might use force in a secessionist conflict not because the use of force is conducive to settling the conflict but because it is in their geopolitical interests.

From this perspective, it is reasonable to argue that geopolitical interests also constitute a dimension of the issue of secession, and it deserves attention in the relevant discussion. Indeed, "all separatist movements operate, expand or shrink in a given and changing geopolitical context. One has to look at geopolitics to understand why some political entities become independent states while others of the same size and importance do not. It is geopolitics that helps us to explain why some secessionist movements are tolerated and others are violently crushed; why some irredentist organizations embrace and others never do."[2] A consideration of geopolitical interests is also especially noteworthy because the effective settlement of a secessionist conflict requires the exclusion of undue interference which can be attributed to the pursuit of geopolitical interests by external actors participating in the secessionist conflict. Undoubtedly, exclusion of undue interference caused by the pursuit of geopolitical interests in secessionist conflicts is largely dependent on the effective application of the current international legal system, although the legal status of geopolitical interests is far from being definite in the current international legal system.

Also related to the participation of external actors in secessionist conflicts, it is necessary to realize that in addition to the use of force, there are also other forms of external participation that deserve serious attention. Not all external participation helps to settle a conflict positively, and there is no reason to condone counterproductive or even detrimental external involvement, even if such counterproductive or detrimental external involvement is not explicitly illegal from the perspective of international law. In this sense, improving external involvement in secessionist conflicts should be regarded as a crucial dimension of the issue of secession,

[2] Malešević and Dochartaigh (2011), p. 232.

although the significance of this point so far has not gained sufficient attention. It is time to pay more attention to external involvement in secessionist conflicts, as counterproductive or even detrimental external involvement can have a rather profound and extensive influence: such involvement in a secessionist conflict can set a precedent, affecting the settlement of other secessionist conflicts on account of the precedential effect. This point becomes more complex when such precedents are followed because they are aligned with the pursuit of geopolitical interests. In addition, counterproductive or even detrimental external involvement can make the conflicting parties more reluctant to cooperate with external actors in conflict settlement. Undeniably, under such circumstances, international cooperation on the peaceful settlement of conflicts, which is advocated by the UN Charter, becomes less likely. For this reason, it is safe to conclude that the pursuit of the aims of the UN requires improved external involvement in secessionist conflicts.

In view of the foregoing, the multi-dimensional nature of the issue of secession is certainly indisputable. The aim of emphasizing secession as a multi-dimensional international legal problem is to reveal that the effective settlement of secessionist conflicts must correspond with their multi-dimensional nature: dimensions including the protection of human rights, self-determination over territorial interests, the use of force and external participation must not be considered in an isolated manner but rather as interrelated facets. The relationships between these dimensions are dynamic rather than static, as "secession was progressive rather than a one-time, clear-cut event"[3] and for this reason, it is ill-advised to overlook any dimension of the issue of secession because overlooking one dimension will affect other dimensions, and finally, this will have an impact on how the whole issue of secession is settled. In short, an approach that focuses on interrelations, development and the whole is required.

1.2 Methodologies

1.2.1 General Methodologies

1.2.1.1 Dialectics

In order to approach the multi-dimensional issue of secession in an interrelated, developed and holistic manner, the dialectic mode of reasoning is well-advised as a methodology in general. Contrary to the metaphysical mode of reasoning, in which objects and processes are observed "in isolation, apart from their connection with the vast whole... in repose, not in motion; as constants, not as essentially variables; in their death, not in their life",[4] in the dialectic mode of reasoning one "comprehends

[3]Thürer and Burri (2009).

[4]Engels (1908), p. 79.

things and their representations, ideas, in their essential connection, concatenation, motion, origin and ending".[5]

Whether intentionally or not, the metaphysical mode of reasoning in addressing the issue of secession is not unusual. To some extent, the commonly applied right-oriented approach is also a reflection of the metaphysical mode of reasoning: the crux of the matter is assumed to be whether there is a legal right to secession, particularly in the unilateral sense; in other words, whether a claim to secession should be recognized according to contemporary international law. Undeniably, there is an element of reasonableness in this idea: rights and duties are standard legal tools for conflict regulation. Nevertheless, one must admit that this idea only works when the settlement of conflict per se has been somewhat standardized from a legal point of view, meaning that, with regard to the rights and duties of conflicting parties, a certain degree of consensus has been established. Unfortunately, such consensus in respect of the rights and duties of conflicting parties in a secessionist conflict, and specifically, the rights and duties of secessionists and non-secessionists, cannot be said to have been established: the divergence of opinions within the international community is invariably noticeable. Therefore, it can be said that applying the right-oriented approach in a secessionist conflict is overlooking the connection between this approach and the standardization of conflict settlement: secessionist conflicts have been confused with other relatively standardized conflicts, in which there is a certain degree of consensus about the mutual rights and duties of conflicting parties from a legal point of view.

Recognizing the connection between the right-oriented approach and the standardization of conflict settlement means that a different approach is required for secessionist conflicts, the settlement of which has not been standardized. In the spirit of dialectics, a conflict-oriented approach is well-advised: the focus of this approach is on how the secessionist conflict can be properly settled rather than whether there is a legal right to secession, particularly in the unilateral sense. Needless to say, compared with the right-oriented approach, the conflict-oriented approach better befits the multi-dimensional nature of the issue of secession: the concern for human rights and self-determination, the fair distribution of territorial interests, violence by internal and external actors, other external involvement during the conflict and the interplay between all these dimensions can be included in the conflict-oriented approach. However, in a right-oriented approach, the same cannot be said: some dimensions, such as a fair distribution of territorial interests between conflicting parties and violence by external actors in support of secessionists, might not be taken into consideration, let alone the interplay between them. In this sense, the right-oriented approach once again reflects the metaphysical mode of reasoning: the origin of secession, namely the distribution of territorial interests, and the motion of secession due to external involvement are largely ignored. Obviously, a metaphysical mode of reasoning tends to underestimate the practical complexity of secessionist conflicts, while the dialectic mode of reasoning can help avoid this problem.

[5]Ibid. pp. 82–83.

In order to render the merits of the conflict-oriented approach inspired by dialectics more understandable, the following points are worth mentioning: firstly, several cases have proven that the settlement of secessionist conflicts is largely dependent on achieving a new balance of interests between secessionists and non-secessionists rather than confirming a static right to secession, particularly in the unilateral sense. The attempted secession of Aceh from Indonesia is a typical case: the violent secessionist conflict ended with a concrete agreement concluded between the conflicting parties. Here, a dynamic negotiating process has replaced the search for a static right to unilateral secession. Of course, a dynamic negotiating process can also lead to a right to consensual secession, as demonstrated in the secession of South Sudan from Sudan. At such time, the right to secession is no longer static and abstract, which cannot help settle practical self-determination conflicts between secessionists and non-secessionists over territorial interests, but becomes a reasonable product of dynamic conflict settlement: the right to secession is based on the agreement concluded between the conflicting parties with regard to a new balance of interests between them, and this right is no longer abstract but clearly defined. Needless to say, a clearly defined right to secession existing in a binding agreement will face fewer challenges than an allegedly abstract one.

Secondly, there is no denying that the development of secessionist conflicts frequently has a lot to do with external involvement, forcible or not. Generally speaking, this interrelation can be better examined under a conflict-oriented approach than a right-oriented approach: under the former one cares about how the interplay between internal actors and external actors would affect conflict settlement, while under the latter one might even fail to realize the existence of such interrelation. Undeniably, overlooking the intricacy of the interplay between different subjects in a secessionist conflict actually renders it less likely for the conflict to be settled in an effective manner: for instance, when "secessionist groups are instigated to actively provoke massive retaliation because they rely on thereby-triggered interventions as decisive help in overcoming the respective states' military, administrative, and financial superiority",[6] such attempts should be frustrated rather than condoned and secessionists should be discouraged from doing so, for the sake of effective conflict settlement. In a right-oriented approach there is not much room to accommodate an analysis of the interplay between internal actors and external actors.

Thirdly, compared with the right-oriented approach, it is obvious that in the conflict-oriented approach the bone of contention is targeted more accurately. Proponents of a right to unilateral secession generally do not argue for an unconditional right to unilateral secession; instead, they usually argue for a right to unilateral secession in a remedial sense: secession is regarded as a remedy to serious human rights violations. Therefore, they simply treat secessionist conflicts as an isolated issue regarding human rights instead of a compound of human rights and territorial interests. In fact, opponents of a right to unilateral secession do not dispute the claim

[6]Janik (2013), pp. 57–58.

to human rights, but they do not think human rights protection can be a reason to ignore the importance of a fair distribution of territorial interests, and they believe that the interrelations between these two aspects should not be misinterpreted. Thus, the real bone of contention is the distribution of territorial interests but not the satisfaction of the human rights claim. Unfortunately, in the right-oriented approach the dimension of territorial interests is usually ignored: this disregard for the territorial interests of non-secessionists caused by a right to unilateral secession has not been taken seriously so the origin of secessionist conflicts is inexplicably reduced to the issue of human rights, as if an unfair distribution of territorial interests would not affect the protection of human rights. This reduction inevitably blurs the true bone of contention, which tends to widen the divergence of opinions between proponents and opponents of a right to unilateral secession. Unlike the right-oriented approach, such reduction does not exist in the conflict-oriented approach, which avoids unnecessary disagreement. Needless to say, minimizing disagreement is a key step towards effective conflict settlement.

Fourthly, compared with the right-oriented approach, the conflict-oriented approach is more effective in preventing abuse of rights. Abuse of a right to unilateral secession is seldom discussed in theory, and this is understandable because the right per se is not universally recognized, so it seems too hasty to consider abuse of such a right. However, in practice this consideration is not hasty at all: cases have demonstrated that secessionists deliberately contributed to humanitarian crises in order to invoke a right to remedial secession. Undeniably, even if a right to remedial secession did exist from a legal point of view, it cannot be understood as granting permission to deliberately provoke humanitarian crises. In this sense, it is meaningful to consider preventing secessionists from abusing an alleged right to remedial secession, despite the notable controversy over this right. Unfortunately, the right-oriented approach is not in a good position to offer a solution: the focus of this approach is on the existence of this right rather than specific problems occurring during the exercise of this right; in the theory of remedial secession, there is no mention of the likelihood of abuse of the right to remedial secession. In short, the right-oriented approach only focuses on the static existence of a right to secession, particularly in the unilateral sense, rather than on the right in motion, namely the practical exercise of this right. In a conflict-oriented approach, such issue will no longer be overlooked because the focus of this approach has shifted from the static existence of a right to secession, particularly in the unilateral sense: this approach focuses on the practical exercise of such a right and avoiding abuse of such a right. After all, abuse of rights itself can lead to or escalate conflicts. On this basis, the conflict-oriented approach that replaces the static right to unilateral secession in theory with a right in practical motion is evidently more advanced.

To sum up, the conflict-oriented approach has brought the discussion regarding the issue of secession closer to secession in practice. This is well-advised as the settlement of this issue has not been standardized to the extent of an abstract right-duty theory. In addition, there is no denying that attempts to apply the right-oriented approach lead to practical problems hindering the effective settlement of secessionist conflicts. Thus, it is reasonable to adopt the conflict-oriented approach, which can avoid those practical problems. Nevertheless, this does not mean that the conflict-oriented approach has totally abandoned basic legal analytical tools such as rights and duties. To the contrary, basic legal analytical tools such as rights and duties still have their place in the conflict-oriented approach, but they do not function as envisioned by proponents of the right to unilateral secession. Further information about this point is to be found in the discussion about legal positivism and natural law.

1.2.1.2 Unity of Deontology and Consequentialism

Clearly, both deontological thinking and consequentialist thinking are embodied in international law and frequently appear in relevant discussion: a classic example of deontological thinking is humanitarian intervention, or the responsibility to protect, while state responsibility or the responsibility of international organizations is a typical expression of consequentialism. To some extent, it is accurate to conclude that, for international law to function effectively, there must be an insistence on the unity of deontology and consequentialism: legally enshrined values must be both the starting point and endpoint for a legal actor. In other words, legal action should be characterized not only by good intentions to uphold enshrined values but also by good outcomes, namely upholding such values in practice. Unquestionably, any action taken with (allegedly) good intentions that fails to bring about a good outcome in practice cannot gain wide acceptance, and when international law condones this kind of action, doubts about the effectiveness of international law become inevitable, in addition to the thorny issue regarding serious damage that may be caused by such action. For this reason, a legal actor certainly needs to make its chosen means compatible with the end it pursues, as misguided means cannot transform good intentions into good outcomes. In short, the unity of deontology and consequentialism requires that the means be compatible with the end, as appropriate means serve as a bridge between good intentions and good outcomes.

In the same vein, the unity of deontology and consequentialism deserves serious attention in the settlement of secessionist conflicts. That is to say, the means adopted to settle a secessionist conflict should be compatible with the end. How should the end here be defined? Many consider the protection of human rights to be the first priority, which is also why remedial secession has been proposed. It would not be wrong to say that the protection of human rights is an end that is pursued in the settlement of secessionist conflicts, but it would definitely be wrong to say that this is the sole end pursued in conflict settlement. As discussed above, the realization of self-determination over territorial interests, the avoidance of violence and the improvement of external involvement are also ends worth pursuing in conflict settlement; in short, it is an overall end to be pursued in the settlement of secessionist conflicts. Therefore, the means adopted to settle a secessionist conflict must be compatible with this overall end, otherwise a good outcome cannot be expected. Unfortunately, misguided means are often adopted, leading to negative outcomes, despite being guided by (allegedly) good intentions: "military interventions such as those by Turkey in Cyprus in 1974, by the North Atlantic Treaty Organization (NATO) in the Federal Republic of Yugoslavia in 1999 and by the Russian Federation in Georgia in 2008, whilst motivated – justifiably or not – by the need to stop serious human rights violations, have themselves led to numerous human rights violations and have not produced lasting solutions for the underlying problems."[7] Given the detrimental influence on the distribution of territorial interests, in addition to numerous human rights violations, humanitarian intervention as a means proved to be incompatible with the overall end pursued in the settlement of secessionist conflicts. The problem of remedial secession is similar: it ignores the right to self-determination of non-secessionists over territorial interests, although it is driven by humanitarian concern. Obviously, both humanitarian intervention and remedial secession focus only on the starting point, but not the endpoint. In other words, they reflect deontological thinking and overlook consequentialist thinking.

Overlooking consequentialist thinking is harmful, for instance, reckless action is therefore encouraged, which usually makes things worse. As mentioned above, (allegedly) humanitarian intervention itself creates numerous human rights violations and offers no practical help, so such action can be deemed reckless. Reckless action cannot be effectively deterred if the terrible consequences thereby caused are not taken seriously. Unfortunately, purely deontological thinking tends to disregard consequences, which largely renders the selection of means unimportant, since dreadful consequences caused by misguided means do not matter. Had serious attention been paid to the inhumane consequences of humanitarian intervention, it would have already been replaced by better means which can lead to humanitarian outcomes. One should never forget that the starting point is unable to justify the endpoint: without proper means a good intention cannot translate into a good outcome but lead to reckless action which does a disservice and cause additional problems. For instance, who is responsible for protecting the human rights of those whose human rights have been severely violated by military action that is in the name of the responsibility to protect? Needless to say, although proponents of humanitarian intervention today would rather refer to humanitarian intervention as the responsibility to protect, consequentialist thinking which is closely linked to responsibility, still fails to sufficiently garner their attention. Therefore, it is still unclear how a legal actor is to assume responsibility when numerous human rights violations have been caused in the course of fulfilling the responsibility to protect. For the same reason, recklessness in fulfilling the responsibility to protect then becomes normal as legal actors are not strictly required to be responsible for the consequences of their recklessness.

Furthermore, overlooking consequentialist thinking can lead to the exploitation of good intentions. As mentioned above, humanitarian concerns by external actors can be exploited by secessionists in their struggle with non-secessionists for territorial interests, which invariably complicates a secessionist conflict. Unfortunately, this

---

[7]Council of Europe Parliamentary Assembly Resolution 1832 (2011): National sovereignty and statehood in contemporary international law: the need for clarification, para. 5.1.

issue seems unlikely to be effectively settled in the context of purely deontological thinking. Driven by purely deontological thinking, legal actors are less likely to consider that their originally good intentions might be maliciously exploited in the end, let alone do they actively avoid such exploitation. It is consequentialist thinking that reminds one of this sad likelihood and motivates one to take the corresponding measures. Once again, it is a matter of the selection of means: legal actors should select means that befit the realization of their good intentions, including avoiding potentially malicious exploitation by others. In short, legal actors should consciously avoid creating room for exploitation of their good intentions in the settlement of secessionist conflicts.

Another delicate issue closely related to deontological thinking is that an allegedly good intention might not be genuinely good. Legal actors are motivated to disguise their self-interested intentions with high-sounding reasoning: the genuine intention of an external actor militarily intervening in a secessionist conflict might be the extension of its geopolitical interests, but it could allege that it acted out of humanitarian concerns. How can one ascertain the real intention of a legal actor? Obviously, condoning the pursuit of geopolitical interests through the use of force is not in accordance with international law, but it is not easy to confirm the connection between military intervention and the pursuit of geopolitical interests if the legal actor has argued that the military intervention was "to protect fundamental values enshrined in the jus cogens and to prevent an impending catastrophe".[8] How can one apply international law to deal with such cases? Undeniably, deontological thinking does not help much in preventing the use of force, as it is extremely difficult to confirm that the genuine intention is definitely not the alleged one. On the other hand, one can rely on consequentialist thinking to confirm that military intervention is not a suitable means of protecting fundamental values enshrined in the jus cogens and actually creates catastrophes, so it should be replaced by a different means. This approach has been applied by the ICJ in the Nicaragua case: according to the ICJ, "while the United States might form its own appraisal of the situation as to respect for human rights in Nicaragua, the use of force could not be the appropriate method to monitor or ensure such respect. With regard to the steps actually taken, the protection of human rights, a strictly humanitarian objective, cannot be compatible with the mining of ports, the destruction of oil installations, or again with the training, arming and equipping of the contras".[9] In short, given that the genuine intention is often hard to ascertain, solely relying on deontological thinking can be highly risky so consequentialist thinking is required, which helps to exclude relevant risks in the application of international law, particularly when fundamental legal values are concerned.

---

[8]Legality of Use of Force (Serbia and Montenegro v. Belgium), ICJ Provisional Measures, Monday 10 May 1999 at 3 p.m., CR 99/15 (uncorrected translation).

[9]Military and Paramilitary Activities in and against Nicaragua (Nicaragua v. United States of America). Merits, Judgement. I.C.J. Reports 1986, p. 134, para. 268.

As once pointed out by Max Weber, "we must be clear about the fact that all ethically oriented conduct may be guided by one of two fundamentally differing and irreconcilably opposed maxims: conduct can be oriented to an 'ethic of ultimate ends' or to an 'ethic of responsibility.' This is not to say that an ethic of ultimate ends is identical with irresponsibility, or that an ethic of responsibility is identical with unprincipled opportunism. Naturally nobody says that. However, there is an abysmal contrast between conduct that follows the maxim of an ethic of ultimate ends--that is, in religious terms, 'The Christian does rightly and leaves the results with the Lord'--and conduct that follows the maxim of an ethic of responsibility, in which case one has to give an account of the foreseeable results of one's action."[10] In the same vein, a legal actor should not overlook the consequences of its action driven by good intentions such as the realization of legally enshrined values; conversely, a legal actor should be genuinely responsible for its action, and (allegedly) good intentions should not be used as an excuse for counterproductive or even detrimental action in the settlement of secessionist conflicts. In this regard, the unity of deontology and consequentialism is undoubtedly necessary from a methodological point of view: this unity encourages the selection of a suitable means, bridging the gap between the good intention of realizing enshrined values and the good outcome that is not contrary to the original intention.

1.2.2 Concrete Methods

1.2.2.1 Legal Positivism and Natural Law

As mentioned above, the rights and duties of secessionists and non-secessionists have not been well established in the current system of international law, and this conclusion is based on a positive analysis. When speaking of legal positivism, one should realize that in international law it does not mean exactly the same as in domestic law, the latter referring to positivism in its classic form, which "endeavors to abstain from any value judgements, asserting that it is possible to have a morally neutral descriptive theory of law. Thus it rejects the main tenet of its counterpart in legal theory, naturalism".[11] Legal positivism in international law has, to a certain degree, incorporated natural law: "Lacking a constitution, the international legal order relies on the sources of international law listed in Art. 38 ICJ Statute, to clarify what qualifies as an international legal norm... Beyond linguistic openness, however, Art. 38 (c) can actually be seen as embracing naturalist notions. The general principles of law, if defined as shared principles embodied in national legal systems, such as equity or good faith (bona fide), allow for the inclusion in law of moral considerations".[12] In the parlance of Simma and Paulus, according to whom "the

[10]Weber (2014), p. 41.

[11]Lachenmann (2011).

[12]Ibid. para. 44.

vision of an international law more amenable to the realization of global values remains compatible with the regime of traditional sources",[13] it can be referred to as "enlightened positivism".[14] Therefore, the positive analysis here is not made in a classic form either: this analysis is not established solely on positive rules, but also on naturalist thinking, which is closely connected with moral values.

It should be noted that adding naturalist thinking to positive rules also befits the discussion about the issue of secession. As a matter of fact, the discussion about secession has already gone beyond positive rules: a typical case is the concept of remedial secession, which has no solid legal foundation but has constantly been a matter for debate. That is to say, insisting on excluding naturalist thinking in relation to secession does not make much sense in the actual discussion and it is fitting to take advantage of naturalist thinking, in order to judge the value of a moral claim such as remedial secession in conflict settlement. Obviously, on the basis of natural law a claim might be considered moral from one perspective but immoral from another perspective, and satisfying such a partially moral claim cannot help to settle a conflict. In order to settle secessionist conflicts in an effective way, it is definitely necessary to reject such partially moral claims. Positive rules cannot offer much help in judging whether a claim is partially moral or not, but naturalist thinking can: if it is confirmed that according to natural law, a supposedly moral claim such as remedial secession is only partially justifiable or even questionable, then the proposition based on this claim is clearly untenable. Similarly, another moral claim which is often witnessed in secessionist conflicts, namely humanitarian intervention, can be scrutinized on the basis of natural law: if humanitarian intervention is also seriously challenged by naturalists, it is difficult to argue that humanitarian intervention is illegal but legitimate. Besides, if one can find inspiration in natural law to fill the void in the positive legal system regarding secession, it would also be conducive to the further development of positive rules.

The further development of the positive rules regarding secession deserves an important place in the positive analysis here. Since the rights and duties of secessionists and non-secessionists have not been well established in the current system of international law, it is reasonable to introduce rules regulating such rights and duties in the international legal system. In other words, the positive analysis conducted in this thesis is not a static one, in which the international legal system is observed as closed and unchanging, but a dynamic one based on the assumption that there is still room for development in this system, particularly as regards questions like secession, which so far have not fully taken root in general international law. Indeed, there have been sporadic international agreements and constitutions of several states, which deal with the rights and duties of secessionists and non-secessionists. Unfortunately, not much attention has been paid to their theoretical contribution: lawyers need to pay more attention to these agreements and constitutions regulating secession, particularly from the perspective of legal reasoning by analogy; such

[13] Simma and Paulus (1999), p. 316.

[14] Ibid. p. 307.

agreements are in a better position to facilitate analogical legal reasoning than general international law. This thesis discusses agreements such as the Comprehensive Peace Agreement concluded between Sudan and South Sudan. This kind of agreement, as well as the constitutions of several states, has provided useful experience for the standardization of the rights and duties of secessionists and non-secessionists in a general sense, and such standardization is quite conducive to the settlement of conflicts for both sides. From this perspective, a dynamic positive analysis based on a developing international legal system, which is in a better position to regulate secessionist conflicts, is certainly meaningful and practical. In addition, given that power politics in general needs to be restricted by the international rule of law, it is accurate to conclude that international law should play a more important role in the issue of secession, otherwise the issue will inevitably be dominated by power politics. In order to trump power politics with the international rule of law, the international legal system must be further developed.

For a better understanding of the merit of a dynamic positive analysis boasting a development-oriented horizon in comparison with a static positive analysis focusing on existing regulations, it must be noted that in the former context, what was once less specifically regulated by international law can attain a more definite legal status through newly established regulations. In other words, ambiguities permeating international law concerning secession, which have caused endless debate and divergence, can largely be removed thanks to newly created regulations. This is not only conducive to the reasonable exercise of conflicting rights to self-determination by secessionists and non-secessionists but also to increasing the reasonableness of external involvement in secessionist conflicts. After all, ambiguous international legal regulations cannot effectively prevent abuse of the right to self-determination, and any abuse of rights contributes to conflicts. When international legal regulations regarding secession are not clear enough, external involvement also lacks clear legal guidance, and under such circumstances problematic external involvement in secessionist conflicts becomes inevitable. Therefore, removing the ambiguities permeating the legal system by creating new regulations undoubtedly deserves serious consideration and endeavors to establish such regulations as a vital addition to the existing legal regulations should become a crucial part of the positivist approach.

The selection of naturalist thinking is particularly noteworthy in the process of establishing new regulations regarding the issue of secession, given that some interpretations of natural law can play a positive role in this process but others cannot. For example, the pursuit of equity in general prompts the establishment of new regulations: the pursuit of equity promotes striking a new balance of interests between secessionists and non-secessionists, which lays the foundation for a binding agreement accepted by both sides. On the other hand, an interpretation of natural law that overlooks the pursuit of equity and the legal interests of one side can hardly contribute to a binding agreement accepted by both sides. From this perspective, it is reasonable to say that although naturalist thinking is not strictly excluded in the discussion of international law, particularly in terms of secession, it certainly does not mean every interpretation of natural law is equally valuable; the selection of interpretations of natural law is indispensable. After all, acknowledging the status of natural law in the current international legal system aims to render this system more competent in response to various issues rather than create more obstacles. When an interpretation of natural law fails to contribute to a solution or even causes additional problems, selecting such interpretation of natural law is certainly not in accordance with the original intention of embracing naturalist notions embodied in Article 38 of the Statute of the International Court of Justice. In short, in order to integrate naturalist thinking with positive rules, it is necessary to make a distinction among various interpretations of natural law in the first place.

1.2.2.2 Historical Review Regarding Secession

The history of secession itself is much longer than the history of secession as an international legal issue. With a view to improving the legal regulation of secession, it is meaningful to conduct a relatively comprehensive historical review of secession, which shall include influential secessionist conflicts, the development of a right to self-determination through historic events as well as political theorists and responses of states and international organizations to (likely) secessionist self-determination. Through such a historical review one can have a better understanding of the kind of legal regulation that is required for effective settlement of secessionist conflicts, as various issues concerning secessionist conflicts can be revealed in this process. When these issues are effectively regulated by legal arrangements, secessionist conflicts can be readily solved.

One must first look at influential secessionist conflicts. The American War of Independence, the Latin American Wars of Independence, the American Civil War, the nationalistic movements in the latter part of the nineteenth century, decolonization in the twentieth century and several cases of secessionist conflicts outside the colonial context have been selected as influential secessionist conflicts for the historical review. Their influence mainly lies in their contribution to the development of a right to self-determination and in the issues raised by the exercise of this right. Needless to say, all these cases are about the practical exercise of a right to self-determination and conflicts between different "selves": one party's right to self-determination becomes the obstacle for another party to exercise the same right; a secessionist conflict, in essence, is a self-determination conflict between secessionists and non-secessionists. Although these cases have not provided a definitive answer to the question as to which one's right to self-determination should take precedence - sometimes the secessionists gained the upper hand and others, the non-secessionists triumphed - they have provided inspiration regarding how to address conflicting rights to self-determination. Such inspiration can prove beneficial when further regulating the exercise of a right to self-determination in secessionist conflicts, regardless of whether they offer positive experiences or negative lessons. For instance, positive experiences regarding the exercise of a right to self-determination, such as applying uti possidetis as a solution to territorial disputes closely related to self-determination, should be confirmed and considered as an integral part of the further regulation while negative lessons regarding the exercise of a right to self-determination, such as abuse of the right to self-determination with the help of external involvement, should be condemned and prevented through the further regulation. Without a review of these cases, neither the positive experiences nor the negative lessons can be applied when further regulating the exercise of a right to self-determination in secessionist conflicts, and this failure to apply them is not conducive to the effective settlement of current and future secessionist conflicts. In short, the effective settlement of secessionist conflicts is largely dependent on the improved regulation of the exercise of a right to self-determination, and this improved regulation is largely established on historical experiences and lessons.

Next, the development of a right to self-determination through historic events as well as political theorists must be analyzed. In addition to influential secessionist conflicts, the development of a right to self-determination is also closely related to other historic events not directly concerned with secession and to political theorists inextricably tied to the concept of self-determination. When it comes to a right to self-determination, historic events such as the French Revolution and First World War, and political theorists such as Lenin and Wilson should not be ignored. Just as both positive experiences and negative lessons can be gleaned from cases of secessionist conflicts, it is also clear that both historic events and political theorists have enriched the meaning of a right to self-determination as well as revealed its inherent defects. The sad fact is that although these theoretical defects embodied in the right to self-determination have been witnessed, the question of how they can be remedied has been left behind. For instance, the question of how such means as the Reign of Terror to pursue self-determination can be replaced by a generally accepted means is left unanswered. Lenin wisely realized that a demand for self-determination is not an "equivalent of a demand for separation, fragmentation and the formation of small states",[15] but his theoretical contribution to the avoidance of such consequences is limited. According to Wilson, in the aftermath of the First World War the holder of the right to self-determination should be decided by the victorious Allies,[16] so he did not bother to consider the distinction between self-determination and other-determination in this context, which amounts to granting certain external actors superior status in self-determination conflicts. Obviously, these unfixed theoretical defects still affect the practical exercise of self-determination in this day and age, and therefore it is necessary to deal with the obstacles caused by these theoretical defects for the sake of the effective settlement of secessionist conflicts. Undoubtedly, theoretical defects regarding the right to self-determination must be corrected in order to prevent this right, which was and is expected to be a blessing, from becoming a curse in practice.

Thirdly, the responses of states and international organizations to (likely) secessionist self-determination should be discussed. Numerous instances have demonstrated how prudent states and international organizations can be when confronted

[15] Lenin (1964), p. 451.

[16] Castellino (2000), p. 18.

with (likely) secessionist self-determination. For instance, in the case of the Aaland islands, the Council of the League of Nations required jurists to rule on the matter of whether Aaland Islanders could claim secession from Finland on the basis of self-determination, and the Report presented to the Council of the League by the Commission of Rapporteurs concluded that "to concede to minorities, either of language or religion, or to any fractions of a population the right of withdrawing from the community to which they belong, because it is their wish or their good pleasure, would be to destroy order and stability within States and to inaugurate anarchy in international life; it would be to uphold a theory incompatible with the very idea of the State as a territorial and political unity".[17] In 1960 the General Assembly of the UN adopted the well-known Declaration on the Granting of Independence to Colonial Countries and Peoples, in which it was stated that "any attempt aimed at the partial or total disruption of the national unity and the territorial integrity of a country is incompatible with the purposes and principles of the Charter of the United Nations".[18] "The United Nations did not treat the emergence of Bangladesh as a case of self-determination despite good grounds for doing so, but rather as a fait accompli achieved as a result of foreign military assistance in special circumstances".[19] In codifying the rules of state succession, representatives of states carefully avoided the very use of the term "secession", preferring to speak about "separation of part of a State".[20] Needless to say, such a prudent attitude constantly demonstrated by states and international organizations towards secessionist self-determination has to be taken into consideration in the settlement of secessionist conflicts: it is well-advised to pursue the realization of self-determination without resorting to secession.

To sum up, through a historical review of secession focusing on self-determination from various perspectives, what must be improved and how to improve it with regard to the legal regulation of self-determination becomes more clear, which is quite helpful in settling secessionist conflicts because the essence of secessionist conflicts is conflicting self-determination between secessionists and non-secessionists.

1.2.2.3 The Principal Contradiction and the Principal Aspect of a Contradiction

"There are many contradictions in the process of development of a complex thing, and one of them is necessarily the principal contradiction whose existence and development determine or influence the existence and development of the other contradictions… whatever happens, there is no doubt at all that at every stage in the

[17]The Aaland Islands Question, LN Doc. B7.21/68/106, 1921, p. 28.

[18]A/RES/1514(XV), para. 6.

[19]Crawford (2006), pp. 415–416.

[20]Kohen (2006), p. 3.

development of a process, there is only one principal contradiction which plays the leading role. . . Therefore, in studying any complex process in which there are two or more contradictions, we must devote every effort to finding its principal contradiction. Once this principal contradiction is grasped, all problems can be readily solved".[21] This analysis can also be applied in the settlement of secessionist conflicts. As mentioned above, secession should be regarded as a multi-dimensional international legal problem, and the interplay among all these dimensions is rather complicated. In order to get to the heart of the problem and take care of every dimension, it seems undoubtedly necessary to grasp the principal dimension whose existence and development determine or influence the existence and development of the other dimensions. So the question becomes: which dimension is the principal one of the issue of secession? In other words, which dimension's existence and development can determine or influence the existence and development of the other dimensions?

It seems that some would say the protection of human rights is the principal dimension, given the undeniable significance of human rights in contemporary international law. Yet, this judgement fails to grasp the real meaning of the principal contradiction, namely the one determining or influencing the existence and development of the other contradictions. There is no denying that the protection of human rights is of the utmost importance, but it is clear that human rights violations are largely determined or influenced by violent struggles over territorial interests, while human rights violations do not determine or influence the violent struggle over territorial interests. As noted by Brilmayer, "what distinguishes separatist from other minority claims is the fact that the group wishes to establish a new state on a particular piece of land",[22] so the wish of secessionists to exclusively occupy a particular piece of land is actually unrelated to generally acknowledged human rights and people who fight for human rights do not need to become secessionists. It is the violent struggle over territorial interests between secessionists and non-secessionists that leads to numerous violations of human rights, not that numerous violations of human rights necessitate the violent struggle over territorial interests. Therefore, it is reasonable to conclude that the principal contradiction discussed here is the distribution of territorial interests instead of the protection of human rights: when secessionists do not give up their wish to exclusively occupy a particular piece of land, the ensuing violent struggle will inevitably frustrate the pursuit of human rights protection. When the distribution of territorial interests is properly addressed, other problems including the protection of human rights can be readily solved. As will be discussed later, effective external involvement in secessionist conflicts entails paying attention to the distribution of territorial interests; external involvement that ignores the distribution of territorial interests is likely to cause unintended consequences, such as encouraging secessionists to create exceptional circumstances for the sake of invoking remedial secession.

[21] Mao (1937).

[22] Brilmayer (1991), p. 193.

It would be accurate to say that if one recognizes that the principal contradiction of the issue of secession is the distribution of territorial interests between secessionists and non-secessionists, one will not support solutions such as remedial secession, as they can only contribute to an unfair distribution of territorial interests. An unfair distribution of territorial interests can only intensify the confrontation between secessionists and non-secessionists, rendering the issue of secession more complicated. Of course, the concern for remedying injured human rights is quite understandable, but this is no reason to believe that an unfair distribution of territorial interests which complicates secessionist conflicts can serve the remedy for injured human rights. Proponents of solutions such as remedial secession fail to realize that confrontations caused by an unfair distribution of territorial interests invariably cast a shadow on the protection of human rights: as noted by Horowitz, "a secession or partition converts a domestic ethnic dispute into a more dangerous international one. And since states are able to procure arms with few of the restraints that periodically bedevil insurgents, the international dispute often involves escalating weapons and the prospect of international warfare".[23] From this perspective, it is clear that ignoring the distribution of territorial interests can endanger the protection of human rights. Remedial secession cannot be genuinely remedial largely because the distribution of territorial interests as the principal contradiction, whose existence and development determines or influences the protection of human rights, is not handled properly here, so it is unlikely to be a reliable solution to secessionist conflicts. Similarly, any other solutions that fail to grasp the principal contradiction of the issue of secession are also ill-advised.

Furthermore, it is necessary to realize that "in any contradiction the development of the contradictory aspects is uneven... Of the two contradictory aspects, one must be principal and the other secondary. The principal aspect is the one playing the leading role in the contradiction. The nature of a thing is determined mainly by the principal aspect of a contradiction, the aspect which has gained the dominant position. But this situation is not static; the principal and the non-principal aspects of a contradiction transform themselves into each other and the nature of the thing changes accordingly. In a given process or at a given stage in the development of a contradiction, A is the principal aspect and B is the non-principal aspect; at another stage or in another process the roles are reversed--a change determined by the extent of the increase or decrease in the force of each aspect in its struggle against the other in the course of the development of a thing."[24] Regarding secession, whether in the contradiction of territorial interests or of human rights protection, two aspects of the contradiction are invariably the secessionists and the non-secessionists. Which should be regarded as the principal aspect? For those that view secessionist conflicts in a static way, the authorities on behalf of the non-secessionists constitute the principal aspect, due to their military, administrative, and financial superiority over the secessionists. For this reason they believe that preventing the escalation of a

[23]Horowitz (2003), p. 55.

[24]See above Note 21.

secessionist conflict means curbing the action of the authorities. However, they fail to realize that their involvement in curbing the action of the authorities can change the contrast in force and make the secessionists become the principal aspect in the development of secessionist conflicts. This is at the root of why some external actors inevitably lend secessionists a hand in the struggle over territorial interests and complicate the secessionist conflict. Therefore, mistaken identification of the principal aspect of a contradiction actually has a negative influence on conflict settlement and should not be overlooked.

In view of the foregoing, effective settlement of secessionist conflicts is closely linked to correctly understanding the principal contradiction, namely the distribution of territorial interests, and correct identification of the principal aspect of the contradiction in the development of secessionist conflicts. Therefore, in any legal arrangement intended for the issue of secession, the distribution of territorial interests and the necessary regulation of the action of secessionists must occupy the foreground.

1.2.2.4 Abstract Legality and Practical Legality

Actors in secessionist conflicts, whether internal or external, can always find a legal justification for their actions: secessionists mainly rely on self-determination and human rights, non-secessionists mainly rely on sovereignty and territorial integrity, and external actors making military interventions rely on humanitarian intervention or other legal justifications such as self-defense and the rescue of nationals abroad. In order to effectively settle secessionist conflicts, one must focus on these legal justifications which should possess not only abstract legality but also practical legality. Abstract legality should not be equated with practical legality and this point is not difficult to understand if one considers that any right is open to abuse; in the same vein, any justification given by actors in the abstract sense can have an element of legality, but one cannot conclude that practical action will be fully justified by such an abstract element of legality. Unfortunately, in secessionist conflicts the distinction between abstract legality and practical legality is made in a discriminatory manner: more often than not, the justification for action given by non-secessionists, who are represented by the authorities, will be scrutinized on the basis of distinguishing abstract legality and practical legality, but the justification for action afforded by secessionists and external actors making military interventions receives no such scrutiny.

To be specific, when the authorities argue for their action against secessionists on the basis of sovereignty and territorial integrity, in which non-secessionist self-determination is embodied, international lawyers are not generally satisfied with this abstract legality and consider issues of practical legality, such as whether anti-secessionist action has caused violations of human rights, and they generally do not believe that an anti-secessionist action having caused numerous violations of human rights can be fully justified from the perspective of international law. However, when secessionists argue for their violent action in pursuit of independence on the basis of self-determination and human rights, fewer international lawyers tend to distinguish abstract legality and practical legality: violations of non-secessionists' right to self-determination over territorial interests and their human rights caused by secessionist rebellions are inexplicably overlooked by many international lawyers, as if abstract legality argued by secessionists could be equated with practical legality. Similarly, when it comes to military interventions made by external actors in secessionist conflicts, too much attention has been given to abstract legality, namely the good or allegedly good intentions of military actions, while little attention has been given to practical legality, namely the actual consequences, as if the actual consequences did not matter as long as the intentions were good or allegedly good. Such absurd phenomena can be witnessed in practice: some external actors have launched military interventions in a way that disregards humanitarian law and still claimed that their use of force was humanitarian intervention, although this is highly problematic from the logical perspective. After all, if non-humanitarian intervention has to follow humanitarian law, there is no reason to conclude that humanitarian intervention does not need to do so. Logically, humanitarian intervention should be required to follow humanitarian law much more strictly than non-humanitarian intervention: because of the specificity of the intervention's aim, the humanitarian standards to be met in humanitarian intervention should be higher. In this sense, the strong opposition of many states to practical humanitarian intervention is quite understandable: the disregard for humanitarian law in practice disconnects the intervention from the humanitarian sense alleged by external actors who make such intervention.

In addition to humanitarian intervention, external actors have also launched military interventions in secessionist conflicts on other legal grounds such as self-defense and the rescue of nationals abroad, according to records of history. Similarly, regardless of the grounds on which the external intervention is based, when it leads to detrimental consequences in practice, its legality deserves reconsideration: abstract legality cannot justify practical harm, and it is also absurd to overlook the practical harm caused by external actors in secessionist conflicts because of their alleged legal intention. Convincing positive external involvement in secessionist conflicts cannot be devoid of positive results and cannot be established solely on good intentions; any good intentions claimed by external actors prove to be somewhat doubtful if they do not lead to good results in practice. To put it simply, external involvement in secessionist conflicts cannot be fully justified on any legal basis if it causes serious harm in practice, such as the escalation of secessionist conflicts and additional human right violations. When practical legality is not required for external involvement in secessionist conflicts, such external involvement which in the abstract sense has an element of legality but is detrimental in practice, is difficult to deter and will render secessionist conflicts more complicated.

Moreover, in failing to scrutinize the justification for action afforded by secessionists and external actors making military interventions based on the distinction between abstract legality and practical legality, a double standard is actually applied in the settlement of secessionist conflicts: practical abuse of a right to self-determination by the secessionists during a secessionist conflict is largely condoned, and the external actors are not held responsible for the escalation of the secessionist conflict and additional human right violations caused by their military involvement, but the authorities acting on behalf of the non-secessionists are strongly criticized for the human right violations caused by their action to maintain sovereignty and territorial integrity, in which the non-secessionist self-determination is embodied. In such circumstances it seems quite natural for one to consider the issue of double standards. After all, if human right violations caused by secessionists in the name of self-determination and by external actors in the name of humanitarian intervention or some other justification can be condoned, it is difficult, if not impossible, to explain why human right violations caused by the authorities, acting on behalf of non-secessionists, in the name of sovereignty and territorial integrity cannot be condoned. Similarly, if the authorities must exercise their sovereign power without violating the right to self-determination and human rights of secessionists, secessionists should also have to exercise their right to self-determination without violating the right to self-determination and human rights of non-secessionists and external actors must perform their humanitarian or other legal pursuits in a way that is more compatible with sovereignty (non-secessionist self-determination) and humanitarian law. Otherwise, such actions should be regarded as a typical expression of double standards: for non-secessionists the complex practical legality is required, while for secessionists and external actors the simple abstract legality suffices.

In view of the foregoing, it is safe to conclude that both simple abstract legality and complex practical legality should be required for actions not only by the authorities on behalf of non-secessionists but also by secessionists and external actors, in order to render secessionist conflicts less complicated and to eliminate this double standard: when complex practical legality is also stressed regarding the actions of secessionists and external actors, it is conducive to the avoidance of abuse of the right to self-determination by secessionists and the optimization of external involvement, and all parties in the secessionist conflict start to be treated in an equal manner. To be more specific, when secessionists are required to exercise their right to self-determination in a way that respects the right to self-determination and human rights of non-secessionists, just as the authorities are required to exercise their sovereign power without violating the right to self-determination and human rights of secessionists, conflicts between these parties are more likely to be settled peacefully. If external actors are required not only to have good intentions but also to ensure good results in practice, the way they undertake their humanitarian or other legal pursuits in secessionist conflicts is more likely to be compatible with requirements based on sovereignty (non-secessionist self-determination) and humanitarian law, thus reducing the need to worry about the escalation of conflicts and additional human right violations caused by external involvement. In short, when complex practical legality is also required of secessionists and external actors, just as it is required of non-secessionists represented by the authorities, the effective settlement of secessionist conflicts becomes more realistic.

1.2.2.5 Responding to Incentives and Facing Trade-Offs

Responding to incentives and facing trade-offs are basic principles of economics summarized by economist Gregory Mankiw.[25] These principles of economics are worth mentioning in the discussion of the issue of secession, mainly because the actors therein do follow these principles in pursuit of their interests, so overlooking such principles would render any legal arrangement less effective in regulating the action of the relevant actors in secessionist conflicts. In short, considering these principles of economics is essential in forming a legal arrangement that can effectively settle the corresponding conflict.

One must first look at the principle stating that people respond to incentives. "An incentive is something that induces a person to act, such as the prospect of punishment or reward. Because rational people make decisions by comparing costs and benefits, they respond to incentives... Public policymakers should never forget about incentives: many policies change the costs or benefits that people face and, therefore, alter their behavior... When policy makers fail to consider how their policies affect incentives, they often end up with unintended consequences... When analyzing any policy, we must consider not only the direct effects but also the less obvious indirect effects that work through incentives".[26] Similarly, lawyers should never forget about incentives: some legal proposals change the costs or benefits that relevant actors face and therefore alter their behavior, so when lawyers fail to consider how their legal proposals affect incentives, they often end up with unintended consequences. When analyzing any legal proposal, one must consider not only the direct effects but also the less obvious indirect effects that work through incentives. On this basis, it is quite understandable why legal proposals like remedial secession would go awry in practice: lawyers that support this idea generally fail to consider the perverse incentive embodied in this idea offered to secessionists. In the parlance of Horowitz, "if independence can only be won legitimately after matters have been carried to extremes, then, by all means, there are people willing to carry them to extremes."[27] Proponents of remedial secession are generally unaware of the calculation of costs and benefits made by secessionists or mistakenly understand this calculation: some secessionists are willing to sacrifice the human rights of their own people in order to unilaterally transform co-ownership of a particular piece of territory into exclusive ownership. Remedial secession happens to offer them this chance, encouraging them to create exceptional circumstances by provoking excessive retaliation. For this reason, it is certainly right to conclude that any legal proposal regarding the settlement of secessionist conflicts needs to observe basic principles of economics, which dominate the actions of the conflicting parties, and to avoid providing perverse incentives.

[25]Gregory Mankiw (2011), p. xix.

[26]Ibid. pp. 7–8.

[27]Horowitz (2003), p. 58.

In the same vein, when positive incentives which can encourage legal actors to improve their actions are absent, it does not bode well for conflict settlement either. Here, military interventions (allegedly) motivated by human rights concerns but actually creating numerous human rights violations in secessionist conflicts come to mind, leading one to wonder why external actors have repeatedly made similar mistakes. Needless to say, there are manifold reasons, and one of them is the lack of incentives for external actors to improve their involvement: when external actors do not actually have to accept the consequences of their counterproductive or even detrimental involvement, they lack the motivation to make any improvement. In this sense, it is reasonable to deduce that providing positive incentives to external actors is of great importance, and the lack of positive incentives is closely related to excessive tolerance of counterproductive and detrimental external involvement. For the sake of conflict settlement, there should be some legal arrangements designed for providing incentives for external actors to avoid counterproductive and detrimental external involvement. This should be regarded as a necessary step to be taken in the standardization of external involvement.

Now the principle that people face trade-offs must be discussed. This principle helps clarify why humanitarian intervention in general cannot be genuinely humanitarian in practice. "There ain't no such thing as a free lunch... To get something that we like, we usually have to give up something else that we also like. Making decisions requires trading off one goal against another".[28] In genuine humanitarian intervention there is also a trade-off, which has been revealed by Alex de Waal and Rakiya Omaar, namely a relatively high number of casualties on the intervening side, "but the demands made upon Western armies by politicians and constituents at home for quick fixes and low casualties"[29] render the required military intervention nearly impossible. In other words, many arguing for humanitarian intervention are actually reluctant to pay the price required by genuine humanitarian intervention. No wonder genuine humanitarian intervention, like the one required in the Rwanda tragedy, is hardly available. Allegedly humanitarian interventions causing numerous human rights violations occur one after another: when intervening forces pursue zero causalities on their own side, it is inevitable for them to resort to military means that can lead to huge costs and suffering on the intervened side. Unless an intervenor is willing to trade its own sacrifice for the protection of human rights of others, genuine humanitarian intervention would invariably be absent in practice, and allegedly humanitarian but actually not humanitarian intervention would occur repeatedly. For this reason, it is necessary to abandon wishful thinking regarding the humanitarian intervention: a genuinely effective means intended for the protection of human rights should be pursued instead of one that can only fulfill this aim in an imaginary sense. Undeniably, no matter how insistently lawyers try to advocate humanitarian intervention, if the intervenors remain unwilling to make the self-sacrifice required

---

[28]Gregory Mankiw (2011), p. 4.

[29]de Waal and Omaar (1994).

by genuine humanitarian intervention, the humanitarian effect of their intervention would persistently remain imaginary.

In view of the foregoing, the objective economic principles governing internal or external actors in secessionist conflicts should be taken into consideration, for the sake of conflict settlement. There is no reason to believe that legal proposals ignoring relevant basic economic principles can contribute positively to the settlement of secessionist conflicts as genuinely helpful legal arrangements must respect such objective economic principles, otherwise ensuing unintended consequences will invariably frustrate their original goal.

1.2.2.6 A Preventive Idea of a Different Type

The application of the preventive idea is not unusual to international lawyers. Boutros Boutros-Ghali, the former Secretary-General of the UN, has provided a classic understanding of the preventive idea in his Agenda for Peace, namely "action to prevent disputes from arising between parties, to prevent existing disputes from escalating into conflicts and to limit the spread of the latter when they occur".[30] In the report by the International Commission on Intervention and State Sovereignty entitled *The Responsibility to Protect,* the responsibility to prevent stands alongside the responsibility to react and the responsibility to rebuild as one pillar of this theory; similar to the understanding expressed by Boutros-Ghali, the responsibility to prevent focuses on the action taken by external actors to deal with deadly conflicts.[31] Therefore, it is reasonable to say that, up to now, external actors have largely been defined as problem terminators rather than problem contributors. Obviously, overlooking the fact that external actors can be identified as problem contributors is detrimental to the realization of preventive intentions: given that the development of secessionist or other internal conflicts is often linked to external involvement, conflict prevention relies not only on productive external action, but also on the avoidance of counterproductive or detrimental external action. In other words, effective conflict prevention also requires external actors to refrain from acting in a counterproductive or detrimental way. To some extent, avoiding such external action seems to be more important: when there is no external action intensifying the tension between the conflicting parties, secessionist or other internal conflicts are less likely to escalate, and when escalation is less likely to occur, there is less need for external actors to become involved. That is to say, if certain external actors had learned to refrain from intensifying the tension between the conflicting parties, they would have spared themselves and other external actors a good deal of additional trouble.

[30]UN Doc. A/47/277, para. 20.

[31]The Responsibility to Protect: Report of the International Commission on Intervention and State Sovereignty, 2001, p. 19.

Undeniably, many secessionist or other internal conflicts have been intensified by external involvement; such external involvement might not be indisputably illegal but it is indisputably conducive to conflict escalation, which renders humanitarian crises more likely to occur. In this situation, conflict prevention should not start with something like an early warning as it is already too late. It would be preferable for external actors to become aware of the need to avoid contributing to the escalation of secessionist or other internal conflicts in the first place. In short, for the sake of conflict prevention, external actors should value their responsibility to refrain specifically from doing anything that is conducive to the escalation of the conflict. Needless to say, if external actors are not required to refrain from acting in a way that is conducive to the escalation of secessionist or other internal conflicts, attempts to prevent these conflicts will largely be in vain. Moreover, it is also unfair to require some external actors to make preventive efforts in secessionist or other internal conflicts, when other external actors have not been required to refrain from contributing to the escalation of the conflict in the first place. Returning to the concept of the responsibility to prevent, its failure to stress the responsibility to refrain actually amounts to forcing the whole international community to be responsible for the counterproductive or detrimental action of some external actors in secessionist or other internal conflicts and there is reason for innocent external actors to question whether a no-fault liability like this is really in accordance with international law. This issue becomes more unbearable when it comes to the responsibility to rebuild: innocent external actors are required to invest large amounts of manpower, material and financial resources in the rebuilding process so they rightly feel it is unfair for them to bear this burden when it was someone else who made a mess of the situation in the first place. Therefore, stressing the responsibility to refrain from doing anything conducive to the escalation of secessionist or other internal conflicts is quite meaningful for the realization of preventive thinking.

Next, it is necessary to find out what kind of external action has proved to be counterproductive or detrimental in secessionist or other internal conflicts, which requires a careful review of the external involvement. Undeniably, the use of force is the most noteworthy type of external involvement in secessionist or other internal conflicts. The influence of the use of force by internal and external actors on the settlement of secessionist or other internal conflicts needs to be thoroughly analyzed. When it is confirmed that the use of force, whether by internal or external actors, is counterproductive or detrimental to the settlement of a conflict, such use of force must be prevented so actors should refrain from acting in this way. In addition to military external involvement, there are a number of other forms of external involvement in secessionist conflicts, including mediation, recognition and delivery of advisory opinions. Similarly, when poorly managed, they can also influence the settlement of secessionist conflicts in a negative manner. In this sense, preventive thinking can also be applied in respect of these forms of external involvement. It is particularly noteworthy that prevention here is targeted at a concrete action which does a disservice to conflict settlement, rather than at a general concept. For example, mediation as a general concept is undoubtedly welcome in conflict settlement but this does not mean that the conflicting parties have to tolerate unsuitable mediators that actually further complicate conflicts; according to preventive thinking, a mediator should refrain from contributing to the complication of a conflict. In short, in order to prevent external involvement from having a negative influence on the settlement of secessionist conflicts, more attention must be paid to unsuitable concrete actions rather than reasonable abstract concepts. Abstract reasonableness is one thing, suitability in practice is another thing, and the latter must never be confused with the former.

Based on this, it is reasonable to deduce that a higher degree of standardization of external involvement is required, in order to prevent external involvement from having a negative influence on the settlement of secessionist conflicts. As revealed above, a reasonable abstract concept can lead to an unsuitable concrete action; thus, to ensure that a reasonable abstract concept will lead to a suitable concrete action, it is necessary to reduce the free space embodied in the abstract concept and directly link this concept with a relatively concrete action. In essence, this necessitates standardization: external actors are no longer allowed to interpret abstract concepts as they please but instead must follow a standardized approach to an abstract concept, and in this way it is less likely for external actors to contribute to the escalation of secessionist conflicts based on their misinterpretation of an abstract concept. Of course, it must be admitted that external actors sometimes deliberately misinterpret abstract concepts, thus contributing to the escalation of secessionist conflicts because it is in their geopolitical interests to do so. In such circumstances standardization becomes particularly significant: a standardized approach to an abstract concept helps exclude the likelihood of the abstract concept being abused by external actors in pursuit of their own geopolitical interests in a secessionist conflict. In addition, a standardized approach to abstract concepts is equally important to external actors that unintentionally misinterpret abstract concepts and contribute to the escalation of secessionist conflicts, since they do not know how to interpret the relevant concepts in a way that can positively contribute to conflict settlement.

To conclude, preventive thinking applied in this thesis is somewhat different from the classic understanding: the point here is not "to do something", but "to refrain from doing the wrong thing"; when actors refrain from doing the wrong thing, they might not have to do something to prevent the escalation of secessionist conflicts, as the escalation itself is usually related to the wrong thing done by actors beforehand. Emphasizing the responsibility to refrain also renders the responsibility to prevent more reasonable from a legal point of view, as the link between responsibility and fault becomes more evident here. Through further standardization of external involvement, the demarcation between "the wrong thing" and "the right thing" becomes clearer, which can be quite conducive to preventing external involvement from having a negative influence on the settlement of secessionist conflicts. Further standardization helps those who do not know how to do it the right way learn to act appropriately and renders those who deliberately act wrongly for the sake of their own geopolitical interests less likely to take such advantage.

1.3 Structure of the Research

This thesis dealing with the theme of secession is composed of four chapters: in Chap. 2 the legal color of secession is carefully explored; in Chap. 3 the discussion centers on the nexus between secession and self-determination conflicts; in Chap. 4 the issue of secession is analyzed in combination with the use of force; and in Chap. 5 attention is paid to improving external involvement in the settlement of secessionist conflicts. In these four chapters the multi-dimensional nature of secession as a legal issue is largely revealed, and the comprehensive solution to this multi-dimensional legal issue is correspondingly structured.

In Chap. 2 the difficult but rather crucial question, namely international legal sources regarding secession, is addressed in a relatively detailed manner. This issue is difficult mainly because "at the international level [there is] neither a universal legislative body corresponding to a national parliament, nor a system for universal judicial jurisdiction which has built up a wide-ranging body of precedent,"[32] and "one is therefore faced with the problem of discovering where the law is to be found and how one can tell whether a particular proposition amounts to a legal rule. This perplexity is reinforced because of the anarchic nature of world affairs and the clash of competing sovereignties."[33] Although difficult, exploring international legal sources is crucial as there are currently a series of distinct legal viewpoints regarding secession: some are legally well-founded while others are not and a thorough exploration of international legal sources helps distinguish those well-founded viewpoints from the rest. According to Article 38(1) of the Statute of the International Court of Justice, international conventions, international custom, the general principles of law recognized by civilized nations, and subsidiary means for the determination of rules of law including judicial decisions and the teachings of the most highly qualified publicists of the various nations need to be considered in a thorough exploration of international legal sources. Thus this chapter is structured correspondingly: the legal color of secession is explored according to these four types of sources. Through this thorough exploration of international legal sources, it is revealed that lex generalis, such as international legal principles, is not in a position to offer a satisfactory solution to secessionist conflicts: the high degree of ambiguity embodied in legal principles invariably leaves them open to numerous and contradicting interpretations. A satisfactory solution to secessionist conflicts is much more concerned with lex specialis, namely an agreement between conflicting parties. In order to formulate such an agreement, the influence of state recognition cannot be ignored: premature recognition disturbs the formulation of an agreement between the conflicting parties and thus negatively affects the solution. Since another major obstacle to the formulation of an agreement between conflicting parties is the divergence of opinion between opponents and proponents of remedial

---

[32]Thirlway (2010), p. 96.

[33]Shaw (2008), p. 70.

secession, it is meaningful to consider moderating the disagreement between them by replacing a remedial right to secession with a right to a remedy.

In Chap. 3 secession is observed from the perspective of self-determination conflicts. This is necessary because "the standard account bases claims to secede upon principles of self-determination of peoples, according to which every nation or people has a right to determine its own destiny".[34] This chapter begins with a review of the historical evolution of self-determination. This historical review offers a relatively complete picture of the evolution of (secessionist) self-determination in theory and in practice, which is helpful in considering the improvement in the theory to make it more suitable in reality. Needless to say, when a theory proves to be unsuitable in reality, not only does it fail to guide the relevant actors in the settlement of real disputes, but the theory itself also becomes a source of dispute. The historical review herein has demonstrated that, despite its entry into the international legal system, the inherent uncertainty about self-determination remains glaring: the holder and the content of the right to self-determination remain controversial, the territorial perspective and the human rights perspective of self-determination are not always clearly distinguished, tension might arise between the principle of self-determination and the principle of territorial sovereignty, and the right to self-determination is open to abuse particularly in the sense of remedial secession. Therefore, it is clear that a wide gap exists between theory and reality in respect of self-determination, and this gap itself contributes to secessionist self-determination conflicts. For the sake of conflict settlement, something must be done to close the gap between theory and reality, and because the existence of this gap can largely be attributed to an inadequate legal framework, the solution undoubtedly entails improving this inadequate legal framework. Specifically, given historical experiences and lessons, improving the legal framework should entail the following points: reasonably defining the holder of a right to self-determination, distinguishing the territorial perspective and the human rights perspective of self-determination, correctly understanding the interrelation between territorial sovereignty and self-determination, and preventing abuse of the right to self-determination. Speaking of preventing abuse of the right to self-determination, it is well-advised to substitute remedial self-determination for secessionist self-determination and to specify the obligations of those who claim to be holders of the right to secessionist self-determination. In an agreement concluded between secessionists and non-secessionists, it is not unrealistic to have all these points well-managed and external actors should make positive contributions to the conclusion of such agreements, as the effective settlement of secessionist conflicts requires constructive external involvement like this.

In Chap. 4 the focus shifts to the highly controversial issue of the use of force in secessionist conflicts. When secession does not involve the use of force, it is much less complex to tackle. Unfortunately, the use of force is often resorted to: secessionists resort to force to oppose parent states, and parent states resort to force to counter the rebellion of secessionists. More often than not in such confrontations a

[34] Brilmayer (1991), p. 179.

third party is more or less visibly involved: the third party could be an international/ regional organization or individual states. The complexity of this issue renders a legal judgment on the use of force rather difficult: from different perspectives there would be different conclusions. For instance, when external actors fight against the authorities in favor of secessionists, from the secessionists' perspective, such external involvement represents the furtherance of self-determination and human rights, but from the perspective of non-secessionists, the military support for the secessionist rebellion is detrimental to their right to self-determination over territorial interests and human rights as both have been severely violated by the secessionist violence. Worse yet, certain well-intended legal interpretations could be maliciously exploited by a conflicting party to achieve its own political aims, or a third party might involve itself in a secessionist conflict out of self-interested motives, but in the name of upholding noble values of international law. How this theoretical and practical conundrum can be properly addressed through the interpretation of international law is the crux of the matter. A detailed discussion about the general prohibition of the use of force and likely exceptions, including the responsibility to protect and the choice between legality and legitimacy, as well as how to escape from the vicious circle of the use of force, will help bring about a reasonable solution to the highly controversial issue of the use of force in secessionist conflicts. It is noteworthy that, compared to the legal judgment on the use of force, preventing the escalation of confrontation between conflicting parties might be more meaningful: lower level of confrontation usually means less violence, and even if the use of force can be abstractly justified, it is still less desirable than non-use of force in practice so, rather than a painstaking search for legal justification for the use of force, an effort to lower the level of confrontation seems more conducive to the avoidance of or decrease in the use of force. Four cases regarding the use of force in secessionist conflicts, namely Katanga, Bangladesh, Kosovo and Crimea, are analyzed in this light.

In Chap. 5 external involvement in the settlement of secessionist conflicts is brought to a comprehensive discussion, for the sake of improvement. This chapter demonstrates that it is definitely insufficient to focus solely on military intervention launched by external actors in secessionist conflicts as other forms of external involvement also play an important role, whether negative or positive, in conflict settlement. In order to avoid counterproductive or detrimental external involvement, external actors must first have a clear picture of the legal issues that are included in a secessionist conflict. Otherwise an external actor might attend to one issue and lose sight of another or overlook the nexus between the legal issues involved in a secessionist conflict. This is the indispensable basis for the standardization of external involvement in secessionist conflicts, which should be characterized by finding a balance between various conflicting interests. In practice, balancing various conflicting interests is closely related to concerting the individual actions of internal and external actors in secessionist conflicts, and for this reason, the UN should play a pivotal role in this regard. In order to fulfill this role, the Security Council and other UN bodies must exercise their power in a more rational manner. In addition to external actors, some specific external actions also deserve special attention: mediation, recognition, response to de facto secession and media coverage of secessionist conflicts, all of which can hamper effective conflict settlement if not managed well. Therefore, it is well-advised to render the exercise of mediating power by external actors more rational through standardization, including emphasizing the observation of legally non-binding UN instruments, replacing unsuitable mediators and eschewing artificial deadlines. The issue of recognition should be handled more cautiously: the significance of non-recognition should be recognized; a wish should not be mistakenly recognized as a legal right; the detrimental effects caused by unilateral secession should also be recognized. As for a reasonable response to de facto secession, it is necessary to bear in mind the Latin maxim *nullus commodum capere potest de injuria sua propria* which can be deemed an aspect of the legal principle of good faith, and the significance of a fair distribution of territorial interests between secessionists and non-secessionists. The influence of the mass media on the settlement of a secessionist conflict should no longer be overlooked either: distorted media coverage will render the public ill-informed, but the public must be well-informed for effective conflict settlement to take place, so it is necessary to take a close look at how distorted media coverage can affect external involvement in conflict settlement.

References

Brilmayer L (1991) Secession and self-determination: a territorial interpretation. Yale J Int Law 16

Castellino J (2000) International law and self-determination. Martinus Nijhoff, Leiden, p 18

Coggins BL (2011) The history of secession: an overview. In: Pavkovic A, Radan P (eds) The Ashgate research companion to secession. Ashgate Publishing Limited, Farnham, p 35

Crawford J (2006) The creation of states in international law. Oxford University Press, Oxford, pp 415–416

Engels F (1908) Socialism: Utopian and scientific (trans: Aveling E). Charles H. Kerr & Company, Chicago, p 79

Gregory Mankiw N (2011) Principles of economics, 6th edn. Cengage Learning, Boston

Horowitz DL (2003) A right to secede? In: Macedo S, Buchanan A (eds) Secession and self-determination. New York University Press, New York

Janik R (2013) The responsibility to protect as an impetus for secessionist movements: on the necessity to re-think territorial integrity. In: Kettemann MC (ed) Grenzen im Völkerrecht. Jan Sramek Verlag, Wien, pp 57–58

Kohen MG (2006) Introduction. In: Kohen MG (ed) Secession: international law perspectives. Cambridge University Press, Cambridge, p 3

Lachenmann F (2011) Legal positivism, para. 3. Max Planck Encyclopedia of Public International Law. Last updated in July 2011

Lenin VI (1964) The socialist revolution and the right of nations to self-determination. In: Lenin VI (ed) Collected works 22. Progress Publisher, Moscow, p 451

Malešević S, Dochartaigh NO (2011) Secession and political violence. In: Pavkovic A, Radan P (eds) The Ashgate research companion to secession. Ashgate Publishing Limited, Farnham, p 232

Mao T-t (1937) On contradiction, August 1937. https://www.marxists.org/reference/archive/mao/selected-works/volume-1/mswv1_17.htm. Last accessed 15 June 2018

Shaw MN (2008) International law, 6th edn. Cambridge University Press, Cambridge, p 70

Simma B, Paulus A (1999) The responsibility of individuals for human rights abuses in internal conflicts: a positivist view. Am J Int Law 93:316

Thirlway H (2010) The sources of international law. In: Evans MD (ed) International law, 3rd edn. Oxford University Press, Oxford, p 96

Thürer D, Burri T (2009) Secession, para. 2. Max Planck Encyclopedia of Public International Law. Last updated in June 2009

de Waal A, Omaar R (1994) Can military intervention be 'Humanitarian'? Middle East Report 187. https://www.merip.org/mer/mer187/can-military-intervention-be-humanitarian. Last accessed 15 June 2018

Weber M (2014) Politics as a vocation (trans: Gerth HH, Wright Mills C). Oxford University Press, Oxford, 1946, moulin digital editions, p 41

Chapter 2
Exploring the Legal Color of Secession

The legal color of secession is worth serious consideration from the perspective of international law. When speaking of legal colors of an act, the instinct response would be "legal" or "illegal": "legal" is always associated with a legal right, while "illegal" is always with a legal prohibition. Will this simple dichotomy also be applicable to secession? Judge Simma of the International Court of Justice in the Kosovo case did not think so. In his declaration he gave his reasons: "it ignores the possible degrees of non-prohibition, ranging from 'tolerated' to 'permissible' to 'desirable'... That an act might be 'tolerated' would not necessarily mean that it is 'legal', but rather that it is 'not illegal'... the narrowness of the Court's approach might constitute a weakness, going forward, in its ability to deal with the great shades of nuance that permeate international law."[1] It is a pity that Judge Simma himself refused to point out whether the unilateral declaration of independence of Kosovo was "tolerated", "permissible" or "desirable". However, it must be admitted that the viewpoint that "legal" and "illegal" might not be the only legal colors of secession is thought-provoking: one is inspired to think how a secessionist dispute can be settled in the current international legal system when secession is deemed not illegal and at the same time not legal. Before discussing the international legal color of secession, it is necessary to clarify how secession acquires an international legal color, so the issue of international legal sources must be discussed in the first place.

Ascertaining sources of international law is not as simple as in domestic law: "at the international level [there is] neither a universal legislative body corresponding to a national parliament, nor a system for universal judicial jurisdiction which has built up a wide-ranging body of precedent."[2] "One is therefore faced with the problem of discovering where the law is to be found and how one can tell whether a particular

[1] Accordance with International Law of the Unilateral Declaration of Independence in Respect of Kosovo, Declaration of Judge Simma, I.C.J. Reports 2010, pp.480–481, paras. 8–9.

[2] See Chap. 1, Note 32.

J. Lu, *On State Secession from International Law Perspectives*,
https://doi.org/10.1007/978-3-319-97448-4_2

proposition amounts to a legal rule. This perplexity is reinforced because of the anarchic nature of world affairs and the clash of competing sovereignties."[3]

Article 38(1) of the Statute of the International Court of Justice (hereinafter may be referred to as ICJ) serves as a guide to law-finding, and there seems to be no other statement as to the sources of international law more authoritative and complete than it.[4] When the ICJ is to decide a dispute submitted to it according to international law, it shall apply (a) international conventions, whether general or particular, establishing rules expressly recognized by the contesting states; (b) international custom, as evidence of a general practice accepted as law; (c) the general principles of law recognized by civilized nations; (d) subject to the provisions of Article 59, judicial decisions and the teachings of the most highly qualified publicists of the various nations, as subsidiary means for the determination of rules of law.

It remains debatable whether this sequence has symbolized a definite hierarchy within these four types of legal sources, as a proposed provision indicating that sources should be applied according to the order in which they are mentioned in that article was rejected during the drafting, but it is relatively clear that a treaty rule or a customary rule will take priority over general principles of law.[5] Article 38(1) proves that, in principle, reasoning in international law is deductive. "One proceeds from the general rule, and then considers the facts of the case and applies the rule to the facts. This form of reasoning is the inversion of both the classical Roman Law and the common law methods, both of which start with the facts."[6] From this perspective, it can be concluded that the Canadian Supreme Court made an evident mistake in its reasoning. Look at the following statement: "Given the lack of specific authorization for unilateral secession, proponents of the existence of such a right at international law are therefore left to attempt to found their argument (i) on the proposition that unilateral secession is not specifically prohibited and that what is not specifically prohibited is inferentially permitted..."[7] According to this statement, an inferentially permitted act can prove the existence of a right, which is obviously not deductive.

It is somewhat understandable that the Canadian Supreme Court made such a mistake because "neither the classical system of Roman law nor the classical common law employed the idea of legal rights. In both cases legal doctrines were based on bringing together facts and their appropriate remedies ... It is not exactly known when European legal scholarship finally moved on from the old Roman and common law of remedies to one of abstract and systematic rights."[8] The idea of

---

[3]See Chap. 1, Note 33.

[4]See e.g. Brownlie (2003), p. 5; Jennings and Watts (1992), p. 24; Hudson (1934), pp. 601 ff. quoted from Shaw (2008), p. 70.

[5]Thirlway (2010), p. 114.

[6]Eleftheriadis (2008), p. 5.

[7]Reference Re Secession of Quebec, [1998] 2 S.C.R. 217, para.111, http://scc-csc.lexum.com/scc-csc/scc-csc/en/item/1643/index.do, last accessed on 15.06.2018.

[8]Eleftheriadis (2008), pp. 2–3.

remedy should deserve particular attention because it might translate into a so-called remedial right, whose (alleged) international legal source should be carefully scrutinized.

2.1 Exploring the Legal Color of Secession in Terms of International Conventions

2.1.1 General Introduction to International Conventions

According to Article 38(1)(a) of the Statute of the ICJ, general or particular international conventions establishing rules expressly recognized by the contesting states are considered as a source of international law. It is noteworthy that an international convention might not be entitled "convention": "Treaties are known by a variety of differing names, ranging from Conventions, International Agreements, Pacts, General Acts, Charters, through to Statutes, Declarations and Covenants."[9] In a strict sense, differing names might imply slight difference: for instance, conventions are usually multilateral treaties dealing with general issues. In this dissertation, for the sake of discussion, the interchangeability of differing names will not be affected due to this slight difference. Whether an international legal instrument can be regarded as an international convention in the sense of Article 38(1)(a) is dependent on the following points: it is about establishing legal rules; these rules are expressly recognized, namely legally binding; these rules apply to contesting states.

According to these three points, a declaration might not always be an international convention in the sense of Article 38(1)(a). The Declaration on the Granting of Independence to Colonial Countries and Peoples is a case in point. This declaration was adopted in 1960 as a General Assembly resolution of the United Nations (hereinafter may be referred to as UN), which is not an international convention in the sense of Article 38(1)(a) of the Statute of the ICJ, as it did not meet all these three points. Meeting the first point is not a problem: this UN document intended to establish a right to independence, or a right for colonies to secede from colonial powers. Then turning to the second point, one cannot say that the General Assembly resolution met this requirement: as a legally non-binding instrument, it is unconvincing that the declaration displayed express recognition. Given that colonial powers cast abstentions to this resolution, their recognition was barely seen. It is particularly noteworthy that compared to recognition granted by other states, recognition granted by colonial powers should deserve more attention. In general, for states which did not own colonies, the granting of independence to colonial countries and peoples was not their business: they were neither beneficiaries of the right to independence nor assumed the obligation to recognize the independence. When it comes to the third point, one should consider the concept of "contesting states" in a

[9]Shaw (2008), p. 93.

context related to independence. Generally speaking, independence of colonial countries and peoples is not an issue between contesting states: colonial countries and peoples did not have statehood, and pursuing independence was pursuing statehood. Of course, when sovereign states other than colonial powers were also involved, this would become an issue between contesting states. However, this declaration did not set out to address relations between colonial powers and other sovereign states, in this sense, it did not meet the third requirement. But is it really meaningful to stick to the literal meaning when the issue of independence is involved? Needless to say, strictly following the literal meaning of Article 38(1)(a) would actually deprive a colonial country and people of the right to conclude an international treaty with a colonial power. From this perspective, it is safe to conclude that if a treaty is concerned with independence, it would be better to interpret "contesting states" as "contesting parties".

By the same token, the Declaration on Principles of International Law Concerning Friendly Relations and Co-operation among states in Accordance with the Charter of the UN,[10] which is also a UN General Assembly Resolution, should not be regarded as an international convention in the sense of Article 38(1)(a). This declaration embodied the following paragraph:

Nothing in the foregoing paragraphs shall be construed as authorizing or encouraging any action which would dismember or impair, totally or in part, the territorial integrity or political unity of sovereign and independent States conducting themselves in compliance with the principle of equal rights and self-determination of peoples as described above and thus possessed of a government representing the whole people belonging to the territory without distinction as to race, creed or color.

This paragraph is regarded by some as 'safeguard clause'.[11] Their interpretation of this paragraph is that the territorial integrity or political unity is no longer under protection when states fail to conduct themselves in compliance with the principle of equal rights and self-determination of peoples as described above and thus do not possess a government representing the whole people belonging to the territory without distinction as to race, creed or color. Thus, a remedial right to secession could be deduced therefrom. In the Kosovo case Judge Yusuf and Judge Trindade have accepted this doctrine. Judge Yusuf argued in his separate opinion that international law does not turn "a blind eye to the plight of such groups, particularly in those cases where the State not only denies them the exercise of their internal right of self-determination, but also subjects them to discrimination, persecution and egregious violations of human rights or humanitarian law. Under such exceptional circumstances, the right of peoples to self-determination may support a claim to separate statehood provided it meets the conditions prescribed by international law... Such conditions may be gleaned from various instruments, including the Declaration on Principles of International Law Concerning Friendly Relations and

[10] A/RES/25/2625.

[11] Kohen (2006), p. 10.

Co-operation among States in Accordance with the Charter of the United Nations".[12] According to Judge Trindade, "what has happened in Kosovo is that the victimized 'people' or 'population' has sought independence, in reaction against systematic and long-lasting terror and oppression, perpetrated in flagrant breach of the fundamental principle of equality and non-discrimination. The basic lesson is clear: no State can use territory to destroy the population".[13]

Such interpretation has met a lot of challenges. "It is one thing to argue that a government may lose its legitimacy if it fails to live up to its fundamental commitments... it is quite another thing to argue that such a loss of legitimacy on the part of a government is transformed into a legal right of the victimized population to secede territory from the state."[14] Moreover, "such a major change in legal principle cannot be introduced by way of an ambiguous subordinate clause, especially when the principle of territorial integrity has always been accepted and proclaimed as a core principle of international law, and is indeed placed before the qualifying clause in the provision in question".[15] It is particularly noteworthy that "the 'safeguard clause' was originally drafted with situations such as South Africa and Rhodesia in mind, without any intention to extend recognition to any 'secession' rights to the majority of the South African and Zimbabwean peoples, as victims of racist regimes. Curiously enough, it was Pretoria's minority regime which encouraged a 'secessionist' policy, through the creation of Bantustan 'independent' States (Transkei, Ciskei, Bophuthatswana and Venda)".[16]

Despite the opposing interpretations, it should be noted that this General Assembly resolution was somehow treated by some as an international convention as they attempted to deduce a right directly from it. Needless to say, this approach, i.e. deducing a right directly from the legal text, is generally accepted in terms of international conventions, but this approach seems rather problematic in terms of a General Assembly resolution. The General Assembly resolution can be treated as evidence of opinio juris,[17] which is a constituent of customary international law. Undoubtedly, one can deduce a right from customary international law, but one certainly cannot deduce a right directly from evidence of opinio juris. If one intends to deduce a right directly from an international instrument, one must first make this

[12] Accordance with International Law of the Unilateral Declaration of Independence in Respect of Kosovo, Separate Opinion of Judge Yusuf, I.C.J. Reports 2010, p. 618, para. 11.

[13] Accordance with International Law of the Unilateral Declaration of Independence in Respect of Kosovo, Separate Opinion of Judge Cançado Trindade, I.C.J. Reports 2010, p.523, para. 176.

[14] Del Mar (2013), pp. 80–81.

[15] Shaw (1997), p. 483.

[16] See above Note 11.

[17] The ICJ treated General Assembly resolutions in the case of *Military and Paramilitary Activities in and against Nicaragua* as evidence of opinio juris, *see Military and Paramilitary Activities in and against Nicaragua (Nicaragua v. United States of America). Merits, Judgement. I.C.J. Reports 1986*, p. 14, para. 188; in the case of *Legality of the Threat or Use of Nuclear Weapons* General Assembly resolutions were also treated as evidence of opinio juris, see *Legality of the Threat or Use of Nuclear Weapons, Advisory Opinion, I.C.J. Reports 1996*, p. 226, para. 73.

international instrument into an international convention because other international instruments alone cannot confirm the existence of an international legal right.

There are international conventions in the sense of Article 38(1)(a) of the Statute of the ICJ, which addressed the issue of secession, despite being much less mentioned compared to the renowned General Assembly resolutions discussed above. Before the Declaration on the Granting of Independence to Colonial Countries and Peoples was adopted by the UN General Assembly, the Treaty Concerning the Establishment of the Republic of Cyprus was concluded among the UK, Greece, Turkey and Cyprus,[18] in which the right of Cyprus to be independent from the UK was confirmed. Nearly 30 years after the adoption of this declaration, the independence of Namibia was finally confirmed in the New York Accords signed by the People's Republic of Angola, the Republic of Cuba, and the Republic of South Africa in 1988.[19] These international conventions had much to do with decolonizing secession, so their heuristic value in the post-colonial era is somewhat limited, as post-colonial secession involves legal issues different from those of decolonizing secession. The Comprehensive Peace Agreement concluded between Sudan and South Sudan can be regarded as an international convention concerned with post-colonial secession in the sense of Article 38(1)(a) of the Statute of the ICJ when "contesting states" is replaced by "contesting parties". Undeniably, the approach to the issue of secession in this agreement deserves serious consideration.

2.1.2 Comprehensive Peace Agreement Between Sudan and South Sudan

One should take a close look at how secession was regulated in the Comprehensive Peace Agreement, which is composed of six agreements, namely the Protocol of Machakos, the Protocol on security arrangements, the Protocol on wealth-sharing, the Protocol on Power-sharing, the Protocol on the resolution of conflict in southern Kordofan/Nuba Mountains and the Blue Nile States and the Protocol on the resolution of conflict in Abyie: in the Machakos Protocol the parties agreed on a broad framework, setting forth the principles of governance, the transitional process and the structures of government as well as on the right to self-determination for the people of South Sudan, and on state and religion; the most notable part of it is that after a 6-year interim period, southern Sudan will have the right to vote in an internationally monitored referendum either to confirm Sudan's unity or to vote for

[18] Treaty Concerning the Establishment of the Republic of Cyprus (Treaty of Nicosia), http://peacemaker.un.org/cyprus-nicosia-treaty60, last accessed on 15.06.2018.

[19] Agreement among the People's Republic of Angola, the Republic of Cuba, and the Republic of South Africa (Tripartite Agreement), http://peacemaker.un.org/angola-tripartite-agreement88, last accessed on 15.06.2018.

secession.[20] Besides, three agreements needed to be finalized in order to achieve a comprehensive peace accord: one on permanent cease-fire arrangements, one on the implementation of all Protocols signed and one on the International/Regional Guarantees; the negotiations between the parties on the Permanent Cease-Fire protocol advanced rather slowly, as they could not reach agreement on a number of issues, such as the redeployment of forces in eastern Sudan and the financing of the Sudan People's Liberation Movement/Army; during the pre-interim and interim period both parties still had negotiations on a Permanent Cease-Fire arrangement.[21]

The legal color of secession, according to this international treaty, can be described as both legal and illegal: if secessionists followed the whole agreement and the referendum confirmed the will of the people to secede, secession was legal or there was a right to secede, but if secessionists did not follow the whole agreement or the referendum did not confirm the will of the people to secede, secession was illegal. Obviously, this agreement combined a right to secession and obligations of secessionists together: in such circumstances, secession was not simply treated as a right or a prohibited act but was comprised of both possibilities. Both secessionists and the sovereign state were entitled to certain rights and assumed corresponding duties at the same time. In essence, the approach adopted in this international convention has not seen secession from the perspective of the traditional dichotomy, namely a pure right or a purely prohibited act, and thus has successfully avoided, in the parlance of Judge Simma, "the great shades of nuance that permeate international law"[22]; although the traditional dichotomy was rejected, the legal color of secession did not become vague, as the agreement clearly provided under which condition there was a right to secession, and under which condition secession was prohibited.

It is worth considering whether this approach is legally more advisable than the traditional dichotomy. When it comes to a secessionist dispute, it is quite natural to adopt the dichotomy focusing on whether there is a right to secession or a prohibition under international law. For the settlement of common disputes, it is not a wrong idea, but for the settlement of secessionist disputes, a second thought is required. Advantages of the approach adopted in the Comprehensive Agreement can be understood from following perspectives:

In the first place, given the practical complexity of secessionist disputes, a simple confirmation of a right to secession or a simple prohibition on secession fails to provide a satisfactory solution. The Comprehensive Peace Agreement has demonstrated how complicated a secessionist dispute might be: its content included democratic governance, wealth-sharing, power-sharing, territorial demarcation and the settlement of armed conflicts and regional conflicts. In general, these points can

---

[20]See the official Website of United Nations Mission in Sudan (UNMIS) regarding the Comprehensive Peace Agreement, https://unmis.unmissions.org/comprehensive-peace-agreement, last accessed on 15.06.2018.

[21]Ibid.

[22]Accordance with International Law of the Unilateral Declaration of Independence in Respect of Kosovo, Declaration of Judge Simma, I.C.J. Reports 2010, p. 481, para. 9.

be classified into different fields of international law such as self-determination, human rights, territorial sovereignty and internal armed conflicts. Undoubtedly, a simple confirmation of a right to secession or a prohibition on secession would not contribute much to a solution to all these issues. The oversimplified assumption of legal relations embodied in the simple confirmation of a right to secession cannot cover those highly complicated legal relations between a secessionist entity and a sovereign state. The simple confirmation of a right to secession assumes that in their legal relations, the secessionist entity is a pure obligee while the sovereign state is a pure obligor. This assumption is certainly problematic: for example, there is no denying that the sovereign state is a holder of a right to self-determination, so the secessionist entity also assumes the obligation to respect the right to self-determination of the sovereign state, particularly when the secessionist entity requires the sovereign state to respect the same right of it. Simply confirming a right to secession is ignoring that the secessionist entity is also an obligor and the sovereign state an obligee. A simple prohibition on secession sounds like a good idea for a sovereign state, but it remains questionable whether it could actually contribute to the settlement of secessionist disputes. Just like the simple confirmation of a right to secession, a simple prohibition on it might also be an oversimplified way of settling secessionist disputes: when those concrete disputing points are not well addressed, a simple prohibition on secession cannot effectively prohibit secession in reality. That is why Sudan finally decided to settle the secessionist issue at the negotiation table. Thanks to the comprehensiveness of the agreement, each aspect of the highly complicated legal relations between the secessionist entity and the sovereign state has been taken care of.

In the second place, a simple confirmation of a right to secession cannot prohibit abuse of such a right. Many are afraid of abuse of sovereignty, so they disfavor a strict prohibition on secession, and those who advocate a remedial right to secession seem to share this viewpoint. Undeniably, power is likely to be abused, but not only power can be abused, a right can also be abused, especially when the boundary of the right is fairly unclear. In general, abuse of rights by states has already aroused attention under international law, but abuse of rights by non-state actors such as a secessionist entity has seldom been discussed. It must be recognized that in discussing a right one should consider preventing likely abuse of this right, and a right to secession is no exception. Unfortunately, preventing the likely abuse of a right to secession is rarely considered. That is why some secessionists, such as the Kosovo Liberation Army (hereinafter referred to as the KLA), did not hesitate to take terrorist action to pursue a right to secession. Did a right to secession include permission for terrorist action? A simple confirmation of a right to secession neither confirms it nor negates it. Following the logic of nulla poena sine lege, the risk of taking terrorist action to pursue a right to secession is rather noticeable. In order to prevent abuse of a right to secession, it is necessary to ascertain the boundary of the right and the consequences of overstepping the boundary, concretizing the abstract right and imposing obligations on the right holder. That is just what the Comprehensive Peace Agreement was about: in this international convention the right to secession was concretized and corresponding obligations were imposed on the right holder. In this context, there is a lower likelihood of the right to secession being abused: unlike a simple confirmation of an abstract right, the boundary of which was unclear, in this international convention the boundary of the right to secession was clarified, and adverse legal consequences of overstepping the boundary discouraged secessionists from abusing this right.

In the third place, the Comprehensive Peace Agreement rejected the traditional dichotomy about secession and introduced a better dichotomy about secession. The traditional dichotomy certainly has its problems, but it does not mean that the dichotomy itself should be abandoned. The importance of the dichotomy between legality and illegality is derived from the requirement of legal certainty. Admittedly, as pointed out by Judge Simma, such dichotomy sometimes oversimplifies the issue: there are acts, the classification of which would be rather difficult, as they neither fall into the typical legal category nor the typical illegal category in the current international legal system. However, it is not a fault of the dichotomy but a fault of international law which is still very underdeveloped: if the legal system were more sophisticated, the classification would not be so difficult. The dichotomy is a requisite: legal certainty cannot be guaranteed without the dichotomy which is closely related to the guiding and regulating function of law. Putting acts into either a "legal" category or "illegal" category is necessary because it sends clear legal signals to legal actors, and only with clear legal signals can law effectively regulate relations between legal actors. When there is a third category, namely "neither legal nor illegal", legal signals sent to legal actors get unclear, and when a "neither legal nor illegal" act caused disputes between legal actors, law can only turn a blind eye to such disputes. When secession is deemed neither legal nor illegal under international law, it is unrealistic to expect that international law can play a pivotal role in the settlement of secessionist disputes. Therefore, in order to ensure legal certainty, including maintaining the guiding and regulating function of law, it is necessary to improve the current international legal system, avoiding or at least reducing "neither legal nor illegal" cases. The Comprehensive Peace Agreement proves to be a valuable attempt: it used "both legal and illegal" to replace "neither legal nor illegal" by specifying under which condition secession was legal and under which condition it was illegal. On the one hand, this approach has adhered to the dichotomy, and the guiding and regulating function of law has thus been maintained. On the other hand, it has avoided the oversimplification caused by the traditional dichotomy: the legal color of secession varied according to the practical implementation of the convention.

2.1.3 Edinburgh Agreement Between the UK and Scotland

The Agreement between the United Kingdom Government and the Scottish Government on a referendum on independence for Scotland (hereinafter referred to as the Edinburgh Agreement) can also be regarded as an international convention in the sense of Article 38(1)(a) on secession. Of course, one may argue that as long as

Scotland has not acquired independence, the Edinburgh Agreement should be deemed a constitutional arrangement, just like an agreement concluded between a regional government and the central government. The problem lies in the legal identity of a secessionist entity: if a secessionist entity is not regarded as a legal subject of international law, the agreement between it and the parent state should be treated as a constitutional arrangement, just like any other agreement between a regional government and the central government; however, when a secessionist entity is regarded as a special legal subject of international law, it is reasonable to treat the agreement between it and the parent state as an international convention. The following discussion is based on that the secessionist entity is regarded as a special legal subject of international law.

Unlike the Comprehensive Peace Agreement which focused on a number of issues, the Edinburgh Agreement focused exclusively on the issue of a referendum on independence. Needless to say, a referendum on independence is an important part of secession, and it is necessary to discern how a referendum on independence can influence the legal color of secession. Therefore, one needs to take a close look at the basic content of the Edinburgh Agreement: the referendum should have a clear legal base, so both governments agreed to promote an Order in Council under Section 30 of the Scotland Act 1998 in the United Kingdom and Scottish Parliaments to allow a single-question referendum on Scottish independence to be held before the end of 2014; the Order put it beyond doubt that the Scottish Parliament can legislate for that referendum, and the referendum legislation should set out the date of the referendum, the franchise, the wording of the question, rules on campaign financing and other rules for conducting the referendum; the referendum should be conducted so as to command the confidence of parliaments, governments and people, and deliver a fair test and a decisive expression of the views of people in Scotland and a result that everyone will respect; both governments were committed, through the Memorandum of Understanding between them and others, to working together on matters of mutual interest and to the principles of good communication and mutual respect.[23]

According to the Edinburgh Agreement, the influence of the result of the referendum on the legal color of secession is somewhat unclear: it was uncertain whether the independence of Scotland became legal or not, when the result of the referendum proved to be pro-secession. Did it mean that the result of a referendum on independence was one thing, the legal effect of the result was another? Such understanding was correct to some extent: when the Edinburgh Agreement was concluded, both parties did not agree on what would happen after the independence referendum; they agreed on this point only a few months before the referendum; even if the result of referendum had proven that more people voted for independence, independence

[23] Agreement between the United Kingdom Government and the Scottish Government on a referendum on independence for Scotland (Edinburgh Agreement), 15 October 2012, http://www.gov.scot/About/Government/concordats/Referendum-on-independence, last accessed on 15.06.2018.

would not happen until negotiations between people representing Scotland and people representing the rest of the United Kingdom have been completed, and these negotiations would include discussion about the allocation of assets and liabilities; in the meantime, Scotland would continue to be part of the UK.[24] In this sense, regulating secession between the UK and Scotland is similar to that between Sudan and South Sudan: a distribution of practical interests between the sovereign state and the secessionist entity was indispensable. The distinction is that the UK and Scotland decided to discuss other issues after the referendum, while Sudan and South Sudan discussed all these issues before the referendum. As a matter of fact, the result of the independence referendum of South Sudan also did not directly bring about an independent effect: both disputing parties agreed that there was a 6-month transition period after the referendum and before South Sudan could declare independence, and during this period both parties were expected to continue to work on post-referendum issues, including oil, debt and currency.[25]

In view of the foregoing, it is clear that an international convention on secession will include a substantive part and a procedural part: the former is about the distribution of substantive rights and duties, and the latter is about procedural rights and duties. Needless to say, the substantive part and the procedural part are inextricably connected with each other, but this connection cannot be misinterpreted. A common misinterpretation is that the pro-secession result of an independence referendum can directly lead to a right to secession.[26] What kind of legal effect an independence referendum might have should depend on the specific provisions in the agreement concluded between the sovereign state and the secessionist entity. In this case, because of the lack of an arrangement for substantive rights and duties between the UK and Scotland, the result of the referendum had little legal effect in the substantive sense, but its legal effect in the procedural sense was evident: if the result of the referendum proved that more people voted for independence, negotiations about the distribution of substantive rights and duties would be started. In the case of South Sudan, the result of the referendum had more legal effect in the substantive sense as both parties already had arrangements for substantive rights and duties between them. Therefore, in order to judge the legal color of secession, focusing on the result of an independence referendum does not suffice, because secession includes both a procedural part and a substantive part, and an

[24]Scottish independence: Post-referendum agreement reached, 18 June 2014, http://www.bbc.com/news/uk-scotland-scotland-politics-27906062, last accessed on 15.06.2018.

[25]Sudan: Second Review Under the 2009-10 Staff-Monitored Program-Staff Report; Staff Supplement; and Statement by the Executive Director for Sudan, IMF Country Report No. 11/86, April 2011, p. 4.

[26]For instance, Quebec as the secessionist entity used to have this misinterpretation, so the Canadian Supreme Court made it clear in the Reference re Secession of Quebec: "the democratic principle identified above would demand that considerable weight be given to a clear expression by the people of Quebec of their will to secede from Canada, even though a referendum, in itself and without more, has no direct legal effect, and could not in itself bring about unilateral secession", see Reference re Secession of Quebec, para. 87.

independence referendum as a procedure cannot reflect the legal color of secession as a whole.

Perhaps the most enlightening point of the Edinburgh Agreement is its emphasis on procedural justice. Procedural justice is mainly about a right for an affected party to participate in the decision-making process. Undoubtedly, bringing procedural justice into an independence referendum is a theme worth considering, because the referendum procedure itself tends to overlook the right to participate of an affected party, when the party does not have a right to vote in the referendum. It might sound somewhat strange, but it is rather common in secession: the secession of Scotland would definitely affect interests of the UK in a severe manner, but the rest of the UK did not have a right to vote in the referendum which could lead to secession. How can procedural justice be guaranteed in such circumstances? The Edinburgh Agreement provided an answer: the UK participated in deciding basic rules of the independence referendum, and thus the right of an affected party to participate in the decision-making process was satisfied.

Undeniably, the importance of procedural justice is often underestimated. Even in the common law system which is deemed to be closely connected with procedural justice, the notion that procedural rights may be sacrificed on the altar of substantive advantage is not strange.[27] In the international legal system, discussion about procedural justice is even rarer. Nevertheless, it is necessary to link the legal color of secession with procedural justice. This point can be understood from following perspectives. Firstly, the right to participate of one affected party can help prevent the other party from abusing its procedural right. A referendum on independence is launched mainly to satisfy the wish of secessionists, so it is a procedural right granted for them. As mentioned above, a right is open to abuse and a procedural right is no exception. There are many possibilities of abusing this procedural right, and those requirements regarding the conduct of the independence referendum embodied in the Edinburgh Agreement can be taken as precautionary measures against abuse of such a procedural right. For example, the wording of the referendum question can be exploited for producing a pro-secessionist result, so the Edinburgh Agreement provided that the referendum question must be fair, easy to understand and capable of producing a result that is accepted and commands confidence; for this sake, the Electoral Commission was required to review the proposed question and any statement that preceded the question and to report to the UK Parliament on the intelligibility of that question.[28] In this process there was active interplay between contesting parties: the Scottish Government would refer the proposed referendum question and any preceding statement to the Electoral Commission for review of its intelligibility; interested parties would be able to submit their views on the proposed wording to the Electoral Commission as part of the Commission's review process; the Electoral Commission would report on the question and this report would be laid before the Scottish Parliament; in turn the Scottish Government would respond to the

[27] Solum (2004), p. 182.

[28] Edinburgh Agreement, paras. 5 and 7.

report, indicating its response to any recommendations that the Electoral Commission might make.[29] Thus it was unlikely for the secessionist entity to exert an undue influence on the result of the referendum by designing a referendum question which was unfair and incapable of producing a result that could be accepted by the other side.

Secondly, procedural justice can help reduce legal controversy surrounding the process of secession. Obviously, the independence referendum itself, as an important part of secession, can contribute much legal controversy: according to the Edinburgh Agreement, potential controversial points could be the legal base of the independence referendum, the legislation power related to the referendum and the wording of the referendum question, etc. As demonstrated in the Edinburgh Agreement, introducing procedural justice could help solve such controversial issues: controversy largely originates from insufficient procedural participation, so a process that provides contesting parties an opportunity to express their different opinions and make joint decisions over controversial points will help reduce controversy. If both the sovereign state and the secessionist entity can jointly decide on details regarding the independence referendum, the independence referendum will therefore cause less controversy, which can contribute a good deal to the exploration of the legal color of secession: undeniably, if the independence referendum itself is controversial, it remains rather doubtful whether the result of it can reflect the genuine will to secede; in such circumstances, the legal color of secession remains unclear. Had the UK not been given the opportunity to participate in deciding those controversial points regarding referendum, it would inevitably have regarded the result of the referendum as controversial and doubt whether it could reflect the will of Scottish people to secede. If the will to secede itself is quite debatable, it will be rather difficult, if not impossible, for the exploration of the legal color of secession to be continued. Therefore, one cannot underestimate the importance of reducing legal controversy surrounding the process of secession, of which the independence referendum is an important part. Clearly, procedural justice is quite helpful in this regard.

Thirdly, procedural justice is closely related to the distribution of substantive rights and duties between disputing parties in secessionist disputes. As discussed before, secession involves regulating various legal relations between a sovereign state and a secessionist entity, and specific regulations are embodied in an agreement reached between them. How can such an agreement be concluded? The answer is through fruitful negotiation. In essence, negotiation is a reflection of procedural justice: negotiation itself signifies that contesting parties participate in the decision-making process, which affords an affected party a meaningful opportunity to present evidence and arguments that are relevant to legal rules and equitable considerations that should govern the dispute as a matter of substantive law.[30] In this sense, it is comprehensible why a claim to unilateral secession should be dismissed from a legal point of view: the claim to unilateral secession inevitably contradicts procedural

---

[29]Ibid.

[30]Solum (2004), p. 316.

justice, because despite being severely affected by the decision of secessionists, a chance for the sovereign state to present evidence and arguments that are relevant to legal rules and equitable considerations that should govern the secessionist dispute as a matter of substantive law, is not fully guaranteed in such circumstances. This chance deprivation unfairly affects not only the distribution of concrete rights and duties between the sovereign state and the secessionist entity but also abstract rights and duties. Obviously, the one, whose rights are affected in the decision-making process, should be included in this process, for the sake of respecting its autonomy and status as an equal legal person[31] under international law. This abstract right of a sovereign state is not well respected in case of unilateral secession. From this perspective, it is necessary to stress the significance of procedural justice in exploring the legal color of secession, in order to have a fair distribution of substantive rights and duties between a sovereign state and a secessionist entity.

To sum up, although procedural justice is seldom discussed in the field of international law, its role in exploring the legal color of secession is worth serious consideration. A secessionist dispute is not only about substantive rights and duties, legal consideration should also be given to procedural aspects. As discussed above, taking procedural justice into consideration of secession is certainly meaningful: reasonable distribution of procedural rights and duties will reduce legal controversy and pave the way for reasonable distribution of substantive rights and duties between a sovereign state and a secessionist entity.

2.1.4 Conclusions and Reflections

In view of the foregoing, it is necessary to conclude international conventions for the settlement of secessionist disputes. In the first place, effectively regulating secessionist disputes requires such conventions concluded between sovereign states and secessionist entities, otherwise one cannot expect international law to play a pivotal role in such disputes: Judge Simma even implied that this is an area "where international law has not yet come to regulate, or indeed, will never come to regulate".[32] From the perspective of dispute settlement, when one realizes that the current legal system cannot deal with a certain issue, one should consider improving the legal system, enabling it to address this issue. Concluding special international agreements to regulate secessionist disputes is improving the current international legal system: these newly formed international instruments have strengthened the regulating and guiding function of international law, enabling the current legal system to regulate those highly complicated legal relations between sovereign states and secessionist entities. Thanks to these specific international instruments, the distribution of rights and duties between them is no longer unclear, which helps

---

[31] Ibid. p. 264.

[32] See above Note 22.

prevent abuse of rights and reduce legal controversy surrounding secessionist disputes.

In the second place, the variety of secessionist disputes requires flexible and individualized legal solutions, and specific international instruments concluded between disputing parties are in a position to provide such solutions. According to what has been discussed above, the settlement of secessionist disputes seems to represent "a central element in the idea of justice" believed by Hart, namely "treat like cases alike and different cases differently".[33] Both the cases of South Sudan and Scotland are about secessionist disputes, so they are like cases in this sense, but each secessionist dispute also has its own feature, so the Comprehensive Peace Agreement focused more on the distribution of substantive rights and duties, while the Edinburgh Agreement stressed procedural justice. The unique feature of each secessionist dispute requires that the solution take on an individualized color, and it seems that only a specific agreement concluded between the contesting parties can guarantee this individualized color at best: it is not only because the contesting parties know their disagreement better than others, but also because their interests should be determined by them. This point will be further discussed from the perspective of self-determination.

Therefore, it can be said that in secessionist disputes international law can play a pivotal role when the legal solution takes good care of the unique feature of a certain dispute, otherwise the contribution of international law in this regard would inevitably be moderate. International agreements concluded between sovereign states and secessionist entities are necessary in the settlement of secessionist disputes, because lex specialis as such is intended for a particular secessionist dispute. This point is actually quite important for one to understand why other sources of international law fail to contribute as much as international conventions to the settlement of secessionist disputes: from international conventions to international custom further to general principles of law, international legal sources become increasingly less particular and more general. The particularity of an individual case and the generality of law will inevitably lead to the consequence known as "hard cases make bad law".

2.2 Exploring the Legal Color of Secession in Terms of International Custom

2.2.1 Composition of International Custom Regarding Secession

When there is no international agreement dealing with a particular secessionist dispute, according to Article 38(1) of the Statute of the ICJ, it is time to consider whether there is international custom addressing this issue. Article 38(1)(b) has

[33] Hart (1961), p. 155.

revealed that international custom contains two parts: one is the material part, i.e. the practice, and the other is the psychological part, i.e. the general belief that the practice is accepted as law (opinio juris). About these two parts there has been a good deal of debate: for instance, "how can a practice ever develop into a customary rule if states have to believe the rule already exists before their acts of practice can be significant for the creation of the rule? Or is it sufficient if initially states act in the mistaken belief that a rule already exists, a case of communis error facit jus (a shared mistake produces law)?"[34] Such controversy reminds one that a cautious attitude to the understanding and application of international custom is required.

When discussing whether there is any international custom regarding secession, it is necessary to review those General Assembly resolutions discussed above, because they can be treated as evidence of opinio juris. For instance, in the case of Legality of the Threat or Use of Nuclear Weapons, the ICJ stated that "the adoption each year by the General Assembly, by a large majority, of resolutions recalling the content of resolution 1653 (XVI), and requesting the member States to conclude a convention prohibiting the use of nuclear weapons in any circumstance, reveals the desire of a very large section of the international community to take, by a specific and express prohibition of the use of nuclear weapons, a significant step forward along the road to complete nuclear disarmament. The emergence, as lex lata, of a customary rule specifically prohibiting the use of nuclear weapons as such is hampered by the continuing tensions between the nascent opinio juris on the one hand, and the still strong adherence to the practice of deterrence on the other".[35] Therefore, only when General Assembly resolutions concerning secession combine with practice concerning secession can international customary law concerning secession come into existence. When it comes to the issue of practice, a fundamental question deserves serious consideration: as a secessionist dispute usually involves a sovereign state and a secessionist entity instead of two sovereign states, is it sufficient to focus only on the practice of sovereign states?

The question whether it is sufficient to focus on practice of sovereign states is closely related to the special legal personality of secessionist entities under international law. A state is a typical subject of international law, but it is no longer the unique subject: as non-state actors appear more and more frequently in the discussion of international law, it would be rather difficult to refuse to treat them as new subjects of international law. For instance, if a right to self-determination is no longer restricted to sovereign states, it will be meaningless to refuse to treat a non-state holder of this right as a subject of international law. In the same vein, exploring the international legal color of secession requires considering the issue of the right to self-determination claimed by secessionist entities, so in this context, it is reasonable to treat them as subjects of international law. Thus the question becomes whether the practice of non-state subjects of international law should be focused on. When it

[34] Thirlway (2010), pp. 102–103.

[35] Legality of the Threat or Use of Nuclear Weapons, Advisory Opinion, I.C.J. Reports 1996, p. 226, para. 73.

comes to the practice of state actors, it is two-sided: "one state asserts a right, either explicitly or by acting in a way that impliedly constitutes such an assertion, and the state or states affected by the claim then react either by objecting or by refraining from objection. The practice on the two sides adds up to imply a customary rule, supporting the claim if no protest is made, or excluding the claim if there is a protest."[36] In the same vain, given that the issue is secession which is about legal relations between a sovereign state and a secessionist entity, it seems unreasonable to exclude practice of the secessionist entity, unless the sovereign state can unilaterally decide their relations. Therefore, when an instance seems to imply customary international law about secession, it should be comprised of practice and shared legal opinion of both sides, namely a sovereign state and a secessionist entity.

2.2.2 *Practice Corresponding to Opinio Juris*

Now one needs to consider the issue whether the Declaration on the Granting of Independence to Colonial Countries and Peoples as evidence of opinio juris could correspond to relevant practice. From the perspective of colonial countries and peoples, they certainly believed that they have the right to independence and acted in this belief. From the perspective of sovereign states, these states should be divided into colonial powers and other states. Because other states (except Dominican Republic) voted for this General Assembly resolution, one can say that they believed that colonial countries and peoples had a right to independence. However, other states were generally unable to provide relevant practice: they were not colonial powers, so they were not in a position to grant independence to colonial countries and peoples in a practical sense. As for colonial powers, because they cast abstentions to this General Assembly resolution, it is hard to say that they believed that colonial countries and peoples had a right to independence under international law. Therefore, when they granted independence to colonial countries and peoples, it is also hard to say that they acted in the belief of a right to independence. In this sense, one cannot simply assert the existence of customary international law with regard to independence or secession in the colonial context.

Then one should turn to the Declaration on Principles of International Law Concerning Friendly Relations and Co-operation among states in Accordance with the Charter of the UN. As mentioned above, it contained the so-called "safeguard clause", from which some intend to deduce a remedial right to secession, to be more specific, a unilateral right to secession in a remedial sense. If such a right is to be deduced in the sense of customary law, only (alleged) opinio juris does not suffice as relevant practice is indispensable. Obviously, the practice of secessionist entities seemingly corresponds to this opinio juris, but the same cannot be said about the practice of sovereign states: only a few states recognized a right to secession in

---

[36]Thirlway (2010), p. 103.

domestic law, and the enforceability of this right remained questionable according to the simple clauses. For instance, a right to secession has been mentioned in Article 72 of the Soviet Constitution: "each Union Republic shall retain the right freely to secede from the USSR".[37] Also in the Preamble of the Czechoslovakian Constitution an inalienable right to self-determination of the Slovak and Czech nations has been recognized "even to the point of separation".[38] Needless to say, without further provisions this right had only symbolic meaning. This symbolic right became an enforceable right thanks to further legal documents that dealt with the distribution of rights and duties arising out of dissolution which can be seen as a special from of secession: in the Alma Ata Declaration relevant parties have achieved mutual recognition as sovereign states and agreed that the Russian Federation would maintain full responsibility for all the rights and obligations of the USSR under the Charter of the United Nations, including the financial obligations[39]; likewise, the Constitutional Act No.541/1992 and No.542/1992 were deemed the most significant legal documents of all those Federal Assembly acts during the dissolution of Czechoslovakia, because the former dealt with the division of property between the Czech Republic and the Slovak Republic and the latter dealt with the dissolution of the federation.[40] Therefore, their consistent practice could correspond to a belief of a right to secession. The problem is that the so-called "safeguard clause" does not suggest a right to consensual secession as such but implies a unilateral right to secession in the remedial sense, so their practice had nothing to do with (alleged) opinio juris as interpreted by advocates of "safeguard clause". From this perspective, one cannot conclude that the practice of these two states helped form customary international law regarding a remedial right to secession, as the belief of a remedial right to secession and the practice of consensual secession do not correspond.

2.2.3 Conclusions and Reflections

It is necessary to distinguish a right to secession and a remedial right to secession. A right to secession includes a right to consensual secession as well as a right to unilateral secession: in this dissertation one can understand whether a right to secession refers to a right to consensual secession or a right to unilateral secession based on the concrete context. A remedial right to secession by nature is a right to unilateral secession: when a secessionist entity and a sovereign state can reach a consensus on secession either through a treaty or custom, the secessionist entity does not need to rely on the remedial nature to justify their action. Given its unilateral character, it can be said that there would be no customary international law about

[37] Weller (2008a), p. 33.
[38] Raič (2002), p. 314.
[39] Škrk (1999), pp. 8–9.
[40] Mikulka (1999), p. 109.

remedial secession, as forming customary international law requires the participation of both conflicting parties. When a secessionist entity claimed a right to unilateral secession on the remedial ground and the sovereign state did not protest, it would not help form customary law on a right to unilateral secession, because non-protest is also a kind of participation with legal effect, so this circumstance at best can help form customary law on a right to consensual secession. Since customary international law is incompatible with unilateral secession, one cannot deduce a remedial right to secession simply because of the so-called "safeguard clause" embodied in the General Assembly resolution.

In addition, it is important to be cautious about the interpretation of opinio juris embodied in General Assembly resolutions. For example, if one deduced that the so-called "safeguard clause" implies a right to unilateral secession, it would be quite difficult to explain why in the Report of the Committee on the Elimination of Racial Discrimination there is such a statement: "international law has not recognized a general right of peoples unilaterally to declare secession from a State. In this respect, the Committee follows the views expressed in An Agenda for Peace...a fragmentation of States may be detrimental to the protection of human rights, as well as to the preservation of peace and security."[41] How to interpret General Assembly resolutions certainly deserves serious consideration, particularly when a General Assembly resolution is treated as an evidence of opinio juris. It seems useful to refer to other documents of the General Assembly to have a less controversial interpretation of a certain paragraph in a General Assembly resolution: maybe an unclear point in one resolution is quite clearly stated in other documents.

Given the variety of secessionist disputes, it would also be unrealistic to assume there could be general customary international law on secession. Secessionist disputes in different states bear distinct appearances: some prove to be violent while others prove to be mild. Secessionist disputes in Canada and Czechoslovakia proved to be mild, and both these two governments were willing to grant independence without first resorting to military means. But secessionist disputes like Aceh and East Timor in Indonesia proved to be totally different: the government was extremely reluctant to grant independence and ready to fight. This sharp contrast is not due to occasional reasons, as pointed out by Barbara F. Walter: "unlike most countries in the world, Canada and Czechoslovakia are ethnically relatively homogeneous. Canada contains concentrated ethnic minorities in Quebec and in Northern Canada where native Americans and Inuit live, but few additional groups with any serious desire to secede. Czechoslovakia contained only two concentrated minority groups—Slovaks and Hungarians—both of whom occupied territory in the secessionist region of Slovakia. The fact that so few potential separatists existed in both countries allowed leaders to negotiate with one group without triggering multiple additional challenges... Jakarta's wars against East Timor and Aceh were not designed solely to maintain sovereignty over these two tiny regions, but to signal to Indonesia's many other minorities that secession would be costly. As one

[41] Report of the Committee on the Elimination of Racial Discrimination, A/51/18 (1996), p. 126.

Indonesian general argued in 2000, giving independence to Aceh could set off 'a violent Balkans style breakup of Indonesia'. Fighting a war against one challenger is the price governments are willing to pay in order to deter additional challengers later on."[42] Obviously, given the particularity of each secessionist dispute, the accumulation of these highly distinct instances seems unlikely to constitute the overall practice and legal opinion required for the establishment of customary international law on secession.

To conclude, one must be cautious about applying customary international law, particularly not confusing the evidence of opinio juris with customary international law: a General Assembly resolution itself is not customary international law but the evidence of opinio juris. As pointed out by the ICJ in the Nicaragua case: "Where two States agree to incorporate a particular rule in a treaty, their agreement suffices to make that rule a legal one, binding upon them; but in the field of customary international law, the shared view of the Parties as to the content of what they regard as the rule is not enough. The Court must satisfy itself that the existence of the rule in the opinio juris of States is confirmed by practice".[43] Given the lack of practice, General Assembly resolutions alone cannot form international customary law. Thus, international customary law does little to help in exploring the legal color of secession.

2.3 Exploring the Legal Color of Secession in Terms of the General Principles of Law

2.3.1 General Introduction to the General Principles of Law

If one needs to be cautious about applying international custom, one needs to be much more cautious about applying general principles of law: the former is more ambiguous than international conventions, while the latter is much more ambiguous than the former. Despite this glaring defect, the raison d'etre of this legal source is still undeniable. As pointed out by Malcolm N. Shaw: "in any system of law, a situation may very well arise where the court in considering a case before it realizes that there is no law covering exactly that point… In such instances the judge will proceed to deduce a rule that will be relevant, by analogy from already existing rules or directly from the general principles that guide the legal system, whether they be referred to as emanating from justice, equity or considerations of public policy. Such a situation is perhaps even more likely to arise in international law because of the

[42]Walter (2009), pp. 7–8.

[43]Military and Paramilitary Activities in and against Nicaragua (Nicaragua v. United States of America). Merits, Judgement. I.C.J. Reports 1986, p. 14, para. 184.

relative underdevelopment of the system in relation to the needs with which it is faced."[44]

In terms of secessionist disputes, the need for the court to decide the case is not that urgent, because disputing parties do not often submit a dispute like this to a court, and compulsory jurisdiction is rarely heard in international law. Nevertheless, there is no denying that disputing parties need legal rules for settling their dispute, just as a judge need such rules to decide the case. Needless to say, a treaty is the best choice, custom is not so good, and the general principles are even worse, given the requirement of legal certainty and the need to reduce controversy. The problem is that for a secessionist dispute, more often than not there would be no agreement beforehand, and as discussed above, customary law is not available either, so in such circumstances, the necessary legal guide seems to depend on the general principles. Owing to the ambiguity of this legal source, its help to the settlement of secessionist disputes is inevitably restricted. Therefore, it is of great importance to encourage negotiation between disputing parties: negotiation helps produce agreement, which is the best choice for the settlement of a dispute. General principles could provide beneficial inspiration, and it could be very helpful to the dispute settlement, but general principles alone are not enough for the effective settlement of secessionist disputes.

Now one should consider what the general principles of law concept is intended to refer to. The ambiguity already appears at this stage. "Some writers regard it as an affirmation of Natural Law concepts, which are deemed to underlie the system of international law and constitute the method for testing the validity of the positive (i.e. man-made) rules. Other writers, particularly positivists, treat it as a sub-heading under treaty and customary law and incapable of adding anything new to international law unless it reflects the consent of states."[45] There is also opinion of including private law and Roman law in the general principles of law concept: "private law, being in general more developed than international law, has always constituted a sort of reserve store of principles upon which international law has drawn. Roman law, as we have seen, was so drawn upon by the early writers on international law, and the process continues, for the good reason that a principle which is found to be generally accepted by established legal systems may fairly be assumed to be so reasonable as to be necessary to the maintenance of justice under any system."[46]

Needless to say, each understanding of the general principles of law concept contains an element of reasonableness. The problem is how the consistency of law can be maintained within one way of understanding and between different ways of understanding. According to the positivist understanding, the general principles of law concept is a sub-heading under treaty and customary law, so general principles concerning secession mainly include state sovereignty, the right to self-determination and protection of human rights. There could be conflicts between

[44] Shaw (2008), p. 98.

[45] Ibid. p. 99.

[46] Brierly (2012), pp. 63–64.

these general principles when applying them to secessionist conflicts: a sovereign state tends to declare the illegality of secession on the basis of state sovereignty, while a secessionist entity tends to base the legality of secession on the right to self-determination. How can the consistency of law be maintained in such circumstances? This point will be thoroughly clarified in the following chapter, as it is the core debate regarding the legal color of secession. Compared with the positive understanding, it is even harder to maintain the consistency within the much less systematized natural law concepts. The social contract theory, as one of the numerous theories that permeate natural law, seems highly concerned with secession. This theory purports to reduce political associations to a fundamental agreement between their individual members, through which these individuals concede certain natural rights of them to the authority of the community in order to escape the brutality of their nonsocial existence or in exchange of the positive benefits of life in a social grouping.[47] "The secessionist would argue that the act of separation by a minority of the society in effect constitutes a simple reassertion of these surrendered rights or, perhaps, an exercise of the residual rights retained by the people concerned."[48] Nevertheless, it is noteworthy that the social contract theory could be interpreted in various ways and thus is not always in favor of secessionists. A review of these various interpretations will contribute to a better understanding of this issue.

2.3.2 *Different Interpretations of the Social Contract Theory Regarding Secession*

2.3.2.1 Thomas Hobbes

One can first look at the idea of Thomas Hobbes. He denied the proposition that those surrendered rights could be reasserted, although he admitted that an abuse of sovereign power would be rather oppressive to individual members. Sovereign power is necessary, as "during the time men live without a common power to keep them all in awe, they are in that condition which is called war; and such a war, as is of every man, against every man."[49] Abuse of sovereign power should be tolerated: "it is true, that a sovereign monarch, or the greater part of a sovereign assembly, may ordain the doing of many things in pursuit of their passions, contrary to their own consciences, which is a breach of trust, and of the law of nature; but this is not enough to authorize any subject, either to make war upon, or so much as to accuse of injustice or in any way to speak evil of the sovereign; because they have authorized all his actions, and in bestowing the sovereign power, made them their own."[50]

---

[47]Buchheit (1978), p. 51.

[48]Ibid.

[49]Hobbes (1962), p. 143.

[50]Ibid. p. 233.

Therefore, "in Hobbes's view, a sovereign could be deposed only if he failed to provide adequate protection against the passions of his subjects directed against each other. The sovereign's own extravagances had to be borne in silence."[51]

The idea of Hobbes, in the parlance of international law, is that abuse of sovereignty is better than a failing state where there is a lack of social order which forms the basis for the protection of basic human rights. When one looks at today's Somalia, Iraq and Libya, one cannot deny that there is an element of truth in the judgment of Hobbes. Obviously, the protection of basic human rights such as a right to life and security requires basic social order, and a civil war can be referred to as the greatest challenge to basic social order. As mentioned before, unilateral secession is likely to incur civil war in countries with numerous ethnic minority groups. Therefore, it is reasonable to doubt whether unilateral secession can actually contribute to the improvement of human rights, given that it might severely disrupt social order. The most important enlightenment of this idea is that the lack of social order is no better than sovereign oppression. Thus, when considering remedies for violations of human rights, it is not enough to focus solely on removing sovereign oppression, as maintaining basic social order at the same time is no less significant: if a remedy intended for removing sovereign oppression is likely to severely disrupt basic social order, the reasonableness of this remedy certainly deserves a second thought. The remedial secession is a case in point: it purely focuses on removing sovereign oppression through unilateral secession, but it neglects that unilateral secession might incur a war between a sovereign state and a secessionist entity, and the horrible nonsocial condition caused by such a war might pose an even greater threat to the protection of basic human rights. Thus, the idea of remedial secession might not bring about remedial effect in practice, given the disruption of social order which could be caused by a secessionist war. It is certainly important to remove sovereign oppression, but unilateral secession does not seem to be a practical way. To conclude, according to the interpretation of Thomas Hobbes, the social contract theory disfavors the idea of secession.

2.3.2.2 Hugo Grotius

The idea of Hugo Grotius deserves serious consideration. Grotius admitted that people retain the right to self-defense when they are confronted with severe oppression, but at the same time he stressed the significance of maintaining social order: "I should hardly dare indiscriminately to condemn either individuals, or a minority which at length availed itself of the last resource of necessity in such a way as meanwhile not to abandon consideration of the common good."[52] This idea, from the perspective of international law regarding secession, inspires one to consider a balance between rights and duties of secessionists. According to this idea,

[51] Buchheit (1978), p. 52.
[52] Grotius (1964), p. 150.

secessionists have the right to self-defense against severe sovereign oppression, but they should not expand this right to such a degree that the common good is under threat. There is no denying that the judgment of Grotius still has much practical sense in this day and age. As Rein Müllerson has summarized: "secessionist movements provoke authorities, often using terrorist methods, calculating (usually correctly) that the latter start using excessive force (e.g. in Kosovo, Chechnya) not only against militants but against civilians as well."[53] Obviously, in exploring the legal color of secession, one should never overlook methods used by secessionists to pursue their goal: a right to resist sovereign oppression does not mean a right to use terrorist methods. It is necessary to consider, what kind of duties secessionists should assume when they are pursuing their right to self-determination, and when they disregarded these duties, such as abandoning the consideration of the common good by using terrorist methods, they also need to be held responsible for that, otherwise terrorist action of secessionists in disregard of the common good can therefore be encouraged. A further discussion of this issue is to be found in the next chapter dedicated to the right to self-determination.

It is particularly noteworthy that Grotius seemed to imply an idea of remedial secession: "this body of which we are treating ... was formed from voluntary compact... it is not right for a part to withdraw from the body unless it is evident that it cannot save itself in any other way... in this respect, the right which the part has to protect itself is greater than the right of the body over the part. The part, in fact, employs the right which it had before entering the association."[54] The body-part metaphor reminds one of a similar application quite long before: the Roman consul Menenius Agrippa was reported to have utilized the organic parable in 494 B.C. to cure the "secession of the commons". Agrippa argued that every part should work in collaboration, and it is in the interest of the entire body as well as its own; when the hand, mouth and teeth decide to subdue the belly by famine through non-cooperation with it, they also reduce themselves and the entire body to the last degree of emaciation.[55] The argument of Agrippa has actually pointed out a practical problem regarding the idea of remedial secession: unilateral secession may not only harm the parent state, but also be detrimental to the secessionist entity. It is especially obvious when it comes to civil war between secessionists and the parent state. If unilateral secession leads to the circumstance described by Hobbes, there will hardly be any effect of self-protection as expected in the theory of Grotius. This point will be further analyzed in the conclusion of the discussion about the general principles of law.

[53]Müllerson (2009), p. 21.

[54]Grotius (1964), pp. 261–262.

[55]Livius (1853), http://www.gutenberg.org/files/19725/19725-h/19725-h.htm#b32, last accessed on 15.06.2018.

2.3.2.3 Emmerich de Vattel

The idea of Emmerich de Vattel is also worth attention. Vattel saw secession not only from the perspective of resisting sovereign tyranny, but also from a consensual perspective. "Since compacts can be broken by the common consent of the parties, if the individuals who compose a Nation should unanimously agree to break the bonds which unite them, they may do so and thereby destroy the State or Nation."[56] However, "civil society is so useful, and even so necessary, to all the citizens that we may well consider it morally impossible that there should be a unanimous consent to break it up without necessity."[57] Besides, "the natural subjects of a prince are bound to him without other conditions than his observance of the fundamental laws . . . it is a further essential and a necessary condition of civil society that subjects remain united to their sovereign as long as it is in their power to do so . . . When, therefore, a city or a province is threatened or is actually attacked, it may not, in order to escape danger, separate from the State of which it forms a part, or abandon its legitimate sovereign, even when they are unable to give it effective help at the moment."[58]

Clearly, the insight of Vattel regarding social contract theory is farsighted, as the idea of consensual dissolution somewhat coincided with the practice of the Soviet Union and Czechoslovakia, although Vattel himself did not favor the idea of consensual dissolution. Moreover, Vattel pointed out that a state and its constituent parts are of such a relation that they have mutual rights and duties, which reveals that under the social contract theory, not only a constituent part could claim a right to secession, but a state could also claim a right to maintain integrity. This point is reminiscent of the legal reasoning of the Reference re Secession of Quebec made by the Canadian Supreme Court: "Quebec could not, despite a clear referendum result, purport to invoke a right of self-determination to dictate the terms of a proposed secession to the other parties to the federation . . . Democratic rights under the Constitution cannot be divorced from constitutional obligations . . . The other provinces and the federal government would have no basis to deny the right of the government of Quebec to pursue secession, should a clear majority of the people of Quebec choose that goal, so long as in doing so, Quebec respects the rights of others."[59] Of course, unlike the reasoning of the Reference re Secession of Quebec, which did not overly accentuate the right of the federal government, Vattel overly accentuated the duty of a city or a province to be loyal to its sovereign. This stance, from the perspective of international law regarding secession, can be interpreted as that state sovereignty usually outweighs secessionist self-determination. The interplay between sovereignty and self-determination under international law will be further discussed in the next chapter.

---

[56]de Vattel (1964), Book 1, Chapter 2 §16.

[57]Ibid. Chapter 17 §200.

[58]Ibid. Chapter 17 §201.

[59]Reference re Secession of Quebec, [1998] 2 S.C.R. 217, para.92.

2.3.2.4 Samuel Pufendorf

Compared with theorists mentioned above, Samuel Pufendorf focused more on the territorial perspective. According to the idea of Pufendorf, secessionists can abandon their state, even though "that State may be seriously weakened, or even entirely drained of its population by the emigration of its citizens in large members... After mankind had multiplied nature desired that it be gathered into civil societies, but she never commanded that this or that state endure and flourish forever".[60] However, secessionists cannot claim the territory: "if citizens wish to emigrate in large groups, they must leave the territory of the state just as individuals must. For all governments would be thrown into confusion, if entire cities and districts could withdraw at their will from their allegiance, and either put themselves under another authority, or set up an independent state."[61]

To separate population and territory in the discussion of secession is a great pioneering work, although its theoretical and practical value have not been fully exploited so far. When it comes to a secessionist dispute, too much emphasis is laid on the democratic or human rights perspective, and there is much less focus on the territorial perspective, as if ownership of the territory were beyond any doubt. As a matter of fact, ownership of the territory deserves no less attention: the territorial claim and the democratic claim of secessionists should be treated separately. Satisfying the democratic claim of secessionists is one thing, satisfying the territorial claim is quite another. It is legally groundless that, in order to satisfy the democratic or human rights claim of secessionists, the territorial claim of them has to be satisfied at the same time. According to the idea of Pufendorf, the concept of remedial secession sounds problematic: why is the remedy territorial alteration instead of emigration? Unlike proponents of remedial secession, Pufendorf clearly realized that the territorial claim of secessionists would lead to severe consequences, which are reminiscent of the judgment of the Indonesian government mentioned before. Based on Pufendorf's interpretation of the social contract theory, it is accurate to say that natural law has no intention to satisfy the wish of secessionists to the prejudice of the parent state.

In addition, emigration can yet function as a solution to a secessionist dispute. For secessionists who strongly wish to get rid of the parent state, emigration can satisfy this wish; for a parent state which stresses the territorial sovereignty, emigration will avoid dismembering or impairing the territorial integrity; for those states which care about secessionists in other states, their wish to protect secessionists will be satisfied by accepting emigrating secessionists, and these states no longer need to worry that human rights of secessionists might not be respected by their parent state, because they get the chance to replace the parent state to protect human rights of secessionists. When other states can open their arms for secessionists, emigration can be a solution satisfying contesting parties at the same time, and it definitely deserves

[60]Pufendorf (1964), Book 8, Chapter 11 §4.

[61]Ibid.

serious consideration. Because contesting parties can be satisfied at the same time, it will also promote international cooperation and reduce confrontation.

Some doubt that these states would refuse to accept secessionists because they might already be over-populated. If so, it is time to question whether these states ever consider that the loss of territory would also increase the tension between territory and population in the parent state, when they actively support the secessionist movement in this state: they do not want to be over-populated, so does the parent state confronted with the threat of losing territory due to the secessionist movement.

2.3.2.5 John Locke

The idea of John Locke cannot be overlooked. The understanding of John Locke of the social contract theory, compared with other theorists mentioned above, highlighted a right to resistance. From the perspective of Locke, "The Liberty of Man, in Society, is to be under no other Legislative Power, but that established, by consent, in the Common-wealth"[62]; what individual members give up to the legislative power upon their entrance into society is limited, and "in the utmost Bounds of it, is limited to the public good of the Society. It is a Power, that hath no other end but preservation, and therefore can never have a right to destroy, enslave, or designedly to impoverish the Subjects."[63] When the rulers exercise a power that the people never put into their hands, "the Body of the People, or any single Man... have no Appeal on Earth, there they have a liberty to appeal to Heaven ... by a Law antecedent and paramount to all positive Laws of men."[64] Despite his clear assent to a right to resistance, Locke has also expressed, "great mistakes in the ruling part, many wrong and inconvenient Laws, and all the slips of humane frailty will be born by the people, without mutiny or murmur. But if a long train of Abuses, Prevarications ... they should then rouse themselves, and endeavor to put the rule into such hands, which may secure to them the ends for which Government was at first erected."[65] Therefore, the right to resistance suggested by Locke is also a limited right.

In fact, both disputing parties in a secessionist dispute can quote the idea of Locke to refute the argument of the other side and defend its own stance. Secessionists would argue that a right to unilateral secession is embodied in a right to resistance, while the parent state could argue that great mistakes in the ruling part is to be born by the people, and the government deserves a chance to correct its mistakes. Perhaps secessionists might argue that due to a long train of abuses and prevarications, a right to unilateral secession should be deemed unequivocal. Then one needs to consider whether a right to unilateral secession is indeed embodied in a right to resistance.

---

[62]Locke (2012), Chapter 11 §22.

[63]Ibid. Chapter 11, §135.

[64]Ibid. Chapter 11, §168.

[65]Ibid. Chapter 11, §225.

Obviously, they have something in common: both rights reflect the wish to remove sovereign oppression. The distinction between them is that unilateral secession contains a territorial claim, but resistance does not necessarily involve this claim. In this sense, it is inaccurate to say that a right to unilateral secession is embodied in a right to resistance: the wish to remove sovereign oppression is one thing, the alteration of territorial ownership is quite another. Locke's interpretation of the social contract theory mainly justified the wish to remove sovereign oppression but did not clarify the issue of territorial ownership. Therefore, according to Locke's interpretation, it is hard to say that under natural law, the secessionist entity is entitled to alter territorial ownership unilaterally due to the right to resistance.

2.3.2.6 Thomas Jefferson

Under the theoretical influence of Locke and Vattel, Thomas Jefferson has set the tenor of the American Declaration of Independence with much stronger emphasis on breaking the old social contract in the event of despotism: "We hold these truths to be self-evident, that all men . . . are endowed by their Creator with certain inalienable Rights . . . . That whenever any form of Government becomes destructive of these ends, it is the Right of the People to alter or abolish it, and to institute new Government. . . . Prudence, indeed, will dictate that Governments long established should not be changed for light and transient causes; . . . that mankind are more disposed to suffer, while evil are sufferable, than to right themselves by abolishing the forms to which they are accustomed. But when a long train of abuses and usurpations . . . evinces a design to reduce them under absolute Despotism, it is their right, it is their duty, to throw off such Government".[66]

Unlike other theorists mentioned above, who did not get the chance to put their ideas into practice, Jefferson was able to put his idea into practice. When an idea is put to the test of practice, some unexpected problems will be revealed, and the social contract theory is no exception. One of the key problems lying in the hypothesis of Jefferson was that he simply assumed that people would always have the same attitude and thus take the same action towards the government. Nevertheless, the reality proved that it was only his personal fantasy: the fight of Loyalists against Patriots demonstrated their determination to preserve the British rule in the North American Continent, but such determination was somehow ignored by Jefferson as a member of Patriots. Thus, this question certainly deserves deliberation: what if one group of people wants to retain the social contract while another group decides to break it? Of course measures Patriots took against Loyalists such as lynching or expulsion[67] should be forbidden and have no heuristic value in this day and age. The answer to this question has extraordinary practical significance in settling secessionist disputes, as a similar problem frequently occurs in this regard: there are people

[66]United States Declaration of Independence (1776).

[67]Jasanoff (2012), pp. 5–53.

who disfavor secession in regions largely inhabited by secessionists, although the voice of such people is less audible. In essence, it could be referred to as self-determination conflicts: distinct "self" has determined distinctly over the fate of the old social contract; secessionists want to break it and become independent, while non-secessionists want to keep it and remain a part of the parent state. Therefore, secessionist disputes are self-determination conflicts between secessionists and non-secessionists, and the legal color of secession is closely related to the settlement of self-determination conflicts. As Jefferson deliberately ignored this problem, his practice of the social contract theory actually did little to help explore the legal color of secession.

2.3.3 *Conclusions and Reflections*

In summary, no definite conclusion can be drawn on the issue of secession according to different interpretations of the social contract theory. Nevertheless, there is no denying that this theory and relevant practice have presented a number of distinct perspectives to analyze and solve this issue: the idea of Hobbes reminded one of the importance of basic social order provided by sovereignty; Grotius implied that resistance against sovereign oppression cannot be a justification for threatening the common good, and he argued for remedial secession in an unconvincing manner; Vattel pointed out that there can be a right to consensual secession but it should be invoked carefully, and a constituent part of a state assumes a loyal duty towards its sovereign, which might be reflected in maintaining territorial integrity; Pufendorf argued that the population can leave, but they cannot claim the territory; Locke affirmed a limited right to resistance but did not deal with the territorial issue; the practice of Jefferson's idea demonstrated that his interpretation overlooked the complexity of reality. Each perspective is like a piece of the jigsaw, and one needs to put them together to get the whole picture of secession. Therefore, it is meaningful to review these different interpretations: this review helps form a comprehensive understanding of secession, and such understanding forms the indispensable basis for the effective settlement of secessionist disputes.

In the same vein, other theories of natural law, private law, Roman law or something which is likely to be classified into the general principles of law can also provide useful perspectives on secession, which can improve the understanding of this issue, thus contributing to settlement. In this sense, the ambiguity of the general principles of law concept will not cause serious problems. What might cause serious problems is that the ambiguity can provide distinct or contradicting interpretations, and the pursuit of consistency between various ideas could therefore be ignored or replaced by selective application. The idea of remedial secession is a case in point. One should have a look at the following statements: "a remedial right to secession constitutes a kind of higher law. It is reminiscent of the classical natural right to resistance against the tyrant. As an ultima ratio, resort to this higher principle is allowed"[68]; "individuals are morally justified in defending themselves against violations of their most basic human rights. When the only alternative to continuing to suffer these injustices is secession, the right of the victims to defend themselves voids the state's claim to the territory and this makes it morally permissible for them to join together to secede."[69] Obviously, these statements reflect selective application of natural law: the right to resistance is overly stressed and other aspects are ignored. Selectively applying natural law cannot make a real contribution to the settlement of secessionist disputes: the right to resistance is open to abuse when the focus of natural law on the public good is ignored; the right to resistance may cause unexpected detrimental consequences, when basic social order is largely disregarded; the disruption of basic social order caused by secessionist wars can also violate most basic human rights. In addition, the focus of natural law on tolerating sovereign power and being loyal to sovereign rulers is hardly seen in the idea of remedial secession: natural law is against excessive sovereign oppression, but it certainly does not mean that natural law encourages disregarding sovereignty; to the contrary, the duty to tolerate sovereign power and to be loyal to sovereign rulers is emphasized in natural law. Clearly, in the idea of remedial secession only the right of a secessionist entity is considered, but its duty is ignored.

As mentioned before, if the idea of Grotius can be taken as the natural legal ground for secessionists to claim a particular piece of territory, the idea of Pufendorf can also be taken as the natural legal ground for a parent state to deny such territorial claim. At such time one should not accept one idea and ignore the other or negate a positive rule based on selective application of natural law. According to the idea of Pufendorf, the positive principle of territorial sovereignty is in accordance with natural law, whereas the idea of remedial secession which intends to negate this principle is not in accordance with natural law. Therefore, it is necessary to pursue the consistency between different interpretations of natural law and consistency between positive law and natural law, otherwise the ambiguity of the general principles of law concept will inevitably cause serious problems: one interpretation of natural law might negate a positive principle, and this interpretation might also be negated by another interpretation; when private law and Roman law also take part in this game of negation, the outcome will be even more unpredictable. In such circumstances, this legal source makes no contribution to the application of international law; conversely, it is destroying the legal nature of international law as such degree of flexibility can no longer be tolerated by legal science.

Of course, pursuing legal consistency is always a challenging task, perhaps more challenging in the field of international law, given the relative underdevelopment of the system. Nevertheless, based on what has been discussed, some key points have already been revealed. First and foremost, one should not understand and apply natural law in a selective manner. Ambiguity is not necessarily bad when the numerous possibilities embodied in it can provoke comprehensive consideration,

---

[68] Peters (2011), p. 104.

[69] Buchanan (2004), p. 354.

while ambiguity is definitely bad when comprehensive consideration is absent and an arbitrary conclusion is to be made. If studying natural law is only intended for supporting an arbitrary conclusion, the comment made by Jeremy Bentham on natural rights is not wrong: "natural rights is simple nonsense: natural and imprescriptible rights, rhetorical nonsense,—nonsense upon stilts."[70] If a review of natural law is aimed at having a comprehensive judgment, natural law definitely makes much sense: multiple perspectives of natural law reflect the complexity of practical disputes, and recognizing the complexity of practical disputes is essential for a solution. Needless to say, when the complexity of practical disputes is overlooked, it is unrealistic to expect a successful solution: as repeatedly mentioned before, secessionist disputes are complicated, given various legal relations involved, such as self-determination, human rights, territorial sovereignty and internal armed conflicts. A selective understanding and application of natural law cannot take care of all these distinct legal relations.

Secondly, one has to be cautious about negating a positive rule when this rule seems contrary to natural law. As mentioned before, some believe that natural law can be used to test the validity of the man-made rules. As commented by Blackstone in the eighteenth century, "This law of nature, being coeval with mankind and dictated by God himself, is of course superior in obligation to any other. It is binding all over the globe in all countries, and at all times; no human laws are of any validity, if contrary to this."[71] The major problem of this opinion is that inconsistency between natural law and positive law usually can be attributed to inconsistency between different interpretations of natural law: negating a positive rule is at the same time negating an interpretation of natural law. "Natural law, therefore, or a similar principle under some other name, is an essential underlying principle of the art of legislation."[72] Ideas of natural law are embodied in positive law, visible or less visible. If there arises any conflict, it is not only a conflict between natural law and positive law, but also a conflict between different ideas of natural law. As introduced before, some interpretations of natural law implied an opposition to unilateral secession, which are embodied in the positive legal system which values territorial sovereignty. Thus, the conflict between a remedial right to secession and the principle of territorial sovereignty is not a pure conflict between a natural right and a positive rule, and one should not overlook the natural legal ground for this positive principle.

Thirdly, understanding and applying natural law should serve the aim of settling concrete disputes. Pursuing legal consistency is closely related to providing successful solutions to concrete disputes. In general, inconsistency in natural law can be attributed to the distinction of focus: disputing parties have contradicting interests, and in order to justify contradicting interests, contradicting interpretations of natural law come into existence, so pursuing legal consistency is at the same time an attempt

[70]Bentham (1843), p. 501.

[71]Commentaries on the Laws of England, Book I, Introduction, quoted from Brierly (2012), p. 20.

[72]Brierly (2012), p. 21.

to reconcile these contradicting interests. When such a reconciliation can be achieved, the dispute will be largely settled. In essence, settling secessionist disputes is an endeavor to balance interests between secessionists and non-secessionists, so understanding and applying natural law should serve this endeavor. Can the focus of natural law on basic social order and the common good contribute to an optimal balance of interests between secessionists and non-secessionists? In general, the contribution is undeniable: both sides can benefit from the maintenance of basic social order and the preservation of common interests. Can the idea of remedial secession contribute to an optimal balance of interests between secessionists and non-secessionists? From the perspective of non-secessionists, the answer is undoubtedly negative because in unilateral secession territorial interests of non-secessionists are disregarded. From the perspective of secessionists, remedial secession seems to satisfy their democratic claim and territorial claim at the same time, but this satisfaction exists only in theory: given the stance of the Indonesian government which resolved to fight a war against existent secessionists in order to deter potential secessionists, one can understand that remedial secession cannot guarantee the interests of secessionists in practice. It is particularly noteworthy that the condition of human rights does not get better in a secessionist war, and a serious sequela of the secessionist war is hardly avoidable.

Fourthly, wrong assumptions of natural law require correction. Assumptions of natural law might not always correctly reflect reality. As mentioned above, the hypothesis of Jefferson did not fully accord with reality: his assumption failed to reflect the will of loyalists. When assumptions prove to be problematic under the test of reality, it is necessary to consider correcting them. Obviously, the assumption embodied in remedial secession that satisfying a territorial claim is necessary for satisfying a democratic claim does not correctly reflect reality. As a matter of fact, the territorial claim tends to impede the satisfaction of the democratic claim. Malcolm N. Shaw wisely pointed out: "what may better be seen as a problem of respect for human rights within a State and the need for the international community to moderate forceful repression of such rights can become transmuted into a territorial issue and accordingly shifted on to a different plane. This process may indeed resist a successful resolution of the problems in question. And it may be argued being counterproductive in leaving unsatisfied the legitimate human rights claims against the State in question."[73] Remedial secession assumes that there are conditions under which "the only alternative to continuing to suffer these injustices is secession", while in reality secession does not prove to be an alternative to continuing to suffer these injustices: to the contrary, secession usually intensifies suffering as there is no reason for a state to tolerate any attempt to dismember or impair its territorial integrity. It is still quite inexplicable that a democratic claim and a territorial claim are bound together. Therefore, it is accurate to consider correcting the assumption of remedial secession: a remedy is the aim and secession is no more than a means, so it is meaningful to consider other means more direct and effective

[73]Shaw (2003), pp. 248–249.

than secession. This point will be further explored in the next chapter focusing on the settlement of self-determination conflicts.

In view of the foregoing, natural law can help explore the legal color of secession rather than directly ascertain the legal color of secession, given various possibilities contained in natural law. By the same token, the general principles of private law and Roman law also fail to directly ascertain the legal color of secession. The major value of the general principles of law lies in its heuristic nature: one is therefore inspired to consider a secessionist dispute from various perspectives, weighing and balancing complicated and contradicting interests of disputing parties. When disputing parties finally strike an optimal balance of interests between them, the legal color of secession will become relatively clear: they might agree on secession, so there is a right to (consensual) secession, or they might agree on non-secession, so there is no need to discuss the legal color of secession any more. In the next chapter dedicated to self-determination conflicts the pursuit of an optimal balance of interests between secessionists and non-secessionists will be further discussed, thus further disclosing the heuristic value of the general principles of law in this regard.

2.4 Exploring the Legal Color of Secession in Terms of Subsidiary Means for the Determination of Rules of Law

2.4.1 *General Introduction to Subsidiary Means for the Determination of Rules of Law*

Judicial decisions and teachings have been specified in Article 38(1)(d) as subsidiary means for the determination of rules of law. "The first three sources of Article 38 are formal sources; those of paragraph (d) are material rather than formal sources, but material sources having a special degree of authority."[74] As "the emphasis in practice has shifted to the contribution made by such (judicial and arbitral) decisions, and away from the views of the most highly qualified publicists of the various nations", the latter will not be specially discussed here and this omission will not be detrimental to exploring the legal color of secession under Article 38(1), because "the judges and arbitrators are more often than not themselves eminent scholars and practitioners, so that the distinction between judicial precedent and teachings is not a sharp one".[75]

Although judicial decisions are material rather than formal sources of international law, "judicial decisions can be of immense importance. While by virtue of article 59 of the Statute of the International Court of Justice the decisions of the

[74]Thirlway (2010), p. 110.
[75]Ibid.

Court have no binding force except as between the parties and in respect of the case under consideration, the Court has striven to follow its previous judgments and insert a measure of certainty within the process: so that while the doctrine of precedent as it is known in the common law, whereby the rulings of certain courts must be followed by other courts, does not exist in international law, one still finds that states in disputes and textbook writers quote judgments of the Permanent Court and the International Court of Justice as authoritative decisions."[76] Although one cannot say that a decision of the court will always be followed in later discussions and contribute to formulating international legal rules, in general "the practice of the court is to examine its own relevant case-law with considerable attention and to depart from it rarely. At the very least, it will constitute the starting point of analysis."[77] As noted by the court in the case concerning the land and maritime boundary between Cameroon and Nigeria, "there can be no question of holding Nigeria to decisions reached by the Court in previous cases. The real question is whether, in this case, there is cause not to follow the reasoning and conclusions of earlier cases."[78]

It is noteworthy that the scope of judicial decisions is not limited to the decisions of international courts and tribunals, because the decisions of national courts are also included. As demonstrated in the Arrest Warrant case, both contesting parties, namely the Democratic Republic of the Congo and Belgium, relied on the decision made by the House of Lords in the United Kingdom in the Pinochet case and by the Court of Cassation in France in the Qaddafi case to argue whether there is any exception to the principle of absolute immunity from criminal process of an incumbent Minister for Foreign Affairs where he or she is accused of having committed crimes under international law, and these decisions rendered by national courts were treated by the ICJ as state practice.[79] Therefore, the decisions of national courts "may play a dual role: on the one hand they may contain a useful statement of international law on a particular point (thus constituting a material source); on the other, the courts of a State are organs of the State and their decisions may also rank as State practice on a question of customary law".[80] It must be noted that judicial decisions discussed here include non-binding judicial opinions, because such opinions can also contain useful statements of international law on a particular point. Besides, given that legal relations between two federal states and legal relations between two sovereign states share a certain degree of similarity, in applying international law, it is also meaningful to consider useful thoughts advanced by national courts in this regard. "One may, finally, also point to decisions by the highest courts of federal states, like

[76]Shaw (2008), p. 110.

[77]Ibid.

[78]Land and Maritime Boundary between Cameroon and Nigeria, Preliminary Objections, Judgment, I.C.J. Reports 1998, p. 275, para. 28.

[79]Arrest Warrant of 11 April 2000 (Democratic Republic of the Congo v. Belgium), Judgment, I.C.J. Reports 2002, p. 3, paras. 56–58.

[80]Thirlway (2010), p. 111.

Switzerland and the United States, in their resolution of conflicts between the component unites of such countries, as relevant to the development of international law rules in such fields as boundary disputes. A boundary disagreement between two US states which is settled by the Supreme Court is in many ways analogous to the International Court of Justice considering a frontier dispute between two independent states, and as such provides valuable material for international law".[81]

As mentioned before, secession is not an issue which is always submitted to a court. Nevertheless, there are still a number of decisions made by international or national courts concerning secessionist disputes. From these decisions, Reference re Secession of Quebec made by the Canadian Supreme Court and the Kosovo Advisory Opinion made by the ICJ are selected for discussion. Undeniably, legal opinions as such are not binding decisions, but given that they contain useful statements of international law on secession, they certainly deserve thorough discussion. Through the discussion of these cases, one can have a basic idea of the role played by this subsidiary source of international law in exploring the legal color of secession.

2.4.2 *Reference re Secession of Quebec*

In exploring the legal color of secession, the Canadian Supreme Court wisely noted that as a judiciary organ it had to avoid being improperly involved in a political controversy. At the outset, the court pointed out that this issue "combines legal and constitutional questions of the utmost subtlety and complexity with political questions of great sensitivity".[82] Due to its political nature, the justiciability is highly questionable: to answer questions of this type "would draw the Court into a political controversy and involve it in the legislative process. In exercising its discretion whether to determine a matter that is alleged to be non-justiciable, the Court's primary concern is to retain its proper role within the constitutional framework of our democratic form of government . . . In considering its appropriate role the Court must determine whether the question is purely political in nature and should, therefore, be determined in another forum or whether it has a sufficient legal component to warrant the intervention of the judicial branch."[83]

Although this point is not discussed from the perspective of international law, there is no denying that in the field of international law similar problems also exist: a court is required to deal with an issue of mixed nature which combines legal and political aspects, rendering it highly likely for the court to be improperly involved in a political debate, and in such circumstances the court must contribute to the solution and avoid improper political involvement at the same time. The experience of the

[81] Shaw (2008), p. 112.

[82] Reference re Secession of Quebec, [1998] 2 S.C.R. 217, para.1.

[83] Ibid. para. 26.

Canadian Supreme Court in dealing with these problems definitely deserves consideration. The above statement of the Canadian Supreme Court conveyed important information: firstly, due to the mixed nature of secession, there arises a need of new legislation to address this issue; secondly, the court should consider proper participation in this legislative process; thirdly, the participation of the court should correspond to its role in the whole legal system. Undeniably, these three points are quite enlightening for one to comprehend the intricate nexus between judicial decisions and the exploration of the legal color of secession. The first point inspires one to consider the interplay between politics and law. In a secessionist dispute, these two perspectives are closely interrelated with each other: when disputing parties are still in the negotiating phase, secession is more of a political problem, or it can be regarded as a matter of future international law; however, when they finally reach an agreement, secession becomes a matter of international law as new legislation is there for regulating this dispute. Of course, before the new legislation, there is international law which can be applied to some aspects of a secessionist dispute, such as human rights law and possibly the law of armed conflict. However, merely applying these legal rules is insufficient to settle a complicated dispute involving various legal relations, and new legislation is by no means dispensable: political negotiation between disputing parties is, meanwhile, a legislative process.

When it comes to legislation, an inevitable question faced by a court is that to what extent it should take part in legislation. It is the second point that requires discussing. Judicial law-making sometimes is inevitable because declaration of non liquet is neither desirable nor appropriate: "while there may not always be an immediate and obvious rule applicable to every international situation, every international situation is capable of being determined as a matter of law."[84] As a matter of fact, "the line between interpretation and law-making is sometimes fluid".[85] Therefore, it is accurate to say that a court actually participates in legislation. In general, how to appreciate the participation of a court in legislation should depend on its contribution to the settlement of a dispute: if judicial law-making genuinely contributes to the settlement of a dispute, the judicial law-making will not be deemed improper, but if judicial law making does a disservice to the settlement of a dispute, the judicial law-making will definitely be criticized. In terms of secessionist disputes, it is a similar story: principally a court cannot make law for disputing parties, and only disputing parties can make law for themselves; however, there is no need to firmly deny judicial law-making if it is accepted by disputing parties. Therefore, the main question about judicial decisions as a subsidiary source of international law is not that these decisions might actually create law rather than purely state law, but that they create bad law which will hamper the settlement of a secessionist dispute.

It is necessary for a court to consider avoiding counterproductive judicial law-making, and the third point is intended for this. As noted by the Canadian Supreme Court, carefully considering the role of the court in the whole legal system

---

[84] Shaw (2008), p. 99.

[85] Wolfrum (2011), para. 46.

can help to solve this problem. Correctly locating its own role requires considering cooperation with other organs in the legal system. According to domestic legal theories, it is closely related to the separation of powers. On the international plane, the separation of powers is rarely discussed, but it still deserves consideration because it can affect the settlement of disputes. Judicial law-making is in principle not in accordance with the separation of powers: a court should not attempt to be a legislator. However, there is no denying that in practice the separation of powers cannot be as clear as in theory: sometimes judicial law-making is both inevitable and necessary due to the practical need. The major problem is to avoid improper judicial law-making, which requires a court to stick to its judicial character and respect the legislative organ. To be specific, a court must carefully consider whether its judicial law-making would prejudice the legislative power or not. When judicial law-making is likely to prejudice the legislative power, it can hardly contribute to dispute settlement in a positive manner; worse still, new disputes can be aroused due to the imbalance between judicative power and legislative power. In terms of secessionist disputes, a court should avoid doing a disservice to negotiation between secessionists and non-secessionists: negotiation between disputing parties is also legislation and should not be affected by judicial law-making, because disputing parties are in a much better position to make law for themselves than a judicial organ. Overlooking this point will not help to settle secessionist disputes and to preserve the judicial nature of a court.

In general, the Canadian Supreme Court has properly dealt with these points in its judicial opinion: "the task of the Court has been to clarify the legal framework within which political decisions are to be taken 'under the Constitution', not to usurp the prerogatives of the political forces that operate within that framework...it will be for the political actors to determine what constitutes 'a clear majority on a clear question' in the circumstances under which a future referendum vote may be taken. Equally, in the event of demonstrated majority support for Quebec secession, the content and process of the negotiations will be for the political actors to settle. The reconciliation of the various legitimate constitutional interests is necessarily committed to the political rather than the judicial realm precisely because that reconciliation can only be achieved through the give and take of political negotiations. To the extent issues addressed in the course of negotiation are political, the courts, appreciating their proper role in the constitutional scheme, would have no supervisory role."[86]

The Canadian Supreme Court admitted that the issue should be left to political negotiation between disputing parties, and the court should focus on its judiciary character instead of taking the place of the negotiators. Therefore, the court managed to avoid declaring non liquet and improper judicial law-making at the same time. Given what has been discussed above, this stance is indeed helpful in settling secessionist disputes. For one thing, the court made proper contribution to new legislation by confirming the necessity of political negotiation: when a court

[86]Reference Re Secession of Quebec, [1998] 2 S.C.R. 217, para. 153.

confirms the necessity of political negotiation, an incentive effect can be generated, as a disputing party used to be reluctant to negotiate will be prompted to negotiate due to the confirmation of the court. Encouraging political negotiation is encouraging new legislation as the latter usually comes as a result of the former. Thus, one can say that the subsidiary legal source sometimes can help formulate a formal legal source which is the best legal source for dispute settlement; undeniably, a formal legal source is more desirable than a subsidiary legal source, and a treaty as a formal source of international law is more desirable than other formal sources of international law. Of course, the Canadian Supreme Court did not think an agreement between the secessionist entity and the sovereign state was an international treaty. However, given that the agreement was about the right to self-determination, which is an international legal right, and the agreement would be concluded between two holders of this international legal right, this agreement is not fundamentally different from a treaty dealing with secession.

For another, the court noted the importance of the separation of powers and avoided likely disputes caused by the imbalance between judicative power and legislative power. With a view to respecting the legislative process, the court highlighted that reconciliation of interests between disputing parties should be achieved through political negotiation and refused to make an arrangement for them by way of judicial law-making. The refusal of a court to distribute interests between disputing parties is quite essential to the settlement of secessionist disputes. As a matter of fact, due to the highly complicated relations between disputing parties, it is hardly possible for a court to make a reasonable distribution for them: as noted by the Canadian Supreme court, "only the political actors would have the information and expertise to make the appropriate judgment"[87]; in such circumstances, it becomes quite necessary to let disputing parties make law for themselves. By letting disputing parties make law for themselves, there is no need to worry that improper judicial law-making would be unfair on one side and therefore do a disservice to the settlement of secessionist disputes; there would be no criticism caused by judicial law-making which prejudiced genuine legislation. Therefore, in terms of secessionist disputes, it is accurate to say that effective dispute settlement requires a court to keep the principle of the separation of powers in mind and respect the right of disputing parties to make law for themselves.

To conclude, the Reference re Secession of Quebec itself did not directly reveal the legal color of secession, but it correctly indicated how the legal color of secession could be revealed. This approach is well-advised, as it helps to settle secessionist disputes in a practical sense: it facilitates the formulation of the best formal legal source and does not cause additional disputes due to the imbalance between judicative power and legislative power. In fact, respecting the right of disputing parties to make law for themselves is respecting conflicting rights to self-determination of disputing parties. How conflicting rights to self-determination can be respected at the same time will be thoroughly discussed in the following chapter.

---

[87]Reference re Secession of Quebec, [1998] 2 S.C.R. 217, para. 100.

2.4.3 *Kosovo Advisory Opinion*

Compared with the Reference re Secession of Quebec, the ICJ Advisory Opinion on Kosovo failed to strike a balance between legislative power and judicative power. According to the Dissenting Opinion of Judge Bennouna: "if it had declined to respond to this request, the Court could have put a stop to any 'frivolous' requests which political organs might be tempted to submit to it in future, and indeed thereby protected the integrity of its judicial function. What is at issue above all in this case is protecting the Court itself against any attempts to exploit it in a political debate, rather than protecting the balance between the principal political organs of the United Nations [the General Assembly and Security Council] ... It should be recalled that, when the Court receives a request for an advisory opinion, pursuant to Article 65 of its Statute, it is not obliged to comply with the request if it considers that giving a reply to the question posed would be 'incompatible with the Court's judicial character'."[88]

"In the Kosovo case, the Court has been confronted with a situation that has never occurred before, since it has ultimately been asked to set itself up as a political decision-maker, in the place of the Security Council. In other words, an attempt has been made, through this request for an advisory opinion, to have it take on the functions of a political organ of the United Nations, the Security Council, which the latter has not been able to carry out."[89]

Judge Bennouna noted the negative consequences caused by confusing judicial function and political function. In essence, it is about balancing judicative power and legislative power when the line between them in this case is somewhat fluid: Security Council resolution 1244 (1999) was treated as a part of international Law in the Kosovo Advisory Opinion, and according to this resolution, the final status of Kosovo was dependent on the outcome of political negotiation between disputing parties, so it was ill-advised for the court to act in the place of the political actors, which would damage the judicial independence and credibility of the court. The insight of Judge Bennouna definitely deserves serious consideration: when disputing parties, namely a sovereign state and a secessionist entity, do not reach an agreement on the distribution of their interests as required by a Security Council resolution, the Court involved in this issue is ill-advised to deliver an opinion in this regard. Obviously, if the opinion of the Court favors one party, it will take this opinion as a strong argument to force the other party to give in in their political negotiation, which actually affects their negotiation. At such time, the judicial independence of the court is inevitably in doubt because the court actually takes sides by delivering this opinion. Of course, if the court comes to a conclusion favoring one party undoubtedly based on its judicial function, it is hardly problematic, but if the court comes to a conclusion favoring one party because of its improper involvement in a

---

[88] Accordance with International Law of the Unilateral Declaration of Independence in Respect of Kosovo, Dissenting Opinion of Judge Bennouna, I.C.J. Reports 2010, pp. 500–501.

[89] Ibid. p. 501.

political debate, it is indisputably problematic. Unfortunately, the Kosovo Advisory Opinion fell into the latter category.

Judge Bennouna also revealed that the way the ICJ exercised its power affected the contribution the court could make to dispute settlement. "All the protagonists in the Kosovo case have stated in advance, in particular before the Court, that the opinion, whatever it may be, will have no impact on their position in relation to the declaration of independence. Therefore, the advisory opinion can only be used as an argument in the political debate taking place between the supporters of recognizing Kosovo's independence and those who are against it…the Court has everything to lose in this political contest, without contributing in any real way either to reducing the tensions caused by the unilateral declaration of independence or to clarifying the functions and responsibility of the United Nations in respect of a territory placed under its administration."[90]

"While the Court cannot substitute itself for the Security Council in exercising its responsibilities, nor can it stand legal guarantor for a policy of fait accompli based simply on who can gain the upper hand. Its duty is to preserve its role, which is to state the law, clearly and independently. That is how it will safeguard its credibility in performing its functions, for the benefit of the international community."[91]

According to Judge Bennouna, the ICJ should have contributed to reducing the tensions caused by the unilateral declaration of independence and clarifying the functions and responsibility of the United Nations in respect of a territory placed under its administration; however, due to its improper involvement in the political debate, the ICJ failed to make this contribution. This point reminds one that the value of judicial decisions in dispute settlement is largely dependent on whether the judicial power is exercised properly: judicial decisions resulting from the improper exercise of judicial power have little value to the settlement of disputes. Realizing this point is important in applying the subsidiary source of international law: clearly, legal opinions which are closely related to the improper exercise of judicial power should not be invoked as subsidiary means for the determination of rules of law in exploring the legal color of secession.

That is to say, before applying a subsidiary source of international law to the settlement of a secessionist dispute, one must examine this source very carefully. In general, the determinative factor is the contribution made by this source to the settlement of a secessionist dispute. Of course, it sounds very abstract and difficult to apply. Nevertheless, given what has been discussed, it is clear that in order to contribute positively to the settlement of a secessionist dispute, a court should not confuse judicative power and legislative power in delivering a judicial decision. A certain degree of cooperation between different organs under the Charter should be required, and this cooperation should be embodied in the exercise of power by any organ under the Charter. Needless to say, this issue is quite complex as the separation of powers between UN organs does not fully correspond with the relevant

---

[90] Ibid. p. 504.

[91] Ibid. p. 505.

description in domestic legal theories. However, despite the concrete difference regarding the separation of powers between domestic law and international law, there is no denying that the necessary cooperation between UN organs will help strike a balance between the judicative power and the legislative power under the international legal system. As mentioned by Judge Keith in his Separate Opinion, "that the Court should address that issue of the appropriateness of an organ requesting an opinion if the request is essentially concerned with the actual exercise of special powers by another organ under the Charter, in relation to the matter which is the subject of the request."[92] Had the Court given sufficient consideration to this point, its contribution to the settlement of the secessionist conflict could certainly have been more positive.

Judge Tomka expressed similar ideas in his Declaration, but from somewhat different perspectives: "through the question put to it by the General Assembly, the Court has become immersed in the disagreements prevailing in the Security Council on this issue, the Council having been still actively seised of the matter but not requesting any advice from the Court. With the answer offered by the majority, the Court takes sides while it would have been judicially proper for it to refrain from doing so."[93]

"As the former President of this Court, the late Manfred Lachs, wisely observed in the case relating to the situation in which the Security Council had been actively exercising its powers, as in the present one, 'it is important for the purposes and principles of the United Nations that the two main organs with specific powers of binding decision act in harmony-though not, of course, in concert-and that each should perform its functions with respect to a situation or dispute, different aspects of which appear on the agenda of each, without prejudicing the exercise of the other's powers'."[94]

"The majority's answer given to the question put by the General Assembly prejudices the determination, still to be made by the Security Council, on the conformity vel non of the declaration with resolution 1244 and the international régime of territorial administration established thereunder."[95]

Therefore, when UN organs fail to act in harmony, it usually signifies an imbalance of powers, which, in general, will have a negative influence on the settlement of a secessionist dispute. Therefore, one must be very cautious about applying judicial opinions in dealing with similar cases. In addition to the proper exercise of power, it is equally important for a court to properly address a vague question posed to it. A vague question allows various ways of interpreting, and not every way of interpreting is meaningful for dispute settlement. Therefore, the

[92]Accordance with International Law of the Unilateral Declaration of Independence in Respect of Kosovo, Separate Opinion of Judge Keith, I.C.J. Reports 2010, pp. 483–484.

[93]Accordance with International Law of the Unilateral Declaration of Independence in Respect of Kosovo, Declaration of Vice President Tomka, I.C.J. Reports 2010, p. 455.

[94]Ibid. pp. 455–456.

[95]Ibid. p. 462.

Canadian Supreme Court also discussed the necessity of clarifying vague questions in the Reference re Secession of Quebec: "If the questions are thought to be ambiguous, this Court should not ... be in a worse position than that of a witness in a trial and feel compelled simply to answer yes or no. Should it find that a question might be misleading, or should it simply avoid the risk of misunderstanding, the Court is free either to interpret the question ... or it may qualify both the question and the answer... ."[96]

The question posed to the ICJ was: "Is the unilateral declaration of independence by the Provisional Institutions of Self-Government of Kosovo in accordance with international law?"[97] This question can be interpreted in various ways leading to various answers. For instance, Judge Yusuf preferred to take it as a question about the legitimacy of secessionist self-determination in the post-colonial era: "the Court had a unique opportunity to assess, in a specific and concrete situation, the legal conditions to be met for such a right of self-determination to materialize and give legitimacy to a claim of separation. It has unfortunately failed to seize this opportunity, which would have allowed it to clarify the scope and normative content of the right to external self-determination, in its post-colonial conception, and thus to contribute, inter alia, to the prevention of unjustified claims to independence which may lead to instability and conflict in various parts of the world."[98] However, the majority of the court refused to see the question in this way: "the General Assembly has requested the Court's opinion only on whether or not the declaration of independence is in accordance with international law. Debates regarding the extent of the right of self-determination and the existence of any right of 'remedial secession', however, concern the right to separate from a State. As the Court has already noted ... and as almost all participants agreed, that issue is beyond the scope of the question posed by the General Assembly."[99]

Due to the refusal to discuss secessionist self-determination, the value of the Kosovo Advisory Opinion was at a large discount: it could not provide much help in exploring the legal color of secession. Worse still, the conclusion of the Kosovo Advisory Opinion that the adoption of the declaration of independence did not violate any applicable rule of international law[100] created an impression that the declaration was in accordance with international law. No wonder the conclusion is open to exploitation for political ends: "Why would secessionist political movements bother to distinguish between a conclusion that the Kosovo declaration of independence did not violate international law and a finding that the declaration was

[96]Reference re Secession of Quebec, [1998] 2 S.C.R. 217, para. 31.

[97]Accordance with International Law of the Unilateral Declaration of Independence in Respect of Kosovo, Advisory Opinion, I.C.J. Reports 2010, p. 407, para. 1.

[98]Accordance with International Law of the Unilateral Declaration of Independence in Respect of Kosovo, Separate Opinion of Judge Yusuf, I.C.J. Reports 2010, p. 618, para. 17.

[99]Accordance with International Law of the Unilateral Declaration of Independence in Respect of Kosovo, Advisory Opinion, I.C.J. Reports 2010, p. 438, para. 83.

[100]Ibid. p. 452, para. 122.

'in accordance with international law'?"[101] Given the incentive effect on secessionist political movements, one should be very cautious about applying the Kosovo Advisory Opinion as a subsidiary source of international law.

2.4.4 *Conclusions and Reflections*

In view of the foregoing, the nexus between judicial decisions as a subsidiary source of international law and the exploration of the legal color of secession is rather intricate, as judicial decisions themselves might contain a number of problems. It must be noted that a court can neither declare non liquet nor create law in interpreting law when confronted with a secessionist dispute. Due to this dilemma it is somewhat understandable that a court could fail to provide a satisfying answer for the settlement of a secessionist dispute. Meanwhile, it is also necessary to pay attention to the successful experience of a court which has avoided likely problems and made contribution to dispute settlement through its judicial opinion. That is to say, one must take a selective attitude towards judicial decisions: not every judicial decision concerning secessionist issue can qualify as a subsidiary source of international law.

By comparing Reference re Secession of Quebec and the Kosovo Advisory Opinion, one can have the impression that the former proved to be more helpful in settling a secessionist dispute than the latter. Reasons have been revealed above, including avoiding improper involvement in political controversy, facilitating new legislation and respecting the right of disputing parties to make law for themselves. These closely interrelated points can be used to analyze whether a judicial decision can qualify as a subsidiary source of international law for the settlement of secessionist disputes, because any disregard for these points inevitably has a negative influence on dispute settlement. A subsidiary source of international law is required because it can help settle secessionist disputes, so judicial decisions must be selected on this basis: if a court is improperly involved in political controversy, negatively interferes in new legislation and fails to respect other actors in the international legal system, its relevant judicial decisions should not be deemed a subsidiary source of international law in exploring the legal color of secession.

Besides, the way a court addresses a secession-related problem in a judicial decision deserves no less consideration. The problem posed to the court might allow various interpretations, and it is important to interpret the problem in a way that will contribute to dispute settlement. Otherwise the court is unlikely to play a positive role in settling secessionist disputes. Therefore, a court must be very cautious about interpreting the problem posed to it, as an improper interpretation will reduce the value of its judicial decision and render it less likely to be regarded as a suitable subsidiary source of international law in exploring the legal color of secession.

---

[101] Falk (2011), pp. 51–52.

Compared with formal sources of international law, it is certain that applying subsidiary sources of international law requires more caution. Obviously, the main reason is that formal sources are law, and subsidiary sources are interpretations of law. Interpretations of law, no matter how authoritative, cannot be equated with law itself. This issue becomes quite complex, given that not every interpretation of law is helpful for the settlement of secessionist disputes, and one way of interpretation could be more helpful than another. At such time, one needs to consider the nexus between the exploration of the legal color of secession and the settlement of secessionist disputes: obviously, in order to effectively settle secessionist disputes, one should consciously compare different interpretations and select the legal interpretation which befits this task. Of course, a legal interpretation which is unhelpful for settling disputes can also be adopted in exploring the legal color of secession. The problem is that, when adopting such an interpretation, the exploration of the legal color of secession cannot contribute to dispute settlement. If dispute settlement is unimportant, this problem can be ignored; however, dispute settlement is actually very important, and it is accurate to say that the exploration of the legal color of secession, including applying subsidiary sources of international law, is intended for the settlement of secessionist disputes.

Therefore, it is quite clear that the exploration of the legal color of secession itself is not the end while the successful settlement of secessionist disputes is the end. The exploration of the legal color of secession serves as a means of finding a suitable solution to secessionist disputes. In general, the means and the end are inseparable: the exploration of the legal color and dispute settlement should be unified in the same process. Nevertheless, given what has been discussed above, a certain degree of separation is witnessed: not every judicial decision can be helpful in settling secessionist disputes, and unhelpful judicial decisions fail to unify the exploration of the legal color of secession and dispute settlement. Already in the discussion of the general principles of law one can realize that there exist numerous possibilities of interpretation, and secession can take on different legal colors according to these different interpretations, but not every interpretation is helpful in settling secessionist disputes. Therefore, it is indeed meaningful to consider how a separation between the means and the end like this can be avoided. In other words, it is unquestionably necessary to enable the exploration of the legal color of secession to contribute positively to the successful settlement of secessionist disputes. How can it be achieved? According to the opinion of the Canadian Supreme Court, the answer is encouraging political negotiation between disputing parties. Given what has been discussed before, the answer is correct: the agreement arising out of political negotiation between disputing parties can unify the exploration of the legal color of secession and the successful settlement of a secessionist dispute. The Comprehensive Peace Agreement between Sudan and South Sudan is a case in point. There is no denying that the agreement successfully unified these two aspects: the revelation of the legal color of secession in this agreement directly contributed to the settlement of this dispute, so the means was not separated from the end.

It is necessary to reflect why an agreement between a sovereign state and a secessionist entity can avoid the separation, but other international legal sources such as the general principles of law and judicial decisions are in a worse position to make it. The balance of interests between disputing parties is the key to success. In general, neither the general principles of law nor judicial decisions can offer a better plan for balancing interests between disputing parties than an agreement concluded between them in practice. Undeniably, in the general principles of law and judicial decisions numerous possibilities of balance can be contained, so the problem is how the most suitable one can be set apart from the rest. Such a problem does not exist when there is an agreement between disputing parties: as demonstrated in the case of South Sudan, the most suitable plan for balancing interests could be confirmed by both disputing parties through political negotiation. Therefore, it is accurate to say that the lack of mechanism for confirming the most suitable plan for the balance of interests between disputing parties renders other international legal sources difficult to avoid the separation between the exploration of the legal color of secession and the successful settlement of secessionist disputes.

Of course, political negotiation is more than a conforming mechanism: it is also a process of creation. The general principles of law and judicial decisions can only offer a framework for balancing interests, as relevant details are largely dependent on specific agreed terms between disputing parties. It should be noted that the settlement of secessionist disputes has much to do with balancing concrete interests, while the general principles of law are generally intended for abstract legal interests, and judicial decisions, as demonstrated in Reference re Secession of Quebec, are not in a better position to decide the concrete distribution of interests between secessionists and non-secessionists than an agreement concluded between themselves. Therefore, creating specific agreed terms to regulate concrete practical interests is indeed indispensable, but this indispensable part is unfortunately missing due to the lack of political negotiation. No wonder the general principles of law and judicial decisions fail to unify the exploration of the legal color of secession and the successful settlement of a secessionist dispute, but an agreement concluded between disputing parties can make it.

Lex specialis represents a dispute-settlement orientation which so far has not gained enough attention in exploring the legal color of secession. For this reason, the exploration of the legal color of secession and the successful settlement of secessionist disputes are not always connected with each other. Many approach the issue of secession from the perspective of a legal right to secession or a prohibition on secession instead of balancing concrete interests between disputing parties. This approach has confused the means and the end: the search for a legal right or a prohibition is intended for dispute settlement and not for its own sake; if a legal right or a prohibition cannot contribute positively to the settlement of disputes, it is necessary to consider new means. Given what has been discussed, it is clear that a simple right to secession or a simple prohibition on secession cannot effectively regulate legal relations between secessionists and non-secessionists. A complicated plan about distributing concrete interests between disputing parties is required, in which there is neither a simple right to secession nor a simple prohibition on secession, but mutual rights and mutual prohibitions which form the balance of concrete interests between disputing parties. This approach to the issue of secession is more suitable, because the priority is given to dispute settlement in exploring the legal color of secession: it is the need for the settlement of disputes that creates legal rights and prohibitions, and there is no reason to focus more on the search of legal rights or prohibitions than on the need for the settlement of disputes.

To conclude, the exploration of the legal color of secession is the means, and the successful settlement of secessionist disputes is the end, and the means should serve the end. For this reason, it is necessary to prevent the separation between the exploration of the legal color of secession and the effective settlement of secessionist disputes. Given what has been discussed above, no other source of international law is better than an agreement concluded between disputing parties for an effective combination of the means and the end.

2.5 Exploring the Legal Color of Secession and State Recognition

2.5.1 General Introduction to State Recognition

It is clear that the nexus between exploring the legal color of secession and state recognition is incredibly complicated, as state recognition itself is a highly debatable issue. Before discussing the nexus, it is necessary to have an overview of state recognition. Generally, there are two theories as to the nature of recognition, that is the constitutive theory and the declaratory theory: according to the constitutive one, "it is the act of recognition by other states that creates a new state and endows it with legal personality and not the process by which it actually obtained independence", so "new states are established in the international community as fully fledged subjects of international law by virtue of the will and consent of already existing states"; the declaratory one "maintains that recognition is merely an acceptance by states of an already existing situation", and "a new state will acquire capacity in international law not by virtue of the consent of others but by virtue of a particular factual situation", so "it will be legally constituted by its own efforts and circumstances and will not have to await the procedure of recognition by other states"; by comparing these two theories, one can conclude that the declaratory theory "is a little more in accord with practical realities".[102]

Generally speaking, either view is partly in accord with practical realities and partly not. "The main criticisms directed at the constitutive school are, first, the anomalous situation that arises where a State is recognized by State A but not by State B, and is therefore both an international person and not an international person at the same time, and, secondly, the fact that the constitutive doctrine gives individual States the arbitrary power to recognize an entity as a State or to withhold

[102]Shaw (2008), pp. 445–446.

recognition."[103] In the declaratory theory these problems seem to be avoided: a new state will acquire capacity in international law by virtue of a particular factual situation, and such a factual situation, according to the Montevideo Convention on the Rights and Duties of States, can be depicted by these criteria, i.e. "an organized government, a defined territory, and such a degree of independence from control by any other states as to be capable of conducting its own international relations".[104] However, it has to be admitted that "the fulfillment of the criteria for statehood... was in no circumstances either self-evident or self-expressive but something that had to be subject to critical judgment and appreciation. In absence of any other determining mechanism, furthermore, the judgment and appreciation had to be that of existing states."[105] Therefore, the declaratory doctrine also gives individual States the arbitrary power to recognize an entity as a State or to withhold recognition. Besides, what should be included in the criteria remains disputable: for instance, it seems insufficient to have just "a rather marginal check on whether or not such violations as apartheid or aggression have occurred in the process of state formation", and more attention should be given to "the entity's internal organization or the way those attributes have been acquired"[106]; according to the Canadian Supreme Court, it is also meaningful for states to consider the domestic law of parent states in granting or withholding recognition of emergent states: "foreign states may also take into account their view as to the existence of a right to self-determination on the part of the population of the putative state, and a counterpart domestic evaluation, namely, an examination of the legality of the secession according to the law of the state from which the territorial unit purports to have seceded."[107] Therefore, although "practice over the last century ... does point to the declaratory approach as the better of the two theories",[108] one still needs to be cautious about applying this theory.

2.5.2 *No Direct Influence of Recognition on the Legal Color of Secession*

How should the nexus between the exploration of the legal color of secession and state recognition be properly understood? In view of the foregoing, it can be said that state recognition, whether constitutive or declaratory, will not have any direct influence on the legal color of secession. As mentioned before, Article 38(1) proved that reasoning in international law is in principle deductive, and judging the legal

[103]Dugard and Raič (2006), p. 100.
[104]Brierly (2012), p. 149.
[105]Craven (2010), p. 242.
[106]Ryngaert and Sobrie (2011), p. 477.
[107]Reference Re Secession of Quebec, [1998] 2 S.C.R. 217, para. 143.
[108]Shaw (2008), p. 447.

color of secession according to state recognition is, in essence, not deductive. That is to say, when international law provides a right to secession, and a secessionist entity conducts secession fully in accordance with the provision, even if all other states refuse to recognize this secessionist entity as an independent state, theoretically its right to secession will not be denied due to the widespread unrecognition; when international law does not provide a right to secession, even if all other states recognize the secessionist entity as an independent state, theoretically no right to secession will be created. In the parlance of the Canadian Supreme Court, "international recognition is not alone constitutive of statehood and, critically, does not relate back to the date of secession to serve retroactively as a source of a 'legal' right to secede in the first place... a change in the factual circumstances may subsequently be reflected in a change in legal status. It is, however, quite another matter to suggest that a subsequent condonation of an initially illegal act retroactively creates a legal right to engage in the act in the first place."[109]

The case of Bangladesh is a good example: Bangladesh declared independence on 17 April 1971; Pakistan did everything to prevent Bangladesh from seceding, but nevertheless, every means including warfare proved to be useless; on 22 February 1974, almost 3 years after Bangladeshi having proclaimed its declaration of independence, Pakistan granted recognition to it; after Pakistan recognized Bangladesh, recognition became universal, and Bangladesh was admitted to the UN on 17 September 1974.[110] Obviously, the recognition of Bangladesh as an independent state granted by Pakistan cannot be interpreted as a recognition of a right to secession and the collective recognition granted by the UN also had nothing to do with a right to secession. "The primary function of recognition is to acknowledge as a fact something which has hitherto been uncertain, namely the independence of the body claiming to be a state, and to declare the recognizing state's readiness to accept the normal consequences of that fact - namely the usual courtesies, rights, and obligations of international relations between states."[111] The recognition of Bangladesh granted by Pakistan can be interpreted as Pakistan's formal acceptance of replacing old legal relations between it and Bangladesh with new legal relations. The collective recognition granted by the UN was to establish legal relations with a new member. It would be difficult to argue that a certain legal judgment on secession was implied in the recognition of Bangladesh.

[109] Reference Re Secession of Quebec, [1998] 2 S.C.R. 217, paras. 142 § 146.
[110] Vidmar (2012), p. 378.
[111] Brierly (2012), p. 151.

2.5.3 *The Influence of Recognition on the Settlement of Secessionist Disputes*

Although state recognition does not have any direct influence on the legal color of secession, it does have a great influence on the settlement of secessionist disputes. Because the exploration of the legal color of secession and the settlement of secessionist disputes should not be separated, it is accurate to say that state recognition plays an important role in exploring the legal color of secession, despite no direct influence on the legal color itself. This might sound rather perplexing, but given practical cases, it becomes easier to understand. When it comes to the Kosovo case, there is no denying that those almost immediate recognitions of Kosovo as an independent state had actually disturbed the political negotiation on the future status of Kosovo between disputing parties: due to these immediate recognitions the secessionist entity gained the upper hand in an unjustified manner and the sovereign state was unfairly prejudiced. As discussed before, political negotiation is usually the key part of exploring the legal color of secession, since the legal color of secession largely depends on the outcome of the negotiation. When the negotiation is disturbed in this way, it is hard to say that the outcome will not be influenced. From this perspective, it is clear that although recognition cannot influence the legal color of secession directly, by influencing political negotiation between a sovereign state and a secessionist entity, recognition can influence the legal color of secession in a less visible way.

Can these immediate recognitions be deemed premature? "These recognitions have been qualified as 'premature' and thus as an illegal interference in Serbia's domestic affairs on the basis of the argument that when the recognitions were granted, Kosovo did not comply with the factual requirements for statehood."[112] Whether the Kosovo issue could be referred to as domestic affairs of Serbia might be debatable, given the profound involvement of the international community, but there is no denying that these recognitions constituted interference in the political negotiation aiming to ultimately settle the issue: when the negotiation is not closed, any recognition of independence will inevitably tip the scale in favor of the secessionist entity, which is clearly to the prejudice of the sovereign state, while this question will not occur when the negotiation is closed and independence is recognized as the outcome of negotiation. For this reason, these recognitions could also be regarded as premature, as they should have arisen after the political negotiation, not during the negotiating process.

Needless to say, this kind of disturbance caused by state recognition in exploring the legal color of secession is a thorny issue, and the current international legal system fails to offer any effective remedy for the prejudiced sovereign state, even if recognition is deemed premature: prejudiced states can argue that premature recognition violates the obligation of non-recognition under customary international law,

[112] Christakis (2011), p. 75.

but this argument will hardly change anything in practice. In this sense, it can be said that it is rather convenient for other states to disturb the exploration of the legal color of secession by granting premature recognition. No wonder the Canadian Supreme Court on the one hand believed that recognition was an exercise of pure sovereign discretion largely dependent on national interest and perceived political advantage to the recognizing state, but on the other hand suggested that foreign states consider the legality of the secession according to the law of the state from which the territorial unit purports to have seceded.[113] Obviously, it serves as a reminder that other states must avoid disturbing the exploration of the legal color of secession by granting premature recognition during political negotiation.

2.5.4 Making Recognition More Rational

Based on this, one can say that recognition might be an arbitrary power of some states to influence the settlement of secessionist disputes in other states: premature recognition will disturb originally normal political negotiation between sovereign states and secessionist entities, thus influencing the outcome of their negotiation and enabling recognition to affect the legal color of secession indirectly. From this perspective, it is necessary to consider reducing the arbitrariness of this power, or making the exercise of this power more rational. As mentioned before, according to the Canadian Supreme Court, it is meaningful to consider improving the criteria for state recognition. From the theoretical perspective, this point of view is quite meaningful: when international legal guidelines about recognition become clearer in this regard, it will be easier for states to avoid abusing this arbitrary power. Unfortunately, there is no guarantee that states or international organizations are willing to follow these guidelines: for instance, the European Community had adopted a Declaration on 16 December 1991 entitled ‘Guidelines on the Recognition of New States in Eastern Europe and in the Soviet Union’, and the Yugoslav Arbitration Commission had taken the view in Opinion No. 5 on 11 January 1992 that Croatia did not meet fully the conditions for recognition laid down in the Guidelines, but the recognition of that state was still granted by the European Community and its member states (together with Austria and Switzerland) on 15 January 1992.[114] Therefore, it is accurate to conclude that improving criteria for state recognition in terms of secessionist disputes is important, while ensuring that states and international organizations follow these criteria is more important: guidelines on recognition alone cannot prevent states from abusing their power in granting recognition.

At this stage it is necessary to mention two Security Council resolutions which not only provided guidelines on (non-)recognition of unilateral secessionist entities

---

[113]See above Note 107.

[114]Shaw (2008), p. 461.

but also helped ensure the observance of guidelines. One is Security Council Resolution 217 (1965), in which the Security Council called upon all states not to recognize Southern Rhodesia and not to entertain any diplomatic or other relations with it[115]; and the other is Security Council Resolution 541 (1983), in which the Security Council called upon all states not to recognize any Cypriot State other than the Republic of Cyprus.[116] If Security Council Resolution 1244 (1999) had also specified that all states should not recognize likely unilateral independence of Kosovo, it would have definitely helped prevent other states from abusing this arbitrary power that improperly influenced the settlement of the secessionist dispute in Serbia. Thus premature recognition can be more effectively avoided. When there seems to be no effective remedy for the consequences caused by premature recognition, it is particularly meaningful to focus on how premature recognition can be avoided. Given the inspiration from Security Council Resolution 217 (1965) and Security Council Resolution 541 (1983), there is no reason to underestimate the role played by Security Council resolutions in avoiding premature recognition, because Security Council resolutions not only provide criteria for state recognition regarding secession but also help ensure that states follow such criteria.

One might argue that the Kosovo case by legal nature is different from the cases of Southern Rhodesia and Northern Cyprus, because in the cases of Southern Rhodesia and Northern Cyprus there was "unlawful use of force or other egregious violations of norms of general international law, in particular those of a peremptory character (jus cogens)."[117] Therefore, there was a clear obligation of non-recognition in the cases of South Rhodesia and Northern Cyprus. However, when it comes to the Kosovo case, the legal premise on which an obligation of non-recognition can be invoked seems not that evident. This question, in essence, concerns the criteria discussed in the declaratory theory: as mentioned above, what should be included in the criteria for state recognition remains debatable, but it is indisputable that recognition should be avoided in cases of violating norms of general international law in the process of pursuing independence. Did the unilateral independence of Kosovo violate norms of general international law? It depends on the way that unilateral independence is interpreted from the perspective of international law. If unilateral independence is interpreted in an extremely narrow way, such as deliberately avoiding any substantial discussion on the principle of self-determination, as the ICJ has done in the Kosovo Advisory Opinion, unilateral independence might not seem to be in violation of norms of general international law. Nevertheless, given the principle of self-determination and that the secessionist dispute is, in essence, a self-determination conflict between the sovereign state and the secessionist entity, unilateral secession is certainly incompatible with the right to self-determination of non-secessionists who are represented by the sovereign state. From this perspective,

[115] Security Council Resolution 217 (1965), para. 6.

[116] Security Council Resolution 541 (1983), para. 7.

[117] Accordance with International Law of the Unilateral Declaration of Independence in Respect of Kosovo, Advisory Opinion, I.C.J. Reports 2010, p. 403, para. 81.

unilateral secession is a violation of norms of general international law, although it might seem less egregious than apartheid or aggression. Obviously, this violation should be taken as the legal premise on which an obligation of non-recognition can be invoked.

In this sense, the examination of the legality of the secession according to the law of the state from which the territorial unit purports to have seceded, as suggested by the Canadian Supreme Court, is not an entirely new criterion for state recognition but a new interpretation regarding the principle of self-determination: to be specific, unilateral secession is usually forbidden in domestic law of parent states which represent non-secessionists, so non-recognition of unilateral independence demonstrates respect for the right to self-determination of non-secessionists in self-determination conflicts. Further discussion about self-determination conflicts is to be found in the next chapter.

To conclude, recognition might prove to be an arbitrary power of states when it disturbs political negotiation between disputing parties in secessionist disputes. By prejudicing parent states, the recognition of unilateral independence disturbs the settlement of secessionist disputes. In this sense, state recognition indeed affects the exploration of the legal color of secession. In order to avoid this issue, the power to grant recognition must be exercised more rationally, which requires improving the criteria for state recognition and ensuring that the criteria can be followed: the latter proves to be more important than the former. In order to guarantee that the criteria will be followed, it is meaningful to consider Security Council resolutions, as criteria regarding (non-)recognition stated in such binding instruments invariably gain more attention of states. Given that creating new states should not violate norms of general international law, the obligation of non-recognition of unilateral independence must be stressed, because by recognizing unilateral independence, the right to self-determination of non-secessionists is not respected.

2.6 Replacing a Remedial Right to Secession with a Right to a Remedy

2.6.1 Moderating Disagreement on Remedial Ways

In view of the foregoing, it is obvious that when disputing parties of a secessionist dispute have reached an agreement on their dispute, whether this agreement concerns secession or non-secession, it can close the chapter of exploring the legal color of secession, because the secessionist dispute has been effectively settled. When there is no such an agreement between disputing parties, exploring the legal color of secession proves to be rather difficult as opinions invariably differ regarding this point. Generally speaking, the core disagreement exists between those arguing for a remedial right to secession and those arguing against it. The voice supporting an unlimited right to unilateral secession is very weak and thus it can be ignored. There is also rare discussion on a prohibition on unilateral secession from the perspective of international law: opponents of unilateral secession usually argue against a right to unilateral secession instead of arguing for a prohibition on it. Therefore, when proponents of unilateral secession mainly argue for a remedial right to secession, correspondingly, opponents of unilateral secession will mainly argue against a remedial right to secession. Given what has been discussed above, although it is impossible to confirm there is a remedial right to secession in a strict legal sense, there is no denying that a remedial right to secession as a remedial plan still gains considerable support. According to Marc Weller, "scholarship has remained divided on this issue, although there is a clear trend towards the acceptance of remedial self-determination."[118] Undeniably, remedial secession as a legal right is inextricably interwoven with remedial secession as a remedial plan: in the doctrine of remedial secession, the line between a right and a remedial plan is fluid. From this perspective, it is wrong to believe that the exploration of the legal color of secession will end because a remedial right to secession does not exist in a strict legal sense. Conversely, the exploration will last as long as disagreement on remedial secession as a remedial plan exists. Thus it is necessary to consider how disagreement on remedial secession as a remedial plan can be moderated.

In general, the key to moderate the divergence of opinion is searching for common ground and enlarging it. Is there any common ground between proponents of a remedial right to secession and opponents of it? When one notes that opponents of a remedial right to secession are mainly against secession, but not against a remedy, the answer is there. Undeniably, both proponents and opponents of a remedial right to secession intend to properly settle secessionist disputes, so both of them need to consider a remedy for victims in such disputes, and therefore on this point they do not have differences. Their differences arise from the next point, namely their understanding of the remedy: proponents of a remedial right to secession associate the remedy with secession while opponents refuse this association. Therefore, it is reasonable to consider replacing a remedial right to secession with a right to a remedy, in order to moderate disagreement between proponents and opponents of a remedial right to secession. Such replacement is well-advised from both the theoretical and practical perspectives.

2.6.2 *Theoretical Advantages of a Right to a Remedy*

Unlike a remedial right to secession, a right to a remedy for victims of gross violations of human rights has already gained widespread consensus: General Assembly resolution 60/147 of 16 December 2005 has adopted Basic Principles and Guidelines on the Right to a Remedy and Reparation for Victims of Gross Violations of International Human Rights Law and Serious Violations of

[118] Weller (2008b), p. 64.

International Humanitarian Law, which stressed that victims shall have equal access to an effective judicial remedy, and states are required to incorporate norms of international human rights law and international humanitarian law into their domestic law, to improve legislative and administrative procedures, to actively prevent and deal with violations and make reparation for harm suffered without any discrimination and exception.[119] Obviously, when there are two remedial plans for addressing gross violations of human rights: one is highly debatable and the other is well-accepted, it is wiser to choose the well-accepted one instead of the highly debatable one. In addition, a right to a remedy instead of a remedial right to secession has avoided transmuting a human right issue into a territorial issue. As mentioned before, the transmutation of a human right issue into a territorial issue cannot contribute to a successful resolution of the problem but aggravate the problem.

Furthermore, if a remedial right to secession is replaced by a right to a remedy, many problems resulting from a remedial right to secession can be avoided. According to a right to remedial secession, a right to unilateral secession is morally justified when there is no other alternative to continuing to suffer severe violations of human rights. This logic is open to numerous challenges. For instance, one might doubt if such a circumstance, in which most basic human rights are continuously violated and there is no other alternative to continuing to suffer these violations but secession, can be confirmed: "it is not entirely excluded that there exists a right of secession in extreme circumstances in which the coexistence of different groups within a State would obviously be impossible in the long run. Such circumstances, however, are hard to fathom and they have, thus far, not been recognized, even in the cases of Biafra, Kosovo, or in Bosnia and Herzegovina."[120] Besides, it is necessary to realize that the extreme circumstance assumed in the theory of remedial secession is not everlasting. As universally acknowledged, secession is a lengthy process, and the unbearably ruthless oppression of human rights tends to come to an end prior to the time secession becomes available. The reason is simple: it is impossible for the international community to turn a blind eye to such issues that can threaten regional or even international peace and security. Regional organizations and the UN Security Council are bound to intervene. In addition, based on the current and historical experience, those great powers boasting a strong sense of justice are also unlikely to look on indifferently. Of course, there will be a divergence of opinion on the suitable way of intervention and the likely outcome of it: for instance, some might prefer a military way and think it would be more effective, while others prefer a non-military way and believe it would be more suitable; this divergence of opinion is understandable, but it is not that understandable when some of this opinion criticize others of that opinion for overlooking human suffering simply because others prefer a different way of relieving human suffering. When the external intervention is there, the

[119] A/RES/60/147, Annex: Basic Principles and Guidelines on the Right to a Remedy and Reparation for Victims of Gross Violations of International Human Rights Law and Serious Violations of International Humanitarian Law.

[120] Nolte (2006), pp. 85–86.

unbearably ruthless oppression will be moderated. Should remedial secession still be considered as an ultima ratio, when the extreme circumstance is no longer extreme? Is it still necessary for the already started secession to be continued?

Besides, it should be noted that "the more appropriate way to address the issue of serious violations of human rights, either collective or individual, is rather through the restoration of the respect of such rights. These kinds of violations are often due to the existence of a particular government following discriminatory policies. By definition, this can be a temporary situation. By contrast, a radical 'solution' such as secession is permanent, or at least, lasting".[121] The appropriateness of the remedy deserves serious consideration. After all, the important thing is not only to offer a remedy, but offer an appropriate remedy, as a less appropriate remedy itself is likely to create new legal problems. Offering a remedy to victims of a secessionist dispute aims to settle this dispute instead of adding new problems to it, and new problems created by an inappropriate remedy tends to complicate the dispute. Returning to the comparison between a remedial right to secession and a right to a remedy, in addition to reasons mentioned above, the latter is more appropriate also because it reflects the focus of the current international legal system more accurately: there is no denying that the focus of the current international legal system is the protection of human rights of victims in secessionist disputes rather than the establishment of exclusive ownership of a particular piece of territory for secessionists. To be more specific, secessionists actually have double identities: one is victims of human rights violations, and the other is alleged exclusive owner of a particular piece of territory; according to contemporary international law, the former identity is generally acknowledged, but the latter is generally unmentioned. Thus, a right to a remedy accurately reflects the focus of the current international legal system, while a right to remedial secession deviates from the focus.

Last but not least, any remedial plan should consider balancing interests between disputing parties, and the remedial plan for victims in secessionist disputes is no exception. It can be said that the remedial plan which can strike a better balance of interests between disputing parties proves to be a better choice. It is time to compare both remedial plans and consider which one can strike a better balance of interests. Given that serious violations of human rights can be temporary but a radical solution such as unilateral secession is generally permanent, a remedial right to secession will cause an imbalance of interests between secessionists and non-secessionists. Of course, from the viewpoint of secessionists, such imbalance does not exist and no other remedy could be better than a remedial right to secession. However, justice in the eyes of victims is not necessarily justice in the legal sense: a victim-oriented perspective is certainly not wrong, but it does not mean that every claim of victims has to be satisfied. As mentioned above, the human rights claim is generally acknowledged in contemporary international law, but the territorial claim is generally unmentioned. Therefore, there is no reason to believe that rejecting the territorial claim of secessionists will cause injustice in the legal sense. Given that a right to a

[121] Kohen (2006), p. 11.

remedy is aimed at rectifying serious violations of human rights and not as radical as unilateral secession, it is not wrong to conclude that this remedial plan can strike a better balance of interests between disputing parties in secessionist disputes.

2.6.3 Practical Advantages of a Right to a Remedy

A remedial right to secession is already problematic in theory, and it becomes much more problematic in practice. It must be admitted that many practical problems concerning a remedial right to secession fall into an area where general international law has not yet come to regulate; in other words, general international law is not prepared for likely unintended consequences caused by a remedial right to secession. Some of these consequences have been mentioned before. For example, a remedial right to secession puts extra pressure on sovereign states with relatively heterogeneous ethnical composition to defend territorial integrity. In general, states with relatively homogeneous ethnical composition tend to be much less sensitive about unilateral secession, because for them it is an event of small probability; even if it really happens, usually there is no need to worry about triggering further potential secessionist tendency. However, states with relatively heterogeneous ethnical composition tend to be highly sensitive about unilateral secession, because for them it is an actual risk; when there is one secessionist attempt, it can encourage further attempts that will disrupt a sovereign state. No wonder Canada and Indonesia approached secessionist attempts quite differently. For this reason, there are always proponents and opponents of a remedial right to secession: for some this right will not bring any substantial risk, so they do not feel the need to oppose it; however, for the other this right will bring incredible risk, so they have no alternative but to oppose it. Therefore, it is improper to discuss a remedial right to secession in a general way. The sympathy for victims in secessionist disputes embodied in a remedial right to secession is quite understandable, but this sympathy cannot be a justification for ignoring disastrous consequences which can be caused by a remedial right to secession. The sympathy for victims in secessionist disputes must be expressed in a more reasonable way, which will not give rise to unintended consequences. From this perspective, a right to a remedy is a better choice. Ethnic conflicts within sovereign states will be further discussed from the perspective of self-determination conflicts in the next chapter.

Besides, there is no denying that a remedial right to secession can motivate extreme secessionists in a perverse way: in order to achieve independence, they will intentionally provoke the authorities to create humanitarian crises. "Secessionist movements often provoke authorities calculating (usually correctly) that the latter will start using excessive force (e.g., in Kosovo, Chechnya and in Macedonia) not only against militants but against civilians as well. This, they hope, will bring them international support and recognition. In many situations one of the crucial questions is: how can the international community encourage respect for human rights, especially minority rights, without encouraging at the same time separatism?"[122] Perhaps the more crucial question is: how does the encouragement to respect human rights become an encouragement to secede? Obviously, it is closely related to the alleged remedial right to secession: "a remedial right... could have the problematic and unintended effect of providing an incentive for groups eager to establish their own states to actively contribute towards the creation of such a situation by provoking massive retaliation, most often against the civilian population".[123] The original intention of proponents of remedial secession does not include the encouragement to secede unilaterally, but it will be really hard, if not impossible, to prevent abuse of this well-intentioned idea. From the viewpoint of extreme secessionists, remedial secession sends such a signal that they can achieve their aim by provoking severe sovereign repression, and they know the price will be the heavy sacrifice of their own people, but for extreme secessionists this price is definitely affordable. In such circumstances, the well-intentioned remedial right to secession might unexpectedly contribute to human rights violations, because of the perverse incentive offered to extreme secessionists. Undeniably, when a remedial right to secession is replaced by a right to a remedy, such perverse incentive will not be provided. The perverse incentive caused by a remedial right to secession will be further discussed later, sometimes in combination with the responsibility to protect.

Furthermore, a remedial right to secession is open to exploitation for geopolitical ends. Needless to say, geopolitics plays an important role in practical secessionist disputes. "Simply put, secessionist claims do not emerge nor do they function in a geopolitical vacuum. Although claims for cultural authenticity, economic interest and state organization are all relevant ingredients of secessionist processes none of them in itself is sufficient to generate these processes or to make them virulent. All separatist movements operate, expand or shrink in a given and changing geopolitical context."[124] A state will choose to assist or instigate secessionist movements in its rivalling state in order to triumph in geopolitical struggles. A typical case is that India chose to assist secessionists of East Pakistan: by contributing to the independence of East Pakistan, India successfully undermined Pakistan's role in South Asia as a reasonably effective counter to India's status as the dominant power in the region.[125] Although at that time a remedial right to secession was rarely heard, India still attempted to justify its assistance for secessionists with the help of a similar idea: "international law recognizes that where a mother State has irrevocably lost the allegiance of such a large section of its people as represented by Bangla Desh and cannot bring them under its sway, conditions are suitable for that section to come into being as a separate state... India would be willing to discuss any cease-fire or withdrawal which would ensure the freedom and aspirations of the people of Bangla

---

[122] Müllerson (2003), p. 128.
[123] Janik (2013), p. 54.
[124] See Chap. 1, Note 2.
[125] Sisson and Rose (1990), p. 207.

Desh."[126] Therefore, one can never underestimate the possibility that a remedial right to secession will be exploited in geopolitical struggles, particularly given that the principle of non-interference in the domestic affairs of other states is currently under severe challenge. In order to avoid this thorny issue, it is necessary to consider replacing a remedial right to secession with another remedial plan. When a remedial right to secession is replaced by a right to a remedy, the possibility of geopolitical exploitation like this can be reduced. The geopolitical aspect of secessionist disputes will be further analyzed in chapters dedicated to the use of force and other external involvement in secessionist disputes.

In addition, there is no denying that the unilateral character of remedial secession is incompatible with practical needs concerning secession. Generally speaking, secession needs to be consensual, because issues such as succession and demarcation of the border require cooperation between disputing parties. Remedial secession seems to assume that these issues could be settled in a unilateral manner: in the name of remedy, the secessionist entity is entitled to unilaterally decide succession and demarcation of the border. This assumption will definitely lead to practical disputes, as there is no guarantee that the decision made by the secessionist entity on succession and demarcation of the border will be fair. In fact, the unilateral character of remedial secession itself enable non-secessionists to claim that the decision is unfair, as their right to participate in the decision on the future status of a particular piece of territory is deprived, so they can argue that it is a violation of the principle of self-determination and refuse to accept the unilateral decision on such grounds. Given such practical issues which can be caused by unilateral secession, a remedial right to secession cannot be deemed a suitable remedial plan. A right to a remedy has nothing to do with unilateral secession, thus avoiding issues such as succession and demarcation of the border. From this perspective, a right to a remedy also proves to be a more suitable choice.

Last but not least, it should be noted that when choosing remedial plans, one must consider practical resistance that can be caused thereby. A remedial plan, no matter how theoretically laudable, will not be a good choice, when it is doomed to provoke incredibly strong practical resistance. Given the likely practical resistance, there is one more reason to replace a remedial right to secession with a right to a remedy. Obviously, a sovereign state is more likely to satisfy human rights claims of secessionists than a territorial claim of them, so a right to a remedy will be confronted with less practical resistance than a remedial right to secession. In other words, a right to a remedy is more likely to be fulfilled than a remedial right to secession. To be specific, practical resistance will invariably affect the remedial effect of a remedial plan: when it is extremely difficult to translate the theoretical remedial effect into the practical remedial effect, the remedial plan definitely does not make much sense. Of course, there is no denying that a right to a remedy will also be confronted with practical resistance: a sovereign state might be quite reluctant to

[126] United Nations Security Council Official Records, 1611th Meeting, 12 December 1971, S/PV. 1611, paras. 124 and 128.

offer the remedy in practice, despite having accepted the right to a remedy in theory. Nevertheless, there is no doubt that a sovereign state will never resist a right to a remedy as firmly as a remedial right to secession: the international pressure caused by human rights violations will generally counteract the reluctance of a sovereign state to offer a remedy, but such pressure can hardly counteract the reluctance to give up ownership of a particular piece of territory. In fact, it is also a question of the executive cost of a remedial plan: practical resistance to a remedial plan entails a certain executive cost, and more practical resistance also means a higher executive cost. Since a right to a remedy requires a lower executive cost, its advantage over a remedial right to secession becomes more obvious.

2.7 Conclusions

The exploration of the legal color of secession begins by examining sources of international law. During this process, it can be ascertained that according to certain international agreements, a right to secession does exist. Of course, it is a right to consensual secession, not a right to unilateral secession. The agreement concluded between both disputing parties can combine the exploration of the legal color of secession and the successful settlement of a secessionist dispute together. The analysis of customary law on secession proves that such a customary right so far does not exist in international law, and a customary right to secession is also unlikely to be formed in the future due to the particularity of each secessionist dispute. Therefore, customary international law has little to contribute to the settlement of secessionist disputes. When it comes to the general principles of law, a certain degree of separation appears between the exploration of the legal color of secession and the successful settlement of secessionist disputes: the general principles of law can be interpreted in various ways, and therefore secession can take on various legal colors. For this reason, it is necessary to interpret and apply this legal source from a dispute-oriented perspective: legal interpretation and application must serve dispute settlement. Based on this, it is well-advised to absorb useful ideas from this vast legal source for the sake of dispute settlement instead of searching for theoretical support for an arbitrary conclusion about the legal color of secession. When it comes to the subsidiary source of international law, there is a similar story: not every judicial decision can contribute to the successful settlement of a secessionist dispute, so a selective attitude is required: when the interpretation and application of international law in judicial decisions does little to help settle disputes, such judicial decisions do not qualify as a subsidiary source of international law in exploring the legal color of secession, because of the separation between the exploration of the legal color of secession and the settlement of disputes.

Recognition also plays an important role in exploring the legal color of secession. However, it does not mean that recognition can decide the legal color of secession in a direct manner: recognition on secession mainly influences the negotiation between disputing parties in secessionist disputes. When the outcome of negotiation is still unclear, recognition of a secessionist entity is premature and creates pressure on a sovereign state to give in. Thus, the legal color of secession can be indirectly influenced by other states. Given that other states might exert improper influence on negotiation between secessionists and non-secessionists through premature recognition, it is necessary to consider reducing the arbitrariness of this power by improving the criteria for state recognition and ensuring that the criteria can be followed. Otherwise the settlement of secessionist disputes is highly likely to be disturbed by premature recognition.

There is severe disagreement on remedies for victims in secessionist disputes. The kernel of the disagreement is surrounding a remedial right to secession. Although a remedial right to secession does not exist in a strict legal sense, remedial secession as a remedial plan still receives considerable support. As a matter of fact, the line between remedial secession as a legal right and remedial secession as a suitable remedial plan is rather fluid, so in order to consummate the exploration of the legal color of secession, it is necessary to address the issue whether remedial secession can be regarded as a suitable remedial plan. As a number of theoretical and practical problems are associated with a remedial right to secession, it is meaningful to replace it with another remedial plan which proves to be less problematic in theory and in practice. In general, a right to a remedy is a more suitable remedial plan, given its theoretical and practical advantages over a remedial right to secession.

Before closing this chapter, it should be restated that the exploration of the legal color of secession is the means and the settlement of secessionist disputes is the end. The means should serve the end instead of doing a disservice.

References

Bentham J (1843) Anarchical fallacies: being an examination of the declaration of rights, The Works of Jeremy Bentham, Band 2, edited by Sir John Bowring, William Tait, Prince Street, p 501

Brierly JL (2012) Law of Nations, 7th edn. Oxford University Press, Oxford, pp 63–64

Brownlie I (2003) Principles of public international law, 6th edn. Oxford University Press, Oxford, p 5

Buchanan A (2004) Justice, legitimacy and self-determination: moral foundations for international law. Oxford University Press, Oxford, p 354

Buchheit LC (1978) Secession: the legitimacy of self-determination. Yale University Press, New Haven, p 51

Christakis T (2011) The ICJ advisory opinion on Kosovo: "Has International Law Something to Say about Secession?". Leiden J Int Law 24:75

Craven M (2010) Statehood, self-determination, and recognition. In: Evans MD (ed) International law, 3rd edn. Oxford University Press, Oxford, p 242

de Vattel E (1964) The law of nations or the principles of natural law (trans: Fenwick CG). Oceana Publications Inc., New York

Del Mar K (2013) The myth of remedial secession. In: French D (ed) Statehood and self-determination: reconciling tradition and modernity in international law. Cambridge University Press, Cambridge, pp 80–81

Dugard J, Raič D (2006) The role of recognition in the law and practice of secession. In: Kohen MG (ed) Secession: international law perspectives. Cambridge University Press, Cambridge, p 100
Eleftheriadis P (2008) Legal rights. Oxford University Press, Oxford, p 5
Falk R (2011) The Kosovo advisory opinion: conflict resolution and precedent. Am J Int Law 105:51–52
Grotius H (1964) De Jure Belli ac Pacis (trans: Kelsey FW) Book I, Chapter 4. Oceana Publications Inc., New York, p 150
Hart HLA (1961) The concept of law. Oxford University Press, Oxford, p 155
Hobbes T (1962) Leviathan, edited by John Plamenatz, Fontana Library, p 143
Hudson MO (1934) The Permanent Court of international justice. The Macmillan Company, New York, p 601 ff
Janik R (2013) The responsibility to protect as an impetus for secessionist movements — on the necessity to re-think territorial integrity. In: Kettemann MC (ed) Grenzen im Völkerrecht. Jan Sramek Verlag, Wien, pp 41–69
Jasanoff M (2012) Liberty's exiles: American loyalists in the revolutionary World. Vintage Books, New York, pp 5–53
Jennings RY, Watts AD (eds) (1992) Oppenheim's international law, 9th edn. Pearson Education, Limited, London, p 24
Kohen MG (2006) Introduction. In: Kohen MG (ed) Secession: international law perspectives. Cambridge University Press, Cambridge, p 10
Livius T (1853) The History of Rome (trans: Spillan D) Book 2. John Childs and Son, Bungay. http://www.gutenberg.org/files/19725/19725-h/19725-h.htm#b32. Accessed 15 June 2018
Locke J (2012) The second treatise of government. Philipp Reclam jun, Stuttgart
Mikulka V (1999) The dissolution of Czechoslovakia and succession in respect of treaties. In: Mrak M (ed) Succession of states. Martinus Nijhoff, Leiden, p 109
Müllerson R (2003) Sovereignty and secession: then and now, here and there. In: Dahlitz J (ed) Secession and international law: conflict avoidance – regional appraisals. United Nations Publications, New York, p 128
Müllerson R (2009) Precedents in the mountains: on the parallels and uniqueness of the cases of Kosovo, South Ossetia and Abkhazia. Chin J Int Law 8:21
Nolte G (2006) Secession and external intervention. In: Kohen MG (ed) Secession: international law perspectives. Cambridge University Press, Cambridge, pp 85–86
Peters A (2011) Does Kosovo lie in the lotus-land of freedom? Leiden J Int Law 24:104
Pufendorf S (1964) De Jure Naturae Et Gentium Libri Octo (trans: Oldfather CH, Oldfather WA). Oceana Publications Inc., New York
Raič D (2002) Statehood and the law of self-determination. Kluwer Law International, Alphen aan den Rijn, p 314
Ryngaert C, Sobrie S (2011) Recognition of states: international law or realpolitik? The practice of recognition in the Wake of Kosovo, South Ossetia, and Abkhazia. Leiden J Int Law 24:477
Shaw MN (1997) Peoples, territorialism and boundaries. Eur J Int Law 8:483
Shaw MN (2003) The role of recognition and non-recognition with respect to secession: notes on some relevant issues. In: Dahlitz J (ed) Secession and international law: conflict avoidance - regional appraisals. United Nations Publications, New York, pp 248–249
Shaw MN (2008) International law, 6th edn. Cambridge University Press, Cambridge, p 70
Sisson R, Rose LE (1990) War and secession: Pakistan, India and the creation of Bangladesh. University of California Press, Berkeley, p 207
Škrk M (1999) Recognition of states and its (Non-) implication on state succession: the case of successor states to the former Yugoslavia. In: Mrak M (ed) Succession of states. Martinus Nijhoff, Leiden, pp 8–9
Solum LB (2004) Procedural justice. South Calif Law Rev 78:182
Thirlway H (2010) The sources of international law. In: Evans MD (ed) International law, 3rd edn. Oxford University Press, Oxford, pp 95–121
Vidmar J (2012) Explaining the legal effects of recognition. Int Comp Law Q 61:378

Walter BF (2009) Reputation and civil war: why separatist conflicts are so violent. Cambridge University Press, Cambridge, pp 7–8

Weller M (2008a) Why the legal rules on self-determination do not resolve self-determination disputes. In: Weller M, Metzger B (eds) Settling self-determination disputes: complex power-sharing in theory and practice. Martinus Nijhoff, Leiden, p 33

Weller M (2008b) Escaping the self-determination trap. Martinus Nijhoff, Leiden, p 64

Wolfrum R (2011) Sources of international law, Max Planck Encyclopedia of Public International Law, last updated in May 2011

Chapter 3
Secession and Self-Determination Conflicts

From the historical perspective, secession is closely related to self-determination. From the American Declaration of Independence in the eighteenth century, to the decolonization movements after the Second World War in the twentieth century, further to post-colonial secessionist movements to this day, such relations are quite evident. Secessionist disputes are, in essence, self-determination conflicts between secessionists and non-secessionists. Lea Brilmayer has once summarized: "the standard account bases claims to secede upon principles of self-determination of peoples, according to which every nation or people has a right to determine its own destiny".[1] Since the nexus between secession and self-determination is undeniable, it is reasonable to argue that, without discussing this nexus, the analysis of secession will prove to be incomplete, if not nonsense. In order to reveal this nexus, a historical review of the evolution of self-determination, particularly in the sense of secession, should occupy the foreground. This historical review can offer a relatively complete picture of the evolution of self-determination which is closely linked to secession in theory and in reality, which is certainly helpful in improving relevant theories, to make them more suitable in reality. Needless to say, when a theory proves to be unsuitable in reality, not only does it cease to contribute to the settlement of practical disputes, but the theory itself also becomes a source of dispute. Moreover, it is of great importance to address actual issues associated with secessionist self-determination, otherwise it is unlikely to prevent self-determination, which was and is expected to be a blessing, from becoming a curse. Only when both theoretical and practical issues concerning self-determination, particularly in the sense of secession, are carefully handled, could self-determination conflicts be effectively settled.

[1]See Chap. 1, Note 34.

J. Lu, *On State Secession from International Law Perspectives*,
https://doi.org/10.1007/978-3-319-97448-4_3

3.1 The Historical Evolution of Self-Determination

3.1.1 Self-Determination in the Eighteenth Century

The American War of Independence should be regarded as a highly influential practice of self-determination in the world history. Thus, the American War of Independence serves as the starting point for this historical review. Self-determination was the keynote of the Declaration of Independence of the United States of America of 4 July 1776: "all men are created equal, that they are endowed by their Creator with certain unalienable Rights, that among these are Life, Liberty and the pursuit of Happiness. — That to secure these rights, Governments are instituted among Men, deriving their just powers from the consent of the governed, — That whenever any Form of Government becomes destructive of these ends, it is the Right of the People to alter or to abolish it, and to institute new Government, laying its foundation on such principles and organizing its powers in such form, as to them shall seem most likely to effect their Safety and Happiness".[2] A few years later this idea was echoed in the French Revolution: the French National Assembly declared in the name of the French people on 17th November 1792 that "it will give help and support to all peoples wanting to recall their freedom. Therefore, the Assembly considers the French authorities responsible to give orders to grant all means of assistance to those peoples, to protect and compensate the citizens who might be injured during their fight for the cause of liberty".[3]

Such claim of peoples to self-government, namely repudiating the right of an elite or an 'alien' people to determine for them and without their consultation their fate, political, cultural, social and economic status, found strong expression in both the American and French revolutions.[4] The expression sounded very exciting, but nevertheless its charm vanished during the operation. As mentioned in the previous chapter, self-determination, in the context of the Declaration of Independence, meant patriot-determination, and loyalist-determination was deliberately excluded: in the name of self-determination Patriots forced Loyalists to accept the determination of Patriots. The question is if the will of Patriots to overthrow the British rule is worth respect, why the will of Loyalists to maintain the British rule is largely neglected? In other words, if Patriots are entitled to determine their fate, why Loyalists are not? If all men are created equal, the political pursuit of Loyalists should deserve equal respect: there is no reason for Patriots to repress the political pursuit of Loyalists, if Patriots really believed that Loyalists were as equal as themselves. From this perspective, it is accurate to say that the practice of self-determination in the American War of Independence took on a color of double standard, which inspired one to consider: when there are distinct ideas regarding determination within the people, whose determination should take precedence? In the American War of

[2]Declaration of Independence of the United States of America of 4 July 1776.

[3]Quoted from Castellino (2000), p. 11.

[4]Raič (2002), p. 173.

Independence an answer was provided: determination of the triumphing party took precedence. Loyalists ultimately lost the battle to Patriots, so the determination of Patriots took priority. Needless to say, this answer was highly problematic and dangerous, as in this sense, self-determination is no more than social Darwinism in disguise: determination of the strongest. In such context, self-determination will inevitably become a catalyst of war between people with distinct opinions about self-determination. Obviously, when this question is not properly addressed, the double standard or social Darwinism inevitably casts a shadow on the exercise of a right to self-determination. Unfortunately, this question is not always properly addressed, as will be demonstrated repeatedly in this historical review.

Another aspect of the practice of self-determination in the American War of Independence deserving equal attention is external involvement in the secessionist conflict. There was no reason to underestimate the role France played in this process: France initially provided Patriots with secret material assistance, then recognized US independence and joined the struggle against Britain. "The reaction of other countries to France's actions was not supportive and revealed that sovereign rights in a states system composed mostly of hereditary monarchies were understood as dynastic rights... The only valid change of title to sovereignty or territory was through freely given consent of the affected monarch, which meant that open siding by a third party with a unilateral secessionist attempt was not considered legitimate. The overwhelming majority of existing states refused to have normal relations with the United States prior to the British acknowledgement of its independence in the preliminary peace treaty of 1782."[5] Needless to say, such reaction of other countries to external involvement in a secessionist conflict is not much concerned with contemporary international law; however, there is no denying that the perspective of territorial sovereignty, the focus on consent of the affected parties and the choice of non-recognition are still worth serious consideration when the legality of external involvement in the context of secessionist self-determination is being discussed.

In the French Revolution, the question regarding self-determination conflicts was not properly addressed either. Liberty, equality and fraternity somehow translated into the Reign of Terror, which was definitely the opposite of these values. Given that Patriots realized their own political pursuit by repressing that of Loyalists, the Reign of Terror could also be understood as a means of realizing self-determination. Therefore, the means of realizing self-determination in self-determination conflicts should be carefully considered: even if there is an indisputable right to self-determination, it will be extremely irresponsible to say that this right can be pursued by any means. Obviously, a means such as the Reign of Terror is likely to violate the right to self-determination of others, and one's right to self-determination should never be a justification for violating that right of others, so there must be legal limitations on the means of realizing self-determination, otherwise a right to self-determination will be open to abuse. Unfortunately, in this regard not much legal

[5] Fabry (2011), p. 255.

progress has been made in theory or in practice, as will be demonstrated later in this historical review.

Apart from what has been mentioned above, a notable feature of double standard regarding self-determination shared by both revolutions is that a certain system which was typically incompatible with self-determination stayed basically intact after these revolutions. The newborn US retained the obnoxious slavery and France fought to keep its colony. These regrettable facts remind one of the importance of combating double standards hidden in self-determination once again.

3.1.2 Self-Determination in the Nineteenth Century

The Latin American Wars of Independence followed the American and French revolutions. "The disintegration of the Spanish imperium in America produced the norm of uti possidetis."[6] "In American Public Law the principle of uti possidetis meant that the boundaries of the new Republic would be the same as those of the old colonial administrative units, which they replaced on gaining independence."[7] At the Congress of Lima in 1847, the Treaty of Confederation was signed, in which the uti possidetis principle was confirmed as a basis for the delimitation of boundaries between the Latin American Republics, and this principle was also reflected in the constitution of Latin American Republics.[8] In the practice of self-determination by Latin American Republics, the territorial perspective was a focal point, which was closely related to the historical experience and practical consideration. To be more specific, "the principle of uti possidetis was formulated to serve a dual purpose: first, a defensive purpose towards the rest of the world, in the form of an outright denial that there was any land without a sovereign (or terra nullius) in the decolonized territories, even in unexplored areas or those beyond the control of the colonizers; secondly, a preventive purpose: to avoid or at least to minimize conflict occurring in the relationships among the successors, by freezing the carved-up territory in the format it exhibited at the moment of independence."[9] Obviously, the second purpose still has current significance: the practice of self-determination could give rise to territorial disputes between newly independent states in Latin America at that time if there was no generally agreed principle to prevent such disputes; in the same vein, at present it will also give rise to territorial disputes if a secessionist entity and a parent state do not reach an agreement on the distribution of territorial interests. In fact, the settlement of territorial issues actually requires a more complicated agreement than a general principle, as a general principle will prove to be ambiguous in some

[6]Franck (1993), p. 5.

[7]Nelson (1973), p. 268.

[8]Ibid. pp. 268–269.

[9]Frontier Dispute, Judgment, I.C.J. Reports 1986, Separate Opinion of Judge ad hoc Abi-Saab, p. 661, para. 13.

circumstances. For instance, although Guatemala and Honduras in the Honduras Borders arbitration were in agreement as to the application of the norm of uti possidetis, they were at odds as to which variation of this doctrine of 1821 to use: Guatemala insisted on applying uti possidetis de facto while Honduras contended that uti possidetis iuris was the right interpretation.[10] "In the end, it would seem that the arbitrators slightly favored the Guatemalan thesis, although quite a number of the points of contention were eventually decided on the basis of equity and justice."[11] It should be noticed that the territorial perspective of self-determination, despite being quite crucial, has not always gained enough attention in the post-colonial self-determination conflicts. As will be demonstrated later, this perspective should never be overlooked for the sake of the settlement of self-determination conflicts.

Meanwhile, it is noteworthy that the modern norm of non-intervention "had its origins in British and American policies outlining acceptable external response to unilateral secessions of Latin American territories from Spain and Portugal".[12] The essence of their perspective is: "while outsiders were free to offer non-forcible assistance in the form of conciliation or mediation proposals to the parties to a secessionist conflict, they were not free to side coercively with either party because that would interfere with the right of a state to determine their own future."[13] In addition to the norm of non-intervention, there was a collateral norm of recognizing de facto statehood: the triumph of secessionists "transformed the situation from one of domestic affairs of the host state, which prohibited unwarranted external intervention, to one in which the very condition of domestic affairs, as far as the territory of the seceded state was concerned, cease to exist."[14] Obviously, both ideas contained an element of reasonableness from the perspective of contemporary international law. The problem is, in practice, intervention can be hidden in conciliation or mediation proposals, when the proposal maker is too powerful to be ignored: powerful outsiders might choose to side with one party by offering a conciliation or mediation proposal in favor of this party. Of course, the prejudiced party can reject this proposal, but it can do nothing to eliminate the influence of this proposal on the negotiation between it and the favored party. For instance, the favored party can employ this proposal as a powerful argument to refuse compromise on its own part and force the prejudiced party to give in during their negotiation. As for the norm of recognizing de facto statehood, there is no denying that it will be highly influenced by the political consideration of recognizing states; moreover, recognition can also constitute a form of intervention when it is granted at the wrong time, which has been discussed in Chap. 2. Therefore, the legal evaluation of external involvement in self-determination conflicts should focus on not only the

---

[10] Honduras borders (Guatemala, Honduras), II UNRIAA. p. 1322.

[11] Klabbers and Lefeber (1993), p. 55.

[12] Fabry (2011), p. 252.

[13] Ibid. p. 253.

[14] Ibid.

form but also its substantive influence, because formally legal external involvement can also be challenged in the substantive sense.

In the nineteenth century the USA provided another influential practice of secessionist self-determination, namely the American Civil War, which was a typical case of self-determination conflicts between secessionists and non-secessionists. Although this theme was coupled with the higher moral cause of emancipating slaves, it was widely agreed that "Lincoln's commitment to emancipating the slaves was tepid and to racial equality rather cool".[15] Thus, it is accurate to focus on the perspective of secessionist self-determination and anti-secessionist self-determination. In the eyes of Southern secessionists, "a nation born in a Declaration of independence from British rule and dedicated to the principle of self-government would find it difficult to sustain popular support for the forcible subjugation of the South just to keep it in the Union",[16] while in the eyes of non-secessionists, the attempt of Southern secessionists was an illegal insurrection, and "the Union refused any form of negotiation that would suggest recognition of the Confederacy as a sovereign state. It also warned Britain and France not to mediate or intervene in any way, for that would be regarded as virtual recognition of the Confederacy and would invite war with the US".[17] Obviously, it was the old question which already existed in the American War of independence: when there is a self-determination conflict, each conflicting party believes its own right to self-determination should prevail. The civil war, just like the Reign of Terror in the French Revolution, was the means they chose to exercise their right to self-determination. In addition, non-secessionists of the US wisely noticed that external involvement could be detrimental to its self-determination, although it might take a seemingly neutral form such as mediation. In general, the major lesson drawn from the American Civil War regarding self-determination can be summarized in two points: one is how a self-determination conflict can be prevented from escalating into a civil war, which definitely requires a more reasonable legal system of self-determination, including limits on the means of pursuing self-determination; the other is how external involvement can play a better role in the settlement of secessionist self-determination conflicts, of which the focus is how an external party can effectively cooperate with both conflicting parties. As demonstrated in the American Civil War, when an external party cannot effectively cooperate with the parent state, it is rather unrealistic to expect this party to play a positive role in settling secessionist self-determination conflicts.

When the nationalistic movements in the latter part of the nineteenth century are taken into account, such as the Italian unification in 1870 and the German unification in 1871, one may feel that unification is another way to exercise self-determination, contrary to secession. In the eyes of Martti Koskenniemi, "the self-determination which identifies the nation as the State could be called the classical, or Hobbesean, conception of self-determination... nationalism buttressed existing States and

[15]Doyle (2011), p. 113.

[16]Ibid. p. 112.

[17]Ibid. p. 115.

created new ones through composition rather than secession".[18] However, it is necessary to note that secession was also hidden in the composition, and similar to pure secession, the success of secession before composition was also closely related to external involvement. For example, the Italian unification owed a good deal to the oral agreement at Plombières made between Napoleon III and Cavour, who was the prime minister of Piemont-Sardinia; according to this agreement France would intervene in northern Italy against Austria in support of Piemont, and Piemont could annex Lombardy, which at that time was under the rule of Austria.[19] In short, France helped Lombardy secede from Austria and become a part of the unified Italy. Similarly, the duchies of Schleswig and Holstein used to be bound to Denmark in a personal union under the Danish crown; Prussia fought against Denmark for the unification of Germany: the first attempt failed, as Russia and Great Britain sided with Denmark; later Prussia together with Austria made a second attempt and this time other powers were not willing to intervene, so Denmark became the loser.[20] Such cases inspire one to consider the nexus between ethnicity and secessionist self-determination. As demonstrated in these two cases, multinational states are prone to the threat of secession; it is not only because of the wish of its ethnic minorities to secede but also because of the action of foreign states sharing the ethnicity with them. Of course, in this day and age few states will act as explicitly as states in the above cases, but it is undeniable that foreign states can still exert their influence in an implicit manner. In such circumstances, a secessionist self-determination conflict is of dual dimension: it is not only a conflict between the ethnic minority and majority within a particular state but also a conflict between this state and a foreign state sharing the ethnicity with the ethnic minority within this state. Therefore, in order to settle secessionist self-determination conflicts in such circumstances, it is not enough to focus on the internal dimension, and the external dimension deserves no less attention.

As a matter of fact, as long as external involvement favors one conflicting party in a secessionist self-determination conflict without solid legal ground, the secessionist self-determination conflict will inevitably gain an external dimension, because the external party interferes with the right to self-determination of one party by siding with the other party. Undeniably, this situation complicates secessionist self-determination conflicts and increases difficulty in settling them, due to the interplay between the internal and the external dimension. Of course, in this day and age external actors will never fail to find a legal justification for their preference for one conflicting party, although there is no guarantee that such legal justification can be widely accepted. In the legal evaluation of external involvement, it is necessary to focus on the legal justification provided by the external actor but more necessary to focus on the actual influence of its external involvement. External involvement that is counterproductive to the settlement of secessionist self-determination conflicts

[18]Koskenniemi (1994), pp. 249–251.

[19]Summers (2007), p. 120.

[20]Ibid. pp. 121–122.

should be condemned, no matter how high-sounding the legal justification is. Although there is no guarantee that such condemnation can contribute a good deal to the improvement in external involvement, at least it can serve as an alert for those which intend to get involved in secessionist self-determination conflicts.

3.1.3 Self-Determination in the First Half of the Twentieth Century

Self-determination is also an important theme in the Russian revolution. Lenin approached this theme from different perspectives. In his eyes, "self-determination implies only the right to secede"[21]; "to accuse those who support freedom of self-determination, i.e., freedom to secede, of encouraging separatism, is as foolish and hypocritical as accusing those who advocate freedom of divorce of encouraging the destruction of family ties"[22]; "from their daily experience the masses know perfectly well the value of geographical and economic ties and the advantages of a big market and a big state. They will, therefore, resort to secession only when national oppression and national friction make joint life absolutely intolerable and hinder any and all economic intercourse."[23] Despite the support for secessionist self-determination, he also pointed out that it was not a categorical right: "the right of nations to self-determination implies exclusively the right to independence in the political sense, the right to free political separation from the oppressor nation. Specifically, this demand for political democracy implies complete freedom to agitate for secession and for a referendum on secession by the seceding nation. This demand, therefore, is not the equivalent of a demand for separation, fragmentation and the formation of small states. It implies only a consistent expression of struggle against all national oppression. The closer a democratic state system is to complete freedom to secede the less frequent and less ardent will the desire for separation be in practice, because big states afford indisputable advantages, both from the standpoint of economic progress and from that of the interests of the masses. . ."[24]; "the most practical procedure is to say a plain 'yes' in favour of the secession of a particular nation rather than in favour of all nations having the right to secede"[25]; "we fight against the privileges and violence of the oppressor nation, and do not in any way condone strivings for privileges on the part of the oppressed nation".[26]

Obviously, the idea of Lenin was influenced by theorists of natural law such as Grotius and Vattel. His theory of secession focused on the struggle against national

[21] Lenin (1964), p. 451.

[22] Lenin (1964), p. 422.

[23] Lenin (1964), p. 423.

[24] See Chap. 1, Note 15.

[25] Lenin (1964), p. 411.

[26] Lenin (1964), p. 412.

oppression, and this remedial color was reminiscent of the metaphor made by Grotius: the social compact is like a body; when a part of the body cannot save itself in any other way, the right which the part has to protect itself is greater than the right of the body over the part.[27] Lenin stressed the considerable benefits of remaining in a community, just like Vattel who argued that civil society was too useful and necessary to be dissolved.[28] In addition to the theoretical inheritance, the metaphor of divorce made by Lenin can be regarded as an innovation. If secession should be treated as divorce, the bilateral character and procedural character of secession must be recognized. As both parties in a divorce have a say in the division of common wealth and the duty of child care and there is a particular procedure for both parties to effectively participate in deciding these issues, both parties in a secession should also have a say in the division of common wealth, particularly the territorial interests, and there should be a corresponding procedure for such division. It seems that Lenin himself did not focus much on shaping a legal institution of secession similar to that of divorce. Nevertheless, given that he has clearly expressed his opposition to the fragmentation of states and likely abuse of secession by oppressed nations, there is no denying that shaping a legal institution of secession similar to that of divorce is in accordance with his intention. Otherwise it will be really difficult to imagine how the fragmentation of states and likely abuse of secession can be prevented.

It must be recognized that the opposition of Lenin to fragmentation of states is definitely farsighted. This idea is echoed by contemporary scholars: for instance, in the report entitled *The Right to Self-determination: Implementation of United Nations Resolutions*, prepared by Hector Gros Espiell, Special Rapporteur of the Sub-Commission on Prevention of Discrimination and Protection of Minorities, it was pointed out that "in certain extreme cases very small States would not be in a position to form real free, independent and sovereign entities and would be unable to discharge the duties that inevitably flow from membership of the United Nations; and because the proliferation of very small States might have the effect of destroying or seriously undermining the very foundations of the existing community of nations, while at the same time giving rise to the problem that this type of very small State might be particularly suited to forms of intervention and/or influence which could well characterize dangerous manifestations of neocolonialism."[29] The judgment that very small States would not be in a position to form real free, independent and sovereign entities has been proved in a number of cases. "Micronesia, the Marshall Islands, Palau, Monaco and Andorra have concluded agreements with other states under which theoretically their absolute freedom of voting in the United Nations could be restricted. By virtue of their respective Compacts of Free Association with the United States, Micronesia, the Marshall Islands and Palau shall in the conduct of

---

[27]See Chap. 2, Note 54.

[28]See Chap. 2, Note 57.

[29]UN Doc. E/CH.4/Sub.2/405/Rev.1 (1980), para. 108.

their foreign affairs 'consult' with the government of the United States."[30] According to the Franco-Monegasque Treaty of 2002, Monaco has to exercise its sovereignty in accordance with the fundamental interests of the French Republic in the political, economic, security and defense areas.[31] "The effect of agreements limiting independence is a complete destabilization of the principle of sovereign equality of the member states on which the United Nations is based."[32] As a matter of fact, even without these agreements, the practical independence of very small states is already highly questionable, and these agreements have highlighted that the theoretical independence of very small states is equally questionable. From this perspective, it is necessary to impose reasonable restrictions on secessionist self-determination, as the likely fragmentation of states resulting from secessionist self-determination is detrimental to the realization of genuine self-determination.

Two points of Lenin's idea require reconsideration in the post-colonial context. One concerns a right to secede as sui generis: as mentioned above, Lenin argued for a right to secession of a particular nation instead of a right to secession of all nations. If it is in the context of consensual secession, this argument will not cause actual problems, because there is lex specialis, namely an agreement between secessionists and non-secessionists, for this sui generis case. Nevertheless, if it concerns unilateral secession which is objected by a parent state, it will lead to serious legal problems. The most glaring one of these problems is that the sui generis concept is open to political exploitation, thus disrupting the functioning of the international legal system: "'Special cases' do not merely dilute the quality of legality of a system: they replace it with a political element, in which the power and commitment of individual actors becomes more significant than the legal rights that they enjoy. Claims that situations are sui generis reduce the universally recognized rights of states, and put them outside the ordinary processes of the making and application of international law".[33] Therefore, applying the sui generis concept must be very prudent, otherwise the universally recognized rights of states will be affected. In a case of unilateral secession, the sui generis concept should not be applied as "a legal argument in order to convince the international community that this case is so unique that it is situated out of the realm of international law and cannot be considered in any way as a 'precedent' for future secessionist attempts".[34] It is of great importance to avoid the precedential effect, but it is hardly possible to avoid the precedential effect simply by claiming sui generis. This point will be further discussed when it comes to secession of South Ossetia and Abkhazia.

[30]Duursma (1996), p. 139.

[31]Franco-Monegasque Treaty 2002, Article 1, para. 2, http://oxcon.ouplaw.com/view/10.1093/law:ocw/law-ocw-rd99.regGroup.1/law-ocw-rd99, last accessed on 15.06.2018.

[32]Duursma (1996), p. 140.

[33]Written Statement of the Republic of Cyprus (2009) requested for the Kosovo Advisory Opinion, para. 77.

[34]Christakis (2011), p. 81.

The other point requiring reconsideration is the judgment of Lenin that a high degree of freedom to secede will lessen the desire for separation. Given the dissolution of the Soviet Union and Czechoslovakia, this judgement did not prove to be persuasive: in the constitution of both countries a right to secessionist self-determination was mentioned, and this degree of freedom to secede was rarely seen in the constitution of most other states; unfortunately, the desire for separation was not lessened due to the extraordinarily high degree of freedom to secede, as both states ended in dissolution. Although there is no reason to believe that a high degree of freedom to secede will lessen the desire for separation, it is still meaningful to consider controlling the desire for separation. As will be discussed later, the control of the desire for separation is dependent on not only internal factors but also external factors.

A few years later after Lenin had published his idea on self-determination, Wilson put the idea of self-determination into practice at the Peace Conference in Paris. Generally speaking, Wilson did not make much effort to solve the problems permeating the exercise of a right to self-determination mentioned before. Double standards, right clashes between different selves, biased external involvement in self-determination conflicts were as glaring as before. "Communities which had been loyal to the Allied Powers, like the Yugo-Slavs, the Polish people, the Czechs and Slovaks and the Romanians, were permitted to form their own states, while other claims were ignored."[35] China, despite being loyal to the Allied Powers, was still deprived of the right to self-determination: the Treaty of Versailles transferred the concessions in Shandong (Shantung) from Imperial Germany to Japan instead of restoring China's sovereign authority,[36] despite the fierce opposition of the Chinese people.

It is necessary to review the criticism from Lansing, who was the U.S. Secretary of State at that time, directed at Wilsonian self-determination: "when the President talks about 'self-determination' what unit has he in mind? Does he mean a race, a territorial area, or a community? Without a definite unit which is practical, application of this principle is dangerous to peace and stability. . . The more I think about the President's declaration as to the right of 'self-determination', the more convinced I am of the danger of putting such ideas into the minds of certain races. It is bound to be the basis of impossible demands on the Peace Conference and create trouble in many lands. What effect will it have on the Irish, the Indians, the Egyptians, and the nationalists among the Boers? Will it not breed discontent, disorder and rebellion? Will not the Mohammedans of Syria and Palestine and possibly of Morocco and Tripoli rely on it? How can it be harmonized with Zionism, to which the President is practically committed? The phrase is simply loaded with dynamite. It will raise

[35] Raič (2002), p. 190.

[36] Part IV, Section VIII of the Treaty of Versailles was entitled Shantung. In this section there were three Articles (Article 156–Article 158). In these Articles it was provided that all rights, title and privileges acquired by Germany regarding the Province of Shantung—particularly those concerning the territory of Kiaochow, railways, mines and submarine cables would be transferred to Japan within 3 months from the coming into force of the Treaty.

hopes which can never be realized. It will, I fear, cost thousands of lives. In the end it is bound to be discredited, to be called the dream of an idealist who failed to realize the danger until too late to check those who attempt to put the principle in force. What calamity that the phrase was ever uttered! What misery it will cause!"[37] Later the criticism of Lansing was echoed by Jennings: "Nearly forty years ago, a professor of political science, who was also president of the United States, President Wilson, enunciated a doctrine which was ridiculous, but which was widely accepted as a sensible proposition, the doctrine of self-determination. On the surface it seemed reasonable: let the people decide. It was in fact ridiculous because people cannot decide until someone decides who the people are."[38]

Lansing realized that the idea of self-determination would inevitably give rise to self-determination conflicts, and Jennings pointed out that Wilsonian self-determination was much concerned with external involvement: at first, an outsider is to decide who the holder of the right to self-determination is. Indeed, "Wilson himself understood who could decide who the people were: as demonstrated by Draft Article III which places the onus on the victorious Allies."[39] Strictly speaking, the expression of "victorious Allies" is not fully accurate, as China was also a member of the Allies but certainly not among the decision makers. Obviously, designating the holder of the right to self-determination seems to be a way of avoiding self-determination conflicts: in such circumstances exist no conflicting rights to self-determination, as one party is deemed the right holder while the other is not. The fundamental problem of this way is that it is self-determination in appearance but other-determination in essence. "The Armenians, Azerbaijanis, Kurds, and Montenegrins, as well as the German, Magyar, and other minorities in the succession states (to take a small sample) did not deem their causes any less worthy of espousal than those of the Poles, the Czechs, or the Serbs."[40] However, the decision makers of the Allies did not think so, so these groups could not acquire the right to self-determination. In the same vein, China was not allowed to resume its sovereign control over Shandong province: China was not a holder of the right to self-determination either, according to the decision makers.

Perhaps the most thought-provoking issue from the practice of the Wilsonian concept of self-determination is how self-determination can be prevented from transmuting into other-determination when external intervention is particularly powerful. As discussed before, when external involvement in self-determination conflicts proves to be biased, self-determination conflicts gain an external dimension: the conflict is not only between original conflicting parties but also between one party and the biased external party. When the external party is powerful enough to decide the result of the self-determination conflict, self-determination has somewhat transmuted into other-determination: self-determination of the prejudiced party

[37] Lansing (1921), pp. 97–98.
[38] Jennings (1956), pp. 55–56.
[39] See Chap. 1, Note 16.
[40] Pomerance (1982), p. 6.

was actually ignored. Obviously, in such circumstances a self-determination conflict is not really settled but temporarily repressed by powerful external intervention; there is no reason to believe that unsettled self-determination conflicts can always be repressed. For this reason, other-determination can become a potential threat to peace and security, so it is of great importance to avoid other-determination: external actors should not interfere in self-determination conflicts to such a degree that it decides the result of such conflicts. A self-determination conflict cannot be effectively settled by granting self-determination to one party and denying that of the other. There are alternatives for settling such conflicts, for instance, focusing on improving the institution of self-determination to enable the coexistence of conflicting self-determination claims. As will be discussed later, by stressing the obligation associated with the right to self-determination and adding procedural restraints, it is possible to enable the institution to accommodate conflicting self-determination claims.

The case of the Aaland Islands submitted to the Council of the League of Nations was about a right to secessionist self-determination. Aaland Islanders claimed secession from Finland on the basis of self-determination, while Finland rejected it and challenged the jurisdiction of the Council of the League. The Council dismissed the challenge from Finland and asked Jurists to rule on the matter. According to the Report of the Committee of Jurists, "the grant or refusal of the right to a portion of its population of determining its own political fate by plebiscite or by some other method, is, exclusively, an attribute of the sovereignty of every State which is definitively constituted".[41] However, "Finland had not yet acquired the character of a definitively constituted State",[42] so "the dispute does not refer to a question which is left by International Law to the domestic jurisdiction of Finland".[43] "Although the principle of self-determination of peoples plays an important part in modern political thought, especially since the Great War, it must be pointed out that there is no mention of it in the Covenant of the League of Nations. The recognition of this principle in a certain number of international treaties cannot be considered as sufficient to put it upon the same footing as a positive rule of the Law of Nations."[44] Furthermore, the commission, "in affirming these principles, does not give an opinion concerning the question as to whether a manifest and continued abuse of sovereign power, to the detriment of a section of the population of a State, would, if such circumstances arose, give to an international dispute, arising therefrom, such a character that its object should be considered as one which is not confined to the domestic jurisdiction of the State concerned, but comes within the sphere of action of the League of Nations."[45]

[41]The Aaland Islands Question: Report of the Committee of Jurists, League of Nations, Official Journal, Special Supp. No. 3 (October 1920), p. 5.
[42]Ibid. p. 14.
[43]Ibid.
[44]Ibid. p. 5.
[45]Ibid.

In the case of the Aaland Islands not only the suitability of external intervention in domestic affairs but also the issue whether abuse of state sovereignty to the detriment of self-determination no longer falls into the category of domestic affairs was involved. In this sense the Report of the committee of Jurists is highly valuable, as such controversial issues which appeared in the case of Aaland Islands still exist in this day and age and are no less controversial. Nevertheless, as its conclusion was much concerned with the secondary status of self-determination in the international legal system at that time, the practical heuristic value of the first report in 1920 on the Aaland Islands question is also discounted. It is noteworthy that there came a second report on the Aaland Islands question in 1921. This Report presented to the Council of the League by the Commission of Rapporteurs actually considered the question from the perspective of natural law and general principles of law. To be more specific, the issue of secessionist self-determination was interpreted from the perspective of remedy and equity:

> Is it possible to admit as an absolute rule that a minority of the population of a State, which is definitely constituted and perfectly capable of fulfilling its duties as such, has the right of separating itself from her in order to be incorporated in another State or to declare its independence? The answer can only be in the negative. To concede to minorities, either of language or religion, or to any fractions of a population the right of withdrawing from the community to which they belong, because it is their wish or their good pleasure, would be to destroy order and stability within States and to inaugurate anarchy in international life; it would be to uphold a theory incompatible with the very idea of the State as a territorial and political unity... The idea of justice and of liberty, embodied in the formula of self-determination must be applied in a reasonable manner to the relations between States and the minorities they include. It is just that the ethnical character and the ancient traditions of these minorities should be respected as much as possible, and that they should be specially authorised to practise freely their religion and to cultivate their language... But what reasons would there be for allowing a minority to separate itself from the State to which it is united, if this State gives it the guarantees which it is within its rights in demanding, for the preservation of its social, ethnical or religious character? Such indulgence, apart from every political consideration, would be supremely unjust to the State prepared to make these concessions... The separation of a minority from the State of which it forms a part and its incorporation in another State can only be considered as an altogether exceptional solution, a last resort when the State lacks either the will or the power to enact and apply just and effective guarantees.[46]

This analysis is reminiscent of the opinion of Grotius, in which unilateral secession, due to its destructive consequences, is generally forbidden but might be admitted as an exceptional remedial solution in extraordinary circumstances. The challenge posed to remedial secession is also applicable here: when the state regains either the will or the power to enact and apply just and effective guarantees, can the separation of a minority still be considered as a last resort? The idea of equity played a key role in this analysis: it has been noted that self-determination of one side in the form of unilateral secession constitutes an unjust indulgence detrimental to the other side, and the right to self-determination must be exercised in a reasonable manner.

[46]See Chap. 1, Note 17.

Obviously, the idea of equity should not be ignored in the settlement of current self-determination conflicts: as unilateral secession was an unjust way of exercising the right to self-determination and can intensify self-determination conflicts, it is necessary to discourage secessionists from acting in this way. This point is worth serious consideration. Further analysis regarding the injustice of exercising the right to self-determination in the form of unilateral secession will be found in the discussion of self-determination from the territorial perspective. In addition, it is noteworthy that this report rejected a right to secessionist self-determination of minorities, but it did not deny the right to self-determination of minorities in the religious and cultural sense. This should be regarded as a great attempt in the settlement of self-determination conflicts: it did not only point out the correct direction of the development of self-determination but also shifted the focus from the right holder to the content of the right. As will be discussed later, this understanding of self-determination is indeed helpful for striking a balance of interests between conflicting parties, thus contributing to an effective solution to self-determination conflicts.

"Although self-determination was proclaimed by the United States and the United Kingdom during World War II, it was mainly because of Soviet pressure that self-determination was included in the Charter of the United Nations."[47] This principle is referred to in Article 1(2) in Chapter I on "purposes and principles": "to develop friendly relations among nations based on respect for the principle of equal rights and self-determination of peoples, and to take other appropriate measures to strengthen universal peace"; self-determination is repeated in Article 55 in Chapter IX on "international economic and social cooperation": "with a view to the creation of conditions of stability and well-being which are necessary for peaceful and friendly relations among nations based on respect for the principle of equal rights and self-determination of peoples, the United Nations shall promote . . ." According to the phrase of these two articles, one could hardly predict how a right to self-determination will be exercised, as the phrase sounds so ambiguous. "On the basis of any reasonable textual construction, the conclusion is inescapable that 'self-determination, in contrast to sovereignty and all that flows from it, was not originally perceived as an operative principle of the Charter; . . . it was one of the desiderata of the Charter rather than a legal right that could be invoked as such'."[48] Of course, the interpretation of a legal principle can never solely be based on the original perception: the interpretation must reflect the actual development of this principle, as time goes by.

[47] Raič (2002), pp. 199–200.

[48] Pomerance (1982), p. 9. The content within single quotation marks is quoted from Blum (1975), p. 511.

3.1.4 Self-Determination in the De-Colonial Era

"Notwithstanding the cautious way in which self-determination is referred to in the UN Charter, there began in the 1950s to be a moral stand taken on the issue by the General Assembly. Furthermore, with the increase in Afro-Asian membership in the 1960s, self-determination became increasingly invoked as a right of dependent peoples."[49] The well-known Declaration on the Granting of Independence to Colonial Countries and Peoples adopted in 1960 by the General Assembly of the UN is a reflection of this trend. As mentioned in Chap. 2, due to the form of General Assembly Resolution, this declaration could not provide rights and duties in a strict legal sense, and it should be taken as a proof of the new interpretation of self-determination: for colonial countries and peoples, self-determination could mean independence. There were also two other alternatives: free association with an independent State or integration with an independent State,[50] as listed in General Assembly Resolution 1541(XV). That is to say, even in the de-colonial era, the exercise of self-determination was not restricted to secession. It is noteworthy that the territorial perspective of self-determination was not overlooked in the context of de-colonization: in the Declaration on the Granting of Independence to Colonial Countries and Peoples, it was stated that "any attempt aimed at the partial or total disruption of the national unity and the territorial integrity of a country is incompatible with the purposes and principles of the Charter of the United Nations"[51]; in General Assembly Resolution 1541(XV), it was stated that "prima facie there is an obligation to transmit information in respect of a territory which is geographically separate and is distinct ethnically and/or culturally from the country administering it".[52] Such statements demonstrated that the drafters of these General Assembly resolutions intended to stress the non-applicability of secessionist self-determination in the non-colonial context. As pointed out by Patrick Thornberry, "the coupling of geography and the ethnic factor is important; without geography, the designation of non-colonial territories as entitled to self-determination was a possibility, though even with this factor, the definition is not perfect if the intention is to exclude all minority groups."[53]

Given the principle of uti possidetis asserted between newly independent republics in Latin America, it is not very difficult to understand why geographical separation was stressed in the exercise of secessionist self-determination: the exercise of secessionist self-determination invariably gives rise to territorial disputes when geographical separation simply does not exist. It was the case in Latin America: former colonies of the Spanish empire geographically bordered each other, so if they did not accept the colonial borders when they became independent

---

[49]Higgins (2003), p. 24.

[50]A/RES/1541(XV), Annex, Principle VI.

[51]A/RES/1514(XV), para. 6.

[52]A/RES/1541(XV), Annex, Principle IV.

[53]Thornberry (1989), p. 874.

of Spanish colonial rule, territorial disputes would be inevitable. Acceptance of the colonial borders helped prevent territorial disputes between newly independent republics. In fact, this also revealed a fundamental distinction between colonial secession and non-colonial secession: due to geographical separation, the territorial relations between colonies and colonial powers were not that complicated, which was favorable for the exercise of secessionist self-determination; because geographical separation usually does not exist in the non-colonial context, the territorial relations between a secessionist entity and a parent state are much more complicated, which should be regarded as an objective reason to reject unilateral secessionist self-determination. It is time to review the remark made by Reisman in terms of post-colonial secession: "in the new context, the travail and duration of 'secession' may prove to be quite different from in the past. In the old world, secession could be taken quite literally to mean as complete a severance as the parties wished. In an interdependent world, there can, in fact, be no such thing as total secession and independence-only reorganization and rearrangement. This will mean that withdrawals will become more protracted and, though there may be violent phases, ultimately each rearrangement will require overlapping bilateral and plurilateral negotiations."[54] This point will be further analyzed later in the discussion of the territorial perspective of self-determination.

Just like in the nineteenth century in Latin America, the principle of uti possidetis was also applied to the newly decolonized Africa. A resolution on border disputes between African states in 1964 was adopted: "considering that border problems constitute a grave and permanent factor of dissention; conscious of the existence of extra-African manoeuvres aimed at dividing African States; considering further that the borders of African States, on the day of their independence, constitute a tangible reality"; the Organization of African Unity "solemnly declares that all Member States pledge themselves to respect the borders existing on their achievement of national independence".[55] About 20 years later, the principle of uti possidetis was reaffirmed by the ICJ in the Frontier Dispute between Burkina Faso and Mali: "at first sight this principle conflicts outright with another one, the right of peoples to self-determination. In fact, however, the maintenance of the territorial status quo in Africa is often seen as the wisest course, to preserve what has been achieved by peoples who have struggled for their independence, and to avoid a disruption which would deprive the continent of the gains achieved by much sacrifice. The essential requirement of stability in order to survive, to develop and gradually to consolidate their independence in all fields, has induced African States judiciously to consent to the respecting of colonial frontiers, and to take account of it in the interpretation of the principle of self-determination of peoples."[56]

[54] Reisman (1990), p. 864.

[55] AHG/Res. 16(I), http://archive.au.int/collect/auassemb/import/English/FIRST%20ORDINARY_E.pdf, last accessed on 15.06.2018.

[56] Frontier Dispute, Judgment, I.C.J. Reports 1986, p. 567, para. 25.

Interestingly, like in the Honduras Borders arbitration, the principle of equity, as an addition to the principle of uti possidetis, once again found its place in the Frontier Dispute between Burkina Faso and Mali: "it will have regard to equity infra legem, that is, that form of equity which constitutes a method of interpretation of the law in force, and is one of its attributes. As the Court has observed: 'It is not a matter of finding simply an equitable solution, but an equitable solution derived from the applicable law.' (Fisheries Jurisdiction, I.C.J. Reports 1974, p. 33, para. 78; p. 202, para. 69.) How in practice the Chamber will approach recourse to this kind of equity in the present case will emerge from its application throughout this Judgement of the principles and rules which it finds to be applicable."[57] Judge Abi-Saab made an addition in his separate opinion: "by proceeding from the geometric concept of a line, which is alone capable of reconciling the principle of uti possidetis with the facts, we can state that there is always a line which defines the outer limit of lawful possession. But the scope of a court's role in identifying that line will vary inversely to the extent of its having taken concrete shape. The fewer the points (or points of reference) involved in its definition, the greater the court's 'degrees of freedom' (in the statistical sense). And it is here that considerations of equity infra legem come into play, to guide the court in the exercise of this freedom when interpreting and applying the law and the legal titles involved."[58]

The practice in Africa proved once again that the territorial perspective of self-determination must be carefully considered. Although the principle of uti possidetis serves as a guide in the exercise of self-determination, there is still ambiguity in this principle. It is suggested that the principle of equity helps clarify such ambiguity. The idea is definitely indisputable, but it must be recognized that equity itself is highly abstract and intangible. That is to say, before applying equity as a method of interpreting the principle of uti possidetis, equity itself requires to be interpreted, and how equity can be convincingly interpreted is already a complex question. As discussed in the judgement on the Frontier Dispute between Burkina Faso and Mali, equity included three possibilities: equity contra legem, equity praeter legem and equity infra legem; the former two possibilities implied an adjustment of respective interests of disputing parties; because the Parties did not entrust the court with the task of carrying out an adjustment of their respective interests, the court must dismiss any possibility of resorting to equity contra legem and equity praeter legem, and choose equity infra legem.[59] Although this approach was not objected by both disputing parties, Burkina Faso considered that it was far from clear what the practical implications would be in this case.[60] Therefore, one can say that equity infra legem is still somewhat intangible. No wonder Judge Abi-Saab expressed in his separate opinion that the solution provided by the court was not

[57]Ibid. pp. 567–568, para. 28.

[58]Frontier Dispute, Judgment, I.C.J. Reports 1986, Separate Opinion of Judge ad hoc Abi-Saab, p. 662, para. 15.

[59]Frontier Dispute, Judgment, I.C.J. Reports 1986, p. 567, para. 28.

[60]Ibid. para. 27.

the best on the basis of considerations of equity infra legem in the interpretation and application of law.[61]

Obviously, even when territorial disputes resulting from secessionist self-determination are not submitted to a judicial organ, it is still necessary for disputing parties as well as external actors involved therein to consider the interpretation and application of international law in this regard. As a crucial part of a secessionist self-determination conflict, the territorial issue must be properly addressed by correctly interpreting and applying international law. Because the settlement of territorial issues is not only concerned with the interplay between disputing parties but also concerned with external involvement, the respect of the ICJ for territorial interests of both Mali and Burkina Faso deserves serious attention of every external actor involved in territorial disputes. As will be discussed later, such respect forms the basis of a solution to territorial disputes resulting from secessionist self-determination.

It must be noted that even the de-colonial self-determination could not get rid of the shadow of other-determination. In 1947 the mandate territory of Palestine was partitioned into one Jewish state and one Arab state by a plan endorsed by the UN General Assembly. When it came to the trust territory of Eritrea, in the Report of the United Nations Commission for Eritrea it was stated that "the claim for independence has to be dismissed, we consider the reintegration of Eritrea into Ethiopia as the only rational and satisfactory solution",[62] "Eritrea shall constitute an autonomous unit federated with Ethiopian under the sovereignty of the Ethiopian Crown".[63] Resolution 1608 (XV) adopted by the General Assembly terminated the Trusteeship Agreement concerning the Cameroons under United Kingdom administration, endorsing the result of the plebiscite that the people of the Northern Cameroons decided to achieve independence by joining the independent Federation of Nigeria.[64] The Republic of Cameroon asked the ICJ to judge and declare that, in the application of the Trusteeship Agreement for the Territory of the Cameroons under British Administration, the United Kingdom failed, with regard to the Northern Cameroons, to respect certain obligations directly or indirectly flowing from that Agreement.[65] The court confirmed that the establishment and the maintenance of the administrative union between the Northern Cameroons and Nigeria was a violation of the Trusteeship Agreement[66]; meanwhile, the court admitted that its judgment would not have practical effect: "the decisions of the General Assembly would not be

[61] Frontier Dispute, Judgment, I.C.J. Reports 1986, Separate Opinion of Judge ad hoc Abi-Saab, p. 663, para. 17.

[62] Report of the United Nations Commission for Eritrea, 5 GAOR (1950) Supplement No. 8 (A/1285) para. 176.

[63] A/RES/390 (V) A, para. 1.

[64] A/RES/1608 (XV), paras. 2 and 4.

[65] Case concerning the Northern Cameroons (Cameroon v. United Kingdom), Preliminary Objections, Judgment of 2 December 1963: I.C. J. Reports 1963, p. 17.

[66] Ibid. p. 32.

reversed by the judgment of the Court. The Trusteeship Agreement would not be revived and given new life by the judgment. The former Trust Territory of the Northern Cameroons would not be joined to the Republic of Cameroon".[67]

Of course, other-determination in such circumstances was different from that in the aftermath of the First World War: unlike the victorious Allies which generally refused to recognize self-determination of colonial countries and peoples, the UN did embrace self-determination of colonial countries and peoples. The problem of other-determination existed in the concrete arrangement made for realizing de-colonial self-determination by the UN. For instance, the termination of the Trusteeship Agreement, in essence, frustrated the legitimate expectation of the Republic of Cameroon to incorporate the Northern Cameroons. That is not to say that the wish of the Northern Cameroons to join the independent Federation of Nigeria demonstrated in the result of the plebiscite should be ignored; the point here is that the UN General Assembly should focus on not only the wish of the Northern Cameroons but also the legitimate expectation of the Republic of Cameroon deriving from the Trusteeship Agreement. Consideration of the legitimate expectation of the Republic of Cameroon did not require the UN General Assembly to declare the result of the plebiscite null and void, but required the UN General Assembly not to endorse it. The conflict between the result of the plebiscite and the Trusteeship Agreement was a reflection of the self-determination conflict between the Northern Cameroons and the Republic of Cameroon; rather than side with the Northern Cameroons by terminating the Trusteeship Agreement, it would have been more well-advised for the UN General Assembly to stay neutral and make efforts to facilitate negotiation between both parties for settling their conflict. Therefore, for the sake of avoiding other-determination, external actors should stay neutral in self-determination conflicts, and refuse to side with one conflicting party against the other, otherwise the incompatibility of self-determination with external involvement will inevitably become more evident.

Also in the de-colonial era, international human rights law started to gain more and more significance. Undoubtedly, this trend has a considerable influence on the development of self-determination. In 1966, the UN adopted two major human rights instruments, namely International Covenant on Civil and Political Rights (hereinafter may be referred to as ICCPR) and International Covenant on Economic, Social and Cultural Rights (hereinafter may be referred to as ICESCR). Common Article 1 of both instruments provides:

> 1. All peoples have the right of self-determination. By virtue of that right they freely determine their political status and freely pursue their economic, social and cultural development.
> 2. All peoples may, for their own ends, freely dispose of their natural wealth and resources without prejudice to any obligations arising out of international economic co-operation, based upon the principle of mutual benefit, and international law. In no case may a people be deprived of its own means of subsistence.

[67] Ibid. p. 33.

3. The States Parties to the present Covenant, including those having responsibility for the administration of Non-Self-Governing and Trust Territories, shall promote the realization of the right of self-determination, and shall respect that right, in conformity with the provisions of the Charter of the United Nations.

It must be admitted that it is somewhat ill-advised to cover the right to self-determination in different contexts in the same article, because it will lead to a misconception that self-determination in different contexts has the same meaning. As the right to self-determination of colonial countries and peoples is closely connected with secession, there is reason for some states to worry that "post-colonial self-determination would necessarily result in the fragmentation of the new nation states, with ethnic groups or religions in one country seeking to secede or to join with the same ethnic or religious population in another country."[68] When ratifying the International Covenant on Civil and Political Rights and the International Covenant on Economic, Social and Cultural Rights, with reference to common Article 1, India declared that "the words 'the right of self-determination' appearing in [this article] apply only to the peoples under foreign domination and that these words do not apply to sovereign independent States or to a section of a people or nation--which is the essence of national integrity."[69] This reservation was objected by several states, for instance, France argued that "this reservation attaches conditions not provided for by the Charter of the United Nations to the exercise of the right of self-determination", and Netherlands argued that "the right of self-determination as embodied in the Covenants is conferred upon all peoples".[70]

How should one understand this divergence? Obviously, it is closely related to the concrete content of self-determination and the concrete holder. If Article 1 means that an ethnic group within one sovereign independent state is entitled to a right to secessionist self-determination, just like colonial countries and peoples that became independent from colonial powers, it is quite understandable that a multi-national state will make a reservation, otherwise the multi-national state will be under threat from dissolution. However, if Article 1 means a right to democratic participation in the political, economic and cultural system of the society, the objection to the reservation is quite reasonable: democratic participation should be conferred upon all peoples. As pointed out by Higgins, "post-colonial, contemporary self-determination has become indissolubly linked with notions of democracy and good governance. The sine qua non to making real the entitlement of all peoples to determine their political and economic systems is to ensure that they can participate in periodic free elections in which they can choose between a plurality of possibilities. Moreover, it is the peoples, and not privileged sector, who should comprise the civil service and the political parties".[71] From this perspective, it is

[68]Higgins (2003), p. 28.

[69]Declarations and Reservations, https://treaties.un.org/Pages/ViewDetails.aspx?src=TREATY&mtdsg_no=IV-3&chapter=4&clang=_en#EndDec, last accessed on 15.06.2018.

[70]Ibid.

[71]Higgins (2003), pp. 29–30.

rather meaningless to argue whether the right to self-determination should be conferred upon the peoples under foreign domination or all peoples, when the concrete content of self-determination is indefinite.

At this stage, it is necessary to consider the legal concretization of self-determination: the reservation and the objection had already proved the necessity of doing so. Of course, common Article 1 of both human rights conventions already further concretized the concept of self-determination, compared with the provision in the UN Charter. Nevertheless, it was far from being enough: there was no clear distinction between self-determination in the colonial context and self-determination in the post-colonial context, and which legal subject has what kind of self-determination in the post-colonial context remains highly indefinite. From this perspective, self-determination is still more of a political character. Nonetheless, "one must... distinguish between the legal right to self-determination and the political expression of the doctrine. The latter will have a far greater application than the former, since it is of the essence that a legal norm connotes a binding obligation and must be carefully defined in the light of related principles. Political principles, in contrast, tend to be broadly based and wide-ranging".[72]

The wide-ranging self-determination has led to numerous problems. As noted by the Committee on the Elimination of Racial Discrimination, "ethnic or religious groups or minorities frequently refer to the right to self-determination as a basis for an alleged right to secession".[73] The findings of the Committee proved that the worry of some states including India is reasonable. The Committee attempted to offer a clarification: "the right to self-determination of peoples has an internal aspect, that is to say, the rights of all peoples to pursue freely their economic, social and cultural development without outside interference. In that respect there exists a link with the right of every citizen to take part in the conduct of public affairs at any level... Governments are to represent the whole population without distinction as to race, colour, descent or national or ethnic origin. The external aspect of self-determination implies that all peoples have the right to determine freely their political status and their place in the international community based upon the principle of equal rights and exemplified by the liberation of peoples from colonialism and by the prohibition to subject peoples to alien subjugation, domination and exploitation".[74] Needless to say, this clarification is still debatable: "What is meant by 'alien' in a pluralistic world, for example, and what is meant by 'subjugation'? Is this, for example, time-limited? If not, at what point does subjugation become assimilation to, or acceptance of, a dominant culture?"[75] What really reassures the multinational states is the judgment of the Committee: "in the view of the Committee, international law has

[72]Shaw (1997), p. 479.

[73]Report of the Committee on the Elimination of Racial Discrimination, A/51/18, p. 125, para. 6.

[74]Ibid. para. 9.

[75]Shaw (2003), pp. 244–245.

not recognized a general right of peoples unilaterally to declare secession from a State."[76]

Nevertheless, because the report of the Committee on the Elimination of Racial Discrimination has no binding force, its judgment cannot terminate debate about secessionist self-determination in the post-colonial context. Besides, even if a general right to secessionist self-determination is not recognized in international law, for some it does not mean that a remedial right to secessionist self-determination in exceptional circumstances, such as in circumstances of massive and severe human rights violations, is certainly excluded. Although there is no widely accepted case about remedial secessionist self-determination so far in practice, it is undeniable that this theory is quite influential in the post-colonial era. Furthermore, this theory is also closely connected with external involvement: the nexus between remedial secessionist self-determination and humanitarian intervention must be carefully considered.

3.1.5 Self-Determination in the Post-Colonial Era

In the post-colonial era, self-determination conflicts between secessionists and non-secessionists within one state become quite common: due to the lack of the legal concretization of self-determination, both secessionists and non-secessionists have their respective definitions of self-determination, and conflicts become hardly avoidable when definitions of both sides cannot be in harmony with each other. Sometimes these conflicts prove to be mild, but most of the time violence is involved. External involvement plays as usual an important role: just like self-determination conflicts which can be either mild or violent, sometimes external involvement is in a peaceful way, but the use of force is getting less exceptional. The interplay between the internal dimension and the external dimension of secessionist self-determination conflicts should deserve more consideration in this day and age, as "a remedial right . . . could have the problematic and unintended effect of providing an incentive for groups eager to establish their own states to actively contribute towards the creation of such a situation by provoking massive retaliation, most often against the civilian population . . . Now that states have become increasingly willing to act in cases of massive human rights abuses by their peers, which would obviously trigger the remedial right to secession, this unintended consequence may be more likely than ever."[77]

First one should get the overall picture for the influence of remedial secessionist self-determination in this era. In 1992 the African Commission on Human and Peoples' Rights was requested by Gerard Moke, President of the Katangese Peoples' Congress, to recognize the Katangese Peoples' Congress as a liberation movement

[76]Report of the Committee on the Elimination of Racial Discrimination, A/51/18, p. 126, para. 11.
[77]See Chap. 2, Note 123.

entitled to support in the achievement of independence for Katanga, to recognize the independence of Katanga and help secure the evacuation of Zaire from Katanga, according to Article 20(1) of the African Charter on Human Rights.[78] Article 20 (1) of the African Charter on Human Rights provides: "all peoples shall have the right to existence. They shall have the unquestionable and inalienable right to self-determination. They shall freely determine their political status and shall pursue their economic and social development according to the policy they have freely chosen." The commission replied: "self-determination may be exercised in any of the following -independence, self-government, local government, federalism, confederalism, unitarism or any other form of relations that accords with the wishes of the people but fully cognizant of other recognised principles such as sovereignty and territorial integrity... In the absence of concrete evidence of violations of human rights to the point that the territorial integrity of Zaire should be called to question and in the absence of evidence that the people of Katanga are denied the right to participate in Government as guaranteed by Article 13(1) of the African Charter, the Commission holds the view that Katanga is obliged to exercise a variant of self-determination that is compatible with the sovereignty and territorial integrity of Zaire."[79] Although the commission refused to recognize that Katanga had a right to secessionist self-determination, the commission did recognize a right to remedial secessionist self-determination to a certain degree.

In the Reference re Secession of Quebec, this approach was once again adopted by the Canadian Supreme Court: "the international law right to self-determination only generates, at best, a right to external self-determination in situations of former colonies; where a people is oppressed, as for example under foreign military occupation; or where a definable group is denied meaningful access to government to pursue their political, economic, social and cultural development. In all three situations, the people in question are entitled to a right to external self-determination because they have been denied the ability to exert internally their right to self-determination. Such exceptional circumstances are manifestly inapplicable to Quebec under existing conditions. Accordingly, neither the population of the province of Quebec, even if characterized in terms of 'people' or 'peoples', nor its representative institutions, the National Assembly, the legislature or government of Quebec, possess a right, under international law, to secede unilaterally from Canada".[80] This reasoning implied that Quebecers could not claim a right to secessionist self-determination because this right existed only in a remedial sense, but Quebecers did not need this remedy as they have not been denied meaningful access to government to pursue their political, economic, social and cultural development.

There is no denying that the intention of advancing remedial secessionist self-determination is not bad: "within a context where the individual citizen is no more

---

[78]Katangese Peoples' Congress v. Zaire, African Commission on Human and Peoples' Rights, Comm. No. 75/92 (1995), para. 1.

[79]Ibid. paras. 4 and 6.

[80]Reference re Secession of Quebec, [1998] 2 S.C.R. 217, para. 138.

regarded as a simple object, international law must allow the members of a community suffering structural discrimination—amounting to grave prejudice affecting their lives—to strive for secession as a measure of last resort after all other methods employed to bring about change have failed".[81] It is absolutely right that the individual citizen should no more be regarded as a simple object: as a matter of fact, individual citizens are active players in secessionist movements, taking advantage of remedial secessionist self-determination. For some secessionists, if a right to secessionist self-determination can be recognized in exceptional circumstances, it will be worthwhile to create such circumstances. As once pointed out by Horowitz: "if independence can only be won legitimately after matters have been carried to extremes, then, by all means, there are people willing to carry them to extremes."[82] At first sight this motivation proves to be rather perverse; nevertheless, given that the ultimate goal of some secessionists is not the removal of sovereign oppression but independence itself, it is still understandable. Contrary to the assumption of remedial secession that secession is a measure of last resort after all other methods employed to bring about change have failed, the failure of all other methods employed to bring about change in practice might be the result of a deliberate choice of some secessionists. "For a secessionist movement's leaders, independence holds the possibility of acquiring high-profile political positions in the new state. Those political positions often imply wealth, prestige, power and lifestyle upgrades. Outside of domestic politics, statehood also carries valuable status for individuals including benefits like legal immunity, sovereign power and control over the new state's diplomatic affairs ... Some have observed that the individual incentives for power and prestige can corrupt the bargaining process on the secessionists' side as nationalist leaders become increasingly dedicated to independence at all cost rather than seeking a more optimal bargain that assures security and well-being for their nation."[83]

Worse still, the increasing will of states to act in cases of massive human rights abuses by their peers unintentionally strengthens this perverse motivation, as demonstrated in the case of Bosnia and Kosovo. It is time to review the strategy adopted by Bosnia's leaders at that time: "first, the Muslims actively lobbied the West to recognize Bosnia's independence, to increase their chance of receiving military assistance if Serb forces attacked. Second, prior to recognition, they strove to avoid using or provoking violence because it could undercut their image as victims of aggression, necessary to qualify for humanitarian intervention. Third, once they could achieve recognition, they planned to declare Yugoslav army troops in the republic a foreign occupying force, so the international community would compel their withdrawal. Fourth, starting in the second half of 1991, the Muslims clandestinely imported weapons and established a militia to enable a rudimentary defense prior to secession".[84] They later admitted that they had no intention of settling the

[81]Tomuschat (2006), p. 41.

[82]See Chap. 1, Note 27.

[83]Coggins (2011), p. 34.

[84]Kuperman (2008), p. 60.

secessionist self-determination conflict through negotiation, and engaging in EC-sponsored negotiations on cantonization in early 1992 was no more than a tactic. In the words of Bosnia's eventual foreign minister, Haris Silajdzic, "all the negotiations were just a farce to buy legitimacy... My strategy was to get Bosnia independent so that it would be granted rights by the international community... My main priority in the whole strategy was to get Western governments and especially the United States to get involved, because [Serbs] had the whole Army."[85] As for the cost of lives, they expected that "secession would lead to an eventual toll at least as high as in Croatia's war—several thousand lives, mostly civilian... which they viewed as a tolerable cost to achieve independence of a unitary Bosnia".[86] Obviously, such costs inherent in remedial secessionist self-determination must be taken into consideration.

Undeniably, the practice in Bosnia did inspire some secessionists in Kosovo, namely the Kosovo Liberation Army (KLM). "Kosovo's relative stability ended in late 1997 when the KLA rose to prominence by repeatedly shooting Serbian police. Belgrade launched a counter-insurgency in late February 1998 starting with attacks on a village and a compound suspected of harboring the rebels in their stronghold of Drenica, killing about 75 Albanians (including civilians). But Serb forces initially refrained from the wholesale violence and ethnic cleansing that had characterized their responses to armed challenges in Croatia and Bosnia, apparently because they now had become aware of the emerging norm and so strove to avoid crossing a line that would again trigger international intervention against them. Despite this relative restraint, the Serb crackdown boosted support for the rebels among Kosovo's Albanians, the Albanian diaspora, and the international community".[87] It must be noted that the target of the KLA included its own group's civilians. According to a report of Human Rights Watch, "the KLA was responsible for serious abuses in 1998, including abductions and murders of Serbs and ethnic Albanians considered collaborators with the state."[88] Just like their counterparts in Bosnia, some secessionists in Kosovo had no intention to pursue a peaceful solution: after Milosevic agreed on the cease-fire and withdrawal of troops from Kosovo to enable displaced Albanians to return to their villages prior to winter in 1998, the KLA took advantage of the cease-fire to reoccupy territory and renew attacks against the Serbs later that year; the Austrian vice president of the Organization for Security and Cooperation in Europe, Willy Wimmer, said that observers of the organization agreed that it was the KLA, not Yugoslav forces, that had systematically evaded the Holbrooke agreement.[89] Similar to the case in Bosnia, this persistence in intensifying conflicts was finally rewarded with a NATO bombing campaign in favor of secessionists.

---

[85]Ibid. p. 61.

[86]Ibid. p. 62.

[87]Ibid. pp. 65–66.

[88]Human Rights Watch, Under Orders: War Crimes in Kosovo, Executive Summary, http://www.hrw.org/reports/2001/kosovo/undword.htm, last accessed on 15.06.2018.

[89]Kuperman (2008), p. 66, Note 41.

Is there any other alternative for external involvement to promote remedial self-determination without bolstering up secessionist movements? The case of Aceh has proved that remedial but non-secessionist self-determination is attainable, and external involvement can make a contribution in this regard. The revolt of Aceh against the Indonesian government can be traced back to 1950s, but it was more regionalist and Islamic than secessionist: many Acehnese wanted Aceh to become a part of an Islamic Indonesian state, but not a secular state; this revolt was settled by granting Aceh special territory status associated with larger autonomy, but this deal was not really honored by the increasingly authoritarian and centralizing Indonesian authorities.[90] From 1976 to 2005, Aceh found itself in an intermittent but often bitter civil war: one side is the Free Aceh Movement, which was dedicated to the independence of Aceh, and the other side is the Indonesian Military, which fought at all costs to prevent secession; in this process, shocking human rights violations began to gain attention of the international community: in the early 1990s, international human rights organizations first began to document reports of large-scale abuses being conducted as part of the military's so-called Military Operations Zone actions; a new generation of Acehnese nationalists began to adopt the idea of remedial secessionist self-determination, defining Aceh's struggle for self-determination in human rights terms and arguing that Indonesian repression justified the independence of Aceh; in 2005 the Helsinki Memorandum of Understanding was signed by the Free Aceh Movement and the Indonesian Government, in which secessionists agreed to give up their demand for independence in exchange for the chance to compete for local political power in a more autonomous Aceh that remains part of Indonesia.[91] It is particularly noteworthy that contrary to the belief of leaders of the Free Aceh Movement that internationalization of the conflict would constrain Indonesia's freedom to conduct military oppression and facilitate Aceh's independence, international actors made clear that the price of their involvement was secessionists' agreement to a peace deal that kept Aceh within Indonesia.[92]

It is time to take a look at the content of the Helsinki Memorandum of Understanding: the remedial character is evident. According to this agreement, Aceh will be governed by a new law, which emphasizes a high degree of autonomy; a Human Rights Court and Commission for Truth and Reconciliation will be established for Aceh; amnesty will be granted to members of the Free Aceh Movement; all civilians who have suffered a demonstrable loss in the conflict will be compensated; the Free Aceh Movement will undertake to demobilize its military troops and the government of Indonesia will reduce its military forces in Aceh; an Aceh Monitoring Mission will be established by the European Union and ASEAN to monitor the implementation of the commitments taken by the parties to this Memorandum of

[90] Aspinall (2011), pp. 459–460.

[91] Aspinall and Zain (2013), pp. 87–88 and 94.

[92] Aspinall (2011), pp. 460–461.

Understanding; a concrete process regarding dispute settlement during the implementation of this Memorandum of Understanding is also provided.[93]

It must be recognized that in some areas, such as the military deal and compensation, more progress has been made; however, in areas concerned with past abuses, inaction has been especially glaring.[94] The Helsinki Memorandum of Understanding confirmed the establishment of a Commission for Truth and Reconciliation in 2005, but it was not until 21 November 2015 that the Aceh provincial parliament announced the appointment of five members of the selection team for the Aceh Truth and Reconciliation Commission (TRC), almost 2 years after the passage of the Aceh TRC bylaw by the Aceh parliament on 27 December 2013.[95] This lateness can be attributed to a variety of reasons: former perpetrators of abuses, from both the military and the Free Aceh Movement, continue to be important actors or veto-players in the post-conflict context, and a formal truth telling process will not be in the interest of both sides; international actors are reluctant to endorse measures which might undermine the peace that has been achieved: Matti Ahtisaari, the chief mediator in the 2005 Aceh negotiations, argued in late 2009 that Aceh did not need a TRC and that such an agency might stimulate resistance which could harm the peace process; even among victims, views are mixed on the desirability of retributive measures vis-a-vis reconciliation; the recovery and reconstruction effort after the devastating Indian Ocean tsunami not only enhanced goodwill between former conflict actors but also provided them with major economic benefits, cementing their commitment to peace.[96] Despite the lateness of the Aceh TRC, Aceh is still often promoted internationally as a role model of how to resolve protracted internal conflicts, as the 2005 Helsinki peace agreement did dramatically lower the level of violence between the two sides.[97] The slow progress regarding the Truth and Reconciliation Commission is undoubtedly regrettable, as it implies that justice is delayed; nevertheless, the steady peace progress has indeed contributed to the avoidance of further injustice: "by stopping the violence it has halted most of the gross and egregious abuses which were part of daily life during the conflict years".[98]

Therefore, it is necessary to consider which mode of settlement of secessionist self-determination conflicts, the remedial but non-secessionist self-determination in Aceh or the remedial secessionist self-determination which had a great influence in Bosnia and Kosovo, is more desirable in the post-colonial context. Obviously, in order to make a choice between these two modes, one must focus on not only the theoretical assumptions regarding self-determination but also actual self-determination conflicts. The settlement of secessionist self-determination conflicts

[93] Memorandum of Understanding between the Government of the Republic of Indonesia and the Free Aceh Movement.

[94] Aspinall and Zain (2013), p. 90.

[95] Amnesty International Public Statement, ASA 21/2976/2015, 30 November 2015.

[96] Aspinall and Zain (2013), pp. 90, 94, 103, 123.

[97] Aspinall and Zain (2013), p. 94.

[98] Aspinall (2008), p. 36.

should be theoretically reasonable and practically effective. Therefore, the following discussion is to deal with theoretical and practical problems revealed in the historical review of self-determination, in the hope that secessionist self-determination conflicts can be avoided or settled in a better way.

3.2 Actively Avoiding or Effectively Settling Secessionist Self-Determination Conflicts

3.2.1 Reasonably Defining the Holder and the Content of a Right to Self-Determination

In the historical review of self-determination, it is clear that the occurrence of self-determination conflicts is closely related to the ambiguity about the holder and the content of a right to self-determination. International law does say something about these points: unfortunately, these general provisions sometimes become the source of conflicts rather than legal grounds on which conflicts can be effectively settled. Therefore, it is necessary to construe international law concerning the holder and the content of a right to self-determination in a manner that helps avoid or settle self-determination conflicts, particularly in the context of secession; when the interpretation alone fails to achieve this aim, specific agreement made by conflicting parties must be taken into consideration, and such agreement focusing on the actual exercise of a right to self-determination is a positive addition to the general principle of international law; external actors with a correct understanding of the theoretical and practical issues regarding self-determination can play a pivotal role in the avoidance or settlement of secessionist self-determination conflicts.

3.2.1.1 Neither Self-Defined Nor Other-Defined

Before the formal entry into international law, the holder and the content of a right to self-determination was frequently self-defined. Patriots in the American War of Independence, colonial peoples under Spanish rule, Southern secessionists in the American Civil War, Italy and Germany in the nationalistic unification, all of them believed that they were exercising self-determination. In a strict sense, this self-defined self-determination contained little legal color and was more of political nature. Obviously, a right holder in the legal sense should not be self-defined but legally approved. Of course, as discussed in Chap. 2, Patriots in the American War of Independence thought that they were legally approved: they were approved by Natural Law. By the same token, other self-defined right holders could also argue that they were legally approved. The question is that in such circumstances it is rather difficult to settle self-determination conflicts between those self-defined right holders: Natural Law might have granted them the right to self-determination, but

Natural Law has not offered a solution to self-determination conflicts between them; in case of conflicts, it is unclear whose natural right should take precedence. No wonder right holders more often than not resorted to war to exercise their right to self-determination: to fight for one's own natural right is quite reasonable. From this perspective, the self-defined manner, or natural law approved manner is problematic: it will inevitably lead to the consequences, in the parlance of Hobbes, that every man is against every man, and such confrontation usually lasts until one conflicting party wins out over the other. Therefore, the institution of self-determination must be improved: for one thing, the wish of self-determination, even if it is of the defeated party in the self-determination conflicts, should not be totally dismissed, otherwise self-determination will mean winner-determination and share the same logic with social Darwinism, and for another, the satisfaction of the wish should not be a reason to disregard peace and security, and it is necessary to consider pursuing self-determination in harmony with peaceful coexistence.

Can other-defined self-determination be regarded as an improvement? In theory it is a possible solution to self-determination conflicts: self-defined right holders might claim conflicting self-determination, which is the origin of self-determination conflicts, so when right holders are no more self-defined but other-defined, the definer can declare that one conflicting party is the right holder and the other is not, in order to avoid self-determination conflicts between them. The problem is that the theoretical assumption is one thing, the practical viability is quite another. Other-defined self-determination characterized the Paris Peace Conference: as mentioned before, the victorious Allies decided who could be holders of the right to self-determination. In fact, this other-defined manner was not well-accepted, particularly because of the unvarnished double standard applied by the victorious Allies: one will doubt whether there is any fundamental difference between other-defined self-determination and other-determination which is the opposite of self-determination, and those who are not designated by the "other" as holders of a right to self-determination will not simply give up claiming this right. It is time to review the statement made by former Russian President Medvedev: "Western countries rushed to recognise Kosovo's illegal declaration of independence from Serbia. We argued consistently that it would be impossible, after that, to tell the Abkhazians and Ossetians (and dozens of other groups around the world) that what was good for the Kosovo Albanians was not good for them. In international relations, you cannot have one rule for some and another rule for others."[99]

Generally speaking, the statement of Medvedev has revealed several problems of other-defined self-determination. In the first place, others usually do not have the same opinion on whether one group of people can be regarded as the holder of a right to secessionist self-determination in a certain case. In such circumstances, a judgment based on the judgment made by Jennings, namely that "people cannot decide until someone decides who the people are",[100] can be made: someone cannot decide

[99]Medvedev, Why I had to recognise Georgia's breakaway regions, Financial Times 2008-08-26.
[100]Jennings (1956), p. 56.

who the people are, until someone else decides who someone is. This sounds like a tongue twister, but it is more of a realistic reflection: if self-determination is other-defined, this "other" should be defined in the first place. Otherwise, this "other" might define the holder differently from that "other", and which definition should prevail will become the preliminary question. One might think that this question can be solved by replacing individual opinions of states with a collective opinion of international organizations. However, there is no reason to believe that when member states are unable to reach a consensus, such disagreement will not influence the formation of the collective opinion of an international organization. Other-defined self-determination can still lead to conflicts when others are of different opinions.

In the second place, there is no guarantee that other-defined self-determination can actually stop a group of people from claiming a right to secessionist self-determination even when they are told by the other that they are not among the holders of such a right. More often than not they will take it as a double standard, regardless of the reasons offered by the other. As a matter of fact, when western countries rushed to recognize Kosovo's independence, not all of them based their argument on secessionist self-determination. There were states which argued for secessionist self-determination, such as Germany, the Netherlands, Switzerland and Finland[101]; there were also states who based their argument on sui generis, such as the UK, France and the USA.[102] Secessionists will not bother to discern why the independence of Kosovo Albanians was recognized: what secessionists in one state will care is the fact that the exercise of secessionist self-determination of their counterparts in another state is allowed, and they should also be allowed to exercise secessionist self-determination. From the legal point of view, this reaction is understandable: currently both remedial secessionist self-determination and sui generis are more of a political nature than a legal nature, as legal conditions for the application of remedial secessionist self-determination or sui generis are by no means definite, so it is quite normal for secessionists to take advantage of this twilight zone. In addition, as mentioned above, others usually do not have the same opinion about whether one group of people can be regarded as the holder of a right to secessionist self-determination in a certain case, so a secessionist entity can focus on the supporting voice and ignore the opposing voice.

In the third place, it is necessary to consider whether the double standard, in the parlance of Medvedev, "one rule for some and another rule for others" can be avoided. In order to avoid the double standard, one must discern why the legal institution of self-determination can contribute to the double standard. As discussed

[101]Kosovo advisory proceedings, Written Statement by Germany, p. 35; Verbatim Record, 10 December 2009, CR 2009/32, p. 15, para. 28; Written Statement of Switzerland, p. 16, paras. 62–63; Written Statement by Finland, p. 4, para. 9.

[102]Kosovo advisory proceedings, Written Statement of the United Kingdom, pp. 9–15; Written Statement by the French Republic, pp. 29–47; Secretary Condoleezza Rice, U.S. Recognizes Kosovo as Independent State, http://2001-2009.state.gov/secretary/rm/2008/02/100973.htm, last accessed on 15.06.2018.

above, although self-determination has entered the international legal system for decades, the relevant legal framework is far from being satisfactory: the line of demarcation between self-determination in the legal sense and self-determination in the political sense remains rather fluid. In such circumstances, the double standard is nothing against expectation. Unless noticeable progress in concretizing the relevant legal framework can be made, such as specifying how self-determination in a remedial sense can be exercised, it is impossible to terminate disagreement on remedial secessionist self-determination between states, and the double standard is hardly avoidable when the current legal framework is general enough to cover various and contradicting interpretations. It is quite interesting to notice that although Medvedev declared that "in international relations, you cannot have one rule for some and another rule for others", Russia still refuses to treat secessionists in Kosovo and secessionists in South Ossetia and Abkhazia in the same way. Perhaps it is easier to realize a double standard being applied by others than oneself.

Therefore, other-defined self-determination is no less problematic than self-defined self-determination: it is unrealistic to expect that self-determination conflicts can be settled when self-determination is other-defined instead of self-defined. It is time to consider whether there is a better option of defining self-determination, which can genuinely contribute to the avoidance or settlement of self-determination conflicts. In view of the foregoing, specifying the content of self-determination instead of determining the holder can be a better option: no matter who claims to be the holder of a right to self-determination, when this legal institution becomes specific enough to exclude unilateral secession, it will be quite difficult for an alleged right holder to insist on secessionist self-determination. In other words, when it becomes legally clear that remedial self-determination cannot be exercised by way of unilateral secession, secessionist self-determination conflicts can be terminated. Of course, it does not mean the problem between secessionists and non-secessionists is settled, but the focus of the problem between them will be shifted from secession to remedy. Undeniably, no other form of self-determination conflicts is more complex than secessionist self-determination conflicts, so making self-determination conflicts less complex can be regarded as a noticeable contribution to the settlement of conflicts. Unfortunately, it is not easy to concretize the legal institution of self-determination in this way: as discussed in Chap. 2, due to particular reasons such as ethnical composition, actual risks and political preference, there will always be states which strongly oppose unilateral secessionist self-determination and states which tend to be more tolerant of unilateral secessionist self-determination. Regardless of attitudes towards remedial self-determination by way of unilateral secession within the international community, it is undoubtedly well-advised to sever the ties between remedial self-determination and unilateral secession from various perspectives, as will be discussed later.

A more realistic way of concretizing the institution of self-determination, for the sake of the avoidance or settlement of self-determination conflicts, is to exclude the unilateralism: no matter who claims to be the holder of a right to self-determination, the alleged right holder should not be allowed to determine in a self-determination conflict unilaterally; in such circumstances, conflicting rights to self-determination can be reconciled; the concrete conflict can be settled due to the reconciliation, and the legal institution of self-determination is concretized at the same time. Several relevant examples have already been discussed in Chap. 2 and this chapter, such as the Comprehensive Peace Agreement between Sudan and South Sudan, the Edinburgh Agreement between the UK government and the Scottish government and the Helsinki Memorandum of Understanding which was signed by the Free Aceh Movement and the Indonesian Government. These examples have proved that disagreement within the international community over the concretization of the institution of self-determination might not matter so much: the most important thing is that the institution of self-determination can be concretized by conflicting parties in self-determination conflicts, particularly in the context of secession. In these agreements, the holder and the content of a right to self-determination are defined in an indisputable manner: the parent state recognized the secessionist entity as the holder of a right to self-determination; meanwhile, the secessionist entity exercised its right to self-determination in such a way as not to abandon consideration of the right to self-determination of the parent state. Obviously, such mutual understanding is the key to the avoidance or settlement of secessionist self-determination conflicts. It is noteworthy that secessionist self-determination will not be a thorny issue when it is exercised in a consensual manner, because in such circumstances, the secessionist entity will not infringe the right to self-determination of non-secessionists. Just as demonstrated by the Comprehensive Peace Agreement, secession as a way of exercising self-determination can be acceptable when it is not a unilateral decision of secessionists in disregard of the same right of non-secessionists.

Therefore, self-determination should be defined by conflicting parties. This point becomes particularly self-evident when one takes into account that the right of self-determination should be conferred upon all peoples, which implies that one's right to self-determination must be exercised without prejudicing self-determination of others, and in order to achieve this aim, peoples with conflicting claims to self-determination need to negotiate with each other, otherwise it will be impossible for the institution of self-determination to accommodate conflicting claims. If such institution always fails to accommodate conflicting claims, the statement that the right of self-determination is conferred upon all peoples will become rather questionable: when the institution only satisfies the self-determination claim of secessionists and ignores that of non-secessionists, it implies that not all peoples are entitled to the right to self-determination. Therefore, remedial secessionist self-determination must be rejected: remedial secessionist self-determination is, in essence, unilateral secessionist self-determination which violates self-determination of non-secessionists over territorial interests, and the remedial aim is not the justification for violating self-determination of others. When the right to self-determination of a group of people is violated, a remedy is undeniably required, but an alleged remedy that will violate the right to self-determination of another group of people must be replaced by a different one which avoids such violations. Only when conflicting parties can negotiate with each other will the exercise of one's self-determination not violate other's self-determination, because the negotiation clarifies the concrete scope of the right to self-determination of each "self": unlike a political right, a legal right definitely requires a relatively clear scope. No one will be in a better position to define this scope than the conflicting parties themselves: they are the best legislators for themselves, and whatever decision made by them will not be accused of applying a double standard in respect of self-determination.

It is noteworthy that although self-determination should be defined by conflicting parties, it does not mean that an external actor cannot contribute to the definition. There is no denying that the successful settlement of the secessionist conflict in Aceh owed a good deal to the positive participation of international actors: by pressuring secessionists to give up the pursuit of independence and the government to moderate repression, international actors helped to reconcile the self-determination conflict between secessionists and non-secessionists. The Helsinki Memorandum of Understanding concluded by the Free Aceh Movement and the Indonesian Government through the mediation of international actors has largely clarified the scope of self-determination of secessionists and non-secessionists and put an end to the self-determination conflict between them. Obviously, when an international actor or actors can facilitate an agreement between secessionists and non-secessionists to bring an end to their self-determination conflict, the international actor or actors are contributing noticeably to the concretization of the institution of self-determination and the settlement of the conflict. External involvement as such in secessionist self-determination conflicts should be encouraged, and at such time it is necessary to consider this question: what makes for successful external involvement? In the case of Aceh, external actors have pressured the secessionists to give up the pursuit of independence, so it is quite meaningful to consider whether this option makes for successful external involvement in secessionist self-determination conflicts. In fact, there exists a different option for external actors, namely pressuring non-secessionists to give up their pursuit of territorial sovereignty, on the basis of the theory of remedial secessionist self-determination. Needless to say, it is necessary to clarify the issue why it is ill-advised to pressure non-secessionists to give up their pursuit of territorial sovereignty in the settlement of self-determination conflicts, which requires a more detailed analysis of problems linked to remedial secessionist self-determination. Therefore, in the following discussion the focus is fatal defects embodied in remedial secessionist self-determination, which affect the avoidance or settlement of self-determination conflicts.

To conclude, self-determination should be neither self-defined nor other-defined but defined by both conflicting parties. Through negotiation conflicting claims on self-determination cease to be in an all-or-nothing game and get the chance of coexistence: the realization of self-determination of one party will not be at the expense of self-determination of the conflicting party. The joint definition of self-determination is undoubtedly a crucial step in avoiding or settling self-determination conflicts, and it is a vital addition to the current international legal system, which increases the legal color of self-determination and renders self-determination less open to political exploitation either by "self" or by "other". External actors can contribute to the joint definition of self-determination if it acts in a right way.

3.2.1.2 Distinguishing the Territorial Perspective and the Human Rights Perspective of Self-Determination

It should be admitted that the territorial perspective and the human rights perspective of self-determination are not always clearly distinguished: the theory of remedial secessionist self-determination even implies that the denial of a human rights claim can be compensated for by satisfying a territorial claim, which definitely confuses a human rights or democratic claim with a territorial claim. Such confusion is not in accordance with international law: both state practice and legal instruments have always demonstrated a very prudent stance on the issue of territorial alteration, and self-determination has not proved to be a reason to change this prudence. It is necessary to review the findings of James Crawford: "State practice since 1945 shows the extreme reluctance of States to recognize or accept unilateral secession outside the colonial context. That practice has not changed since 1989, despite the emergence during that period of twenty-three new States. On the contrary, the practice has been powerfully reinforced. Of the new states which have emerged since 1945 outside the context of decolonization, only one case may be classified as a successful secession in the sense described above, viz Bangladesh. The indications are that the United Nations did not treat the emergence of Bangladesh as a case of self-determination despite good grounds for doing so, but rather as a fait accompli achieved as a result of foreign military assistance in special circumstances... In all other cases which might otherwise be classified as unilateral secession (Senegal, Singapore, the Baltic States and Eritrea) the consent of the relevant parties was given before independence was externally recognized as accomplished, and the process was accordingly not unilateral."[103] That is to say, most cases of successful secession should not be regarded as unilateral secession, and the rare successful case of unilateral secession cannot be attributed to the exercise of a right to self-determination. How should this point be understood according to international law, particularly given the right to self-determination?

In order to clarify this issue, the distinction between unilateral secession and consensual secession must be accentuated: unilateral secession is self-determination of secessionists while consensual secession is self-determination of both secessionists and non-secessionists. As discussed before, the right to self-determination is conferred upon all peoples, so not only secessionists but also non-secessionists can claim self-determination, and not only self-determination of secessionists but also self-determination of non-secessionists deserves respect. Therefore, it is quite understandable that the emergence of Bangladesh was not treated as a case of self-determination despite good grounds for doing so: if it were treated as a case of self-determination, it would be extremely difficult to explain why only self-determination of secessionists was respected. In the case of consensual secession this difficulty does no longer exist as secession here is based on self-determination of both secessionists and non-secessionists. In this sense, it is reasonable to deem the

[103] See Chap. 1, Note 19.

extreme reluctance of States to recognize or accept unilateral secession an inevitable result of following international law which requires respecting self-determination of both secessionists and non-secessionists.

In fact, even in the colonial context whether the independence of colonial countries and peoples should be deemed unilateral secessionist self-determination deserves further consideration. As mentioned in Chap. 2, the independence of Cyprus and Namibia had nothing to do with unilateral secession: the independence of Cyprus was based on the Treaty Concerning the Establishment of the Republic of Cyprus, and the independence of Namibia was based on the Agreement among the People's Republic of Angola, the Republic of Cuba, and the Republic of South Africa. Other cases of independence of colonial countries and peoples might not be based on a concrete agreement, but they are still not much of a typically "unilateral" character: due to the fact that "control over land had significantly decreased in value and the global spread nationalism had increased the costs of holding on to far flung territories", some colonial powers chose to acquiesce in the independence of its colonies.[104] This acquiescence is noteworthy not because that it demonstrated that colonial powers recognized that colonial countries and peoples were entitled to a right to independence based on self-determination: as discussed in Chap. 2, colonial powers did not vote for the Declaration on the Granting of Independence to Colonial Countries and Peoples. This acquiescence is noteworthy mainly because it demonstrated that even in the colonial context, the alteration of territorial relations did not purely result from unilateral determination in practice.

Therefore, the careless attitude towards territorial alteration, which is found in the idea of remedial secessionist self-determination, is not in accordance with international law. In fact, this careless attitude towards territorial alteration itself is in contradiction with self-determination: satisfying the claim made by secessionists on exclusive ownership of a particular piece of land in disregard of opposition of non-secessionists is violating the right to self-determination of non-secessionists over territorial interests. As noted by Higgins: "the insistence by certain leaders of ethnic minorities that they have the right to secede by virtue of self-determination, often deprives the entire people of a state of their real right to self-determination—their right to determine their own political and economic destiny, on the basis of pluralism and choice."[105] Brilmayer also expressed a similar opinion focusing on the democratic perspective: "If one were to consult the secessionists, in many cases one would find a desire to secede. How then can it be consistent with democracy to deny a right to secede? The fallacy of this argument is obvious; it assumes that the relevant individuals to consult are the members of the secessionist group. In consulting the population of the entire state, one might find that a majority overall wished to remain a single country. What has not been explained is why only the separatists need be consulted".[106] To be fair, proponents of remedial secessionist self-determination

[104]Coggins (2011), p. 30.
[105]Higgins (2003), pp. 30–31.
[106]Brilmayer (1991), p. 185.

have explained why only the separatists need be consulted: to put it simply, secessionists are victims of brutal sovereign oppression and deserve a remedy, and this remedy is secession and there is no alternative.

This explanation seems reasonable mainly because truth and fallacy are mixed together. A human rights or democratic claim is embodied in the idea of remedial secessionist self-determination, and according to contemporary international law, such claim should be satisfied: international law no longer ignores grave human rights violations caused by brutal sovereign oppression, and the thriving development of human rights law is an evidence of this trend. Nevertheless, satisfying a human rights or democratic claim is one thing, endorsing remedial secessionist self-determination is quite another: when the satisfaction of a human rights claim is somehow translating into territorial alteration through unilateral determination, definite international legal grounds for such translation are still absent: "Writers appear to prefer to preface remedial secession with '(Possibly)', 'may perhaps', '[t]here must, at least, be . . .', or justify it in a circular way by referring to '[a] number of commentators'".[107] When it comes to commentators and international legal rights, it is meaningful to review the judgment of Horowitz: "international law has always placed great emphasis on the writings of jurists, but traditionally for their synthesis of legal rules and for their influence on state practice that could then change the law, not for the direct creation of new rights by cobbling together new formulations. Such a practice is particularly doubtful when it is recalled that international law is a field in which judicial and bureaucratic institutions far outrun representative ones. It is dangerous and undemocratic to allow commentators to become legislators".[108]

Therefore, the position of remedial secessionist self-determination in international law cannot be secured mainly through writings of jurists. One needs to focus more on the inherent reasonableness of this theory and possible problems which might be caused by implementing this theory, in order to judge whether this theory should have a place in the current international legal system. One unreasonable point has already been mentioned: remedial secessionist self-determination ignores the right to self-determination of non-secessionists over territorial ownership, and it means that a human rights claim is confused with a territorial claim here, or these two different claims are bound together. At such time one needs to question the necessity of doing so, because the satisfaction of one claim actually has nothing to do with the satisfaction of the other. As noted by Brilmayer, "the remedy for maltreatment is better treatment by the current government, not permission to set up a new state in the same location. Maltreatment alone does not give rise to a territorial claim; such claims must be independently established... the minority cannot justifiably claim the remedy of secession unless it can convincingly assert a claim to territory. What distinguishes separatist from other minority claims is the fact that the group wishes to establish a new state on a particular piece of land."[109]

107 Summers (2007), p. 347.

108 Horowitz (2003), p. 70.

109 Brilmayer (1991), pp. 188 and 193.

Besides, remedy generally means to restore injured rights so as to revive the balance of legal interests between conflicting parties rather than grant a brand new right to one conflicting party and create new imbalance. Needless to say, human rights of secessionists, which are violated by brutal state oppression, should be restored as required by international human rights law, so satisfying the human rights claim should be included in the concept of remedy. However, when granting exclusive ownership of a particular piece of land to secessionists is also included, the concept of remedy becomes quite perplexing: no matter how brutal state oppression might be, it is certain that there is no violation of exclusive ownership of a particular piece of land claimed by secessionists, because they are not entitled to it at all. When secessionists are not entitled to exclusive ownership of a particular piece of land, granting them such territorial ownership is certainly beyond the general meaning of remedy: it is not restoring injured rights but creating a new right. Obviously, secessionists, as the beneficiary of this new right, will welcome this creation, but as the prejudiced party, non-secessionists will invariably oppose it. If proponents of remedial secessionist self-determination indeed want to settle secessionist conflicts in practice, they should distinguish the restoration of the balance of legal interests and the readjustment of legal interests between conflicting parties: the former as a remedy is legally approved and less likely to create new imbalance of legal interests while the latter as a remedy is rather untypical and highly likely to cause new problems.

At such time, it is necessary to point out that secession in the de-colonial context is fundamentally different from that in the post-colonial context: when colonial countries and peoples seceded from colonial powers, they were actually restoring exclusive territorial ownership injured by colonial powers for a long time. As wisely noted by Brilmayer: "colonialism represents a special case because the colonial powers were particularly lacking in justification for their original territorial conquest. Colonial powers possessed no colorable claims to the territories they conquered. Once conquered, the colonies were not incorporated into the nation but were retained as overseas possessions".[110] That is to say, secessionist self-determination in the de-colonial context is undoubtedly remedial secession, as colonial countries and peoples are entitled to exclusive ownership of a particular piece of land, and secession is the way to restore their exclusive ownership injured by colonial powers. However, secessionists in the post-colonial context are not entitled to exclusive ownership of a particular piece of land in the first place, let alone restore it through secession. Thus, it is right to conclude that secession of colonial countries and peoples from colonial powers is the restoration of the balance of legal interests between them, while secession in the post-colonial context is the readjustment of legal interests between secessionists and non-secessionists.

It is noteworthy that the significance of the territorial issue is invariably neglected by proponents of remedial secessionist self-determination. Although reasons for such neglect have not been specified, it is clear that such neglect is detrimental to

[110]Brilmayer (1991), p. 196.

the settlement of self-determination conflicts between secessionists and non-secessionists in reality: such neglect results in the incorrect assumption that the core of self-determination conflicts is human rights instead of entitlement to territory. Proponents of remedial secessionist self-determination fail to understand that it is the territorial claim of secessionists that aggravates the sovereign oppression, not that the human rights claim of secessionists triggers the aggravation of sovereign oppression. In other words, the real aim of some secessionists is not the fulfillment of human rights but independence, and what really offends a sovereign state is not the pursuit of human rights but the pursuit of independence. In such circumstances, the key to the settlement of secessionist conflicts is the renunciation of independence: when secessionists renounce independence, sovereign oppression will correspondingly be moderated and the fulfillment of human rights becomes more likely. This process has been demonstrated in the case of Aceh. Therefore, it must be admitted that in reality, the moderation of sovereign oppression of secessionists is largely dependent on secessionists themselves: when they give up their territorial claim, the self-determination conflict between them and the sovereign state which is on behalf of non-secessionists will noticeably de-escalate, and human rights will generally be better respected thanks to a lower degree of tension. Unfortunately, the theory of remedial secessionist self-determination does not encourage secessionists to give up the territorial claim. Worse yet, remedial secessionist self-determination motivates secessionists to pursue independence in a perverse manner: in order to meet the precondition of remedial secessionist self-determination, secessionists deliberately contribute to human rights crises. Undeniably, such unintended consequences are closely related to the neglect of the significance of the territorial perspective embodied in self-determination conflicts between secessionists and non-secessionists.

More importantly, satisfying the territorial claim of secessionists can be detrimental to human rights protection. "Contrast Yugoslavia, with six or seven groups and the complex alignment they created, making it difficult for any one group to dominate, with the more dangerous situation in Bosnia, in which three groups confront each other... The right direction for international boundaries is upward, not downward, so that states are so heterogeneous that no one group can plausibly dominate others."[111] When there is no one group can plausibly dominate others, there is no reason to worry that the dominant position of one group can be abused and therefore others can be bullied, so it does bode well for human rights protection. However, secession is to reduce the ethnic heterogeneity, which might lead to more intense confrontation between ethnic groups. Undeniably, such intense situation will cast a shadow on human rights protection. In addition, "the treatment of minorities in smaller states is less visible to outsiders".[112] When maltreatment of minorities becomes less visible in a secessionist state, human rights protection offered by the international community definitely becomes less available for the suffering

[111] Horowitz (2003), pp. 54–56.

[112] Ibid. p. 54.

minorities. When speaking of human rights protection of minorities in the aftermath of an alleged remedial secession, one certainly needs to give more serious consideration to the analysis made by Horowitz: secessionists as minorities once having been oppressed by the majority in the undivided state may have accumulated many grudges, so they tend to release their grudges against minorities in the region when they become the majority in the secessionist region, and thus minorities in the secessionist region may be particularly vulnerable to the expression of violent hostility and settlement of old scores, as demonstrated by the fate of Serbs and Roma in Kosovo, of Biharis in Bangladesh, of Sikhs and Hindus in Pakistan at the time of partition, of Muslims in India at the same time, and of Georgians in Abkhazia, etc.[113] Therefore, it is quite problematic to argue that the satisfaction of the territorial claim of secessionists will definitely be conducive to human rights protection: the interrelation between secession and human rights protection in practice is more complicated than it is assumed in the theory of remedial secessionist self-determination.

The second report on the Aaland Islands question of the League of Nations reveals that satisfying the territorial claim of secessionists can also discourage sovereign states from granting more democratic rights to secessionists: "what reasons would there be for allowing a minority to separate itself from the State to which it is united, if this State gives it the guarantees which it is within its rights in demanding, for the preservation of its social, ethnical or religious character? Such indulgence, apart from every political consideration, would be supremely unjust to the State prepared to make these concessions."[114] It is particularly noteworthy that when the state feels these concessions unjust, it can suspend them, as demonstrated in the reaction of the Spanish government to the Catalan independence referendum.[115] In such circumstances, it can be said that the territorial claim severely affects the satisfaction of democratic claims: originally, no remedy is needed, but the territorial claim creates the need for remedies.

Proponents of remedial secessionist self-determination generally argue that a right to secession should be recognized when there is no other alternative to continuing to suffer severe violations of human rights.[116] As a matter of fact, the assumption that secession is the only means is rather questionable, as victimized ethnic groups, such as Kurds in Iraq, Ibos in Nigeria, Acehnese in Indonesia, have vacillated between secessionists and autonomists, and the case of Ibos in Nigeria particularly deserves consideration: in 1966 Ibos suffered two serious pogroms in

---

[113]Ibid.

[114]See Chap. 1, Note 17.

[115]After the independence referendum, Rajoy announced in Madrid that his government would take steps to enact Article 155 of the Spanish Constitution for the first time in Spanish history, thereby suspending Catalan regional autonomy and paving the way for new regional elections, see Cristina Burack, Spanish government threatens to revoke Catalan autonomy, 19.10.2017, http://www.dw.com/en/spanish-government-threatens-to-revoke-catalan-autonomy/a-41027163, last accessed on 15.06.2018.

[116]See Chap. 2, Note 69.

Nigeria, which convinced them that they could not even live in Nigeria; in 1967 they tried secessionist self-determination by establishing Republic of Biafra; in 1970 they were defeated by Nigerian government forces and then reintegrated into Nigerian politics.[117] Although the observer mission in 1968 insisted that there was no genocide, "it is equally impossible to rule out the possibility that incidents comparable to the scale and quality of the Srebrenica massacre during the Bosnian civil war might have happened, which both the International Court of Justice and the International Criminal Tribunal for the Former Yugoslavia (ICTY) have qualified as an act amounting to genocide."[118] The reintegration of Ibos into the Nigerian Federation, as well as other cases mentioned above, proves that "it looks to outsiders at any given moment as if secession is 'the only way' minorities can participate in determining their own future, but there is more fluidity to ethnic politics than those who write about populations that are unalterably hostile to each other have sensed."[119]

To sum up, it is ill-advised to advocate remedial secessionist self-determination which has gratuitously bound the claim to territory and the claim to human rights together. The human rights claim of secessionists definitely deserves respect, but the satisfaction of their claim to human rights does not mean their claim to territory must also be satisfied. International law invariably shows a very prudent stance on the issue of territorial alteration and the principle of self-determination does not change this point, so a careless attitude towards territorial alteration is not embodied in this principle. Besides, secession as a remedy for human rights violations is not well justified: in addition to the lack of clear legal grounds, remedial secessionist self-determination fails to optimize the balance of interests between secessionists and non-secessionists, tends to have unintended consequences, and poses actual threats to human rights protection of ethnic minorities. Furthermore, the assumption that secession is the only alternative to continuing to suffer severe violations of human rights does not correspond to real ethnic politics.

3.2.1.3 Correctly Understanding the Interrelation Between Territorial Sovereignty and Self-Determination

It seems that for proponents of remedial secessionist self-determination, the interrelation between the principle of territorial sovereignty and the principle of self-determination can be reduced to an issue of priority. Which claim should take priority when non-secessionists claim territorial sovereignty and secessionist claim secessionist self-determination? The answer provided by proponents of remedial secessionist self-determination seems to be in pursuit of a balance: in general, territorial sovereignty claimed by non-secessionists should take priority, but in exceptional circumstances, for instance, when secessionists are severely oppressed

[117] Horowitz (2003), p. 61.
[118] Lahmann (2009).
[119] See Chap. 1, Note 27.

and victimized by sovereignty, secessionist self-determination claimed by secessionists should take priority. As described by Buchanan, "unilateral secession should only be permitted in cases where a persisting pattern of fundamental injustices robs the state of legitimacy. The same serious injustices that give credibility to secessionist demands also delegitimize the state, voiding its right to territorial integrity and thereby clearing the way for lawful unilateral secession."[120] Similarly, Orentlicher expressed that "international law has long disfavored separatist claims. But alongside this general disapproval, international instruments and other relevant sources have long reserved a possible exception: implicit in international law's core commitment to basic human rights and democratic principles is recognition of a last-resort, remedial right for a subnational group to secede when these rights are denied its members."[121] Cassese argued that "denial of the basic right of representation does not give rise per se to the right of secession. In addition, there must be gross breaches of fundamental human rights, and, what is more, the exclusion of any likelihood for a possible peaceful solution within the existing state structure."[122]

Such understanding of the interrelation between the principle of territorial sovereignty and the principle of self-determination is open to question. Firstly, it assumes that a choice must be made between territorial interests of non-secessionists and human rights protection of secessionists, as if they were irreconcilable with each other in exceptional circumstances. Such assumption is undoubtedly misleading: it is territorial interests pursued by non-secessionists and secessionists that are irreconcilable with each other, not territorial interests of non-secessionists and human rights protection of secessionists. Obviously, non-secessionists want to share territorial ownership with secessionists, but secessionists want exclusive territorial ownership, and therefore secessionists do not directly fight for democratic governance in order to satisfy their human rights claim but choose to fight for secession, although secession is more strongly opposed by the authorities, compared with the fight for democratic governance. It should be noted that non-secessionists will not oppose the human rights claim of secessionists as strongly as the territorial claim of them. The case of Aceh has proved this point: when secessionists renounced the territorial claim but kept claiming human rights, sovereign oppression was still relieved. Therefore, territorial interests of non-secessionists and human rights protection of secessionists are not irreconcilable, and it is co-ownership of the territory claimed by non-secessionists and exclusive ownership claimed by secessionists that are irreconcilable. Misunderstanding about this point is detrimental to the observance of both legal principles. The impairment of territorial sovereignty is more evident, as territorial sovereignty is somehow considered less significant than the self-determination of secessionists: proponents of remedial secessionist self-determination tend to downplay this impairment by arguing that "since the possibility of impairment of territorial integrity is not totally excluded, it is logically

[120]Buchanan (2004), p. 288.

[121]Orentlicher (2003), p. 25.

[122]Cassese (1995), pp. 119–120.

admitted."[123] What proponents of remedial secessionist self-determination fail to realize is that impairing territorial integrity is, in essence, violating the right of non-secessionists to determine the destiny of the territory shared with secessionists: once again, it must be borne in mind that not only secessionists but also non-secessionists are entitled to determine the destiny of the territory, according to the principle of self-determination, and ignoring the right to self-determination of non-secessionists is also in violation of this principle.

Secondly, proponents of remedial secessionist self-determination correctly understand the importance international law attaches to human rights protection and the close connection between human rights and the right to self-determination, but they fail to understand why international law places much weight on territorial sovereignty. To be more accurate, proponents of remedial secessionist self-determination fail to appreciate how sensitive states might be, when it comes to secession: "not surprisingly, existing States have shown themselves to be 'allergic' to the concept of secession at all times. Their representatives even carefully avoided the very use of the term 'secession' when involved in codifying the rules of State succession, preferring to speak about 'separation of part of a State'. This aversion is not simply terminological. It is evidence that states are not willing to allow even a potential consideration that secession is a situation governed by international law, even after the success of a secessionist State."[124] Therefore, respecting the principle of territorial sovereignty is freeing states of the fear of secession at the same time. Is there any evidence that the fear of secession has been alleviated thanks to acceptance of self-determination? The answer is negative: as mentioned in Chap. 2, only a few states have recognized secessionist self-determination in their respective constitutional frameworks; prior to the adoption of the Declaration on Principles of International Law concerning Friendly Relations and Co-operation among States in accordance with the Charter of the United Nations, many states expressed their concern about the effect self-determination might have on the stability of state boundaries during the negotiations, and the wording of the final draft did take their concern into account[125]; as discussed earlier in this chapter, only some of those states having recognized the independence of Kosovo clearly argued for secessionist self-

[123] Ibid. p. 119.

[124] Kohen (2006), pp. 3–4.

[125] For instance, the representative of Kenya stated that "although the principle applies to all peoples, even in independent countries, it would be an interference in the domestic affairs of sovereign states if the commission drew up rules for the secession of, to use the words of the 1967 United Kingdom proposal, 'a territory which is geographically distinct and ethnically and culturally diverse from the remainder of the territory of the state administering it'(see UN Doc A/AC.125/SR.107, p. 88, 5 Nov. 1969). The final draft did not contain such open-ended expression, but the representative of India still emphasized that self-determination should not prejudice territorial sovereignty: "the right of self-determination did not apply to sovereign and independent states or to integral parts of their territory or to a section of a people or nation. Without such an understanding, the principle of self-determination would lead to fragmentation, disintegration and dismemberment of sovereign states and members of the United Nations. The danger in that context would be particularly acute in the case of states having multi-racial and multi-lingual populations".

determination in their respective statements. Based on this, it is correct to conclude that the assumption made by proponents of remedial secessionist self-determination about the interrelation between the principle of territorial sovereignty and the principle of self-determination is generally not in accordance with the reality.

Thirdly, proponents of remedial secessionist self-determination seem to believe that allowing secessionists to secede in exceptional circumstances can keep a balance between conflicting claims of secessionists and non secessionists. In fact, it cannot because of the perverse incentive embodied in remedial secessionist self-determination: secessionists might actively contribute to such exceptional circumstances in order to achieve their aim of being independent. As mentioned before, the genuine aim of some secessionists is not to moderate sovereign repression but to establish an independent state, so they have the motivation to create exceptional circumstances. "In the 1980s and early 1990s, Sikh separatists in the Indian Punjab were willing to attack Hindus in order to precipitate attacks on Sikhs elsewhere in India, so as to convince Sikhs that secession was the only solution. There is no shortage of methods to satisfy tough standards of victimization or oppression. A right to secede could indeed contribute to the sense that secession is the only way."[126] That is to say, contrary to the expectation of proponents, remedial secessionist self-determination is to tip the scale in favor of secessionists in reality: they can deliberately create exceptional circumstances and then claim that there is no alternative for them but to secede. The Kosovo case discussed above also proved that some secessionists pursued their political end by actively contributing to the aggravation of the humanitarian situation. In other words, given the complexity of the reality, proponents of remedial secessionist self-determination should reconsider the interrelation between the principle of territorial sovereignty and the principle of self-determination: the priority between them should not be decided on the basis of exceptional circumstances, and it is necessary to consider how such exceptional circumstances take place. In practice, remedial secessionist self-determination might not only fail to strike a balance between non-secessionists claiming territorial integrity and secessionists claiming self-determination but also give rise to more conflicts which can threaten social stability and human rights of both sides.

Fourthly, proponents of remedial secessionist self-determination fail to draw on similar historical experience. As demonstrated in the historical review of the evolution of self-determination, territorial disputes in the name of self-determination occurred repeatedly. How these disputes were settled at that time should not be disregarded because it can be helpful for dispute settlement in this day and age. When speaking of historical experience regarding territorial dispute settlement, the principle of uti possidetis largely applied to Latin American and Africa must be mentioned. This principle, in general, has proved to be a successful solution to territorial disputes in the name of self-determination: to be more specific, self-

---

[See Report of the Special Committee on Principles of International Law concerning Friendly Relations and Co-operation among States, UN Doc. A/8018 (1970), p. 110, para. 219].

[126]See Chap. 1, Note 27.

determination conflicts over territorial ownership have mostly been avoided on the basis of uti possidetis. The success of this solution deserves serious consideration: reasonable elements should be distilled and applied to other similar disputes. Obviously, the success of uti possidetis has much to do with the prohibition on unilateral alteration of borders, and in such circumstances no one is allowed to unilaterally alter territorial relations in the name of self-determination in disregard of the objection of other relevant parties. The reasonableness of this prohibition is quite noteworthy: parties involved in a territorial dispute are equal subjects under international law, so no subject should have the privilege of dealing with territorial interests of other subjects against their will, otherwise it will violate equity and justice. Unfortunately, proponents of remedial secessionist self-determination fail to draw on this valuable experience: remedial secessionist self-determination actually confers on secessionists a privilege of dealing with territorial interests in disregard of the objection of non-secessionists. Given that the right to self-determination should not transmute into a privilege of secessionists: under international law secessionists and non-secessionists should be deemed equal and both are entitled to the right to self-determination, so such a privilege is incompatible with equity and justice. Therefore, the unreasonableness of remedial secessionist self-determination is quite evident. This unreasonable element of remedial secessionist self-determination is certainly detrimental to the settlement of self-determination conflicts between secessionists and non-secessionists.

Fifthly, proponents of remedial secessionist self-determination seem to be overly optimistic about the situation after unilateral secession. As a matter of fact, this optimism is rather groundless: the impairment of territorial sovereignty might not contribute that much to the realization of self-determination of secessionists in practice, contrary to the assumption of proponents of remedial secessionist self-determination. One reason has been analyzed before: very small States would not be in a position to form real free, independent and sovereign entities, and they might be particularly suited to forms of intervention and/or influence[127]; very small states such as Micronesia, the Marshall Islands, Palau, Monaco and Andorra have concluded agreements with other states, under which theoretically their absolute freedom of voting in the United Nations could be restricted.[128] In the same vein, it is unclear whether secessionist states of very small size can really enjoy the right to self-determination, particularly given the tension between the state emerging from unilateral secession and the parent state. When speaking of the tension created by unilateral secession, its threat to the realization of self-determination should never be underestimated. not only is the sovereign oppression detrimental to self-determination, severe international confrontation is also harmful to the realization of self-determination in practice. As noted by Horowitz, "recognition of a right to secede is thus likely to be, not the end of an old bitterness, but the beginning of new bitterness... If it does not solve boundary problems, secession does do something

[127] UN Doc. E/CH.4/Sub.2/405/Rev.1 (1980), para.108.

[128] See above Note 30.

else. A secession or partition converts a domestic ethnic dispute into a more dangerous international one. And since states are able to procure arms with few of the restraints that periodically bedevil insurgents, the international dispute often involves escalating weapons and the prospect of international warfare. Consider the nuclear armaments possessed by India and Pakistan and the recurrent warfare between those states."[129] That is to say, unilateral secession cannot settle self-determination conflicts between secessionists and non-secessionists but turns internal conflicts into international conflicts. In this sense, the remedial effect of secessionist self-determination is once again open to question, as it is hard to conclude that international confrontation is definitely more favorable than internal confrontation. If the old confrontation between secessionists and non-secessionists is deemed harmful to the realization of self-determination of secessionists, there is no reason to believe that the new confrontation between the secessionist state and the parent state can be harmless in this regard.

To conclude, the way proponents of remedial secessionist self-determination interpret the interrelation between the principle of territorial sovereignty and the principle of self-determination is problematic or detrimental. A correct understanding of the interrelation between these two legal principles should include the following points: it is unnecessary to make a choice between territorial sovereignty claimed by non-secessionists and human rights claimed by secessionists because they are not irreconcilable, and it is co-ownership of the territory claimed by non-secessionists and exclusive ownership claimed by secessionists that are irreconcilable with each other; despite the significance of self-determination, it is not a reason to downplay the principle of territorial sovereignty; remedial secessionist self-determination fails to strike a balance between territorial integrity claimed by non-secessionists and self-determination claimed by secessionists in practice, as such a right to secede will inevitably motivate secessionists in a perverse manner; when an inexplicable privilege is created for secessionists to alter territorial relations unilaterally, it does not bode well for the settlement of self-determination conflicts between secessionists and non-secessionists; secession itself cannot remove confrontation between secessionists and non-secessionists but turns internal confrontation into international confrontation.

3.2.2 *Preventing Abuse of a Right to Self-Determination*

It should be admitted that abuse of a right to self-determination invariably contributes to self-determination conflicts. In view of what has been discussed above, transforming a right to self-determination into a right to unilateral secession is abusing this legal right, which generally contributes to self-determination conflicts between secessionists and non-secessionists. Therefore, it is quite meaningful to

[129]See Chap. 1, Note 23.

consider how such abuse of a right to self-determination can be effectively avoided. Obviously, preventing abuse of a right to self-determination requires not only replacing the wrong understanding with a correct understanding of legal rules and actual questions but also positive action based on the correct understanding. The following discussion will focus on a correct understanding of legal rules and actual questions and positive action based on this understanding.

3.2.2.1 Remedial but Not Secessionist Self-Determination

In view of what has been analyzed, remedial secessionist self-determination contains both an element of truth and an element of fallacy: no one can deny that there should be a remedy for an injured right to self-determination, but it is unreasonable to associate the remedy with secession. It is reasonable to argue for remedial secession when a right to secessionist self-determination is injured, but when there is no such a right in the first place, claiming a right to secessionist self-determination in a remedial sense is rather illogical. When it comes to a remedy in the legal sense, one needs to discern at first which right is injured and consider remedying this injured right, because considering remedying a non-existent right is not only a misapplication of law but also a disservice to the solution to real problems.

Which rights might have been injured when secessionist self-determination is proposed as a remedy for such injury? It seems that in general these rights can be categorized as "basic human rights" or "fundamental human rights".[130] In addition, due to the fact that victims, whose basic human rights have been violated or fundamental human rights have been breached, generally belong to an ethnic minority, it can be said that minority rights have also been injured. When it comes to the right to self-determination, the issue becomes more complicated. Perhaps it would be better to clarify this issue with the aid of the concept of external self-determination and internal self-determination. In the parlance of Thornberry, "the external dimension or aspect defines the status of a people in relation to another people, State or Empire, whereas the democratic or internal dimension should concern the relationship between a people and 'its own' State or government".[131] From this perspective, when the authorities violate basic human rights of an ethnic minority, a right to internal self-determination is suspected of being violated. Despite the suspicion, it is rather difficult to confirm the violation of this right in a strict sense, because whether an ethnic minority can be taken as "a people" remains debatable. "The existence of distinct peoples within states is often contested: some states may recognise them, others may not".[132] For this reason, to confirm a violation of human rights and minority rights is not a big problem, but it would be quite difficult to confirm that there is definitely a violation of the right to self-

[130]Orentlicher (2003), p. 25; Buchanan (2004), p. 354; Cassese (1995), p. 120.
[131]Thornberry (1993), p. 101.
[132]Summers (2013), p. 235.

determination. Nevertheless, there is no need to focus too much on the issue whether there exists a violation of the right to self-determination: as long as the violation of the more concrete human rights and minority rights can be effectively rectified, the likely violation of the more abstract right to self-determination will also be rectified.

The violation of human rights and minority rights should be condemned rather than condoned, and international law is dedicated to providing remedies for these injured rights: ICCPR, ICESCR and other international instruments have proved this point. The problem is never whether there should be a remedy or not but whether the proposed remedy itself is suitable or not. In the parlance of Tomuschat, a right solution should consist of "exploring the suitability of an envisioned method of furthering the goal to be achieved, without dealing a lethal blow to the framework which secures the viability of international law as a system, the principles and rules of which are recognized by all the members of the international community".[133] Undoubtedly, unilateral secession as a legal remedy for injured human rights and minority rights proposed by secessionists and proponents of remedial secessionist self-determination is not suitable: a right to remedial secessionist self-determination is open to abuse, which would further aggravate the conflict between secessionists and non-secessionists and contribute to more violations of human rights and minority rights.

It is necessary to review the points which can lead to abuse of remedial secessionist self-determination. One point concerns the legal identity of secessionists, namely whether secessionists can be taken as a people entitled to self-determination under international law. In the theory of remedial secessionist self-determination this issue is ignored, which has attracted criticism as it is "tantamount to saying that when a national, religious or linguistic minority is seriously discriminated against, then it becomes a 'people'."[134] Because the issue regarding the holder of a right to self-determination has been discussed above, it will not be repeated here, and one just need to bear in mind that a right is open to abuse when the right holder is indefinite. The focus here is that through remedial secessionist self-determination, the originally intended goal cannot actually be attained: unlike the assumption made by proponents of remedial secessionist self-determination that secession is the means and remedy is the aim, for some secessionists, secession is the aim and remedy is nothing. Because secession is only allowed in exceptional circumstances according to remedial secessionist self-determination, there is incentive for some secessionists to create such exceptional circumstances: as mentioned before, Sikh separatists in the Indian Punjab deliberately chose to attack Hindus in order to precipitate attacks on Sikhs elsewhere in India, so as to create the impression that secession was the only remedy; in order to obtain a right to remedial secessionist self-determination, former Bosnian leaders believed the cost of thousands of civilian lives was tolerable; the KLA made every effort, including abductions and murders of Serbs and ethnic Albanians considered collaborators with the state, to provoke the authorities to

[133]Tomuschat (2006), p. 40.

[134]Kohen (2006), pp. 10–11.

retaliate excessively. Obviously, such consequences run counter to the good intention of proponents of remedial secessionist self-determination, and exercising remedial secessionist self-determination as such is also abusing this right: remedial secessionist self-determination is not intended to encourage secessionists to realize their political aim unscrupulously but intended to remedy injured human rights and minority rights; when consequences run counter to the original intention, it is accurate to argue that there exists abuse of the right.

Worse still, following the logic of remedial secessionist self-determination, it is impossible to avoid such abuse: as long as the exceptional circumstance is the precondition for a right to unilateral secessionist self-determination, there is incentive for some secessionists to create the exceptional circumstance. Undeniably, proponents of remedial secessionist self-determination have very kind intention: they focus on the deterrent effect of this right; they believe that the authorities will be deterred by this right and refrain from taking extreme measures which might severely injure human rights and minority rights of secessionists; in this sense, there is a better chance of achieving the purposes of international law. Unfortunately, they fail to realize that in such circumstances, not only the authorities but also secessionists need to be deterred: unless both parties can be deterred, it is impossible to prevent the conflict between them from escalating. Generally speaking, it is erroneous to assume that secessionists are only passive victims of sovereign oppression: given what has been discussed above, a secessionist group is an active actor in self-determination conflicts. For this reason, secessionists should not be treated as a pure right holder without effective legal restraints, otherwise it will be impossible to deter them from abusing their right and intensifying the conflict. To be fair, proponents of remedial secessionist self-determination do not totally forget to impose legal restraints: for instance, Cassese argued that the denial of the basic right of representation is not sufficient to invoke a right to secession, and there should be gross breaches of fundamental human rights and no other peaceful solution within the existing state structure, if secessionists want to invoke a right to secession.[135] The problem is that such restraints cannot actually deter secessionists from abusing this right: such restraints only enhance the cost for some secessionists to pursue secession but not effectively discourage them from pursuing secession by creating exceptional circumstances. In order to discourage secessionists from doing so, the key is to disconnect secession from remedy: only when unilateral secession is no longer deemed a likely remedy for injured rights in exceptional circumstances will secessionists lose enthusiasm for creating exceptional circumstances.

That is to say, remedial secessionist self-determination must be transformed into remedial but not secessionist self-determination. Needless to say, proponents of remedial secessionist self-determination will question the remedial effect when the ties between remedy and unilateral secession are severed, particularly given exceptional circumstances. At such time, it is necessary to consider this issue: the avoidance of exceptional circumstances and unilateral secession as a remedy in

---

[135]Cassese (1995), pp. 119–120.

exceptional circumstances, which is more desirable? This question is meaningful mainly because remedial secessionist self-determination and the avoidance of exceptional circumstances are incompatible with each other: as discussed above, a right to unilateral secessionist self-determination in exceptional circumstances invariably gives some secessionists a strong incentive to create exceptional circumstances, in which gross breaches of fundamental human rights take place, and this incentive renders the avoidance of exceptional circumstances impossible. Therefore, a choice must be made between these incompatible options. If one admits that the avoidance of gross breaches of fundamental human rights is more desirable than any remedy for existing gross breaches of fundamental human rights, one will also admit that unilateral secession as a remedy in exceptional circumstances is not that desirable, given that before secession becomes a remedy for gross breaches of fundamental human rights, the strong incentive to create an exceptional circumstance will have resulted in gross breaches of fundamental human rights in the first place. From this perspective, it is unnecessary to worry about the remedial effect because when exceptional circumstances are avoided thanks to a lack of perverse incentives, the consideration of a remedy in exceptional circumstances is not required. Therefore, compared with a painstaking search for a justification for a right to secessionist self-determination in exceptional circumstances, considering the avoidance of exceptional circumstances proves to be more meaningful, which requires transforming remedial secessionist self-determination into remedial but not secessionist self-determination.

Besides giving some secessionists a strong incentive to create exceptional circumstances, remedial secessionist self-determination also inadvertently encourages secessionists to overlook the right to self-determination of non-secessionists over territorial interests: remedial secessionist self-determination seems to suggest that the right to self-determination of secessionists is sufficient to determine the future of a particular piece of territory, and the future of the particular piece of territory has nothing to do with the right to self-determination of non-secessionists. As discussed above, the point of view is legally unjustified: if co-ownership of the territory is transformed into exclusive ownership, such transformation should not be decided by one co-owner but all co-owners. Undoubtedly, territory concerns fundamental interests of both secessionists and non-secessionists, so both parties should have a say in the decision concerning their fundamental interests. In such circumstances, secessionists are obliged to exercise their right to self-determination without prejudicing the right to self-determination of non-secessionists. If secessionists exercise their own right to self-determination in disregard of the same right of non-secessionists, they actually violate their legal obligation. Unfortunately, the theory of remedial secessionist self-determination inadvertently encourages such violation in the name of remedy. From this perspective, transforming remedial secessionist self-determination into remedial but not secessionist self-determination is definitely necessary: the pursuit of remedy cannot be a justification for disregarding rights of others, so secessionists should not be allowed to determine territorial ownership unilaterally in the name of remedy and disregard the right to self-determination of non-secessionists in this regard.

It is particularly noteworthy that the "not secessionist" means itself is conducive to the "remedial" end. As discussed above, it is the claim to exclusive territorial ownership made by secessionists and the claim to co-ownership made by non-secessionists that are irreconcilable with each other. If secessionists are no longer allowed to claim exclusive territorial ownership and are transformed into pure advocates of human rights or democracy, the degree of confrontation between them and non-secessionists will certainly be lowered. Needless to say, it forms the indispensable basis for the restoration and promotion of human rights and democracy: when there exists a high degree of confrontation between one group of people and another, violent hostility is hardly avoidable, and it is quite unrealistic to expect an improvement in human rights and democracy in such circumstances. Remedial but not secessionist self-determination lowers the degree of confrontation between secessionists and non-secessionists, thus helping avoid violent hostility, which forms the basis for the restoration and promotion of human rights and democracy, as demonstrated in the case of Aceh.

Last but not least, it must be admitted that compared with remedial but not secessionist self-determination, remedial secessionist self-determination is less likely to contribute to mutual understanding and mutual respect between secessionists and non-secessionists. According to the theory of remedial secessionist self-determination, secessionists have another identity, namely victims of human rights violations. Needless to say, non-secessionists will have different attitudes towards these two identities: they definitely will not have any sympathy for secessionists, but it is hard to say that they also have no sympathy for victims of human rights violations. When these two identities are combined, as suggested in the theory of remedial secessionist self-determination, non-secessionists generally ignore the identity of secessionists as victims of human rights violations due to their struggle for territorial interests: if secessionists clearly demonstrate their disrespect for the right to self-determination of non-secessionists over territorial interests, non-secessionists will similarly ignore human rights of secessionists in return. Obviously, such interaction which rejects mutual understanding and mutual respect is undesirable. How can one change undesirable interaction as such? The answer lies in transforming secessionists into pure advocates of human rights or democracy: after such a transformation, there will be no disrespect for the right to self-determination of non-secessionists over territorial interests, and when the territorial self-determination of non-secessionists is no longer disregarded by secessionists, the identity of secessionists as victims of human rights violations is more likely to get recognized by non-secessionists. Such desirable interaction is demonstrated in the Aceh case: the successful settlement of secessionist conflicts is largely dependent on the restoration of mutual understanding and mutual respect between secessionists and non-secessionists. Given this point, remedial secessionist self-determination must be replaced by remedial but not secessionist self-determination.

To conclude, given the inherent defects of remedial secessionist self-determination discussed above, it is well-advised to transform remedial secessionist self-determination into remedial but not secessionist self-determination, which helps optimize the exercise of self-determination and lower the chance of abuse of this right.

3.2.2.2 Specifying Obligations on Holders of the Right to Secessionist Self-Determination

It must be noted that abuse of the right to self-determination is closely related to the vagueness of obligations holders of such a right should assume. Perhaps some might even question whether there exists any obligation for holders of the right to self-determination under international law, as this point has not been definitely confirmed in international instruments. Nevertheless, the necessity of imposing obligations on holders of the right to self-determination proves to be undeniable in practice: as mentioned repeatedly before, if one actor exercises its own right to self-determination without respecting this right of another, self-determination conflicts will frequently occur. From this perspective, no one can deny that respecting the right to self-determination of another must be an obligation of any holder of the right to self-determination. Therefore, even if the importance of imposing obligations on holders of the right to self-determination in international instruments is not stressed, this point still plays a pivotal role in settling self-determination conflicts.

Based on this, it is time to discuss what should be obligations of secessionists when they claim a right to secessionist self-determination. Needless to say, the highly generalized obligation to respect the right to self-determination of non-secessionists over territorial interests needs to be transformed into more specific obligations, otherwise it will have little practical sense. What kind of specific obligations can be derived from this highly generalized obligation? One can draw some inspiration from the constitutional frameworks of states that have recognized secessionist self-determination, in order to answer this question. Perhaps some may question why such inspiration is derived from domestic law: generally speaking, it is because that, in a strict sense, there are few international instruments which explicitly provide secessionist self-determination; of course, the constitutional frameworks of states which have recognized secessionist self-determination are also scarce but still more than typical international instruments. This is actually quite understandable when one notices that secessionist self-determination is usually provided in an agreement between secessionists represented by a secessionist entity and non-secessionists represented by the parent state, and the controversy over the legal identity of a secessionist entity exists invariably there: whether and when a secessionist entity can be regarded as a legal subject of international law remains highly debatable. For those regarding a secessionist entity as a legal subject of international law, an agreement between it and the parent state will be regarded as an international instrument, while for those refusing to regard a secessionist entity as a legal subject of international law, an agreement between it and the parent state will be regarded as a constitutional arrangement. In general, fewer will regard a secessionist entity as a legal subject of international law, so an agreement between it and the parent state is more often regarded as a constitutional arrangement. From this perspective, it is not worthwhile to focus too much on this debate: the point is not whether this bilateral agreement between a secessionist entity and the parent state should be regarded as an international instrument or a constitutional arrangement but whether this agreement has translated the highly generalized obligation to respect the right to self-determination of non-secessionists over territorial interests into specific procedural and substantive obligations, which is the key to standardizing secessionist self-determination and decreasing its political nature. In this way, more rational exercise of a right to self-determination can be expected.

As discussed in Chap. 2, only a few states have mentioned secessionist self-determination in their constitutional law; moreover, the actual possibility of exercising secessionist self-determination varies from one to another: it must be admitted that the stipulation is one thing, the practical exercise is another; theoretical existence cannot be equated with practical viability. When the stipulation concerning secessionist self-determination is too general and fails to clarify how it can actually be exercised, such stipulation might conversely contribute to self-determination conflicts rather than provide a solution to these conflicts. For instance, in the 1974 Constitution of the Socialist Federal Republic of Yugoslavia (hereinafter referred to as SFRY), the stipulation concerning secessionist self-determination was too general to be enforced: section 1 of the Basic Principles stated that "the nations of Yugoslavia, proceeding from the right of every nation to self-determination, including the right to secession..."[136]; meanwhile, it must be noted that border readjustments of the Federation were only permitted with the consent of all six republics and the two autonomous territories, according to Article 5.[137] Obviously, a right to secessionist self-determination and the obligation associated with this right did exist in this constitutional framework, but it was unclear how this right and obligation could be put into practice. When relevant parties were at odds over the practical exercise of secessionist self-determination and unable to reach an agreement, intensified self-determination conflicts would hardly be avoidable: the occurrence of violent secessionist wars at that time has proved this point. Therefore, a general stipulation concerning secessionist self-determination, which fails to clarify how it can actually be exercised, is undesirable or destructive: the practical viability of secessionist self-determination weighs no less than the theoretical existence.

Compared with the constitution of the SFRY of 1974, the practical viability of secessionist self-determination stipulated in the 1947 Constitution of the Union of Burma seemed to be better: there was a supplementing mechanism for putting secessionist self-determination into practice. Secessionist self-determination was stipulated in Chapter 10 of the constitution, and the whole Chapter was dedicated to it. At first, Art. 201 stated that "every State shall have the right to secede from the Union in accordance with the conditions hereinafter prescribed".[138] Such conditions

[136]Summers (2007), p. 54, Note 182.

[137]Raič (2002), p. 313, Note 25.

[138]The whole text could be found on the website: https://www.ilo.org/dyn/natlex/docs/ELECTRONIC/79573/85699/F1436085708/MMR79573.pdf, last accessed on 15.06.2018.

are included: (1) the right of secession shall not be exercised within 10 years from the date on which this Constitution comes into operation; (2) a state wishing to exercise the right of secession shall have a resolution to that effect passed by its State Council with no less than two-thirds of its total number of members having voted in its favour; (3) a plebiscite will be taken for the purpose of ascertaining the will of the people of the State concerned, supervised by a Plebiscite Commission consisting an equal number of members representing the Union and the State concerned; (4) all matters relating to the exercise of the right of secession shall be regulated by law.[139] Similarly, the 1994 Ethiopian Constitution also stipulated a supplementing mechanism to translate secessionist self-determination into practice. At the outset of Art.39 it is stated that "every Nation, Nationality and People in Ethiopia has an unconditional right to self-determination, including the right to secession".[140] Then the procedure for exercising this right is stipulated: (1) a demand for secession has to be approved by a two-thirds majority of the members of Legislative Council of the Nation, Nationality or People concerned; (2) a referendum organized by the Federal Government must take place within 3 years from the time it received the concerned council's decision for secession; (3) the demand for secession is supported by majority vote in the referendum; (4) Federal Government has transferred its powers to the council of the Nation, Nationality or People who has voted to secede; (5) the division of assets is effected in a manner prescribed by law. In the same article, the definition of "Nation, Nationality or People" can be found: "a group of people who have or share large measure of a common culture or similar customs, mutual intelligibility of language, belief in a common or related identities, a common psychological make-up, and who inhabit an identifiable, predominantly contiguous territory."[141]

Obviously, when the supplementing mechanism is also provided in the constitutional framework, the exercise of secessionist self-determination is less likely to intensify self-determination conflicts between secessionists and non-secessionists. Obligations specified in this mechanism help prevent secessionists from abusing a right to secessionist self-determination: whenever they intend to invoke secessionist self-determination, they have to fulfill these obligations in the meantime, which requires them to exercise secessionist self-determination in a given way rather than ad libitum. Therefore, the actual exercise of self-determination by secessionists will not prejudice the right to self-determination of non-secessionists, thus contributing to the avoidance of secessionist self-determination conflicts. More importantly, only when obligations of secessionists are specified in the constitutional framework does it become possible to judge whether secessionists have fulfilled the highly

[139] Ibid.

[140] The whole text can be found on http://www.wipo.int/edocs/lexdocs/laws/en/et/et007en.pdf, last accessed on 15.06.2018.

[141] Ibid.

generalized obligation to respect the right to self-determination of non-secessionists over territorial interests or not. Otherwise, if non-secessionists accuse secessionists of violating their right to self-determination and secessionists deny this accusation, it will be quite difficult, if not impossible, to make a judgment on this issue based on the overly generalized stipulation concerning secessionist self-determination, as both conflicting parties can argue that they are exercising their right to self-determination and the opponent is violating this right. In such circumstances, the exercise of secessionist self-determination is actually not regulated by law because according to the overly generalized stipulation, how secessionist self-determination can be exercised is still indefinite. In other words, when obligations of secessionists concerning secessionist self-determination are not specified, it is unlikely to confirm whether there is abuse of secessionist self-determination, let alone prevent such abuse. Specifying obligations of secessionists is necessary as secessionist self-determination needs to be exercised in a right way, and it is hardly possible to confirm the right way when the stipulation concerning secessionist self-determination is overly generalized.

When speaking of confirming the right way of exercising secessionist self-determination, the importance of this issue becomes particularly conspicuous when terrorist means are suspected of being involved. In general, judging whether an act can be referred to as an act of terrorism is not that difficult; nevertheless, when it is connected with secessionist self-determination, the situation becomes quite different. "One of the historical obstacles confronting the achievement of an internationally agreed definition of terrorism, as a crime under international law, has been support by some governments for the legitimacy of the use of force by peoples subjected to oppressive regimes... Even as the scope of the international law covering terrorism is expanding, this scope remains determined in part by the scope of the right of self-determination".[142] Some argue that "the threat to start a secessionist movement will normally increase the repression suffered by the population concerned. In such instances, the international community should not lightly accept any allegation that 'acts of terrorism' are being committed by the victims",[143] while others argue that "it is important not to confuse national liberation warfare with an open licence to engage in acts of terrorism or other grave violations. Such atrocities are never permissible, even in the cause of an internationally lawful struggle of anti-colonial liberation".[144] How should this issue be understood?

Obviously, the occurrence of this issue is closely related to the lack of the specification of obligations of likely holders of the right to secessionist self-determination, which has created an impression that they can pursue secessionist self-determination ad libitum, in disregard of interests of other relevant parties. Needless to say, even if there is no solid legal ground to accuse secessionists of employing terrorist means to pursue self-determination, when what they do is not

[142]Clapham (2006), pp. 46 and 63.
[143]Tomuschat (2006), p. 42.
[144]Weller (2008), p. 30.

different from typical acts of terrorism, pursuing self-determination in this way will still violate self-determination of non-secessionists and escalate self-determination conflicts between them. In such circumstances, both parties have victims suffering from intensified violence: it must be admitted that repressing violence employed by some secessionists is actually necessary as there is no reason to let innocent civilians become victims of the violence employed by some secessionists. Of course, these secessionists might be victims of sovereign repression before they employ violence, but the victim identity cannot create a right to generate more victims. Allowing victims to create more victims will not provide a solution to the conflict, and the settlement of conflicts requires freeing conflicting parties from the vicious circle of violence. For this sake, any violent means which will increase tension between secessionists and non-secessionists should not be allowed in pursuing self-determination: when secessionist self-determination is recognized in a constitutional framework or an international instrument, how it should be exercised needs to be provided explicitly in the meantime, in order to guide secessionists away from an obnoxious exercise of secessionist self-determination and avoid escalating self-determination conflicts which will create more victims from both sides.

It is noteworthy that specifying obligations of secessionists is in the interest of not only non-secessionists but also secessionists themselves. Obviously, such specification largely ensures that self-determination of non-secessionists is not disregarded when secessionists pursue their self-determination. In such circumstances, secessionists will face less opposition in pursuing self-determination: by fulfilling obligations they demonstrate their respect for the right to self-determination of non-secessionists, which helps reduce confrontation between both sides. More importantly, when obligations of secessionists regarding the exercise of self-determination are explicitly provided, and secessionists have fulfilled these obligations, there is no reason for non-secessionists to refuse to recognize their right to self-determination. It should be noted that when obligations associated with a right to self-determination are specified and fulfilled by secessionists, non-secessionists are also under clear obligation to recognize the legal effect of the action of secessionists, otherwise non-secessionists breach the constitutional arrangement or the international instrument which specifies such obligations. In such circumstances, the right to self-determination of secessionists is actually better guaranteed: it will be quite difficult for non-secessionists to argue that their right to self-determination over territorial interests is violated when secessionists have fulfilled obligations specified in a constitutional arrangement or an international instrument. In the same vein the parent state can no longer deny secessionist self-determination due to violation of territorial sovereignty.

To conclude, in order to prevent abuse of the right to self-determination, particularly in the sense of secession, obligations concerning self-determination need to be specified. It is undesirable or even destructive when there is only a generalized stipulation of secessionist self-determination and no mention of how it should be exercised: according to such stipulation, there is actually no effective legal regulation of self-determination, so abuse of this right is unlikely to be prevented. Specifying obligations of a right holder helps prevent abuse of secessionist self-determination, which is quite conducive to the de-escalation of self-determination conflicts, and therefore is in the interests of both sides. Meanwhile, specifying obligations of a right holder also helps realize the right to self-determination of secessionists, due to reduced opposition and increased legal color.

3.2.2.3 Making External Involvement Constructive in Secessionist Self-Determination Conflicts

In the historical review, the close nexus between secessionist self-determination and external involvement is clearly revealed. Based on this, it is accurate to say that the discussion of secessionist self-determination is definitely incomplete when external involvement in secessionist self-determination conflicts goes unmentioned. Needless to say, it is a very complicated issue which can be discussed from numerous perspectives. In Chap. 4 external involvement will be considered from the perspective of the use of force, while Chap. 5 is to deal with the issue about improving the participation of external actors in secessionist conflicts. Discussion in this chapter is centered on several general problems regarding external involvement which is closely related to the prevention of abuse of secessionist self-determination and the de-escalation of secessionist self-determination conflicts. To some extent, Chaps. 4 and 5 can be regarded as the specification of ideas discussed here.

In the first place, it seems necessary to explain why it is stressed here that external involvement should be constructive. Generally speaking, when it comes to external involvement, it is the issue of legality that is invariably being discussed: for instance, whether external involvement should be regarded as a violation of internal affairs or a violation of the national unity and the territorial integrity, what kind of external involvement is forbidden and what kind of external involvement can be allowed. Undeniably, such discussion is necessary and meaningful, but it proves to be inadequate: what is really required is not only legal external intervention but constructive external intervention which is conducive to the settlement of conflicts. There is no denying that there can be seemingly legal but actually counterproductive external involvement, or "illegal but legitimate" and counterproductive external involvement.[145] If it is admitted that external involvement is aimed at settling conflicts, one may assume that considering its legality is insufficient, and it is

[145]The Independent International Commission on Kosovo thought that "the NATO military intervention was illegal but legitimate", see The Independent International Commission on Kosovo, The Kosovo Report, Oxford University Press, 2000, p. 4. In Parliamentary Assembly Resolution 1832 (2011), the Council of Europe has admitted: "military interventions such as those by Turkey in Cyprus in 1974, by the North Atlantic Treaty Organization (NATO) in the Federal Republic of Yugoslavia in 1999 and by the Russian Federation in Georgia in 2008, whilst motivated—justifiably or not—by the need to stop serious human rights violations, have themselves led to numerous human rights violations and have not produced lasting solutions for the underlying problems." See Parliamentary Assembly Resolution 1832 (2011): National sovereignty and statehood in contemporary international law: the need for clarification, para. 5.1.

necessary to consider whether external involvement is constructive or not in actual secessionist self-determination conflicts. After all, the pursuit of legality is not the end of law, but the end of law is to effectively settle conflicts through the pursuit of legality. If external involvement is deemed counterproductive in the settlement of secessionist self-determination conflicts, no matter how hard proponents of external involvement work at justifying its legality or legitimacy, external involvement will still fail to gain widespread acceptance. Worse still, if there have been a large number of cases of legal or legitimate but counterproductive external involvement, it will inevitably give rise to serious doubts about international law itself: people might query if there is something wrong with international law, whether international law still possesses the guiding function and the regulating function, why international law encourages counterproductive external involvement... Therefore, simply focusing on the issue of legality is insufficient, and the legality of external involvement needs to be considered in combination with constructiveness.

When it comes to constructiveness, needless to say, it is closely connected with the effective settlement of conflicts. When external involvement facilitates the de-escalation of secessionist self-determination conflicts, it should be deemed constructive, as de-escalation is key to the settlement of conflicts; furthermore, when external involvement helps strike a balance of interests between secessionists and non-secessionists, it should be deemed constructive, as the settlement of conflicts is largely dependent on a balance of interests between both conflicting parties. Constructive external involvement in secessionist self-determination conflicts must be to the advantage of both secessionists and non-secessionists: to be more specific, external involvement should not be biased, so preference for one side should not be allowed. Obviously, it is easier said than done: sometimes it is even hard to realize that there exists a preference which is detrimental to the process of striking a balance of interests between conflicting parties. For instance, if external involvement is guided by the theory of remedial secessionist self-determination, it will be really hard to expect such external involvement to be unbiased, because the theory itself proves to be biased: in order to satisfy the claim to human rights of secessionists, the ill-founded claim to exclusive territorial ownership is also satisfied, which demonstrates an undoubted preference for secessionists. Guided by such theory, it is unrealistic to expect external involvement to facilitate de-escalation of secessionist self-determination conflicts: the loss of territorial interests means nothing to external actors, but it means a lot to non-secessionists which are represented by the parent state. If external involvement guided by the idea of remedial secessionist self-determination is to force a parent state to give up its territorial interests, the secessionist self-determination conflict will actually be expanded: originally such conflict exists only between secessionists and non-secessionists, and now a new dimension is added, that is the confrontation between external actors and the parent state which is on behalf of non-secessionists. Obviously, in such circumstances secessionist self-determination conflicts actually become more complicated. Because the upgraded complexity of conflicts will hinder settlement in practice, external involvement guided by the theory of remedial secessionist self-determination is unlikely to be constructive. Based on this, for the sake of constructiveness, external actors should consciously abstain from preference: they need to treat both secessionists and non-secessionists on an equal footing and help strike a balance of interests between them.

When it comes to the issue about striking a balance of interests between secessionists and non-secessionists, one must admit that it is highly intricate. As mentioned above, human rights and territorial ownership are concerned. What does international law say about this issue? International law has stressed the protection of human rights and the maintenance of territorial sovereignty but did not mention the distribution of interests between secessionists and non-secessionists. That is to say, secessionists and non-secessionists should pursue a balance of interests between them based on the protection of human rights and the maintenance of territorial sovereignty. Accordingly, external actors involved in such conflicts are required to have due regard to both the protection of human rights and the maintenance of territorial sovereignty, in order to make their involvement constructive. As discussed before, these two aspects are actually closely related with each other, although this nexus is not always correctly interpreted by external actors, which renders external involvement unhelpful, if not counterproductive. A common mistake made by external actors in this regard is that they consciously or unconsciously neglect the importance of the territorial dimension of the secessionist self-determination conflict and fail to appreciate that such neglect will have detrimental effects on human rights protection. Undeniably, when secessionists and non-secessionists cannot peacefully settle their disputes over territorial ownership, the effective protection of human rights is out of the question: in order to strengthen human rights protection in such circumstances, the first step should be to replace violence with peace, which requires pressuring both sides to relinquish violent means. More often than not, external actors focus on pressuring the parent state on behalf of non-secessionists to relinquish violent means against secessionists for the sake of their human rights, but forget to pressure secessionists in equal degree to relinquish violent means to pursue exclusive territorial ownership. When secessionists pursue exclusive territorial ownership in a violent way, not only the maintenance of territorial sovereignty but also the right to self-determination and human rights of non-secessionists are severely affected. In such circumstances, it is quite understandable that a parent state, despite being under huge external pressure, might still choose using force against violent secessionists: it is an attempt not only to maintain territorial sovereignty but also to protect non-secessionists. In this sense, solely pressuring the parent state on behalf of non-secessionists to relinquish violence is actually futile.

In order to make external involvement constructive, external actors need to pressure both the secessionist entity and the parent state to settle their dispute over territorial ownership in a peaceful manner. Only when violence can largely be replaced by peace, can human rights protection be strengthened. Territorial sovereignty or non-secessionist self-determination will not be violated, even if the peaceful negotiation between secessionists and non-secessionists leads to consensual secession: "international law has not recognized a general right of peoples unilaterally to declare secession from a State... This does not, however, exclude the possibility of arrangements reached by free agreements of all parties concerned."[146] Obviously, international law does not forbid secessionists and non-secessionists to distribute their own interests by free agreements, and territorial interests are no exception. Moreover, concluding agreements is a typical form of exercising self-determination, through which a balance of interests between conflicting parties can be struck. When there is no free agreement to readjust territorial interests between secessionists and non-secessionists, it is accurate to say that secessionists should not be allowed to make readjustments unilaterally: the maintenance of territorial sovereignty implies that international law values the stability of borders, and it is hard to say that unilateral readjustments are compatible with the requirements of stability. Besides, unilateral readjustments only embody self-determination of secessionists and exclude self-determination of non-secessionists, which is destructive to a balance of conflicting interests. Therefore, it is certainly well-advised for external actors to prevent secessionists from attempting unilateral secession and facilitate agreements between secessionists and non-secessionists on the territorial issues in secessionist self-determination conflicts. When there exist such agreements, striking a balance of interests between secessionists and non-secessionists is no longer a problem: this balance will definitely ease the tension between conflicting parties which forms the basis for the improvement in human rights, and will help preserve the stability of borders because unilateral action is replaced by consent. External involvement facilitating the conclusion of constructive agreements dealing with secessionist self-determination conflicts is therefore constructive.

In view of the foregoing, it is not wrong to say that constructive external involvement in secessionist self-determination conflicts largely depends on the cooperative interplay between three parties, namely external actors, secessionists and non-secessionists: external actors need to cooperate with both secessionists and non-secessionists, which can improve the internal cooperation between secessionists and non-secessionists, and it is quite unrealistic to expect external involvement to improve the cooperation between secessionists and non-secessionists when external actors neglect the cooperation with non-secessionists or even act against the parent state. In such circumstances, confrontation rather than cooperation is to be expected. Therefore, NATO's involvement in Kosovo was a sheer failure while the EU's involvement in Aceh was a laudable success: NATO failed to cooperate with the Yugoslavian authorities to prevent Kosovo secessionists from employing violence to pursue independence, which also discouraged the secessionist entity from cooperating with the parent state, while the EU did cooperate with the Indonesian authorities to require Aceh secessionists to relinquish violence, which also helped form the basis for the cooperation between the parent state and the secessionist entity. Obviously, when secessionists realize that external actors lack the sincerity to cooperate with non-secessionists, they are not motivated to cooperate with non-secessionists either; worse yet, secessionists will be discouraged from making compromises or even act more egregiously if they know external actors are also against the parent state; in such circumstances, there is only the cooperative interplay

[146] Report of the Committee on the Elimination of Racial Discrimination, UN Doc. A/51/18, p. 126.

between external actors and secessionists, and constructive external involvement is out of the question because of the lack of the cooperative interplay between secessionists and non-secessionists as well as between external actors and non-secessionists. Conversely, when secessionists realize the sincerity demonstrated by external actors to cooperate with non-secessionists, they are also motivated to cooperate with non-secessionists; meanwhile, secessionists are encouraged to make compromises and exercise more restraint as they do not want to be placed under external pressure in addition to the high internal pressure; in such circumstances all cooperative interplay required in constructive external involvement is there: cooperative interplay between secessionists and non-secessionists, cooperative interplay between external actors and secessionists and cooperative interplay between external actors and non-secessionists. Needless to say, only when external actors can cooperate with both secessionists and non-secessionists do they truly fulfill the obligation to cooperate required by general international law in dispute settlement, and the settlement of secessionist self-determination conflicts should not be an exception.

Last but not least, constructive external involvement needs to provide positive incentives for both conflicting parties in secessionist self-determination conflicts. The issue about incentive has been repeatedly mentioned before: when some secessionists deliberately create exceptional circumstances in order to invoke a right to remedial secessionist self-determination, they are motivated by a perverse incentive emanating from remedial secessionist self-determination. To be more exact, this perverse incentive emanates from both the theory and the practice: "any remedial right would not have been more than a mere paper tiger due to the lack of enforcement", but "things have changed in light of new developments regarding outside interference in civil wars", and "states have become increasingly willing to act in cases of massive human rights abuses by their peers".[147] For this reason, "secessionist groups are instigated to actively provoke massive retaliation because they rely on thereby-triggered interventions as decisive help in overcoming the respective states' military, administrative, and financial superiority".[148] Obviously, external involvement should not be exploited by secessionists in this way, and such perverse incentive for secessionists should be eliminated. When external involvement no longer provides a perverse incentive for secessionists to actively provoke massive retaliation, such malicious exploitation of external involvement can be avoided.

As for a positive incentive for the parent state on behalf of non-secessionists provided by constructive external involvement, it has not been explicitly mentioned before. Nevertheless, given what has been discussed above, it is not difficult to discern that constructive external involvement, in general, should provide incentives for the parent state to respect democratic claims made by secessionists, which is much concerned with the improvement of the constitutional framework aimed at strengthening the guarantee of minority rights. In order to provide such incentives, it

[147] Janik (2013), p. 54.

[148] Ibid. pp. 57–58.

is quite logical to say that external actors need to work at keeping secessionists within the parent state, as the EU has done in the Aceh case: the improvement of the constitutional framework aimed at strengthening the guarantee of minority rights is only meaningful when secessionists are still minorities within the parent state, because when secessionists are no longer minorities within the parent state, there is no need to consider improving the constitutional protection of secessionists in the sense of national minorities. From this perspective, when external actors rush to recognize a secessionist entity, it is hard to say that such external involvement can provide a positive incentive for states involved in secessionist self-determination conflicts to improve their constitutional frameworks aiming to strengthen the guarantee of minority rights. Therefore, it is accurate to say that when external actors really want to motivate states involved in secessionist self-determination conflicts to improve democratic governance, particularly in terms of human rights and minority protection, they should make an effort to keep secessionists within parent states in the first place, which is the logical precondition of improving the constitutional protection of secessionists in the sense of national minorities. The importance of this point has been implied in the second report on the Aaland Islands question in 1921: "what reasons would there be for allowing a minority to separate itself from the State to which it is united, if this State gives it the guarantees which it is within its rights in demanding, for the preservation of its social, ethnical or religious character? Such indulgence, apart from every political consideration, would be supremely unjust to the State prepared to make these concessions."[149] Therefore, constructive external involvement in secessionist conflicts should be aimed at discouraging secessionists from pursuing independence and urging the parent state to improve the constitutional protection of secessionists in the sense of national minorities.

To conclude, in order to make external involvement in secessionist self-determination conflicts more constructive, a comprehensive consideration is required, which should include aspects such as de-escalating secessionist self-determination conflicts, striking a balance of interests between secessionists and non-secessionists, protecting human rights and maintaining territorial sovereignty at the same time, promoting cooperative interplay and providing positive incentives. In fact, these aspects are not isolated but closely interrelated with each other. A detailed discussion about this complicated interrelation is to be found in Chaps. 4 and 5.

References

Aspinall E (2008) Peace without justice? The Helsinki Peace process in Aceh. Centre for Humanitarian Dialogue, Geneva

Aspinall E (2011) Aceh: the secession that never was. In: Pavkovic A, Radan P (eds) The Ashgate research companion to secession. Ashgate Publishing Limited, Farnham, pp 459–462

[149]See Chap. 1, Note 17.

Aspinall E, Zain F (2013) Transitional justice delayed in Aceh, Indonesia. In: Jeffery R, Kim HJ (eds) Transitional justice in the Asia-Pacific. Cambridge University Press, Cambridge, pp 87–123

Blum YZ (1975) Reflections on the changing concept of self-determination. Israel Law Rev 10:511

Brilmayer L (1991) Secession and self-determination: a territorial interpretation. Yale J Int Law 16:177–202

Buchanan A (2004) Justice, legitimacy and self-determination: moral foundations for international law. Oxford University Press, Oxford

Cassese A (1995) Self-determination of peoples: a legal reappraisal. Cambridge University Press, Cambridge

Castellino J (2000) International law and self-determination. Martinus Nijhoff, Leiden, p 11

Christakis T (2011) The ICJ advisory opinion on Kosovo: "Has international law something to say about secession?". Leiden J Int Law 24:73–86

Clapham A (2006) Secession, terrorism and the right of self-determination. In: Kohen MG (ed) Secession: international law perspectives. Cambridge University Press, Cambridge, pp 46–64

Coggins BL (2011) The history of secession: an overview. In: Pavkovic A, Radan P (eds) The Ashgate research companion to secession. Ashgate Publishing Limited, Farnham, pp 23–44

Doyle DH (2011) An attempt at secession from an early nation-state: the confederate States of America. In: Pavkovic A, Radan P (eds) The Ashgate Research Companion to Secession. Ashgate Publishing Limited, Farnham, pp 103–116

Duursma J (1996) Fragmentation and the international relations of micro-states. Cambridge University Press, Cambridge

Fabry M (2011) International involvement in secessionist conflict: from the 16th century to the present. In: Pavkovic A, Radan P (eds) The Ashgate research companion to secession. Ashgate Publishing Limited, Farnham

Franck T (1993) Postmodern tribalism and the right to secession. In: Brölmann C, Lefeber R, Zieck M (eds) Peoples and minorities in international law. Martinus Nijhoff, Leiden, pp 3–28

Higgins R (2003) Self-determination and secession. In: Dahlitz J (ed) Secession and international law: conflict avoidance – regional appraisals. United Nations Publications, New York

Horowitz DL (2003) A right to secede? In: Macedo S, Buchanan A (eds) Secession and self-determination. New York University Press, New York, pp 50–76

Janik R (2013) The responsibility to protect as an impetus for secessionist movements — on the necessity to re-think territorial integrity. In: Kettemann MC (ed) Grenzen im Völkerrecht. Jan Sramek Verlag, Vienna, pp 41–69

Jennings I (1956) An approach to self-governance. Cambridge University Press, Cambridge, pp 55–56

Klabbers J, Lefeber R (1993) Africa: lost between Uti possidetis and Self-determination. In: Brölmann C, Lefeber R, Zieck M (eds) Peoples and minorities in international law. Martinus Nijhoff, Leiden, pp 37–76

Kohen MG (2006) Introduction. In: Kohen MG (ed) Secession: international law perspectives. Cambridge University Press, Cambridge

Koskenniemi M (1994) National self-determination today: problems of legal theory and practice. Int Comp Law Q 43:241–269. https://doi.org/10.1093/iclqaj/43.2.241

Kuperman AJ (2008) The moral hazard of humanitarian intervention: lessons from the Balkans. Int Stud Q 52:49–80

Lahmann H (2009) Biafra conflict, paras. 31 and 32. Max Planck Encyclopedia of Public International Law. Last updated in August 2009

Lansing R (1921) The peace negotiations: a personal narrative. Houghton Mifflin, Boston, pp 97–98

Lenin VI (1964) The right of nations to self-determination. In: Lenin VI (ed) Collected Works 20. Progress Publisher, Moscow

Nelson LDM (1973) The arbitration of boundary disputes in Latin America. Neth Int Law Rev 20:267–294. https://doi.org/10.1017/S0165070X0002163X

Orentlicher D (2003) International responses to separatist claims: are democratic principles relevant? In: Macedo S, Buchanan A (eds) Secession and self-determination. New York University Press, New York, pp 19–49

Pomerance M (1982) Self-determination in law and practice. Martinus Nijhoff, Leiden

Raič D (2002) Statehood and the law of self-determination. Kluwer Law International, Alphen aan den Rijn

Reisman M (1990) International law after the Cold War. Am J Int Law 84:864

Shaw MN (1997) Peoples, territorialism and boundaries. Eur J Int Law 8:478–507

Shaw MN (2003) The role of recognition and non-recognition with respect to secession: notes on some relevant issues. In: Dahlitz J (ed) Secession and international law: conflict avoidance – regional appraisals. United Nations Publications, New York, pp 243–258

Summers J (2007) Peoples and international law: how nationalism and self-determination shape a contemporary law of nations. Martinus Nijhoff, Leiden

Summers J (2013) The internal and external aspects of self-determination reconsidered. In: French D (ed) Statehood and self-determination: reconciling tradition and modernity in international law. Cambridge University Press, Cambridge, pp 229–249

Thornberry P (1989) Self-determination, minorities, human rights: a review of international instruments. Int Comp Law Q 38:867–889

Thornberry P (1993) The democratic or internal aspect of self-determination with some remarks on federalism. In: Tomuschat C (ed) Modern law of self-determination. Martinus Nijhoff, Leiden, pp 101–138

Tomuschat C (2006) Secession and self-determination. In: Kohen MG (ed) Secession: international law perspectives. Cambridge University Press, Cambridge, pp 23–45

Weller M (2008) Why the legal rules on self-determination do not resolve self-determination disputes. In: Weller M, Metzger B (eds) Settling self-determination disputes: complex power-sharing in theory and practice. Martinus Nijhoff, Leiden, pp 17–46

Chapter 4
Secession and the Use of Force

If secession does not involve the use of force, this issue will be much less complex. Unfortunately, the use of force is often resorted to: secessionists resort to force to oppose parent states, and parent states resort to force to counter the rebellion of secessionists. As observed by Weller, "unless defeated by the government, secessionist campaigns will persist with varying degrees of violence… Some are simmering at a lower level of terrorist violence, others amount to more regular internal armed conflicts, with secessionist groups maintaining control over significant swaths of territory to the exclusion of the central government."[1]

More often than not in such conflicts, external involvement is to be found, more or less visibly: an external actor could be an international/regional organization or individual states. External actors will always find a reason for their involvement, and one of them is humanitarian intervention. Some prefer to replace humanitarian intervention with the responsibility to protect, but there actually is no fundamental distinction between them. Obviously, when an external actor coercively interferes in a secessionist conflict, the issue becomes more complicated, practically and theoretically. Many researchers focus on the legal justification for such external intervention, and of course, searching for the legal justification is not wrong, but if it is not aimed at effectively settling the secessionist conflict, the practical value of this search is questionable: as will be discussed later, the use of force which proves to be counterproductive in conflict settlement might be justified from a certain perspective of international law. In addition, it is quite meaningful to consider avoiding the external use of force in secessionist conflicts: non-military means are undeniably more desirable than military means, given that the use of force against another sovereign state is in principle prohibited under contemporary international law, the search for a legal justification for external intervention is generally painstaking, and there is no guarantee that the outcome of the search will be widely accepted. Avoiding the use of force is also significant because the external use of force in

[1]Weller (2008), p. xi.

J. Lu, *On State Secession from International Law Perspectives*,
https://doi.org/10.1007/978-3-319-97448-4_4

secessionist conflicts tends to provide a perverse incentive for secessionists, as mentioned in Chap. 3.

Therefore, in this chapter the legal discussion about the use of force is closely connected with an effective solution to secessionist conflicts: the effectiveness of the use of force should never be deemed unrelated to the legality of the use of force, so the positive contribution to the settlement of the conflict should be regarded as an integral part of the justification for the use of force. Besides, difficulty in avoiding the use of force is to be analyzed: if the use of force in certain circumstances can be justified, it is definitely necessary to prevent such circumstances from being deliberately created, otherwise it will be impossible to uphold the general prohibition on the use of force if exceptional circumstances become the "new normal". In fact, consciously preventing exceptional circumstances which are deliberately created is in line with not only the general prohibition on the use of force but also other legal principles enshrined in the Declaration on Principles of International Law Concerning Friendly Relations and Co-operation among states in Accordance with the Charter of the UN, such as state sovereignty, non-interference in domestic affairs and peaceful settlement of disputes. In order to ensure that the international legal system normally functions, consciously preventing exceptional circumstances from being deliberately created should be deemed indispensable. After a general discussion, four relevant cases will be studied. The study of cases will follow the idea embodied in the general discussion.

4.1 Internal Use of Force and External Use of Force in Secessionist Conflicts

4.1.1 Force Used by Conflicting Parties

The internal use of force concerns secessionists and non-secessionists, which has not been explicitly regulated by international law. As noted by Christakis, outside the colonial context "the sovereign states concerned have not only the possibility to regulate secession internally in their respective domestic orders, but also have the right to take all measures compatible under international law, including police measures and the use of force, in order to protect their territorial integrity against these secessionist attempts".[2] Meanwhile, it should be noted that international law does not deny the possibility that secessionists can protect their wish to secede against attempts to maintain territorial sovereignty made by non-secessionists. That is to say, general international law prohibits neither sovereign states on behalf of non-secessionists from using force against secessionists nor secessionists from using force against sovereign states. Clearly, such situation does not bode well for the settlement of secessionist conflicts: when the regulation of the use of force is absent,

[2]Christakis (2011), p. 80.

it is logical to expect the escalation of violence between secessionists and non-secessionists, which can lead to loss of lives and human suffering. As observed by Coggins, "secessionist conflicts constituted nearly half of the major violence between states and non-state actors in the 20th century ... they kill more people because they are more frequent and tend to last much longer than interstate wars."[3]

For this reason, international law has started to limit the internal use of force on a case-by-case basis. As noted by Pellet, "it is quite usual for the UNSC to call upon States to seek a peaceful solution to their disputes with non-State parties to an internal conflict... since the end of the 1970s, the Council and the General Assembly call upon 'all the parties to the (armed) conflict' or 'all interested parties' (including non-governmental entities) to seek a peaceful settlement."[4] Security Council resolutions 1199 (1998) and 1203 (1998) are typical examples: both Security Council resolutions condemned all acts of violence by any party, as well as terrorism in pursuit of political goals by any group or individual; not only was Yugoslavia required to cease all action by the security forces affecting the civilian population and order the withdrawal of security units used for civilian repression, but also the Kosovo Albanian leadership was required to condemn all terrorist action and pursue their goals by peaceful means only.[5]

Based on this, one can conclude that currently the stance of international law on the internal use of force in secessionist conflicts is that both secessionists and non-secessionists should limit their violent actions: neither side is allowed to pursue its goal by resorting to force. Obviously, this stance embodies a conflict-oriented thought instead of a right-oriented thought: the top priority is to lower the degree of violence which leads to loss of lives and human suffering from both sides, and neither conflicting party should claim its own right in disregard of the right claimed by the other. At first glance, such restraints on the force used by secessionists and non-secessionists seem to be unnecessary because general international law does not require so. However, it is actually quite meaningful as both sides can benefit from such restraints: basic human rights are largely preserved because the level of violence between the conflicting sides is dramatically lowered. Moreover, as discussed before, secessionist self-determination conflicts should be settled through negotiation, which can be expected only when international law clearly dissuades or even prevents conflicting parties from pursuing a military solution. From this perspective, the limitation or prevention of the internal use of force embodied in UN Security Council resolutions is definitely an important addition to general international law: in this way, the principle of peaceful settlement of disputes, which used to be only applicable to international disputes, can be officially applied to internal disputes and helps avoid warfare which can be deemed one of the greatest threats to human rights protection.

---

[3]See Chap. 1, Note 1.

[4]Pellet (2013).

[5]S/RES/1199 (1998), paras. 4 and 6, S/RES/1203 (1998), paras. 3, 4 and 10.

Nevertheless, it is necessary to consider what happens if conflicting parties refuse to follow the principle of peaceful settlement of secessionist conflicts, especially when intensifying violence is actually a part of the strategy employed by one conflicting party. In other words, what should be done when a conflicting party endeavors to evade the obligation to pursue a peaceful solution to a secessionist conflict in a sly way? For instance, Bosnia's Muslim president, Alija Izetbegovic, one of the three Muslim representatives at the EC's negotiations in Lisbon, later admitted that "our tactics were to buy time.... [pursuing] a zig-zag line for independence... so the international community would defend this country"[6]; with regard to the cantonization proposed by the EC, another Muslim representative, Rusmir Mahmutcehajic explained that "to reject it outright would identify us as guilty for obstructing the agreement and this could obstruct getting recognition"[7]; the eventual foreign minister of Bosnia and negotiating representative, Haris Silajdzic, even revealed that "all the negotiations were just a farce to buy legitimacy... My main priority in the whole strategy was to get Western governments and especially the United States to get involved, because [Serbs] had the whole Army".[8] Undeniably, when one conflicting party endeavors to evade the obligation to pursue a peaceful solution to a secessionist conflict, it is unrealistic to expect the other party to stick to this obligation. In such circumstances, the limitation or prevention of the internal use of force will not work effectively. Therefore, the issue of evading the obligation to pursue a peaceful solution should be addressed, and it should be realized that addressing this issue is largely dependent on making the peaceful settlement of secessionist disputes in the interests of conflicting parties. Otherwise there will always be incentive for conflicting parties to evade the obligation to pursue a peaceful solution when peaceful negotiation appears worthless to them.

Perhaps one might question why peaceful settlement might not prove to be in the interests of conflicting parties in a secessionist conflict: in order to answer this question, it is necessary to point out the interplay between peaceful settlement, violence and human rights in the first place. In a secessionist conflict, when violence can be replaced by peaceful settlement, gross breaches of fundamental human rights can largely be avoided; conversely, when violence cannot be replaced by peaceful settlement, gross breaches of fundamental human rights can hardly be avoided. For those who need to avoid a humanitarian catastrophe, peaceful settlement is in their interests and they are not motivated to avoid peaceful negotiation, but for those who need the humanitarian catastrophe, peaceful settlement is not in their interests and they are motivated to avoid peaceful negotiation. Therefore, one needs to consider this question: in a secessionist conflict, which side needs a humanitarian catastrophe, secessionists or non-secessionists? In actual secessionist conflicts where violence is involved, usually both secessionists and non-secessionists are perpetrators and

[6]Kuperman (2008), p. 61.
[7]Ibid.
[8]Ibid.

victims at the same time, so from this perspective it is hard to tell which side needs a humanitarian catastrophe. The answer to this question is actually closely related to incentives provided by international law, to be more specific, general international law, because specific instruments such as UN Security Council resolutions mentioned above usually provide identical incentives for both sides to relinquish the use of force.

When it comes to general international law, incentives for non-secessionists and secessionists to relinquish the use of force are quite different, which can largely be attributed to the distinction of identity: non-secessionists in international law are represented by a sovereign state while secessionists are represented by a secessionist entity. As a traditional legal subject of international law, a sovereign state has to fulfill the obligation to protect human rights during peacetime and the humanitarian obligation during wartime. Such legal obligation actually provides a relatively strong incentive for a sovereign state on behalf of non-secessionists to exercise restraint in using force, as the unrestricted use of force can lead to severe human rights violations, which is likely to place the sovereign state under huge international pressure or even trigger humanitarian intervention. Thus, a sovereign state needs to avoid humanitarian catastrophes and is not motivated to avoid peaceful negotiation. However, general international law fails to provide an identical incentive to a secessionist entity. As a secessionist entity so far has not become a typical subject of international law, its legal obligation is far from being clear. That is to say, even when the use of force by secessionists has caused severe human rights violations, they do not need to worry much about international pressure as they are not explicitly obliged by international law to respect human rights. As for humanitarian obligations of secessionists, it is also quite difficult to confirm such obligations in secessionist conflicts in practice: according to Common Article 3 to the Geneva Conventions of 1949, it is likely to address the issue of humanitarian obligation of secessionists; however, as Nair has observed, it remains quite unclear how to determine the legal nature of "intermediate, gray situations of political violence. The gray situation can be distinguished from situations of 'normal' crime or war".[9] Therefore, it is accurate to say that the lack of clear legal obligation under international law is unlikely to provide an incentive for secessionists to exercise restraint in using force.

Such difference between non-secessionists and secessionists emanating from general international law will certainly lead to practical problems: "imagine the head of a human rights organization having to explain to a government why the organization condemns the army's violence in the search of terrorists – yet never says a word about organized rebel attacks on civilian targets. One could say one is strictly applying a humanitarian legal framework and the bombings have not reached the required threshold – but this is unlikely to convince any government that there is no bias involved."[10] As pointed out by Watkin: "if a human rights body does not also

[9]Nair (1998), p. 11.
[10]Clapham (2006), p. 50.

direct its attention to the actions of a nonstate actor in terms of compliance with international humanitarian law, it may leave the perception of not being evenhanded. The body may even come to be seen as a tool for restricting the activities of one party to a conflict".[11] How human rights organizations should participate in an armed conflict between secessionists and non-secessionists will not be discussed here, and the point here is the consequences of the asymmetric restraint on the internal use of force. Obviously, such asymmetric restraint on the use of force favors secessionists and places non-secessionists at a disadvantage, which is unlikely to work out: when non-secessionists feel discriminated against because of legal restraints, it is unrealistic to expect that they will observe such restraints without reluctance; when secessionists can launch attacks on non-secessionists without restraint, it is reasonable to assume that non-secessionists will fight back. The use of force in such circumstances is more likely to be upgraded rather than downgraded. When the use of force is being upgraded, the humanitarian situation is gradually escalating into a humanitarian catastrophe. In this sense, one can conclude that sovereign states cannot effectively exercise restraint implied in general international law in using force when secessionist entities can use force without similar restraint.

Besides, it should be noted that in order to protect the right to self-determination of non-secessionists over territorial interests, sovereign states sometimes are forced to use violence against peaceful secessionists. The Catalan Independence Referendum is a typical case in point: in order to stop Catalan secessionists from unilaterally altering territorial co-ownership through the referendum, the Civil Guard fired rubber bullets on the crowds who turned out to vote in the poll.[12] Such violence is detrimental to the human rights of secessionists, but when non-violent means such as suspending the referendum law passed by the Catalan parliament[13] could not stop secessionists, the Spanish government actually did not have a better option to protect the right to self-determination of non-secessionists over territorial interests. There is no denying that as a sovereign state bound by international human rights law, it is not allowed to use violence against secessionists due to the obligation to protect their human rights; however, a sovereign state also assumes the obligation to protect human rights and the right to self-determination of non-secessionists over territorial interests and thus needs to prevent secessionists from violating these rights. Such need becomes more urgent when secessionists become violent, like the KLA and the Free Aceh Movement. If non-violent means cannot even prevent peaceful secessionists, as demonstrated in the Catalan case, it is certainly unrealistic to expect that armed secessionists can be prevented in this way. From this perspective, it is more problematic to simply criticize sovereign states for failing to fulfill the obligation to

---

[11] Watkin (2004), p. 30.

[12] Caroline Mortimer, Catalan referendum: Jeremy Corbyn urges Theresa May to intervene 'to find political solution to the crisis', https://www.independent.co.uk/news/uk/politics/catalonia-independence-referendum-jeremy-corbyn-theresa-may-violence-intervention-mariano-rajoy-a7976976.html, last accessed on 15.06.2018.

[13] Spain Catalonia: Court blocks independence referendum, https://www.bbc.com/news/world-europe-41196677, last accessed on 15.06.2018.

protect human rights of secessionists: critics only see that the human rights of secessionists are violated by sovereign states in self-determination conflicts but ignore that the human rights of non-secessionists are also violated by armed secessionists, so they simply accuse sovereign states of using violence against secessionists and disregard that such violence actually protects the human rights and the right to self-determination of non-secessionists. From this perspective, these critics are advocating a selective protection of human rights, which is not in accordance with the purposes of international human rights law. Therefore, for the sake of human rights protection, it is necessary to avoid such situation that sovereign states are caught in conflicting obligations, the key to which lies in restraining secessionists.

Of course, the most important thing is to restrain secessionists from using violence. As mentioned before, secessionists lack the incentive to exercise restraint in using force. From the lack of incentive for secessionists to exercise restraint in using force one cannot explain why they need the humanitarian catastrophe and are motivated to avoid peaceful negotiation. The need for humanitarian catastrophe and the motive in avoiding peaceful negotiation should be understood on the basis of the perverse incentive provided by remedial secession discussed before: if unilateral secession is only allowed in case of humanitarian catastrophes, in order to achieve independence, humanitarian catastrophes are undoubtedly worth pursuing. From this perspective, peaceful negotiation is certainly not in the interests of those secessionists who are willing to sacrifice their own people for the sake of unilateral secession: the peaceful settlement of secessionist conflicts tends to exclude humanitarian catastrophes, and when humanitarian catastrophes are excluded, the wish for unilateral secession based on such exceptional circumstances goes unrealized. For this reason, leaders of Bosnian secessionists endeavored to evade the obligation to pursue a peaceful solution, and such evasion existed not only in negotiation but also in battlefield: "Bosnia's Muslim-controlled government and army repeatedly resisted ceasefires, even though the main victims of continued fighting were fellow Muslims, because of the expectation that such suffering would attract humanitarian military intervention sufficient to help them win the war".[14] The first commander of UN peacekeepers in Bosnia, General Lewis Mackenzie, thought that the Muslim-led "Bosnia Presidency was committed to coercing the international community into intervening militarily"[15]; his successor, General Michael Rose, reported that the Muslim side rejected ceasefires because "if the Bosnian Army attacked and lost, the resulting images of war and suffering guaranteed support in the West for the 'victim State'".[16]

Therefore, the motive of secessionists in evading the obligation to pursue a peaceful solution has much to do with not only remedial secession but also the availability of humanitarian intervention. As observed by Janik, "the combination of remedial secession and Responsibility to Protect thus provides an entirely new

[14]Kuperman (2013), p. 304.
[15]Mackenzie (1993), p. 159.
[16]Rose (1998), p. 141.

impetus for secessionist struggles. While Responsibility to Protect provides armed groups with the military help they need in encountering an otherwise clearly superior enemy, the right to remedial secession constitutes the legal basis for their claim to secession after their fighting is over or as a means to end it. The prospects for successful secessions have thus never been better."[17] In such circumstances, it proves to be quite difficult to limit or prevent the internal use of force in secessionist conflicts: the peaceful settlement of secessionist conflicts requires both non-secessionists and secessionists to pursue a peaceful solution, and a peaceful solution is certainly out of the question when non-secessionists are encouraged to pursue it and secessionists are encouraged to avoid it. Hence, it is necessary to discourage secessionists from avoiding peaceful negotiation and to render humanitarian catastrophes not worth pursuing for them. Obviously, for this sake, one needs to reconsider both remedial secession and humanitarian intervention from the perspective of international law. As remedial secession has been much discussed in previous chapters and this chapter is dedicated to the use of force, the following discussion is centered on humanitarian intervention, namely the external use of force.

4.1.2 Force Used by External Actors

Contrary to the internal use of force which is indirectly regulated by general international law through the medium of human rights protection, general international law has relatively sophisticated regulations governing the external use of force. Needless to say, these regulations governing the external use of force are also applicable to secessionist conflicts. A correct understanding of these regulations is a challenging task as they are open to various interpretations, and the level of difficulty is further enhanced given the complexity of secessionist conflicts. Thus, the whole issue proves to be quite confusing. Nevertheless, when one has the effective settlement of secessionist conflicts as the aim, the whole issue becomes less confusing: although there are numerous ways of interpreting these legal regulations, it is clear that not every way is conducive to the settlement of conflicts, so selecting interpretations should be based on the contribution to conflict settlement. Whether the external use of force in a secessionist conflict can be legally justified should largely depend on whether the external use of force has played a negative or positive role in conflict settlement: the justification for the external use of force cannot be convincing when the external use of force fails to contribute to the settlement of the secessionist conflict and creates other problems.

The nexus between the convincing justification for the external use of force and the effective settlement of secessionist conflicts is a very interesting issue. According to the Parliamentary Assembly of the Council of Europe: "military interventions such as those by Turkey in Cyprus in 1974, by the North Atlantic Treaty

---

[17] Janik (2013), p. 69.

Organization (NATO) in the Federal Republic of Yugoslavia in 1999 and by the Russian Federation in Georgia in 2008, whilst motivated – justifiably or not – by the need to stop serious human rights violations, have themselves led to numerous human rights violations and have not produced lasting solutions for the underlying problems."[18] This remark has revealed that the external use of force can be justified from one dimension but condemned from other dimensions: obviously, when the external use of force can only be justified in a selective manner, such justification is certainly unconvincing; worse still, selectively-justified external use of force, as listed above, cannot contribute to the settlement of secessionist conflicts. For this reason, the justification for the external use of force must be considered in a comprehensive manner instead of a selective manner, otherwise the use of force which does a disservice to the settlement of conflicts can be condoned. If it is admitted that the external use of force should be convincingly justified and play a positive role in conflict settlement, a comprehensive justification for the external use of force should be pursued under international law, and the selective justification proves to be inadequate, even detrimental.

In view of the foregoing, the discussion of the external use of force here is of a comprehensive nature and settlement-oriented, which actually are two sides of the same coin. In the first place, there will be a general introduction to legal regulations governing the external use of force (Sect. 4.1.2.1). Based on this, the highly controversial theme, namely the responsibility to protect will be specifically analyzed (Sect. 4.1.2.2). After the specific analysis, there will be a review of a legal judgement made on the NATO bombing of Yugoslavia, which actually reflected the complex relationship between the naturalist perspective of international law focusing on morals and the positivist perspective focusing on practical legal rules: the general prohibition on the use of force and the responsibility to protect as a likely exception also reflect this complex relationship to a large extent (Sect. 4.1.2.3).

4.1.2.1 General Introduction to Legal Regulations Governing the External Use of Force

A general introduction to legal regulations governing the external use of force should include the general prohibition, the complex interplay between the general prohibition and other principles of international law, and legal justifications, explicitly provided or merely inferred, for the exceptional use of force.

[18] Parliamentary Assembly Resolution 1832 (2011): National sovereignty and statehood in contemporary international law: the need for clarification, para. 5.1.

a. Article 2(4) of the UN Charter: Necessary Condition and Sufficient Condition

The general prohibition on the external use of force is enshrined in the UN Charter. According to Article 2(4): "all Members shall refrain in their international relations from the threat or use of force against the territorial integrity or political independence of any state, or in any other manner inconsistent with the Purposes of the United Nations." Obviously, the article itself is stressing cooperative interplay between the general prohibition on the use of force and other international legal principles: "the territorial integrity or political independence" indicates the principle of state sovereignty and non-interference in domestic affairs; "Purposes of the United Nations" are specified in Article 1, in which the principle of the peaceful settlement of disputes [Article 1(1)], self-determination [Article 1(2)] and international cooperation [Article 1(3)] are embodied. The principle of good faith is not directly involved, but given the indissoluble link between good faith and international cooperation, there is no reason to deduce that force can be used in disregard of the principle of good faith. Needless to say, Article 2(4) reminds one to consider this issue: when members fail to refrain in their international relations from the threat or use of force, it might have an extensive influence including violating the sovereignty of one state, constituting interference in domestic affairs, endangering international peace and security, repressing self-determination and undermining international cooperation. That is to say, disregarding the general prohibition on the external use of force is closely related to violations of other principles of international law, and in order to uphold these legal principles, a state shall conduct its international relations without resorting to the threat or use of force.

It should be noted that the violation of the territorial integrity or political independence is not based on the subjective judgment of an intervening state. In the Corfu Channel case, the UK argued that its forcible intervention in Albanian territorial waters was to search for evidence, in order to ascertain which state had to be responsible for laying naval mines which had led to the destruction of two British warships, and therefore it did not violate Article 2(4) because its action did not threaten the territorial integrity or political independence of Albania.[19] The ICJ rejected this claim, arguing that "the alleged right of intervention [was] the manifestation of a policy of force, such as has, in the past, given rise to most serious abuses and such as cannot... find a place in international law".[20] In addition, the court wisely pointed out that such a right in the present case "would be reserved for the most powerful states, and might easily lead to perverting the administration of international justice itself".[21] Through the reasoning of the ICJ it is quite understandable why the violation of the territorial integrity or political independence cannot be based on the subjective judgment of an intervenor: if military intervention can be condoned simply because the intervenor alleges that it has no intention to

[19] Corfu Channel case, Judgement of April 9th 1949: I.C.J. Reports 1949, p. 34.

[20] Ibid. p. 35.

[21] Ibid.

make violations and it intervenes out of a reasonable intention, international law is unlikely to control the external use of force because every intervenor can allege that it intervenes out of a reasonable intention, even if their real intention hidden in the reasonable appearance is illegal. Even if the real intention is just the one alleged by the intervenor, there is no denying that a legal intention is one thing, a legal intervention is quite another, and thus the intention alone cannot justify the relevant intervention.

The logical nexus between a legal intention and the legal use of force is worth serious attention. A legal intention is the necessary condition for the use of force to be legal but not the sufficient condition.[22] That is to say, the use of force without a legal intention is certainly illegal, but the use of force is not necessarily legal when there is a legal intention. Whether the use of force is legal or not depends on a very complicated consideration which requires more than a legal intention: for instance, when the outcome of the use of force proves to be detrimental, there is sufficient reason to doubt the practical legality of the use of force in this case, no matter how noble the (alleged) intention is. Otherwise it will be unlikely to stop military interventions which create more problems and contribute nothing to the underlying issue, despite the good intention alleged by intervenors. Military interventions of this type were not rarely found in secessionist conflicts: as summarized in the above-mentioned instrument of the Council of Europe, military interventions by Turkey in Cyprus in 1974, by NATO in the Federal Republic of Yugoslavia in 1999 and by the Russian Federation in Georgia in 2008 fell into this category. It is definitely correct to believe that a good intention cannot be equated with the legal use of force, and the detrimental outcome caused by the use of force should not be ignored in judging the practical legality of the use of force, if one does not want to encourage seemingly legal but definitely counterproductive military intervention. For this reason, it is necessary to make a distinction between a necessary condition for the use of force to be legal and a sufficient condition for that. This point becomes particularly significant when one considers the legal justification for the exceptions to the general prohibition on the use of force.

b. Exceptions to the General Prohibition: Abstract Legality and Practical Legality

As for exceptions to the general prohibition on the use of force, some are explicitly provided in the UN Charter while others are not. According to Chapter VII entitled "Action with Respect to Threats to the Peace, Breaches of the Peace, and Acts of Aggression", it is clear that any use of force shall be of a collective nature, namely on the basis of the decision made by the UN Security Council, and the individual use of force is only an exception in case of self-defense. At such time, the problem of distinguishing a necessary condition and a sufficient condition recurs: is self-defense

[22] See Chap. 1, Sect. 1.2.2.4.

or the decision made by the UN Security Council a necessary condition for the use of force to be legal or a sufficient condition? Considering such problem is actually quite necessary in discussing secessionist conflicts: for instance, when India militarily intervened in the secessionist conflict between Pakistan and Bangladesh, self-defense was the primary legal justification; if the military interventions by Turkey in Cyprus in 1974, by NATO in the Federal Republic of Yugoslavia in 1999 and by the Russian Federation in Georgia in 2008 were on the basis of decisions made by the UN Security Council, how these cases should be judged from a legal point of view remains highly controversial given the disastrous results. That is to say, one needs to consider not only whether the use of force can be regarded as self-defense or the execution of the decision made by the UN Security Council but also practical controversies aroused by the use of force, as such controversies might still exist even when the use of force can be somewhat justified by self-defense or the execution of the decision made by the UN Security Council.

One can first take a look at self-defense, the definition of which is still under debate. Although some writers, such as Brownlie, argue that the right to self-defense provided in Article 51 is limited to cases in which an armed attack has occurred against a State,[23] others maintain that the phrase "inherent right" in this article preserves the pre-Charter customary right.[24] The latter view was shared by the ICJ in the Nicaragua case: "Article 51 of the Charter is only meaningful on the basis that there is a 'natural' or 'inherent' right of self-defense, and it is hard to see how this can be other than of a customary nature, even if its present content has been confirmed and influenced by the Charter".[25] In its advisory opinion on the Legality of the Threat or Use of Nuclear Weapons, the ICJ affirmed this approach and declared some constraints on the exercise of this "inherent right" in addition to those specified in Article 51: "The submission of the exercise of the right of self-defense to the conditions of necessity and proportionality is a rule of customary international law."[26] When Article 51 is understood in the sense of the customary legal right of self-defense, it is difficult to exclude the rescue of nationals abroad.[27] In addition, this exclusion "is made more difficult by the amount of State practice since 1945 in support of military intervention to protect nationals abroad in time of emergency and the failure of courts and political organs of the United Nations to condemn such action".[28] It is also concluded in Oppenheim's International Law as follows: "there has been little disposition on the part of States to deny that intervention properly

---

[23]Brownlie (1981), pp. 272–275.

[24]John R. Dugard, First report on diplomatic protection, A/CN.4/506, 7 March 2000, para. 57.

[25]Military and Paramilitary Activities in and against Nicaragua (Nicaragua v. United States of America). Merits, Judgement. I.C.J. Reports 1986, p. 94, para. 176.

[26]Legality of the Threat or Use of Nuclear Weapons, Advisory Opinion, I.C.J. Reports 1996, p. 245, para. 41.

[27]John R. Dugard, First report on diplomatic protection, A/CN.4/506, 7 March 2000, para. 58.

[28]Ibid.

restricted to the protection of nationals is, in emergencies, justified."[29] The rescue of nationals abroad can be a reason for some states to intervene in secessionist conflicts: for instance, this reason was employed by Belgium as a justification for its military intervention in the Katanga secessionist crisis.

It is noteworthy that despite the amount of State practice since 1945 in support of military intervention to protect nationals abroad in time of emergency and the failure of courts and political organs of the United Nations to condemn such action, states still refuse to recognize the rescue of nationals abroad as an integral part of self-defense in a formal way: in the *first report on diplomatic protection*, a draft article which was to confirm and also to restrict a right to the rescue of nationals abroad,[30] proposed by John Dugard, the Special Rapporteur for the International Law Commission (hereinafter may be referred to as ILC), found no support and was deleted. How should this paradox be understood from the perspective of international law? In the first place, it is necessary to point out that the failure of courts and political organs of the United Nations to condemn the rescue of nationals abroad might not imply a genuine recognition. The issue caused by the rescue of nationals abroad does not necessarily require a judicial settlement as it can be settled in a diplomatic way: in such circumstances, such issue is not referred to a court, and the court fails to condemn the rescue of nationals abroad not because it is legal but because the court does not get the chance to express its opinion. In addition, as discussed in Chap. 2, due to the underdevelopment of international law, on a certain point the stance of international law can be rather ambiguous: the failure of courts to condemn might not because it is legal, but because it is not unambiguously illegal according to international law. That political organs of the United Nations fail to condemn can also partly be attributed to this reason. Apart from the underdevelopment of the legal system, political consideration plays a key role in the failure of political organs of the United Nations to condemn: when members of these organs believe that the condemnation might not be in their own interests, they will abstain from condemning. Moreover, it must be noticed that the most powerful political organ of the United Nations, namely the Security Council, has a relatively exclusive structure: it is highly likely that states intending to condemn such action are not participating in the decision-making process of the Security Council. Therefore, the failure of political organs of the United Nations to condemn the rescue of nationals abroad might have nothing to do with recognition in a legal sense.

In the second place, a formal recognition of the rescue of nationals abroad as an integral part of self-defense might lead to more abuse of this right. Needless to say,

---

[29] Jennings and Watts (1992), p. 440.

[30] This article reads as follows: "The threat or use of force is prohibited as a means of diplomatic protection, except in the case of rescue of nationals where: (a) The protecting State has failed to secure the safety of its nationals by peaceful means; (b) The injuring State is unwilling or unable to secure the safety of the nationals of the protecting State; (c) The nationals of the protecting State are exposed to immediate danger to their persons; (d) The use of force is proportionate in the circumstances of the situation; (e) The use of force is terminated, and the protecting State withdraws its forces, as soon as the nationals are rescued."

the original intention of Dugard is to prevent the abuse of this right: "from a policy perspective it is wiser to recognize the existence of such a right, but to prescribe severe limits, than to ignore its existence, which will permit States to invoke the traditional arguments in support of a broad right of intervention and lead to further abuse."[31] The problem is that there is no reason to believe severe limits can work effectively when the right is formally recognized in codified international law. From the perspective of a customary legal right of self-defense, severe limits are invariably associated with the right; unfortunately, states generally invoke the customary legal right and ignore customary legal limits associated with it, such as necessity and proportionality, although these customary legal limits were emphasized by the ICJ. For this reason, it is certainly overly optimistic to calculate that these limits can work effectively when they are formally introduced into codified international law. As long as the observance of these limits mainly relies on the self-discipline of states claiming a broad right of intervention, and no concrete responsibility is provided when states claiming a broad right of intervention fail to observe these limits, abuse of this right is unlikely to be prevented by introducing this right into codified international law. Although the codification of a customary legal right cannot encourage states claiming this right to observe relevant limits, it can encourage states to justify their intervention on this legal ground. When more and more states exercise a broad right of intervention in disregard of relevant limits, more abuse of this right can be expected. In this sense, the rejection of the draft article aimed at confirming as well as restricting a right to the rescue of nationals abroad is quite understandable or even well-advised.

In the third place, it must be realized that arguing for a broad right of intervention, such as recognizing the rescue of nationals abroad as an integral part of self-defense, actually favors strong states and places weak states at a disadvantage. In the Corfu Chanel case, the ICJ argued that a broad right of intervention was reserved for the most powerful states: the intervening state actually need not be most powerful because being more powerful than the state being intervened will suffice: even when a broad right of intervention is unambiguously confirmed, it is clear that states are still discouraged from exercising this right against states more powerful than themselves, so more often than not this right will be exercised against weaker states which have no advantage in the military confrontation. Obviously, arguing for a broad right of intervention can strengthen practical inequality between states, and strengthening practical inequality goes against legal principles aimed at fostering equality between states. As discussed above, the general prohibition on the use of force interacts with other principles of international law: broadening the right of intervention requires shrinking sovereignty. As noted by Kingsbury, "there is thus a relationship of mutual containment between sovereignty and inequality. The system of sovereignty at least notionally precludes some forms of inequality, while helping to exclude other forms of inequality from real consideration. Conversely, inequality

[31] John R. Dugard, First report on diplomatic protection, A/CN.4/506, 7 March 2000, para. 59.

limits sovereignty."[32] When the problem of increasing practical inequality between states is not effectively addressed, arguing for a broad right of intervention, such as recognizing the rescue of nationals abroad as an integral part of self-defense, is certainly risky. Besides, it is also a problem of maintaining the consistency of the international legal system: in general, self-defense does not weaken principles of international law, so it is allowed to be an exception to the general prohibition on the use of force; nevertheless, when it is interpreted in a way which is likely to weaken principles of international law, the consistency of the international legal system is undoubtedly affected. Therefore, it is wise to reject the draft article proposed by Dugard.

In view of the foregoing, there is no denying that whether the use of force can be regarded as self-defense and whether self-defense is exercised in accordance with international law should be considered as a whole, which embodies the necessity of distinguishing a necessary condition and a sufficient condition: when the abstract legality of self-defense is not confused with the practical legality of its exercising, the nexus between the exception and the prohibition can be better understood. To be more specific, self-defense is a legal justification for the use of force in the abstract sense, but justifying the use of force requires more than the abstract legality, particularly given that self-defense in practice might be exercised in disregard of relevant limits; when self-defense is exercised in disregard of relevant limits, it only possesses the abstract legality which merely fulfills a necessary condition for the use of force to be legal; when self-defense is exercised in accordance with relevant limits, it possesses the practical legality that fulfills the sufficient condition for the use of force to be legal. Meanwhile, when discussing legal justification for the use of force, one needs to take the distinction of power between states into consideration: the legal justification should not help strengthen practical inequality between states, such as creating more chance for powerful states to use force, and it should not go against legal principles that foster equality between states, such as the principle of sovereignty. In fact, this approach can also be applied to the analysis of those justifications for the use of force not explicitly provided in the UN Charter, such as intervention by invitation.

The legality of intervention by invitation was confirmed by the ICJ in the case concerning armed activities on the territory of the Congo: the presence of foreign troops does not violate the general prohibition on the use of force when it goes with consent.[33] Given that the use of force in such circumstances does not seem to go against principles fostering equality between states, the consistency of the international legal system seems to be unaffected. In this sense, intervention by invitation has a certain degree of abstract legality, so it is understandable that it was confirmed by the ICJ. Nevertheless, focusing on the abstract legality is not sufficient in discussing an exception to the general prohibition on the use of force, since the

[32]Kingsbury (1998), p. 602.

[33]Armed Activities on the Territory of the Congo (Democratic Republic of the Congo v. Uganda), Judgment, I.C.J. Reports 2005, paras. 42–53.

practical legality deserves no less consideration: the ICJ carefully analyzed the duration of the consent and concluded that the presence of foreign troops became illegal because the consent was withdrawn.[34] Intervention by invitation can also occur in secessionist conflicts, and the military intervention by Turkey in Cyprus in 1974 seemed to be an example. In this case, the invitation was seemingly treaty-based. In 1960 a set of treaties, which were designed to create an independent Cyprus where the interests of both Greek and Turkish Cypriots would be protected, were concluded between the UK, Greece, Turkey and Cyprus.[35] Article 4 of the Treaty of Guarantee provides:

> In the event of a breach of the provisions of the present Treaty, Greece, Turkey and the United Kingdom undertake to consult together with respect to the representations or measures necessary to ensure observance of those provisions.
>
> In so far as common or concerted action may not prove possible, each of the three guaranteeing Powers reserves the right to take action with the sole aim of re-establishing the state of affairs created by the present Treaty.[36]

Due to the open conflict between the two Cypriot communities, the right to take action was invoked by Turkey to justify its use of force in Cyprus, while the government of Cyprus argued that the consent of Cyprus to the treaty was coerced and the reliance of Turkey on the treaty violated jus cogens norms forbidding forcible intervention in the domestic affairs of a sovereign state.[37] Needless to say, the effect of this treaty is highly debatable. However, attention needs to be focused on this point: whether the consent of Cyprus to the treaty was coerced or not, the military intervention of Turkey could not be justified. When the consent was coerced and the treaty was null and void ab initio, the intervention was illegal due to the reason the government of Cyprus put forward. When the consent was not coerced and the treaty was valid, the intervention was illegal on account of treaty violations: according to Article 4 of the treaty, the action taken by Turkey has to be limited to the sole aim of re-establishing the state of affairs created by the treaty, while assisting the Turkish Cypriots in establishing their own autonomous "state" in northern Cyprus certainly runs counter to this aim. Clearly, if the treaty can be interpreted as providing an implicit right to intervention and relevant limits, Turkey also needed to prove that the practical exercise of the right to intervention was within relevant limits provided in the treaty, in order to justify its use of force in Cyprus. It is undoubted that militarily assisting the Turkish Cypriots in establishing their own autonomous "state" was not in accordance with the treaty.

Now one should take a look at the other explicitly provided exception to the general prohibition on the use of force, that is the collective use of force based on the decision made by the UN Security Council. Is the approach discussed above still

---

[34]Ibid.

[35]Wippman (2000), p. 316.

[36]Treaty of Guarantee, Art. 4, 382 UNTS 3 (1960).

[37]Wippman (2000), pp. 316–317.

applicable here? In order to answer this question, it is necessary to consider whether issues of strengthening inequality between states and disregarding limits on the use of force still exist in such circumstances. Unfortunately, the collective use of force is not immune therefrom. The system of the UN Security Council was designed in a way that focuses on effectiveness, which was indicated in Article 24(1) of the UN Charter: "in order to ensure prompt and effective action by the United Nations, its Members confer on the Security Council primary responsibility for the maintenance of international peace and security, and agree that in carrying out its duties under this responsibility the Security Council acts on their behalf". Undeniably, it is not easy to strike a balance between effectiveness and equality: states not having participated in the decision-making process of the Security Council might therefore have a strong sense of insecurity. As expressed by the Permanent Representative of Algeria with regard to the UN's increasing concern over human rights: "we do not deny that the United Nations has the right and duty to help suffering humanity. But we remain extremely sensitive to any undermining of our sovereignty, not only because sovereignty is our last defense against the rules of an unequal world, but because we are not taking part in the decision making process of the Security Council..."[38] Therefore, a decision made by the UN Security Council is also likely to strengthen inequality between states, and a decision made by the UN Security Council might also be questioned by states from a legal point of view. In fact, Article 24(2) of the UN Charter also provides limits for the Security Council: "in discharging these duties the Security Council shall act in accordance with the Purposes and Principles of the United Nations". However, it still fails to reassure states like Algeria: just like limits on the customary legal right of self-defense, the observance of which mainly relies on self-discipline of states which claim this right, the observance of limits on the action of the Security Council is also largely dependent on self-discipline of the Security Council.

Another thorny issue regarding the collective use of force based on the decision made by the UN Security Council is that such decision is open to various interpretations, so the practical limits on the military intervention authorized by the UN Security Council will inevitably become rather ambiguous. The military intervention in Libya authorized by UN Security Council Resolution 1973(2011) is a case in point. With regard to the interpretation and implementation of this decision, serious doubts were expressed. According to Russia, "the international community is alarmed by statements that compliance with Security Council resolutions on Libya in the NATO interpretation is a model for the future actions of NATO in implementing the responsibility to protect... The demand for a quick ceasefire turned into a full-fledged civil war, the humanitarian, social, economic and military consequences of which transcend Libyan borders. The situation in connection with the no-fly zone has morphed into the bombing of oil refineries, television stations

[38]Abdallah Baali, Permanent Representative of Algeria, Statement to the Informal Thematic Consultations of the General Assembly, to Discuss the Four Clusters Contained in the Secretary-General's Report In Larger Freedom, Cluster III: Freedom to Live in Dignity, 19 April 2005.

and other civilian sites. The arms embargo has morphed into a naval blockade in western Libya, including a blockade of humanitarian goods... These types of models should be excluded from global practices once and for all".[39] Even proponents of the NATO intervention in Libya admitted that "there is some substance in the criticism of NATO overreach with even those most generously inclined having to concede that NATO stretched its mandate to the absolute limit"; an operation conducted on a much more restrained basis would be more desirable "in the interests of giving no excuse to those who were always going to argue that giving the military option an inch would be bound to result in taking a mile and in the interests of preserving the maximum possible chance of consensus for action in the future when the next extreme situation arose".[40] It should be noted that when the decision made by the UN Security Council does not specify limits on the use of force, it does not mean that the military intervention is boundless. The intervenor is obliged to control its action according to the purposes and principles of the United Nations: if the Security Council as the decision maker is obliged to observe the purposes and principles of the UN, as provided in Article 24(2) of the UN Charter, there is no reason to believe that the intervenor authorized by the Security Council can disregard these limits. Of course, apart from the UN Charter, there should be other necessary restraints for the collective use of force, which will be discussed later in the analysis of concrete cases.

In view of the foregoing, it is accurate to say that the same approach can be applied here. The legality of the collective use of force is dependent on making and enforcing decisions: when relevant limits are not observed in making or enforcing decisions, the abstract legality and the practical legality are likely to be separated from each other, so the collective use of force cannot be fully justified. To be more specific, an authorization of the UN Security Council is merely the necessary condition for the use of force to be legal, through which an abstract legality is provided, and in order to justify the use of force, the practical legality dependent on details of making and enforcing UN Security Council decisions is required in addition to the abstract legality. Undoubtedly, this general conclusion will not be changed in terms of external intervention in secessionist conflicts. Based on this, given the practical consequences of the military interventions by Turkey in Cyprus in 1974, by NATO in the Federal Republic of Yugoslavia in 1999 and by the Russian Federation in Georgia in 2008, even if they had been launched on the basis of decisions made by the UN Security Council, they still could not be thoroughly justified from a legal point of view.

[39]United Nations Security Council, 66th year, 6627th meeting, 4 October 2011, S/PV.6627, p. 4.
[40]Evans (2011), p. 10.

4.1.2.2 An Analysis of the Responsibility to Protect

The responsibility to protect as a legal notion was firstly brought forward in the Report of the International Commission on Intervention and State Sovereignty in 2001. Although authors of this report described the responsibility to protect as a new approach,[41] its central idea is certainly not new: "delivering practical protection for ordinary people, at risk of their lives, because their states are unwilling or unable to protect them."[42] This is the central idea of humanitarian intervention which is a controversial concept of natural law, and its history can be traced back to arguments of writers such as Grotius, Gentili and Vattel.[43] Authors of this report declared that "any new approach to intervention on human protection grounds needs to meet at least four basic objectives: to establish clearer rules, procedures and criteria for determining whether, when and how to intervene; to establish the legitimacy of military intervention when necessary and after all other approaches have failed; to ensure that military intervention, when it occurs, is carried out only for the purposes proposed, is effective, and is undertaken with proper concern to minimize the human costs and institutional damage that will result; and to help eliminate, where possible, the causes of conflict while enhancing the prospects for durable and sustainable peace".[44] As a matter of fact, these objectives, to a large extent, can also be found in "conditions that are commonly asserted in the writings of various publicists and by the few States to have exceptionally explicitly referred to a right (whether legal or moral) of humanitarian intervention".[45] Due to this high degree of homogeneity and for the sake of discussion, in the following analysis humanitarian intervention is to be treated as a synonym for responsibility to protect.

a. Intervention but Not Humanitarian

Generally speaking, humanitarian intervention can be divided into two modes, i.e. the individual mode and the collective mode: the former is not authorized by the UN Security Council, while the latter is authorized by the UN Security Council. The individual mode usually gains much less support, compared with the collective mode. In order to understand this point, it is necessary to review comments made by the British Foreign Office regarding humanitarian intervention: "In fact, the best case that can be made in support of humanitarian intervention is that it cannot be said to be unambiguously illegal. To make that case, it is necessary to demonstrate, in particular by reference to Article 1(3) of the UN Charter, which includes the

[41]The Responsibility to Protect: Report of the International Commission on Intervention and State Sovereignty, 2001, p. 11.

[42]Ibid.

[43]Lowe and Tzanakopoulos (2011), para. 4.

[44]See above Note 41.

[45]Lowe and Tzanakopoulos (2011), para. 39.

promotion and encouragement of respect for human rights as one of the Purposes of the United Nations, that paragraphs 7 and 4 of Article 2 do not apply in cases of flagrant violations of human rights. But the overwhelming majority of contemporary legal opinion comes down against the existence of a right of humanitarian intervention, for three main reasons: first, the UN Charter and the corpus of modern international law do not seem specifically to incorporate such a right; secondly, state practice in the past two centuries, and especially since 1945, at best provides only a handful of genuine cases of humanitarian intervention, and, on most assessments, none at all; and finally, on prudential grounds, that the scope of abusing such a right argues strongly against its creation. As Akehurst argues, 'claims by some states that they are entitled to use force to prevent violations of human rights may make other states reluctant to accept legal obligations concerning human rights'. In essence, therefore, the case against making humanitarian intervention an exception to the principle of non-intervention is that its doubtful benefits would be heavily outweighed by its costs in terms of respect for international law. (footnote omitted)"[46]

It seems that the approach adopted by the British Foreign Office here, in terms of humanitarian intervention, is quite similar to the one applied before: not only the abstract legality but also the practical legality is taken into account. The abstract legality is much concerned with the promotion and encouragement of respect for human rights based on the assumption of proponents; with regard to the practical legality, more issues including the incompatibility with contemporary international legal structure, inadequate state practice and abuse of such a right must be considered. Undeniably, these reasons are powerful arguments against humanitarian intervention in an individual mode. Is humanitarian intervention in a collective mode immune from such critical remarks? Given the statement of the Permanent Representative of Algeria cited before, the answer proves to be disappointing. The report of the former UN Secretary-General Kofi Annan entitled "We the peoples: the role of United Nations in the twenty-first Century" also confirmed this point: "some critics were concerned that the concept of 'humanitarian intervention' could become a cover for gratuitous interference in the internal affairs of sovereign states. Other felt that it might encourage secessionist movements deliberately to provoke governments into committing gross violations of human rights in order to trigger external interventions that would aid their course. Still others noted that there is little consistency in the practice of intervention, owing to its inherent difficulties and costs as well as perceived national interests – except that weak states are far more likely to be subjected to it than strong ones. I recognize both the force and the importance of these arguments. I also accept that the principles of sovereignty and non-interference offer vital protection to weak and small states. But to the critics I would pose this question: if humanitarian intervention is, indeed, an unacceptable assault on sovereignty, how should we respond to a Rwanda, to a Srebrenica – to

[46]British Foreign Office (Foreign Policy Document No. 148): British Year Book of International Law, Vol. 57 (1986), p. 619.

gross and systematic violations of human rights that affect every precept of our common humanity?"[47]

It is somewhat curious to see that Annan declared here that the inviolability of sovereignty was the reason for the ineffective response to gross and systematic violations of human rights that affect every precept of our common humanity, because in his autobiography entitled "Interventions: A Life in War and Peace", the reason seemed to be different: when it comes to the ineffective response to the Rwanda tragedy, Annan revealed that "our greatest fear at that moment, given the precarious position of the UN peacekeeping at the time, was for another military disaster to befall a peacekeeping operation leading to significant causalities... in the post-Somalia international climate, there was no appetite in the international community for taking even the slightest risks with the lives of peacekeepers, certainly not in the United States. A small-scale encounter with only a few casualties would have set off a withdrawal by the Security Council and the collapse of yet another peacekeeping mission, perhaps triggering the collapse of the entire peace process."[48]

It is necessary to consider which reason hinders an effective response to gross and systematic violations of human rights that affect every precept of our common humanity, the inviolability of sovereignty or the practical cost suffered by the intervenor. Given that the inviolability of sovereignty failed to stop the military intervention by the NATO in Yugoslavia and this intervention was zero-casualty for their own side, there is reason to believe that the practical cost suffered by the intervenor rather than the inviolability of sovereignty hinders effective responses to humanitarian crises. The military intervention by the NATO in Libya also confirmed that if the humanitarian intervention could be conducted in a way avoiding casualties on the intervenor, potential intervenors would not be deterred. The major problem is, when humanitarian intervention authorized by the UN Security Council is conducted in this way, can it still be referred to as humanitarian intervention? In fact, reducing intervening cost usually leads to huge cost suffered by the intervened side, which is creating additional violations of human rights. In short, the means adopted by an alleged humanitarian intervenor are incompatible with the humanitarian end advocated by it. Yugoslavia refuted the humanitarian nature of the NATO bombing before the ICJ on this basis: "the modalities selected disqualify the mission as a humanitarian one. Bombing the populated areas of Yugoslavia and using high performance ordnance and anti-personnel weapons involve policies completely inimical to humanitarian intervention... The selection of a bombing campaign is disproportionate to the declared aims of the action. Thus, in order to protect one minority in one region, all the other communities in the whole of Yugoslavia are placed at risk of intensive bombing."[49]

[47]UN Doc. A/54/2000, para. 217.

[48]Annan and Mousavizadeh (2012), pp. 53–54.

[49]Legality of Use of Force (Yugoslavia v. USA), ICJ Provisional Measures, Monday 10 May 1999 at 10 a.m., CR 99/14.

Perhaps it is the most noteworthy issue about the right to humanitarian intervention or the responsibility to protect. Needless to say, in order to translate the abstract legality into the practical legality, the means play a pivotal role, otherwise the humanitarian nature of intervention cannot be actually guaranteed. The significance of means selected in achieving humanitarian ends has been confirmed by the ICJ in the Nicaragua case: "while the United States might form its own appraisal of the situation as to respect for human rights in Nicaragua, the use of force could not be the appropriate method to monitor or ensure such respect. With regard to the steps actually taken, the protection of human rights, a strictly humanitarian objective, cannot be compatible with the mining of ports, the destruction of oil installations, or again with the training, arming and equipping of the contras".[50] Unfortunately, the compatibility of the means with the humanitarian end is still largely ignored by (alleged) humanitarian intervenors, as demonstrated in the case of Yugoslavia and Libya. It is necessary to discern why incompatible means are often selected to achieve humanitarian ends. One major reason has already been pointed out: an intervenor is not prepared to suffer high cost such as a relatively high level of casualties, and therefore its intervention can hardly be humanitarian. As indicated by Alex de Waal and Rakiya Omaar: "most modern military forces are equipped for and trained to fight high-technology wars with the aim of securing a quick victory... Humanitarian intervention demands a different set of military skills... They stressed extreme patience, a high level of confidence between troops and people, and a military strategy that was an intrinsic part of an overall political and economic plan... furthermore, it was politically acceptable for intervening forces to sustain a relatively high level of casualties... Radical changes in military doctrine and training will be needed if armies are to carry out humanitarian tasks. But the demands made upon Western armies by politicians and constituents at home for quick fixes and low casualties make the required changes difficult."[51]

In addition, although proponents of humanitarian intervention are inexplicably confident that military coercion will bring about a humanitarian effect, this confidence usually cannot stand the test of the complicated reality: for instance, when the military coercion is too weak, the intended aim of deterring the oppressive regime cannot be achieved; when the military coercion is too strong, the escalation of tension and the collateral civilian damage will be inevitable. It seems that in such a dilemma an (alleged) humanitarian intervenor will choose to replace human rights violations caused by the oppressive regime with human rights violations caused by itself, as demonstrated in the case of Yugoslavia and Libya. Strictly speaking, such replacement is meaningless: the genuine improvement of the humanitarian situation is not dependent on the change of human rights violators, and there is no reason to condone human rights violations simply because violators act in the name of human rights protection. Undoubtedly, "a right to use force on humanitarian grounds can only exist if, in that particular context, there is a military option that can improve the

[50]See Chap. 1, Note 9.

[51]See Chap. 1, Note 29.

humanitarian situation. Where there is no such option, there is no right. Or, if there is a right, it is a right only in the most abstract of senses: the right to do something which cannot be done… in many, perhaps most, conflicts a foreign military intervention offers no realistic prospects of accomplishing any humanitarian objective. In these cases the use of force would be unnecessary (or even counterproductive) – and therefore illegal".[52] Also for this reason, the British Foreign Office declared that "state practice in the past two centuries, and especially since 1945, at best provides only a handful of genuine cases of humanitarian intervention, and, on most assessments, none at all".[53]

Returning to the question posed by Annan, it is clear that something should be done to stop gross and systematic violations of human rights that affect every precept of our common humanity, but his conclusion that implies realizing a humanitarian goal by using force certainly deserves reconsideration: the case of Rwanda has proved that the force required in a real humanitarian crisis is what states generally are unwilling to contribute, while cases of Kosovo and Libya have proved that the force states are willing or even eager to contribute is not required or even detrimental. If one really wants to settle humanitarian crisis by using force, one should focus on not only the gravity of the humanitarian crisis but also whether the crisis can be relieved by military intervention, by what kind of military intervention and who is willing to launch this kind of military intervention. As correctly pointed out by Verdirame: "an issue which is for the lawyers, rather than the strategists, to address is the legal standard that should apply to the question of whether the intended humanitarian objective … can be achieved through the proposed use of force… force should be used only as a last resort. This is sensible. But, particularly where no indication is given that the chances of success in accomplishing the humanitarian objectives have formed part of the assessment of legality, this condition could quite easily be read as endorsing the dangerous logic of 'force is better than nothing'. The absence of a non-forcible alternative cannot alone justify the use of force, in either a legal or a strategic sense. The use of force must, on its own terms, offer at least a credible prospect of providing substantial humanitarian relief."[54] Therefore, it is right to conclude that the greatest obstacle to the idea of humanitarian intervention in international law is not principles such as sovereignty, non-interference in domestic affairs or peaceful settlement of disputes, but the humanitarian aim embodied in itself: in general, it is quite difficult to realize the humanitarian aim by using force, and it does not become easier when the use of force is authorized by the UN Security Council.

That is to say, the focus should be shifted from "intervention" to "humanitarian": the humanitarian aim which is enshrined in a series of UN documents, such as the UN Secretary-General report *We the peoples: the role of United Nations in the twenty-first Century (A/54/2000)*, the report *A More Secure World: Our Shared*

[52] Verdirame (2013).

[53] See above Note 46.

[54] Verdirame (2013).

Responsibility (A/59/565) of the UN High-level Panel on Threats, Challenges and Changes in 2004, the UN Secretary-General report *In Larger Freedom: Towards Development, Security and Human Rights for All* (A/59/2005), the 2005 World Summit Outcome (A/RES/60/1) and the report *Implementing the Responsibility to Protect* (A/63/677) of 2009 should be borne in mind; as for how to realize the humanitarian aim, it is necessary to throw off the yoke of the use of force. "There is an ideal form of such intervention that few would object to: when a governing power is so tyrannous that its crimes can be remedied only by external intervention, and the world community is united in demanding such action. The problem is that few if any cases of military intervention that cite this doctrine come close to the ideal."[55] A governing power might be rather tyrannous, but it is not a reason to believe its crimes can be remedied by external intervention, let alone remedied only by external intervention. Perhaps its crimes can be punished by external intervention, but punishment cannot be equated with a remedy. Confusing punishment with a remedy is actually a very important but usually ignored issue regarding the humanitarian intervention. As noted by Luban, "War is a blunt instrument. Despite easy talk about 'surgical' strikes and 'precision' attacks, the fact is that warmaking wreaks damage across entire towns, cities, and territories. Wars are the equivalent of natural disasters like floods and hurricanes, and even the most discriminate war breaks whatever it touches. Thus, if war is retributive punishment, we must acknowledge that it is collective punishment, indeed collective corporal punishment."[56] In short, external intervention is to punish both the (assumed) tyrannous regime and the people under this regime; because people are actually punished rather than healed in such circumstances, as demonstrated in the case of Libya, perhaps it is more accurate to refer to such external intervention as punitive intervention instead of humanitarian intervention.

It should be noted that proponents of the responsibility to protect do not totally ignore the devastating outcome produced by the military intervention, so the responsibility to rebuild is mentioned: "if military intervention action is taken – because of a breakdown or abdication of a state's own capacity and authority in discharging its 'responsibility to protect' – there should be a genuine commitment to helping to build a durable peace, and promoting good governance and sustainable development... Ensuring sustainable reconstruction and rehabilitation will involve the commitment of sufficient funds and resources and close cooperation with local people, and may mean staying in the country for some period of time after the initial purposes of the intervention have been accomplished."[57] The problem is that proponents seem to have overestimated the willingness and ability of the international community in the cause of rebuilding. It is noteworthy that in the 2005 World Summit Outcome Document, the responsibility to rebuild was omitted from the

[55]See Chap. 1, Note 29.

[56]Luban (2011), p. 36.

[57]The Responsibility to Protect: Report of the International Commission on Intervention and State Sovereignty, 2001, p. 39.

principle of the Responsibility to Protect: the reason seemed to be the creation of the Peacebuilding Commission by Member States, as it provides a framework and mechanism at the UN for addressing rebuilding.[58] Definitely, the reason is not convincing: "why should one (experimental) instrument that would help implement the responsibility to rebuild be the reason for abandoning the much larger, more important norm?"[59]

Albrecht Schnabel has provided more convincing reasons for the omission: "first, focusing on an 'easy way out' by committing to prevention and reaction, resulting in few actual obligations and even less subsequent action, fraught with the usual political squabbling and skillfully ambiguous diplomatic activity, provides a more comfortable approach to embracing R2P. Second, the fear of the tremendous costs attached to a rebuilding commitment – and possibly a failure to fully appreciate the significance of the ability to prevent an escalation and the recurrence of violence – will make the responsibility to rebuild a very hard sell. Third, there might be reasonable worries that a 'rebuilding commitment' could quickly and uncontrollably evolve into applications outside strict R2P contexts (i.e. the prospect or presence of grave humanitarian disasters, mass violence and as a follow-up to prior military intervention) and might thus trigger a great multitude of lengthy post-conflict quagmires."[60]

Given these reasons for the omission of the responsibility to rebuild, it is clear that the cool commitment of the international community to the responsibility to rebuild is much concerned with the devastating outcome produced by the military intervention and the lack of confidence in a quick recovery. The self-interested motive of intervenors is somewhat understandable, but from the perspective of victims of the military intervention, it is rather problematic as it means that victims thereof might have to swallow the pain and loss caused by the so-called humanitarian intervention all by themselves. Thus, the problem regarding humanitarian intervention is more than the lack of practical humanitarian effect, and that the intervenor actually is not effectively bound by definite legal responsibility for the severe damage caused by the intervention is another argument to reject humanitarian intervention. Undoubtedly, when (alleged) humanitarian intervenors are allowed to act without restraint such as definite legal responsibility, one can say that international law is encouraging reckless action: intervenors do not have to carefully think about the consequences of their action, since they are not strictly bound to make up for their mistakes. From this perspective, it becomes clearer why some alleged humanitarian intervenors did not bother to use high performance ordnance and anti-personnel weapons: they know that they do not have to assume any responsibility for the damage caused by using them, no matter how severe the damage might be. Obviously, given that victims

[58] See the official website of the International Coalition for the Responsibility to Protect (ICRtoP), http://www.responsibilitytoprotect.org/index.php/about-rtop/related-themes/2417-pbc-and-rtop, last accessed on 15.06.2018.

[59] Schnabel (2012), p. 57.

[60] Ibid.

generally need to absorb all the damage caused by (alleged) humanitarian intervention, it becomes more necessary to consider pursuing the humanitarian aim without resorting to force.

b. Humanitarian Pursuit Without the Use of Force: Responsibility to Refrain

After negating military intervention, one should consider what can be done to improve the humanitarian situation, particularly given the necessity of avoiding humanitarian crises. The Report of the International Commission on Intervention and State Sovereignty in 2001 also dealt with this topic in the chapter entitled the Responsibility to Prevent. What will be discussed here is different from the responsibility to prevent discussed in this report where external parties are mainly taken as crisis terminator: it is actually more necessary to focus on their identity as crisis contributor. An external party can easily become a crisis contributor, and such possibility is also recognized in this report in a fairly implicit manner: "in zones of potentially catastrophic conflict where external actors have significant interests (and usually more than a few rivalries), coordination of preventive actions can be especially difficult. This provides easy ammunition for indigenous actors to exploit divisions among external players".[61] Perhaps it is not very accurate to take it as exploitation by indigenous actors when external players are eager to be exploited for the sake of their own interests. An external actor can act out of self-interest, which might be rather detrimental to the effective prevention of humanitarian crises; worse still, the self-interested action can be seemingly irreproachable as it is not explicitly illegal according to international law. What France has done to the Rwanda tragedy is a case in point.

Rwanda has long suffered from the power struggle between the ethnic minority Tutsi and the ethnic majority Hutu, and France chose to support the Hutu-dominated government of the President Habyarimana in the civil war between the government and the predominantly Tutsi Rwandese Patriotic Front (RPF). According to Human Rights Watch, for France "backing Rwanda offered the chance not just to outdo Belgium but also to humiliate the Anglo-Saxon forces thought to be behind the largely English-speaking RPF... The French dreaded an upset in Rwanda, which they had come to regard as part of their backyard... In addition to these general considerations, French policymakers also supported Rwanda in order to have a firm base for dealing with potential crises in Zaire... As the Rwandan army expanded from fewer than 10,000 to more than 30,000 soldiers, the French played an important role in training both the combatants and soldiers who would in turn serve as instructors for others... France officially supported peace efforts and was one of the sponsors of the Arusha Accords which stipulated the withdrawal of all foreign troops, except those involved in bilateral military cooperation arrangements... On

[61]The Responsibility to Protect: Report of the International Commission on Intervention and State Sovereignty, 2001, p. 26.

August 26, 1992, three weeks after the first part of the Accords was signed, Ambassador Martres formally agreed with the Rwandan government to expand the limited French military training program to the whole Rwandan army… In February 1993 French authorities once more proved their support by sending more than 500 troops to 'indirectly command' and assist the Rwandan forces in halting the RPF advance. They also stepped up delivery of arms and ammunition, sending up to twenty tons of arms a day, enough to cut into the stocks of the French army itself. After a visit to Rwanda to assess the situation, then Minister of Cooperation Marcel Debarge reported to Mitterrand that the 'indirect military support' provided by France was not enough and that a 'real intervention force' (une véritable force d'interposition) was necessary to enforce the Arusha Accords… French diplomats worked so hard to get a U.N. peacekeeping force to replace its soldiers in aiding their ally that, according to one member of the Security Council, the effort became 'a standing joke'."[62]

In a strict sense, what France has done was not indisputably in violation of international law; nevertheless, this not explicitly illegal action was definitely detrimental to the effective prevention of humanitarian crises, as the military support was conducive to the escalation of the tension between conflicting parties; with the escalation of the tension a humanitarian crisis was increasingly unlikely to be prevented. From this perspective, not only should France be blamed for supporting the government militarily, the external actor that unofficially supported the RPF should also be blamed: both of them were crisis contributors because their military support encouraged both conflicting parties to disobey the Arusha Accords, and by providing military support, they helped aggravate the dreadful humanitarian situation into a humanitarian catastrophe. Therefore, when it comes to the prevention of humanitarian crises, it is quite important for external actors to avoid being crisis contributors. When there are less crisis contributors, the problem of lacking competent crisis terminators will be less worrisome: the demand for crisis terminators depends on the supply of humanitarian crises; when there are fewer crisis contributors, the supply of humanitarian crises is doomed to drop; when there are fewer humanitarian crises, the lack of competent crisis terminators becomes a less thorny issue. Returning to the Rwanda case, ethnic conflicts between Hutus and Tutsis would not have escalated into the catastrophic degree if both the government and the RPF had failed to get military support from the external actors, and more peacekeepers would not have been required if ethnic conflicts had not escalated into the catastrophic degree. Needless to say, a certain degree of military preparation is indispensable for either an escalation of the tension or a humanitarian catastrophe; when conflicting parties are not militarily prepared, either an escalation of the tension or a humanitarian catastrophe lacks the material basis and thus can be avoided. According to Human Rights Watch, "Colonel Rwagafilita, Habyarimana's close associate, told the general who directed French military cooperation in Rwanda

[62]Human Rights Watch, Leave None to Tell the Story: Genocide in Rwanda, Choosing War, https://www.hrw.org/reports/1999/rwanda/Geno1-3-11.htm#P867_332547, last accessed on 15.06.2018.

that the Tutsi 'are very few in number, we will liquidate them'."[63] Obviously, had there been no French military support, they would have been less likely to establish this kind of confidence: the UN peacekeeping operation would have proved to be a formidable obstacle to the liquidation. Perpetrators in the tragedy of Rwanda dared to ignore the UN peacekeeping operation, largely because they obviously outdid peacekeepers in the military sense with the help of France.

Based on this, it is meaningless to require states to take high risks and accept significant causalities for the humanitarian cause while turning a blind eye to the active contribution of some states to humanitarian crises in the meantime. In preventing humanitarian crises, it is not only what external actors should do but also what they should refrain from doing that matters: external parties should not act in a self-interested way which is not explicitly illegal but certainly detrimental to the prevention of humanitarian crisis. Perhaps it can be referred to as the responsibility to refrain. Given that states are still quite reluctant to take high risks and accept significant causalities for the humanitarian cause, arguing for the responsibility to refrain is meaningful: when external actors pay attention to the responsibility to refrain, an escalation of ethnic violence becomes less likely, which certainly helps reduce the likelihood of humanitarian catastrophes. When the number of humanitarian catastrophe drops, states are less likely to be required to take high risks and accept significant causalities for the humanitarian cause. It is in the interests of both the side which is open to humanitarian catastrophes and the side which is required to offer humanitarian protection. One must admit that the reluctance of states which are not crisis contributors to take high risks and to accept significant causalities for the humanitarian cause is quite understandable, from the perspective of state responsibility. According to the theory of state responsibility, a state has to assume the responsibility for an act which is attributable to the state under international law,[64] so such liability is largely based on fault. For states who do not contribute to humanitarian crises, they have reason to doubt whether it is fair to require them to offer humanitarian protection by taking high risks and accepting significant causalities, because it amounts to a no-fault liability. Obviously, if some states could have borne in mind the responsibility to refrain and avoided being crisis contributors, other states would not have to assume the responsibility for acts which cannot be attributed to them.

Also in the sense of state responsibility, the responsibility to refrain proves to be logically more justifiable than the responsibility to protect. Unlike the responsibility to protect, which practically requires states to assume a responsibility for acts which cannot be attributed to them, the responsibility to refrain requires every state to act with a responsible attitude and avoid becoming a crisis contributor. That is to say, the responsibility is directly connected with the act, and a state does not have to take responsibility for the act of another state, particularly when taking this responsibility

[63] Ibid.

[64] ILC Articles on the Responsibility of States for Internationally Wrongful Acts (2001), Articles 1 and 2.

involves high risks and significant casualties. It must be noted that although proponents of humanitarian intervention now prefer to talk of the "responsibility to protect"[65] rather than the "right to intervene", they are not willing to accept the generally accepted concept of responsibility in international law: for them "the core function of the notion of responsibility to protect is to fix a clear set of rules, procedures, and criteria, with whose assistance it can be determined whether the community of States as an organized whole has a responsibility to intervene",[66] and they fail to consider high risks and significant casualties involved in fulfilling the responsibility to protect, and therefore it is not surprising that the force required in a real humanitarian crisis is what states generally are unwilling to contribute, and the force states are willing or even eager to contribute is not required or even detrimental. In order to replace a right which is associated with a high degree of autonomy and self-interest with a responsibility which is associated with self-restraint and self-sacrifice, it is meaningful to require states to refrain from doing a disservice to the improvement of humanitarian situation in the first place, not only because it is easier to exercise self-restraint than self-sacrifice including taking high risks and accepting significant casualties, but also because when every state refrains from doing a disservice to the improvement of the humanitarian situation, there will be less humanitarian crises, and thus such self-sacrifice is less likely to be required.

Moreover, arguing for a responsibility to refrain is also an effective way to prevent a conflicting party from exploiting external intervention. One should think about the worry mentioned in the Secretary-General report of Annan that secessionists can be encouraged to deliberately provoke governments into committing gross violations of human rights in order to trigger external interventions that will aid their course,[67] the judgment of General Lewis Mackenzie that the Muslim-led "Bosnia Presidency was committed to coercing the international community into intervening militarily"[68] and the revelation by Bosnia's Muslim president Alija Izetbegovic that their tactics were to buy time for the pursuit of a zig-zag line for independence and let the international community play the role as their defender.[69] Obviously, in order to cut down the supply of humanitarian crisis, secessionists must be discouraged from deliberately provoking governments into committing gross violations of human rights, and the responsibility to refrain can play a key role for this sake: self-restraint exercised by external actors in secessionist conflicts can help reduce the possibility that external involvement might be maliciously exploited by a conflicting party. Returning to the Bosnian case, the Muslim-led Bosnia presidency would not have been committed to coercing the international community into intervening militarily, if external actors had been well-known for their self-restraint in

[65] The Responsibility to Protect: Report of the International Commission on Intervention and State Sovereignty, 2001, p. 11.

[66] Winkelmann (2010).

[67] UN Doc. A/54/2000, para. 217.

[68] See above Note 15.

[69] See above Note 6.

secessionist conflicts. After all, for external actors participating in an internal conflict, the point is not being active but being constructive,[70] and active but destructive external involvement is definitely not as good as the exercise of self-restraint. It is accurate to refer to external interventions which can be exploited by secessionists to aid their course as destructive because external interventions like this actually boost the supply of humanitarian crises in such circumstances. Stressing the responsibility to refrain, in appearance, is to prevent a conflicting party from exploiting external intervention while in essence, is to reduce the supply of humanitarian crises. When external actors can help reduce the supply of humanitarian crises, it is more meaningful than peacekeeping efforts in actual humanitarian crises: prevention is better than cure, so it is better to stop humanitarian crises from happening than to deal with them after they have happened.

Therefore, it is definitely well-advised to pay more attention to the idea of the responsibility to refrain: external actors should not only focus on the "set of rules, procedures, and criteria, with whose assistance it can be determined whether the community of States as an organized whole has a responsibility to intervene"[71] but also focus on their acts which are conducive to the escalation of conflicts that can render humanitarian crises more likely to occur. There is no reason to condone the disservice done by some states in preventing humanitarian crises while requiring the international community to take high risks and accept significant casualties in dealing with such crises, otherwise the supply of humanitarian crises cannot be reduced when such disservice is condoned, and states who did not contribute to humanitarian crises but are required to assume the costly humanitarian responsibility will always think that it is unfair on them and thus be reluctant. Stressing the responsibility to refrain helps eliminate the disservice done by some states in preventing humanitarian crises, and the supply of humanitarian crises can therefore be reduced, which is in the interests of not only victims of potential humanitarian crises but also the international community which is not truly ready to assume the costly humanitarian responsibility. If at that time France and other external actors had refrained from interfering in the ethnic power struggle in Rwanda in such an active manner, the tragedy of Rwanda could have been avoided or at least the UN peacekeeping operation could have proved to be relatively adequate to respond to the ethnic conflict. In order to realize the responsibility to refrain, it seems also necessary to establish a set of rules, procedures, and criteria, with whose assistance it can be determined whether external actors have contributed to the escalation of an internal conflict, which might lead to a humanitarian crisis. Otherwise it is inevitable to require states who did not contribute to humanitarian crises to assume the costly humanitarian responsibility, despite their reluctance and the lack of the solid legal basis for such a requirement.

[70]United Nations Security Council, 66th year, 6627th meeting, 4 October 2011, S/PV.6627, pp. 3 and 5.

[71]See above Note 66.

It is noteworthy that, compared with the responsibility to protect, the responsibility to refrain is more compatible with the UN Charter and the corpus of modern international law. Obviously, the respect for the legal principle of non-interference in domestic affairs is embodied in the responsibility to refrain. In fact, not only this principle, other principles such as non-use of force and peaceful settlement of disputes are also respected. It must be realized that respecting these legal principles in dealing with secessionist conflicts helps much in improving humanitarian situations: as discussed above, the aggravation of humanitarian situations has much to do with the escalation of secessionist conflicts, and the escalation of conflicts can largely be avoided if both conflicting parties can relinquish the use of force and stick to the peaceful settlement of their conflicts. For this sake, external actors should refrain from doing a disservice that can escalate conflicts, such as what France has done in the case of Rwanda. Undeniably, applying legal principles of international law such as non-use of force and peaceful settlement of disputes and requiring external actors to exercise self-restraint supplement each other in addressing secessionist conflicts, which also renders the responsibility to refrain more desirable than the responsibility to protect, as a means to realize the humanitarian pursuit. Ensuring the consistency of the international legal system should be considered in dealing with secessionist conflicts and pursuing humanitarian values.

Of course, it is also necessary to point out that in order to achieve the humanitarian aim, the responsibility to refrain is only a necessary condition but not a sufficient one: as mentioned above, both what external parties should do and what they should refrain from doing are of great importance in improving humanitarian situation. When external actors do something they should refrain from doing, which is detrimental to the pursuit of the humanitarian aim, a responsibility to refrain should be argued. Similarly, a responsibility to act should be argued when external actors fail to do what they should do, which also amounts to a disservice to the pursuit of the humanitarian aim. Of course, the responsibility to act cannot be mistaken for humanitarian intervention in the sense discussed above: as analyzed before, the humanitarian effect of this kind of intervention is, to a large extent, nothing more than wishful thinking. External involvement required for the humanitarian sake should be effective in practice. What kind of external involvement will be effective in practice? Such involvement has much to do with positive interplay between internal actors and external actors involved in a conflict: positive interplay means not only that external involvement should not contribute to the escalation of the conflict but also that external actors can help in offering an ultimate solution to the conflict. In terms of secessionist conflicts, positive interplay between internal actors and external actors means not only that external involvement will no longer be exploited by secessionists in their struggle against non-secessionists but also a positive contribution made by external actors to the settlement of the secessionist conflict. A typical case of positive interplay between internal parties and external parties has already been mentioned before: in the case of Aceh, external involvement did not contribute to the escalation of the conflict and the external actors did contribute noticeably to the settlement of the secessionist conflict. Further discussion about positive interplay between internal actors and external actors involved in secessionist conflicts will be found later, which focuses on escaping the vicious circle of the use of force.

4.1.2.3 The Legal Judgment by the Independent International Commission on Kosovo

a. Legality or Legitimacy

The legal judgment made by the Independent International Commission on Kosovo on the use of force by the NATO reads as follows: "the NATO military intervention was illegal but legitimate. It was illegal because it did not receive prior approval from the United Nations Security Council. However, the Commission considers that the intervention was justified because all diplomatic avenues had been exhausted and because the intervention had the effect of liberating the majority population of Kosovo from a long period of oppression under Serbian rule."[72] Before analyzing reasons provided by the commission, it is necessary to say something about the paradoxical saying "illegal but legitimate". Generally speaking, illegal and illegitimate are closely connected with each other, just like legitimate and legal, so "illegal but legitimate" seems rather confusing. Nevertheless, for a Continental European scholar, it is not a problem: "illegal" refers to existing international law whereas "legitimate" is an extra-legal judgment which refers to policy or morals. Although the problem in such circumstances seems to be solved, another issue resulting from such understanding needs to be addressed: one should follow international law or follow morals? Obviously, when one is to follow international law, one must refrain from such an act because it is illegal; when one is to follow morals, one is actually encouraged to act in this way because it is justified from this perspective. As one cannot be required to refrain from an act and encouraged to act at the same time, it is impossible to require one to follow both international law and morals in such circumstances. A choice must be made: one should either follow international law and violate morals or follow morals and violate international law. The NATO has allegedly chosen the latter, so the use of force was "illegal but legitimate". Therefore, the major question here seems to be which combination constitutes a better choice: legal but illegitimate, that is following international law and violating morals, or illegal but legitimate, that is following morals and violating international law. Can one get out of this dilemma? In fact, one need not consider this issue in this case as the dilemma is a fake one: reasons provided for legitimacy are insufficient, and even the commission has recognized this point to a certain degree.

According to the commission, the legitimacy of the NATO military intervention emanated from the exhausting of peaceful alternatives and the liberation of Kosovo Albanians from oppression under Serbian rule. Before analyzing these legitimate

[72] The Independent International Commission on Kosovo, The Kosovo Report, Oxford University Press, 2000, p. 4.

justifications, it is necessary to quote another conclusion from the same report: "the legitimacy of such use of force will always be controversial, and will remain so, so long as we intervene to protect some people's lives but not others".[73] Although it is inexplicable why the Independent Commission Report on Kosovo still insisted that the NATO military intervention was illegal but legitimate while recognizing the controversy over the legitimacy of such use of force, there is no denying that a third perspective should be added to legitimate justifications mentioned above, that is indiscriminate humanitarian protection. This perspective is quite understandable, given that the NATO bombing in Yugoslavia did cause severe human rights violations.[74] Because the NATO air strike against Yugoslavia protected Kosovo secessionists but caused many casualties of Serbian civilians, the legitimacy of the use of force in this regard simply did not exist: it is hard to conclude that killing and injuring Serbian civilians can be morally justified; from a moral point of view, Serbian civilians deserve no less protection than Kosovo secessionists; sacrificing Serbian civilians for the sake of protecting Kosovo secessionists can only be justified when the double standard is widely and formally recognized. It should be noted that ignoring indiscriminate humanitarian protection is not only untenable from a moral point of view but also in violation of human rights law: according to the Universal Declaration of Human Rights, the entitlement to rights and freedoms is without distinction of any kind,[75] so the discriminatory protection itself concerns violation of human rights law rather than merely a controversy over legitimacy. Perhaps the Independent Commission has its own understanding of indiscriminate protection, which can explain why the intervention to protect some people's lives but not others is legitimately controversial rather than illegal, but the Independent Commission should have made this point in a convincing manner.

[73]Ibid. p. 298.

[74]For instance, Brownlie pointed out that there was "the use of very powerful modern weapons in urban areas, the offensive generally against the economy of a whole country, and the use of cluster bombs. Many civilians were killed or maimed, hospitals were damaged and internal refugee flows induced", see Brownlie and Apperley (2000), p. 910.

[75]The first three articles of the Universal Declaration of Human Rights:

Article 1

All human beings are born free and equal in dignity and rights. They are endowed with reason and conscience and should act towards one another in a spirit of brotherhood.

Article 2

Everyone is entitled to all the rights and freedoms set forth in this Declaration, without distinction of any kind, such as race, colour, sex, language, religion, political or other opinion, national or social origin, property, birth or other status.

Furthermore, no distinction shall be made on the basis of the political, jurisdictional or international status of the country or territory to which a person belongs, whether it be independent, trust, non-self-governing or under any other limitation of sovereignty.

Article 3

Everyone has the right to life, liberty and security of person.

As for the exhaustion of peaceful alternatives, can one say that the exhaustion of peaceful avenues be a sufficient reason for the use of force? Given what has been discussed above, the answer is negative: the exhaustion of peaceful avenues is a necessary reason for the use of force but not a sufficient one, and only when the use of force can achieve the end which cannot be achieved by peaceful avenues can the reason for the use of force be deemed sufficient, so when there is no reason to believe that the use of force can make it, it is still unjustified to use force even when all peaceful revenues have been exhausted. Did the use of force achieve the intended aim? If the intended aim was to cause numerous human rights violations, the NATO military intervention definitely made it, given that the intervention not only caused numerous human rights violations but also the serious sequelae: according to Human Rights Watch, "immediately following NATO's arrival in Kosovo, there was widespread and systematic burning and looting of homes belonging to Serbs, Roma, and other minorities and the destruction of Orthodox churches and monasteries. This destruction was combined with harassment and intimidation designed to force people from their homes and communities. By late-2000 more than 210,000 Serbs had fled the province; most of them left in the first six weeks of the NATO deployment. Most seriously, as many as one thousand Serbs and Roma have been murdered or have gone missing since June 12, 1999."[76] If the intended aim is to improve the humanitarian situation, it is hard to conclude that the NATO intervention has made a better contribution than peaceful means in this regard. When the use of force cannot contribute more than peaceful means, the exhaustion of peaceful means fails to become a sufficient reason to use force: that peaceful means do not work well is not a proof that force is certainly better. If the Independent Commission intended to demonstrate the legitimacy of the NATO military intervention, stressing the exhaustion of peaceful alternatives is certainly not enough, and it needed to stress the positive contribution of the intervention to the improvement of the humanitarian situation. The exhaustion of peaceful alternatives itself cannot prove the effectiveness of the use of force from the perspective of morals or policy: the use of force can be justified not solely because all diplomatic avenues have been exhausted, but because it does improve the humanitarian situation. The Independent Commission seemed to have confused the necessary reason with the sufficient reason.

Another noteworthy issue is that the exhaustion of peaceful means can be attributed to different reasons: sometimes it is the fault of the external intervenor. When the exhaustion of peaceful means is the fault of the intervenor, whether the exhaustion of peaceful means should be regarded as a necessary reason for the use of force certainly requires reconsideration. As will be further discussed in the case study, the exhaustion of peaceful means can largely be attributed to the fault of the NATO states; to some extent it seemed to be the result deliberately pursued by the U. S.-led NATO. For instance, one of the prominent American diplomats involved in the Rambouillet conference, Ambassador Christopher Hill, informed the Washington Post that the US representatives knew that there was a "zero point

[76]See Chap. 3, Note 88.

zero" chance that Serbs would agree to what they were offered at Rambouillet; another participant at Rambouillet even told the press off the record that "we intentionally set the bar too high for the Serbs to comply", which was corroborated by a curious statement the U.S. Secretary of State Madeleine Albright made in an interview to the New York Times: according to Albright, Rambouillet was the key to "getting [the Europeans] to agree to the use of force".[77] Obviously, if such exhaustion of peaceful means can be condoned, upholding principles such as peaceful settlement of disputes, international cooperation and good faith is simply out of the question. In short, the exhaustion of peaceful means might result from the deliberate pursuit by an intervenor, which is suspected of violating international legal principles. This issue deserves serious consideration, given that it is necessary to prevent a potential intervenor from sabotaging the chance of peaceful settlement. Because the exhaustion of peaceful means as the legal ground for the use of force is actually open to manipulation, and an intervenor tends to exploit this ground, it is quite problematic to regard the exhaustion of peaceful means as a necessary condition for the use of force, let alone as a sufficient condition.

Then one should consider whether the liberation of Kosovo Albanians from oppression under Serbian rule provides legitimacy for using force. In the first place, it is rather ill-advised for an independent commission to talk like an advocate of the Kosovo Liberation Army, as it is highly likely to raise doubts about the neutrality of the independent commission. The independent commission could have adopted more neutral expressions, such as protecting Kosovo Albanians from humanitarian catastrophes, which sound definitely more legitimate than the one-sided "liberation". From a point of morals or policy, it is difficult to argue that liberation gains a higher degree of acceptance than protecting ethnic minorities from humanitarian catastrophes within the international community. The degree of acceptance should not be ignored when discussing a justification from a point of morals or policy. When a certain moral orientation is not widely accepted, legitimacy based on which is open to challenge. In the second place, the formulation "liberating the majority population of Kosovo from a long period of oppression under Serbian rule" seems to imply that oppression resulted only from the Serbian rule but not from the secessionist entity: as recorded by Human Rights Watch, the Kosovo Liberation Army was also responsible for severe human rights violations, including abductions and murders of Serbs and ethnic Albanians considered collaborators with the state.[78] In the third place, it is clear that the liberation of secessionists has not been generally accepted as an international moral rule: even in the Kosovo case, Western officials repeatedly declared that NATO would not be the "air force of the KLA".[79] Even if the independent commission intended to establish a new moral rule, it needed to offer convincing argument rather than directly took the liberation of secessionists as a self-evident moral rule. Therefore, the liberation of Kosovo secessionists from

[77]Grigorian (2006), p. 52.
[78]See Chap. 3, Note 88.
[79]Kuperman (2008), Note 57.

oppression under Serbian rule failed to justify the use of force by the NATO from a point of morals or policy.

In view of the foregoing, the dilemma between illegality and legitimacy actually did not exist in the case of Kosovo: the use of force by the NATO was illegal and illegitimate, which did not only violate international law but also cannot be well justified from a point of morals and policy. In this case, the separation between law and morals did not lead to real inconsistency between them: as a matter of fact, the inconsistency between international law and morals, or positive law and natural law, is seriously exaggerated here. Positive international law actually does not prevent good deeds of external actors but it does prevent alleged good deeds. Some argue that the emphasis on general principles such as sovereignty and the ban on the use of force will frustrate volunteers who want to contribute to humanitarian operation,[80] based on what has been discussed above, this worry is largely unfounded: genuine volunteers who can really improve the humanitarian situation, as were required in the case of Rwanda, are scarce, while unwanted volunteers who can only make things worse, such as the NATO in the case of Kosovo, need to be frustrated by general principles of international law, and the issue that unwanted trouble makers cannot be effectively frustrated by international law is actually something worth worrying.

b. The Pursuit of Consistency Between Legality and Legitimacy

To some extent, it is accurate to say that the prevention of alleged good but actually harmful deeds is an important theme through the evolution of international law from the stage of natural law to the stage of positive law: the prototype of humanitarian intervention can be traced back to the idea of just war, which includes a wide range of just causes for waging wars, and as natural law was gradually replaced by positive law, the range of just causes shrank. Grotius, who is deemed the one having laid the foundation of the Westphalian system, generally limited just causes to self-defense, the protection of property and the punishment of offenders in the second book of his work entitled De Jure Belli ac Pacis. It is particularly noteworthy that from the work of Grotius one can realize that even for naturalists, just cause is merely a necessary condition instead of a sufficient condition for the use of force: "we must proceed to correct an error, in order to prevent any one from thinking that, where a right has been adequately established, either war should be waged forthwith, or even that war is permissible in all cases. On the contrary it frequently happens that it is more upright and just to abandon one's right. That we may honourably neglect the care of our own lives in order that, to the best of our ability, we may safeguard the life and eternal salvation of another… This fact of itself much the more urges us not to follow up our own interests, or what may be due to us, so far as to cause others the suffering that wars bring with them. That war is not to be undertaken for every just

[80]Henkin (1999), p. 10.

cause is the advice of Aristotle and of Polybius".[81] It seems that even naturalists at that time also admitted that an alleged good or just deed might not be a genuinely good or just deed, and from a point of morals or policy, even if there is a right to intervene, it is still more desirable not to exercise it. Obviously, this idea should be regarded as the natural legal basis for the general prohibition on the use of force embodied in positive law. In this sense, it can be argued that not only humanitarian intervention but also opposition to humanitarian intervention has a moral basis. It is a pity that proponents of humanitarian intervention in the case of Kosovo somehow ignored this moral basis on which the opinion opposing humanitarian intervention was established.

Therefore, the violation of the general prohibition on the use of force is violating not only positive law but also its moral basis. From this perspective, illegality will invariably be associated with illegitimacy. In order to deal with this issue, proponents of humanitarian intervention should endeavor to address inconsistency between different moral grounds rather than consciously ignore the moral basis against humanitarian intervention. A selective promotion of morals is unconvincing, and the conclusion from a selective promotion of morals is inevitably open to challenge. Worse still, the selective promotion of morals will render the dilemma between legality and legitimacy more common: when the moral basis for the general prohibition on the use of force is ignored and the moral basis for humanitarian intervention is overly emphasized, the separation and inconsistency between legality and legitimacy becomes a salient issue. If one refuses to ignore the moral basis for the general prohibition on the use of force, the separation and inconsistency between legality and legitimacy will be replaced by consistency. It must be admitted that the pursuit of consistency between legality and legitimacy is of great importance, otherwise upholding positive international law will be quite difficult. Obviously, if states invariably violate positive law in the name of pursuing legitimacy, it will be unrealistic to expect that the current legal system can function effectively. The current legal system will also seem redundant, as morals or policy almost takes its place: states might resort to positive rules only when morals or policy does not serve their own interests. Is such interplay between positive law and natural law, or law and morals worth pursuing?

Perhaps this is the most thought-provoking issue arising out of the conclusion made by the independent commission that the NATO bombing was illegal but legitimate. What kind of interplay between the positive prohibition on the use of force and moral speculations is worth pursuing? To refer to humanitarian intervention as a moral speculation is proper in essence: as discussed above, so far the humanitarian effect of such intervention has not been really demonstrated because the objective consequence of such intervention cannot be deemed humanitarian despite any humanitarian intention, so referring to humanitarian intervention as a moral speculation is suitable. In order to answer this question, it is necessary to review that the Group of 77 and China "reject the so-called 'right' of humanitarian

[81] Grotius (1964), p. 567.

intervention, which has no legal basis in the United Nations Charter or in the general principles of international law".[82] It is particularly noteworthy that at the same time these states "further stress the need for scrupulously respecting the guiding principles of humanitarian assistance, adopted by the General Assembly in its resolution 46/182, and emphasize that these principles are valid, time-tested and must continue to be fully observed… humanitarian assistance should be conducted in full respect of the sovereignty, territorial integrity, and political independence of host countries, and should be initiated in response to a request or with the approval of these States".[83] The guiding principles of humanitarian assistance adopted by the General Assembly in its resolution 46/182 was characterized by humanity, neutrality and impartiality. According to the stance of the Group of 77 and China, the humanitarian pursuit is worth affirming, but it is necessary to make this pursuit in accordance with positive rules, so the interplay between law and morals in the case of Kosovo is not worth pursuing: the positive prohibition on the use of force should not simply be outweighed by a moral speculation, and one must render the moral pursuit compatible with positive rules. This is how the consistency between legality and legitimacy should be pursued from the viewpoint of the Group of 77 and China.

In fact, not only the Group of 77 and China think this way. In the report *Implementing the Responsibility to Protect* of the UN Secretary-General, a similar idea can be found: "as demonstrated by the successful bilateral, regional and global efforts to avoid further bloodshed in early 2008 following the disputed election in Kenya, if the international community acts early enough, the choice need not be a stark one between doing nothing or using force. A reasoned, calibrated and timely response could involve any of the broad range of tools available to the United Nations and its partners. These would include pacific measures under Chapter VI of the Charter, coercive ones under Chapter VII and/or collaboration with regional and subregional arrangements under Chapter VIII. The process of determining the best course of action, as well as of implementing it, must fully respect the provisions, principles and purposes of the Charter. In accordance with the Charter, measures under Chapter VII must be authorized by the Security Council".[84] Undeniably, this idea discouraged humanitarian pursuit which is incompatible with positive provisions. In other words, the pursuit of legitimacy should not be at the expense of legality. Is such interplay between positive law and natural law, or law and morals more desirable?

Undoubtedly, a better balance between law and morals can be struck in such circumstances: "illegal but legitimate" should be replaced by "legal and legitimate"; the consistency between law and morals should be pursued, for the sake of not only upholding positive international law but also realizing humanitarian values. It must be admitted that the fundamental divergence between proponents and opponents of

[82]Declaration of The South Summit, para. 54, http://www.g77.org/summit/Declaration_G77Summit.htm, last accessed on 15.06.2018.

[83]Ibid.

[84]UN Doc. A/63/677, p. 9.

humanitarian intervention lies in "intervention" but not "humanitarian": positivists definitely have no reason to oppose the humanitarian pursuit, but they have sufficient reason to oppose the use of force in the name of humanitarian pursuit; if proponents of humanitarian intervention can separate humanitarian pursuit and the use of force, they will find themselves confronted by less opposition. If proponents of humanitarian intervention nowadays can learn from their precursor Grotius, who believed that it is more upright and just to abandon one's right to wage a war, they will not easily lead themselves into the dilemma between legality and legitimacy. The inconsistency between law and morals here is not because law refuses to recognize moral values but because law refuses to recognize certain means of pursuing moral values. Such refusal is definitely necessary: numerous facts have proved that military intervention as a means in practice has nothing to contribute to the humanitarian cause, and proponents of humanitarian intervention cannot deny this point if they do not choose to ignore human rights violations caused by alleged humanitarian intervention. In short, both positive law and natural law, or law and morals have enshrined humanitarian values, and their major divergence is that law has excluded certain means of pursuing humanitarian values while morals have not. It is clear that ignoring this exclusion provided by positive rules is violating international law, but it is hard to conclude that pursuing humanitarian values in accordance with positive legal restrictions will violate morals: natural law or morals do not exclude war as a means of realizing humanitarian aims, but it does not mean that natural law or morals have a preference for military means, so it is accurate to say that as long as humanitarian aims can be achieved, applying peaceful means instead of military means is also in accordance with natural law or morals. Just war definitely does not mean only war is just, and no war is unjust. Therefore, the inconsistency between law and morals argued by proponents of humanitarian intervention is misleadingly exaggerated, and a better balance between law and morals can be struck when the pursuit of humanitarian values is in compliance with positive legal restrictions: in such circumstances, the dilemma created by proponents of humanitarian intervention between legality and legitimacy no longer exists as both law and morals can be followed at the same time.

The interplay between positive law and natural law can also be understood from the perspective of abstract legality and practical legality discussed before. Undeniably, the dilemma between law and ethics created by proponents of humanitarian intervention also lies in the confusion between abstract legality and practical legality. Deontological ethics are generally associated with abstract legality: the use of force can be deemed justified when it is (allegedly) motivated by humanitarian concerns, but whether the use of force can really help improve the humanitarian situation, or whether it will create additional human rights violations in practice, seems to be somewhat ignored by deontological ethics. From this perspective, it is no wonder that the NATO bombing could be deemed legitimate by the independent commission despite practical damage caused thereby. As demonstrated before, abstract legality alone is no more than a necessary condition for the use of force, and what really counts is practical legality, namely the practical improvement in the humanitarian situation resulting from the military intervention. Because such improvement is hardly found, proponents of humanitarian intervention actually lack sufficient grounds to justify the use of force. A real dilemma between the legal requirement of refraining from the use of force and the moral requirement of using force to improve humanitarian situation can only exist when the intervention actually improves the humanitarian situation, and when there is no such improvement, there exists no real dilemma between law and morals. Proponents of humanitarian intervention assume that there would be such a dilemma, partly because they fail to distinguish between abstract legality and practical legality: the moral speculation that the military intervention can improve the humanitarian situation is mistaken for the practical outcome, which is another reason why the inconsistency between law and ethics has been exaggerated. When the moral speculation is not mistaken for the practical outcome, the interplay between positive law and natural law regarding the use of force certainly becomes more harmonious.

To conclude, it is erroneous to judge the use of force in the name of humanitarian pursuit as illegal but legitimate: in the first place, upholding positive international law becomes more difficult in such circumstances, as it seems to allow violations of positive rules in the name of pursuing legitimacy; in the second place, it largely ignores the moral basis of positive rules against the use of force and leads to a selective promotion of morals; in the third place, it fails to contribute to a constructive interplay between law and morals and misleadingly exaggerates the inconsistency between law and morals.

4.1.3 Escaping the Vicious Circle of the Use of Force

After discussing the internal use of force and external use of force separately, it is necessary to look at the interplay between them. As mentioned repeatedly above, between the internal use of force and external use of force there is a high degree of interplay, the complexity of which sometimes is beyond imagination. Unfortunately, such complexity is more often than not underestimated, and therefore the external use of force, despite good intention, hardly leads to a good outcome. The external use of force in secessionist conflicts is no exception: it is repeatedly witnessed that the external use of force, whilst motivated by humanitarian concerns, has itself led to numerous human rights violations and failed to provide a lasting solution to such conflicts. It must be admitted that the failure of the external use of force can largely be attributed to the complex interplay between the external use of force and internal use of force; to be more specific, the external use of force is likely to trigger a vicious circle of violence, which will inevitably do a disservice to the improvement in the humanitarian situation.

In the first place how the external use of force can trigger a vicious circle of violence needs to be explained. Such vicious circle of violence is not rare in secessionist conflicts: as noted by Tomuschat, confrontations between secessionists and non-secessionist often "end up in a vicious circle of violence and counter-violence".[85] As for what triggers the vicious circle, Tomuschat did not give a clear answer; but he pointed out that "the threat to start a secessionist movement will normally increase the repression suffered by the population concerned".[86] Therefore, it can be said that both the threat to start a secessionist movement and the increase of repression constitute the basis for the vicious circle of violence. Following this logic, it is clear that the vicious circle is largely triggered by the threat to start a secessionist movement: when there is no such threat, repression is less likely to be increased, so the confrontation is less likely to translate into the vicious circle of violence. Thus, it is necessary to consider this problem: why do secessionists take the strategy of threatening to start a secessionist movement? In order to understand this issue, one also needs to consider why secessionists do not take this strategy earlier.

According to statements of Kosovan secessionists, one can have some clues to this issue. Led by Ibrahim Rugova and his Democratic League of Kosovo (LDK), Kosovan secessionists, despite declaring themselves independent from Serbia and establishing their own parallel government institutions, did not take up arms to establish sovereignty; such passive resistance did not give rise to the intensification of the conflict between secessionists and non-secessionists; nevertheless, it must be realized that they also wanted to use force but refrained from doing so because they were intimidated by the military superiority of the parent state: Mehmet Kraja, the LDK cofounder, revealed that they were not peaceful but they thought that it was impossible for them to defeat Yugoslavian government forces; Rugova himself said that they were not certain how strong the Serbian military presence in the province actually was, but they did know that it was overwhelming and they had nothing to set against the tanks and other modern weaponry in Serbian hands.[87] Therefore, it is accurate to say that "the threat that states are ready and willing to use massive force to crush insurgent movements would usually prevent the latter from resorting to violence".[88] However, such equilibrium is changed by the possibility of external force against the government which used to have a deterrent effect on secessionists. The final outcome of the Croatian and Bosnian struggles for independence, where Serbia had been defeated with the help of external actors, created for Kosovan secessionists an impression that they had to take up arms in order to make the international community care about their cause.[89] For this reason, the passive resistance was replaced by violent movement. Emrush Xhemajli, a top KLA commander, confirmed: "When we took the decision to start the war in 1993 . . . we thought it was essential to get international support to win the war. You could not stand against the world . . . we thought that with the international community on our side, we could win the war. But otherwise we would plan for a 10- to 15-year war,

[85] See Chap. 3, Note 143.

[86] Ibid.

[87] Kuperman (2008), pp. 65 and 68.

[88] Janik (2013), p. 57.

[89] Ibid.

with a strategy to get the international community on our side."[90] Of course, these secessionists did not forget the price they had to pay for getting international support. The Albanian negotiator at Rambouillet, Dugi Gorani, admitted that "every single Albanian realized that the more civilians die, intervention comes nearer... The more civilians were killed, the chances of international intervention became bigger, and the KLA of course realized that. There was this foreign diplomat who once told me 'Look unless you pass the quota of five thousand deaths you'll never have anybody permanently present in Kosovo from the foreign diplomacy'."[91] Compared with statements made by Bosnian representatives cited before, one can notice the striking similarity of strategies adopted by secessionists. It seems that the remark made by General Mackenzie, the first commander of UN peacekeepers in Bosnia, could also be applied to Kosovo: secessionists were committed to coercing the international community into intervening militarily.

Thus, the external use of force does not only trigger the vicious circle of violence but also strengthens it: originally, it was an internal war, and it acquires the color of international armed conflict when external actors are militarily involved. In such circumstances, one must consider this issue: how can the external use of force aimed at improving the humanitarian situation avoid morphing into something which is against this aim? Needless to say, triggering and strengthening the vicious circle of violence is aggravating the humanitarian situation, and settling such issue requires improving the interplay between the external actors and the conflicting parties, the core of which is to escape the vicious circle of the use of force. Therefore, it is necessary to discourage secessionists from taking arms: as demonstrated above, the passive resistance of secessionists will not lead to a murderous secessionist war. How can secessionists be discouraged from taking arms? It is time to consider restoring the equilibrium which is changed by the possibility of external force against the government which used to have a deterrent effect on secessionists. For instance, the external actors should consider taking measures against violent secessionists. Timothy Crawford argued that the NATO should have "tried to deter both the Serbs and the KLA from escalating, and to push them toward a compromise solution"[92]; to be more specific, the NATO should have "tried to make two credible yet contradictory threats — to intervene if Belgrade escalated the heavy-handed repression in Kosovo, and to abandon and isolate the KLA if it continued to provoke Serb retaliation and oppose a negotiated solution".[93] According to Timothy Crawford, "NATO did not take feasible measures to restrain the KLA as it stepped up the pressure on Belgrade at the end of 1998. This failure is the key reason why the October cease-fire broke down in January, a crucial turning point on the path to war

[90] Kuperman (2008), p. 69.

[91] Allan Little, "Moral Combat: NATO At War", A BBC2 special, 9pm Sunday 12 March 2000, http://news.bbc.co.uk/hi/english/static/events/panorama/transcripts/transcript_12_03_00.txt, last accessed on 15.06.2018.

[92] Crawford (2001/2002), p. 501.

[93] Ibid. p. 503.

two months later".[94] One should ask whether the threat to abandon and isolate the KLA could be convincing when the threat to intervene was there. As a matter of fact, it is nearly an impossible task: abandoning the KLA and intervention cannot exist at the same time; abandoning the KLA means restoring the equilibrium which can deter secessionists from pursuing violence, while intervention means changing the equilibrium; a choice must be made from these two options, as in practice one cannot restore and change something at the same time.

Therefore, in order to discourage secessionists from taking arms, it is necessary to restore the equilibrium and let secessionists be deterred by the military superiority of non-secessionists. In fact, external actors in the case of Aceh followed this doctrine: contrary to the belief of leaders of the Free Aceh Movement that internationalization of the conflict would constrain Indonesia's freedom to conduct military oppression and facilitate Aceh's independence, international actors made clear that the price of their involvement was secessionists' agreement to a peace deal that kept Aceh within Indonesia.[95] That is to say, "two credible yet contradictory threats" suggested by Timothy Crawford is unnecessary, a credible threat against secessionists is enough for avoiding the escalation of secessionist conflicts. After all, when secessionists can be deterred by the military superiority of non-secessionists, they will choose the peaceful means, as expected by the international community, to pursue their political aim, which is in accordance with humanitarian values pursued by international law. It cannot be denied that international law never sees the pursuit of independence superior to humanitarian values. Even according to proponents of humanitarian intervention, the pursuit of independence is not superior to humanitarian values: the pursuit of independence is actually the pursuit of sovereignty; if non-secessionists are not allowed to uphold sovereignty at the expense of humanitarian values, there is no reason to allow secessionists to pursue sovereignty at the expense of humanitarian values. In the same vein, if external actors believe that they have the right to intervene against a government, in order to safeguard humanitarian values, they should not deny that the government also has the right to crush a secessionist movement and prevent a full-scale secessionist war which would involve more deaths and suffering. According to Kuperman, "by autumn 1998, Serbia's counter-insurgency had virtually eliminated the rebels' ability to launch attacks, while inflicting relatively few civilian casualties. But when U.S. Ambassador Richard Holbrooke threatened NATO air strikes—compelling Serbian forces to cease fire and retreat—the rebels were able to regroup, reoccupy abandoned territory, and further escalate the war".[96] This conclusion coincided with the statement of Agim Ceku, the KLA's eventual military leader: "the cease-fire was very useful for us, it helped us to get organized, to consolidate and grow. We aimed

[94]See above Note 92.

[95]See Chap. 3, Note 92.

[96]Kuperman (2008), p. 71.

to spread our units over as much territory as possible. We wanted KLA units and cells across the whole of Kosovo".[97]

In view of the foregoing, it is ill-advised to change the equilibrium between secessionists and the government on behalf of non-secessionists by the external use of force, as a vicious circle of violence can be triggered thereby. For the humanitarian sake, it is necessary to escape the vicious circle of violence: as mentioned above, when secessionists do not take up arms, the secessionist conflict will be less likely to escalate into an internal and international armed conflict which can cause numerous human right violations of both secessionists and non-secessionists. Although international law does not clearly prohibit secessionists from taking up arms, given its devastating consequences and the importance of maintaining international peace and security, one must consider preventing secessionists from taking up arms: a Pandora's Box is opened when secessionists switch from pacifism to rebellion. As the external use of force largely contributes to this switch, it is reasonable for external parties to consider renouncing the use of force in secessionist disputes. At such time one might question how the government can be deterred from severely violating human rights of secessionists when there is no humanitarian intervention. In order to answer this question, one should not forget the fact that when Kosovo secessionists passively resisted the authorities, they did not suffer from severe human rights violations. Humanitarian crises generally occur in the background of fierce confrontation: cases mentioned above such as Bosnia, Aceh and Rwanda are all associated with such background. When such background does not exist, a government is unlikely to use excessive force against secessionists: as discussed before, under contemporary international law sovereign states are discouraged from causing numerous human rights violations, not only because they are bound by human rights law, but also because they do not want to be placed under international pressure; conversely, secessionists dare not provoke the government into creating human rights violations, not only because their obligation to respect human rights is indefinite, but also because they want to exploit international pressure on the government to achieve their political aim. Therefore, it is safe to conclude that rather than worry about the excessive use of force by the government against secessionists, one should first worry about the secessionist rebellion which can lead to a vicious circle of violence.

It must be realized that renouncing the external use of force is easier said than done: as mentioned in the report *Implementing the Responsibility to Protect* of the UN Secretary-General, when the international community fails to act early enough, the choice seems to be a stark one between doing nothing and using force.[98] That is also why General Mackenzie said that the international community was coerced into intervening militarily.[99] For this reason, it seems that the viability of renouncing the external use of force actually has much to do with the choice being left. The

[97] See above Note 91.

[98] UN Doc. A/63/677, p. 9.

[99] See above Note 15.

Secretary-General believed that an early action could lead to a better choice, and this judgment is definitely correct, but solely focusing on early action is insufficient because early inaction is equally important. As discussed in the responsibility to refrain, humanitarian crises can largely be attributed to problematic actions of external actors, the illegality of which might not be indisputably confirmed while the damage of which to the settlement of the underlying issue is evident, so requiring external actors to refrain from such actions is quite important in preventing humanitarian crises. The case of Kosovo is no exception: as mentioned above, if U.S. Ambassador Richard Holbrooke had not threatened Yugoslavia with NATO air strikes and compelled Serbian forces to cease fire and retreat, the rebels would not have been able to regroup, reoccupy abandoned territory and further escalate the war, and thus a large amount of civilian casualties could have been avoided. Therefore, solely stressing early action might not be really helpful, given that it can be a redundant disservice which renders conflict settlement more difficult, and in such circumstances, the choice is actually made by external actors to be a stark one between doing nothing and using force. Therefore, it is quite meaningful to stress the importance of inaction: external actors should consciously refrain from doing a disservice, which is also a contribution to the settlement of conflicts. When external actors can refrain from doing a disservice, secessionist conflicts are less likely to escalate, so the international community will not face the stark choice between doing nothing and using force in pursuing humanitarian values. Only in this way can the external use of force be really renounced.

To conclude, for the sake of escaping the vicious circle of the use of force, it is necessary to renounce the external use of force which tends to change the equilibrium discouraging secessionists from taking up arms to intensify the conflict, and for the sake of renouncing the external use of force, it is necessary to stress the inaction of external actors, given that counterproductive action can aggravate the situation and eventually make the choice for the international community limited between doing nothing and using force. In other words, escaping the vicious circle of the use of force in secessionist conflicts largely depends on constructive inaction of external actors, and any action that contributes to the choice limited between doing nothing and using force should be avoided. It is really difficult to resist the dangerous logic that force is better than nothing when the choice seems to be limited between them, although force is actually not better than nothing. That is also why humanitarian intervention, despite being not humanitarian in practice, is still advocated by its proponents. External actors can play a more positive role in escaping the vicious circle of the use of force when they can realize the importance of refraining from counterproductive actions.

The following discussion is centered on four cases regarding the use of force in secessionist conflicts, through which one can get a more explicit picture of how the external use of force influenced secessionist conflicts and how counterproductive external involvement contributed to the vicious circle of the use of force. Lessons drawn from these cases will help external actors avoid acting counterproductively in secessionist conflicts and render the interplay between external actors and conflicting parties more positive.

4.2 Cases Regarding the Use of Force in Secessionist Conflicts

4.2.1 Katanga

The case of Katanga is quite noteworthy because in this case the UN fought directly against the secessionist entity: the military intervention was carried out by the UN force in the Congo in order to implement Security Council resolutions. In the history of the UN such action is rare: as mentioned in the Kosovo Advisory Opinion, the standard practice of the UN, to be more specific, of the UN Security Council, against unilateral secession is to condemn its illegality[100] rather than rectify this illegality directly through military intervention. Besides, this case has raised several problems concerning the use of force, which deserve serious consideration even in this day and age.

In 1960 the Congo obtained independence from Belgium. Soon after its independence came the violent secessionist movement of Katanga. Moise Tshombe, the premier of the province of Katanga, called for Belgian troops to intervene in the province. Soon after the Belgian intervention Katanga formally declared independence. The leaders of the central government appealed to the UN for military assistance to counter the intervention of Belgium,[101] and the Security Council adopted a resolution which called upon the government of Belgium to withdraw its troops and authorized the Secretary-General to take the necessary steps to provide the Congolese government with military and technical assistance until the national security force might be able to fully meet their tasks.[102] According to the Secretary-General Dag Hammarskjöld, the participation of the UN in the Congo should be understood in this manner: "the United Nations units must not become parties in internal conflicts, that they cannot be used to enforce any specific political solution of pending problems or to influence the political balance decisive to such a solution."[103]

Later the situation got more complicated as the leaders of the central government also appealed to the Soviet Union for military intervention.[104] Such possibility of intervention was precluded by another resolution, in which the call upon Belgium to withdraw its troops was reaffirmed and all states were requested to refrain from any action that might tend to impede the restoration of law and order in the country or undermine its territorial integrity and political independence.[105] Meanwhile,

---

[100]Accordance with International Law of the Unilateral Declaration of Independence in Respect of Kosovo, Advisory Opinion, I.C.J. Reports 2010, para. 81.

[101]U.N. Doc. S/4382 (1960), O.R., 15th year, Supp. July–Sept. 1960, p. 11.

[102]S/RES/143 (1960).

[103]First Report by the Secretary-General on the Implementation of Security Council Resolution S/4387 of 14 July 1960, S/4389, p. 5.

[104]Buchheit (1978), p. 145.

[105]S/RES/145 (1960).

Tshombe opposed the UN intervention, and Hammarskjöld replied that such resistance would lead to legal consequences laid down in the Charter.[106] It should be noted that, even in this situation, Hammarskjöld did not forget the principle of non-intervention in internal affairs: "the entry of these military elements does not represent any interference in the internal affairs of the Republic of the Congo, including its provinces, or impede or modify in any way the free exercise of rights to act, in legal and democratic forms, in favour of one or another solution of such constitutional problems as may in due time arise for the Congolese people."[107] Even Belgian expressed a similar stance: "Belgian troops were obliged to intervene solely in order to save the lives of fellow-countrymen who were in a great danger, lacking any of the protection which a State must afford to private individuals. This intervention implies no interference in the internal affairs of the Congo... The Belgian Government is grateful to the United Nations for having undertaken speedily and effectively a mission of public welfare."[108]

Hammarskjöld managed to reach an agreement with Tshombe for the entry of UN troops into Katanga on certain conditions.[109] Obviously, this was not the intervention that the central government of the Congo had expected: "the actions and attitudes of the United Nations, and in particular of its Secretary-General, came under severe criticism from the Prime Minister of the Congo".[110] In response to this criticism, Hammarskjöld restated that "the ultimate purpose of the United Nations services to the Republic of the Congo is to protect international peace and security, and that, to the extent that the difficulties facing the Republic are not of a nature to endanger international peace, they are not of our concern."[111] The central government of the Congo pointed out: "there were official negotiations between the United Nations representative and this puppet of the Belgians and their allies who were under orders to carry out in Katanga the plan of aggression directed by the Belgian Government against the Republic of the Congo... We cannot accept this because we are convinced that no nation in the world can accept further domination once it has won back its independence. If the Council's resolutions were to continue to be wrongly interpreted, they would lead not to the complete liberation of the Congo but to the effective reconquest of our country".[112]

The situation got more eventful, as the new born Republic of the Congo experienced a constitutional crisis and the Prime Minister Lumumba got assassinated in

[106] Second Report by the Secretary-General on the Implementation of Security Council Resolutions S/4387 of 14 July 1960 and S/4405 of 22 July 1960, S/4417, para. 6.

[107] Ibid.

[108] Ibid. para. 5.

[109] United Nations Security Council Official Records, 887th Meeting, 21 August 1960, S/PV.887, paras. 68–69.

[110] Ibid. para. 8.

[111] Ibid. para. 11.

[112] Ibid. para. 70.

February 1961.[113] Katanga itself suffered the secession of North Katanga during January 1961.[114] In the wake of Lumumba's death the Security Council adopted resolution 161 which aimed to prevent the occurrence of civil war in the Congo: "[the Security Council] urges that measures be taken for the immediate withdrawal and evacuation from Congo of all Belgian and other foreign military and paramilitary personnel and political advisers not under the United Nations Command, and mercenaries".[115] The second resolution regarding the Congo in this year marked a radical shift from non-interference to anti-secession: one of the purposes of the UN with respect to the Congo is to "maintain the territorial integrity and the political independence of the Republic of the Congo."[116] This new approach was concluded in the report of the UN Secretary-General U Thant in this way: "the United Nations has avoided any intervention in the internal politics of the country beyond the opposition to secession in general required by the Security Council resolutions..."[117]

In the case of Katanga, force was used by four parties: the central government of the Congo, secessionist entity of Katanga, foreign troops mainly of Belgium and UN troops. The legality of the use of force by the central government to cope with the situation has been affirmed by S/RES/143 (1960). The illegality of the use of force by Belgium has not been directly affirmed in the several resolutions mentioned above, but Belgium was repeatedly required to withdraw its force out of the territory of the Congo, despite the cause Belgium had offered for its use of force, that is the rescue of nationals abroad. As discussed before,[118] the rescue of nationals abroad is not generally recognized as an exception to the general prohibition on the use of force, so Belgium could not justify its use of force on this basis. Moreover, the military action of Belgium was definitely inconsistent with other principles and purposes of the UN Charter, as it served as a military obstacle for the central government of the Congo to exercise sovereignty over Katanga. Belgium could have avoided such result, for instance, it could have withdrawn its troops with nationals rescued within a reasonable period. More importantly, given its explanation that its military action implied no interference in the internal affairs of the Congo, Belgium should have assumed the obligation to avoid any exploitation of its intervention by the secessionist entity, otherwise such an explanation would certainly be unconvincing. Therefore, it was quite reasonable for the central government of the Congo to believe that what happened in Katanga was an aggression directed by the Belgian Government against the Republic of the Congo: Belgium was certainly aware of the fact that its military presence in Katanga could be

[113] Buchheit (1978), p. 149.

[114] Ibid.

[115] S/RES/161 (1961), para. 2.

[116] S/RES/169 (1961).

[117] Report by the Secretary-General on the Implementation of the Security Council Resolutions of 14 July 1960, 21 February and 24 November 1961, S/5240, para. 37.

[118] See b. in Sect. 4.1.2.1 of this chapter, pp. 169 – 173.

exploited by secessionists, thus intensifying the conflict between the provincial authorities and the central authorities, but Belgium did not bother to avoid these problems. Compared to the relentless effort made by Hammarskjöld not to be a party in internal conflicts, the partiality of Belgium in the internal conflict of the Congo was evident. Thus, there was no denying that the use of force by Belgium violated the principle of non-interference in internal affairs, which also cannot be justified by the rescue of nationals abroad. Based on this, it can be said that the secessionist conflict escalated as the principle of non-interference in internal affairs was violated.

For the sake of conflict settlement, the UN should have required Belgium to cease interference in internal affairs of the Congo and facilitate negotiation between secessionists and the central government: the former formed the basis for the latter, given that secessionists largely relied on external involvement to rebel against the central government. Unfortunately, the performance of the UN was far from being satisfying. The fundamental problem of the UN action lied in the fact that it did not effectively stop the interference of Belgium; conversely, the UN was somewhat exploited as a cover for the interference of Belgium, thus further complicating the conflict. To be specific, although Belgium gave "the formal assurance of the Belgian Government of completion of the withdrawal of all combat troops within, at the most, eight days",[119] it was considered by Hammarskjöld that "some delay in the evacuation from Kamina and Kitona of non-combat personnel should not be attributed to Belgian resistance to the move, but results from the responsibility, which will now be that of the United Nations, of assisting the country in the maintenance of the substantial Congolese population so fully dependent on the bases for the security of their work and income".[120] Clearly, it was highly problematic to let Belgium perform the responsibility of the United Nations in this case, given that at the outset Belgium appeared as an intervention maker with partiality for the secessionist entity in the Congo crisis. There was no guarantee that Belgium would abstain from such partiality when performing the UN task in the Congo. Worse still, interference favoring the secessionist entity was camouflaged with the UN task, so it became less noticeable. No wonder the central government of the Congo strongly protested against this arrangement and argued that it "had no other aim than to allow Belgian military personnel and civilians to disguise themselves as United Nations troops without being discovered."[121] Relevant evidence was also found: in Leopoldville at least seventy Belgian paratroopers wearing the uniform, arm-band and beret of the United Nations were arrested, as they were from the Belgian Sabena Airline, aircraft of which had endangered the internal security of the Republic by bringing insulting

[119] United Nations Security Council Official Records, 887th Meeting, 21 August 1960, S/PV.887, para. 29.

[120] Ibid.

[121] S/PV.887, para. 86.

and provocative pamphlets from Brussels.[122] Besides, so-called Belgian volunteers were still sent to train the militia of Tshombe.[123]

It must be admitted that in order to deescalate a secessionist conflict, external actors including the UN should attempt to gain the trust of conflicting parties. Obviously, the success of a UN mission is highly dependent on the understanding of parties involved. Hammarskjöld was definitely aware of it, and therefore he had negotiation with Tshombe, leader of Katanga province. It was quite confusing that when he decided to allow Belgium to participate in the UN mission in the Congo, he did not consult with the central government of the Congo. Undoubtedly, this would impair the trust of the central government of the Congo in the UN mission. When there was a lack of consultation and the chance of making objections, it was no wonder that "the actions and attitudes of the United Nations, and in particular of its Secretary-General, came under severe criticism from the Prime Minister of the Congo".[124] As an external actor, Belgium itself should have refrained from taking part in the UN mission, given its special relationship with both sides in the secessionist crisis and the fact that so-called Belgian volunteers were still training the militia of the secessionist entity. Because Belgium could not gain the trust of the central government and was regarded as an enemy, it was quite inexplicable that Belgium could be involved in the UN mission which was aimed at settling the secessionist conflict. Hammarskjöld should have made an arrangement that could gain the trust of not only the secessionist entity but also the central government, for the sake of conflict settlement.

Another notable issue regarding the UN action lies in the request made by the Congo government to suppress the secessionist movement aided by Belgium. Hammarskjöld rejected this request and insisted that the secessionist struggle was only a problem of the Congo but not a problem of the UN[125]; nevertheless, as the crisis kept aggravating, the attitude of the Security Council changed, and in S/RES/169 (1961) a different approach was adopted, that is meeting the request of the Congo government and fighting against secessionists. It was particularly noteworthy that U Thant, the successor of Hammarskjöld, stressed in his report that "the principle of non-interference in the internal political affairs of the Congo... has been observed and the United Nations has scrupulously avoided any support for or opposition to any Congolese official or candidate, whether in the national or provincial governments... the United Nations has never used the arms at its disposal to further the political aims of any group or individual in the country, or to interfere with its political processes. Even with regard to secession, civil war and the elimination of mercenaries, the employment of the Force has been in the most limited manner, with limited objectives, without the Force itself taking any military

[122] S/PV.887, para. 88.
[123] S/PV.887, para. 94.
[124] See above Note 110.
[125] UN Doc. S/4389, p. 5 and S/4417, para. 6.

initiatives, and only then as a last resort".[126] According to this report, it is clear that the approval of the UN Security Council alone is insufficient to justify the external use of force in a secessionist conflict: even when there exists a Security Council approval on the external use of force, its legality is still subject to the compliance with general principles such as non-interference in internal affairs and other relevant limits. Otherwise there is no need for U Thant to emphasize the principle of non-interference in internal affairs and other limits on the use of force which was already approved by the Security Council. A few years later, in the report entitled *Respect for Human Rights in Armed Conflicts,* U Thant repeated that the United Nations forces in the Congo were required to "observe the principles and spirit of the general international conventions applicable to the conduct of military personnel"[127]; meanwhile he implied the practical difficulty of complying with humanitarian law: "since in United Nations peace-keeping forces the responsibility for the training and discipline of troops has thus far rested with each national contingent rather than with the Organization, it is suggested that improved legal protection of human rights in such operations is likely to come from wider acceptance and application of the humanitarian conventions by contributing States than it is from having the United Nations undertake obligations whose discharge would involve the exercise of an authority it has not yet been granted".[128] On this basis, it is accurate to say that external actors must also strive to observe general principles such as non-interference in internal affairs and requirements of humanitarian law, even when they are allowed to use force in dealing with secessionist crises.

Perhaps the most important inspiration from the case of Katanga regarding the external use of force is that a comprehensive approach was adopted: compared with the judgment made by the independent commission on the NATO bombing in Yugoslavia, which simply focused on the lack of Security Council approval, the Secretary-General definitely took a much more comprehensive perspective in judging the legality of the UN force in the Congo. According to U Thant, the Security Council approval of using force should not be regarded as a license to ignore general principles such as non-interference in internal affairs, and it was necessary to consider relevant limits on the use of force stipulated in humanitarian law, although it was not easy to observe such limits in practice. From the perspective of conflict settlement and humanitarian protection, it must be admitted that the comprehensive approach adopted by the Secretary-General is more sensible than the simple approach by the independent commission. Obviously, if the legality of the use of force concerns only the Security Council approval but not the practical outcome, legal but counterproductive use of force will be encouraged. This question should not be overlooked as such use of force should also be condemned rather than condoned: there is no reason to condone the use of force authorized by the Security Council, when it is detrimental to the settlement of the conflict and human rights

[126]UN Doc. S/5240, paras. 37 and 38.

[127]UN Doc. A/7720, para. 9.

[128]Ibid. para. 114.

protection. As mentioned above, the use of force by Turkey in Cyprus in 1974, by the NATO in the Federal Republic of Yugoslavia in 1999 and by the Russian Federation in Georgia in 2008 were unwanted not only because they were not authorized by the Security Council, but also because they created additional human rights violations and failed to provide a lasting solution to the secessionist conflicts. Therefore, the comprehensive approach adopted by U Thant is still of great significance in judging the legality of the use of force by external actors in this day and age: Security Council approval is not everything, and one should not overlook general principles and humanitarian rules. In other words, the Security Council approval is the necessary condition for the legal use of force, and confusing this necessary condition with the sufficient condition is something which should be avoided.

4.2.2 Bangladesh

The case of Bangladesh is especially noteworthy because it is a rare case of successful secession against the will of the parent state and mainly dependent on an external military intervention. In discussing this case one can discern how geopolitics can influence the outcome of a secessionist conflict under the cover of international law, particularly with the help of the exception to the general prohibition on the use of force. For this reason, it seems quite meaningful to consider how the negative influence of geopolitics can be eliminated in applying international law to secessionist conflicts.

The partition of the independent India in 1947 left the Muslim state of Pakistan in a position of being itself a divided country: West Pakistan and East Pakistan (Bangladesh) were separated geographically by thousands of kilometers of Indian territory, and this distance existed not only geographically but also historically, socially, linguistically and culturally; unfortunately, these disparities kept growing during the early years of independence due to economic and political factors; after General Ayub resigned, General Yahya became president, and the state gradually returned to civilian rule; a general election on the principle of one man one vote was planned to elect a constituent assembly, which was intended to have 300 seats; due to the proportion of population, 162 seats would be elected in East Pakistan and 138 in West; Mujib's Awami League, an East Pakistan nationalist organization, had won 160 out of 162 seats, and the winner in West Pakistan was Bhutto's Pakistan's People's Party.[129]

The election did not dispel the shadow cast on the political future of Pakistan: Mujib won his overwhelming victory on the basis of the "Six Points", which demanded a federal government so weak that it was tantamount to an acknowledgement of the secession of East Pakistan, and this idea was not shared by Bhutto; due to

[129]Sisson and Rose (1990), pp. 8–34; Buchheit (1978), pp. 199–203.

the fundamental divergence between the East and the West, the National Assembly was indefinitely postponed, which triggered an immediate hostile reaction in East Pakistan, and the Yahya government started to increase the strength of armed force in the East; there were negotiations between Yahya, Bhutto, and Mujib, which remained unfruitful; on the night of March 25th, 1971, the armed forces of West Pakistan launched attack to suppress the secessionist tendencies of the East; President Yahya gave several reasons for this military action, including treason, creation of turmoil, terror and insecurity, which could be attributed to Mujib and his Awami League.[130]

Militarily, the East was no match for the West, but India was right behind the East, and this state was powerful enough to overcome the West. Early in the war India had allowed East Pakistan guerrillas to use Indian territory as a safe haven, and later India supported secessionists more actively by providing arms and ammunition to the secessionists; due to the increasing amount of refugees from East Pakistan flowing into India and more frequent border clashes, an open warfare between India and Pakistan broke out,[131] and India granted recognition to Bangladesh without any hesitation. The military victory of India served to secure the independence of Bangladesh from Pakistan.

The role of the UN in the Bangladesh case was inactive and unproductive. The Security Council gave a reason for its inactivity in S/RES/303(1971), that is the lack of unanimity of its permanent members, and decided to refer the question to the General Assembly. The General Assembly issued a resolution requiring an immediate ceasefire and withdrawal of armed forces of both sides from each other's territory.[132] India refused to accept it[133] and argued in the meeting of the Security Council that "we have a clear and formal understanding with the Government of Bangla Desh that the armed forces of India shall remain in Bangla Desh only as long as the people and Government of Bangla Desh require and welcome their presence. The alternative to those arrangements would have been chaos and repression in East Bengal and a misinterpretation of our intentions by interested parties... India would be willing to discuss any cease-fire or withdrawal which would ensure the freedom and aspirations of the people of Bangla Desh, and which would ensure the vacation of aggression by Pakistani troops from Indian territory".[134] In addition, the Indian representative expressed that "international law recognizes that where a mother State has irrevocably lost the allegiance of such a large section of its people as represented by Bangla Desh and cannot bring them under its sway, conditions are suitable for that section to come into being as a separate state".[135] The Pakistani representative

---

[130]Sisson and Rose (1990), pp. 111–133 and 154–156; Buchheit (1978), pp. 203–206.

[131]Sisson and Rose (1990), pp. 206–215.

[132]A/RES/2793 (XXVI).

[133]United Nations Security Council Official Records, 1611th Meeting, 12 December 1971, S/PV. 1611, para. 16.

[134]Ibid. paras. 100 and 128.

[135]Ibid. para. 124.

refuted: "let us accept the fact that there is such a theory of the mother State, that if a part of the mother State wants to release itself from the mother, it must find its own conditions for freedom. I accept that position, although I do not find authentic or reliable evidence for the mother State concept or theory that has been propounded by the Indian Foreign Minister. But if there is such a concept, who is the mother and who is the child? The mother is East Pakistan and the child is West Pakistan, because it is in East Pakistan that the majority of our people live. Fifty-six per cent of our people live in East Pakistan and the rest live in West Pakistan. The mother naturally must be the 56 per cent and not the 44 per cent".[136]

Only when the Pakistani Army surrendered in Bangladesh did the Indian government express the intention to end the conflict.[137] The Security Council was then able to issue a resolution which "demands a durable cease-fire and cessation of all hostilities in all areas of conflicts be strictly observed and remain in effect until withdrawals take place, as soon as practicable, of all armed forces to their respective territories and positions which fully respect the cease-fire line".[138] According to the phrase of this resolution, it seemed that India did not have to withdraw its army immediately. The final success of secession was marked by the formal recognition granted by Pakistan, and soon after that Bangladesh was admitted into the UN.

There were three parties using force in this case: Pakistan, Bangladesh and India. Unlike the case of Katanga, resolutions of the Security Council did not shed much light on the Bangladesh case, so the discussion here is largely based on general international law. First one should have a look at the internal use of force between conflicting parties, to which following perspectives of international law are related: non-interference in internal affairs, self-determination and human rights protection in armed conflicts. Clearly, from the perspective of non-interference in internal affairs, the conclusion can be very simple: the internal use of force cannot be scrutinized according to international law. From the perspective of self-determination or human rights protection in armed conflicts, discussion about the internal use of force will become very lengthy, and the conclusion might be quite indefinite. For this reason, it seems well-advised to discuss the internal use of force from the perspective of non-interference in internal affairs and avoid discussing it from perspectives of self-determination and human rights protection in armed conflicts. Nevertheless, given the practical outcome of the secessionist war in Bangladesh, such mono-perspective consideration is not viable: the huge number of refugees flowing beyond the border created by the secessionist war inevitably added an international color to the internal conflict; the settlement of the secessionist conflict required a balance of conflicting claims to self-determination; overlooking human rights protection in an armed conflict was not only detrimental to the settlement of the conflict, but also cast a shadow on international peace and security.

[136] Ibid. para. 185.

[137] United Nations Security Council Official Records, 1616th Meeting, 16 December 1971, S/PV. 1616, para. 5.

[138] S/RES/307(1971).

Therefore, when it comes to the internal use of force, solely focusing on one perspective of international law, such as non-interference in internal affairs, does not help settle the practical issue, and the practical complexity of secessionist conflicts such as the case of Bangladesh invariably requires a multi-perspective consideration.

Needless to say, a multi-perspective analysis means more than discussing the internal use of force from different perspectives of international law: the interplay between conflicting parties and the external actors should also be included. Undeniably, the contribution of India to the escalation of the secessionist conflict between West Pakistan and East Pakistan can never be underestimated: military training and other forms of assistance were offered by India for secessionists in East Pakistan; had there not been such strong support of India, whether East Pakistan guerrillas could have survived the military attack launched by the Pakistani Army was certainly questionable.[139] How should the contribution of India to the escalation of the secessionist conflict be evaluated according to international law? From the stance of Pakistan, it was certainly illegal as the principle of non-interference in internal affairs was violated; nevertheless, one could also argue that violation of self-determination could not be considered as something within internal affairs: India implied this idea by arguing that international law recognized secessionist self-determination to some extent.[140] This seems to be a dilemma but actually it is not that complex: the principle of non-interference in internal affairs is actually consistent with the promotion of self-determination, particularly in self-determination conflicts; even if international law recognized secessionist self-determination to some extent, it did not mean that international law refused to recognize non-secessionist self-determination; in order to promote conflicting claims of self-determination, non-interference in internal affairs is actually a necessary choice because interference favoring one side will inevitably hinder the pursuit of self-determination by the other side. Thus, India actually violated non- secessionist self-determination by interfering in internal affairs of Pakistan. Given that the secessionist conflict actually escalated into a humanitarian crisis, India should be criticized for not only violating non-interference in internal affairs and non-secessionist self-determination but also for contributing to humanitarian crisis. Therefore, the international community should have forced India to cease its illegal interference, for the sake of not only upholding international legal rules but also settling the conflict. Had there not been the interference of India, the escalation of the self-determination conflict between secessionists and non-secessionists could have been avoided, and thus the aggravation of the humanitarian situation was also less likely to occur.

Speaking of the aggravation of the humanitarian situation, one should note that India justified its use of force in Bangladesh with a humanitarian excuse: India refused to withdraw its troops out of East Pakistan by arguing that it would have led to chaos and repression in East Bengal and endangered the freedom and aspirations

[139]See above Note 131.

[140]See above Note 135.

of the people of Bangladesh.[141] It must be admitted that the justification offered by India did not sound very convincing. Firstly, if India did care about chaos and repression in East Bengal, it should not have contributed to chaos and repression in East Bengal by training, arming and harboring militant secessionists; secondly, it was wrong to conclude that the freedom and aspirations of secessionists were the freedom and aspirations of the people of Bangladesh: Biharis living in Bangladesh stood by the Pakistan army against secession, and the pro-secessionist intervention made by India was against their freedom and aspirations. Of course, there is no denying that the normal order in East Pakistan should be ensured and the freedom and aspirations of the people of Bangladesh, including both secessionists and non-secessionists, should be respected; however, India was not in a position to fulfill this task by using force. This task should be fulfilled by a neutral external actor which could respect the pursuit of self-determination of both secessionists and non-secessionists, and India was unlikely to respect the pursuit of non-secessionist self-determination due to geopolitical reasons: "Pakistan's role in South Asia as a reasonably effective counter to India's status as the dominant power in the region would be seriously undermined, in part because the remnant Pakistan was likely to identify itself more with the Islamic states of Southwest Asia than with South Asia once East Pakistan had been lost."[142] Geopolitical influence in applying international law should no longer be ignored when the fulfillment of international legal rights is affected thereby. In the Bangladesh case, self-determination of non-secessionists was impeded by not only an alleged right to intervene but also self-proclaimed self-defense. India mainly based its military intervention on self-defense, and it is understandable given that the right to self-defense was better established than the right to intervene.[143] The problem is that the practical use of force by India against Pakistan could hardly be referred to as self-defense.

In general, it is more accurate to refer to the direct military action of India against Pakistan as self-inflicted defense, or instigation of defense. Long before the air strike carried out by the Pakistani air force against India on 3 December 1971, India launched an operation getting the freedom fighters (Mukti Bahini) in Bangladesh together and training and arming them; the Mukti Bahini was formed in January 1971 and for the next 10 months people who came across the border were selected for training; by September-November 1971, these forces were infiltrated into Bangladesh for covert missions, including sabotage of lines of communication and command and control centers.[144] It is clear that self-inflicted defense is different from self-defense recognized in international law: the former is incompatible with the legal purpose of maintaining international peace and security. In the 1970 Friendly Relations Declaration, a prohibition on indirect force can be found: "every State has the duty to refrain from organizing, instigating, assisting or

---

[141] See above Note 134.

[142] See Chap. 2, Note 125.

[143] Gray (2010), p. 622.

[144] Kasturi and Mehra (2001), p. 24.

participating in arts of civil strife or terrorist acts in another State or acquiescing in organized activities within its territory directed towards the commission of such acts, when the acts referred to in the present paragraph involve a threat or use of force."[145] Given the indirect force used by India, perhaps the air strike carried out by the Pakistani air force against India was closer to the concept of self-defense. Nevertheless, it must be admitted that the air strike against India was ill-advised: thanks to the Pakistani air strike, India eventually got the chance to transform covert military intervention into overt military intervention which further complicated the secessionist conflict. In the name of self-defense, India successfully amplified its geopolitical interests at the expense of sovereignty and territorial integrity of Pakistan and self-determination of non-secessionists in Pakistan.

Such abuse of self-defense driven by geopolitical interests could have been and should have been prevented. Had the Security Council decided to maintain the territorial integrity of Pakistan, just like in the case of Katanga, there would have been a different result; had the interference tantamount to indirect intervention made by India in internal affairs of Pakistan been condemned timely by the Security Council, violations of self-determination of non-secessionists in Pakistan might have been avoided; had the Security Council made a systematic plan aimed at avoiding the escalation of the secessionist conflict and eliminating the counterproductive influence of India, the humanitarian situation could have been improved. Unfortunately, the Security Council failed to act this way to prevent abuse of self-defense driven by geopolitical interests. Perhaps it might seem somewhat strange that in such circumstances the responsibility to refrain, which is repeatedly mentioned in this chapter, is replaced by the responsibility to act. How should one understand this point? Given the settlement of conflicts and the humanitarian aim, the significance of the harmony between the responsibility to refrain and the responsibility to act is quite understandable: counterproductive action, such as the contribution made by India to the escalation of the secessionist conflict which led to numerous human right violations in Pakistan, must be avoided and therefore the responsibility to refrain needs to be stressed, but in order to eliminate the influence of such counterproductive action, something must be done by external actors such as the Security Council to abate the secessionist conflict and improve the humanitarian situation, and thus the responsibility to act needs to be stressed. Stressing the responsibility to act becomes particularly noteworthy when geopolitical interests are involved, as counterproductive action of external actors driven by geopolitical interests, such as the military intervention by India, must be stopped, otherwise it is unlikely to restore the positive interplay between internal actors and external actors. After all, it is unrealistic to expect external actors to give up their geopolitical interests willingly, so someone else should do something to stop them from acting counterproductively in conflict settlement. It was a pity that this task was unfulfilled in the case of Bangladesh, and this lesson should be borne in mind in dealing with similar cases in this day and age.

[145] A/RES/25/2625, Annex, Principle 1, para. 9.

4.2.3 Kosovo

Unlike the cases of Katanga and Bangladesh, in which the use of force directly decided the outcome of the secessionist conflict, in the case of Kosovo the decisive role of the use of force proved to be somewhat indirect: the declaration of independence was issued by the Kosovo authorities in 2008 while the military strike of the NATO was conducted in 1999. Nevertheless, the nexus between them is undeniable. Much about the NATO's use of force has already been discussed before and will not be repeated here. The main point here is some details which are often ignored but can contribute significantly to conflict escalation and deviation from the purposes and principles of the UN.

In the first place, one should look back at the statement of Dugi Gorani, an Albanian negotiator at Rambouillet, who was told by a foreign diplomat that the quota of five thousand deaths had to be passed to realize their secessionist pursuit.[146] Undeniably, it was encouraging secessionists to aggravate the humanitarian situation and escalate the secessionist conflict, and such external involvement was counterproductive, even detrimental. Unfortunately, this was not a rare situation in the Kosovo crisis. According to the interview made by Kuperman, Shkelzen Maliqi, a politician turned journalist, said that during the pacifist phase, foreign diplomats, for example, Americans and Swedes—in private would say, 'you need to fight.'[147] The KLA's Xhemajli said that Western officials, in meetings with KLA representatives in Europe prior to the uprising of 1998, contradicted their governments' official stance against rebellion: "at the diplomatic level, the diplomats always repeated the official position. But at other levels—for example, the intelligence services—they were more realistic about the way the Balkans were heading."[148]

Therefore, the issue of external actors being a double-dealer in secessionist conflicts should not be ignored: official stance and unofficial action should be in consistency, so external actors should not officially argue for a peaceful solution while unofficially encourage secessionists to take up arms. Being a double-dealer is more than a political issue, given the deviation from the purposes and principles of the UN. In essence, the inconsistency between official stance and unofficial action of some external actors in the Kosovo crisis represented an attempt to dodge observing the purposes and principles of the UN: principles of non-use of force, peaceful settlement of disputes, non-interference in internal affairs, international cooperation, self-determination, sovereignty and good faith can be compromised when external actors officially argue for a peaceful solution and unofficially encourage secessionists to take up arms. The case of Kosovo did demonstrate how harmful such external involvement can be: it provided perverse incentive for secessionists, intensified the secessionist conflict, reduced the chance of a peaceful settlement, aggravated the humanitarian situation, endangered state sovereignty and non-secessionist

[146]See above Note 91.

[147]Kuperman (2008), p. 70.

[148]Ibid.

self-determination due to the increasing will of external actors to intervene. Given these harmful effects, such external involvement should no longer be condoned: an official stance should be consistent with unofficial action, so external actors should both argue for a peaceful solution officially and refrain from encouraging secessionists to take up arms unofficially, and in this way the escalation of a secessionist conflict is less likely to occur, which helps replace the use of force with a multi-cooperative solution, as demonstrated in the case of Aceh. Obviously, such replacement is quite necessary: many thorny issues caused by the use of force, such as additional human rights violations, violation of sovereignty and violation of non-secessionist self-determination, no longer baffle and tear the international community apart when the use of force can be replaced by a peaceful solution. To conclude, requiring external actors to avoid being a double-dealer is to respect the purposes and principles of the UN, which not only helps prevent external actors from acting counterproductively but also saves the painstaking efforts made by external actors to justify their use of force in secessionist conflicts.

In the second place, it is necessary to consider whether the ultimatum made by external actors prior to their military intervention is in accordance with international law. At the Rambouillet Conference Belgrade was given an ultimatum, but this ultimatum was rejected by Belgrade, and soon afterwards came the air campaign of the NATO against Yugoslavia. It must be admitted that when the ultimatum itself was not in accordance with international law, the rejection of which was justified and the military intervention caused by the rejection was groundless. In other words, if the ultimatum referred to legal obligations of Yugoslavia under international law, Yugoslavia had no reason to reject it, but if this ultimatum was not concerned with legal obligations of Yugoslavia under international law, no one had the right to force Yugoslavia to accept it. As for the scope of legal obligations of Yugoslavia, it could be ascertained according to general international law and relevant UN documents.

First one should look at the contents of the ultimatum, i.e. the clauses of the Interim Agreement for Peace and Self-Government in Kosovo. The agreement dealt with multifarious issues, including an end of use of force, a new constitution for Kosovo, issues regarding police and civil public security, elections and economic issues and implementation.[149] Generally speaking, these topics did not only concern obligations of a sovereign state but also self determination of secessionists and non-secessionists. For this reason, it is worth considering whether issues concerning the self-determination conflict between secessionists and non-secessionists should be included in an ultimatum: an ultimatum is hardly compatible with the right to self-determination because an ultimatum is aimed at forcing the recipient to accept something against its own will, which actually translates self-determination into other-determination. To be exact, it was quite reasonable that certain issues, such as an end of using force, were included in the ultimatum: Yugoslavia had the obligation to settle the conflict in a peaceful manner, according to UN Security Council

[149] UN Doc. S/1999/648, Annex: Rambouillet Accordes—Interim Agreement for Peace and Self-Government in Kosovo.

resolutions,[150] and such obligation would not be affected by its own will, but when it came to constitutional issues, they should not be included in the ultimatum in disregard of the will of the people in Yugoslavia. If all peoples of Yugoslavia could be simply divided as Kosovan secessionists and the rest, the central government of Yugoslavia was undeniably the representative of the rest, so it could represent the rest to exercise their right to self-determination. In this sense, Yugoslavia had the right to disagree on the ultimatum, when this ultimatum was aimed at dealing with the right to self-determination of non-secessionists in Yugoslavia. In other words, the self-determination conflict as a constitutional issue should be left to negotiations between conflicting parties but not decided by external actors in an ultimatum.

The most curious point of this ultimatum was the military privilege demanded by the NATO. One should take a look at the following statement: "NATO personnel shall enjoy, together with their vehicles, vessels, aircraft and equipment, free and unrestricted access throughout the FRY [Federal Republic of Yugoslavia] including associated airspace and territorial waters. This shall include, but not be limited to, the right of bivouac, maneuver, billet, and utilization of any areas or facilities as required for support, training, and operations."[151] Needless to say, the existence of such a demand in the ultimatum was hardly explicable from the perspective of international law. According to general international law, principles of sovereignty and self-determination usually are not compatible with any military privilege of external actors. This point will not be changed even if the sovereign state is required to settle a conflict in a peaceful manner. When Security Council resolutions were taken into consideration, it was also unlikely to infer a military privilege like this therefrom: these resolutions were aimed at an end of the use of force and the verification of it, searching for a political solution, addressing the refugee issues and providing humanitarian aid.[152] Clearly, none of these arrangements necessitated the military privilege demanded by the NATO. Thus, Yugoslavia had sufficient grounds to reject the unjustified military annex.

In view of the foregoing, this ultimatum contained both justified and unjustified elements. It is meaningful to consider these questions: had the ultimatum not contained those unjustified elements, would it have been more acceptable to Yugoslavia? Was it really necessary to include those unjustified elements in the ultimatum? Should an ultimatum that contains such unjustified elements be condoned rather than condemned? These questions are meaningful not only because they affect the effective settlement of secessionist conflicts but also because they affect the observance of international law: undeniably, the ultimatum made by external actors prior to the military intervention must be in accordance with international law, otherwise there will exist a privilege superior to law, which can lead to detrimental effects. Obviously, the military privilege demanded by the NATO, together with the

[150] S/RES/1160 (1998), para. 1; S/RES/1199 (1998), para. 4.

[151] UN Doc. S/1999/648, Appendix B, para. 8.

[152] S/RES/1199 (1998), S/RES/1203 (1998), S/RES/1244 (1999).

constitutional arrangement, led to the failure of the Rambouillet negotiation. Given the fact that the Serb delegation had expressed its support to a political agreement, but charged that the negotiation at Rambouillet was changed at the last minute to suit the Albanian secessionists, and continued to reject any discussions of the military annex,[153] it is reasonable to deduce that Yugoslavia had nothing against an end of the use of force but something against the constitutional agreement and was totally against the military annex. Thus, it is safe to conclude that the negotiation in Rambouillet would have had a positive outcome if the ultimatum had not contained the constitutional agreement and the military annex.

Then one needs to consider the necessity of including the unjustified elements in the ultimatum. There is no denying that if there exists such necessity, it should not be disregarded. Did such necessity exist in this case? To answer this question, one needs to consider if the justified elements are indissolubly linked with the unjustified elements, which requires examining the relations between ceasefire, the constitutional arrangement and military privileges. Undoubtedly, they are not indissolubly linked with each other: a ceasefire could exist even without adopting a constitutional arrangement or granting military privileges. This was demonstrated in Security Council resolutions mentioned above, in which neither a concrete constitutional agreement nor military privileges of external actors like those demanded by the NATO were stressed, while the ceasefire was repeatedly stressed. Therefore, the ceasefire as the justified element was not indissolubly linked with the unjustified elements such as the constitutional arrangement and the military annex in the ultimatum, which proves that the necessity of including the unjustified elements in the ultimatum does not exist. It is particularly noteworthy that the top priority in this case was to protect innocent civilians from violence, and anything else was obviously less significant compared with it. In this sense, it is not difficult for external actors to make a choice between an end of the use of force, a certain constitutional arrangement and military privileges when these goals cannot be achieved at the same time: the ceasefire outweighs anything else.

That is to say, at the Rambouillet conference the NATO should have had secured the ceasefire in order to protect civilians in Kosovo and averted an aggravating humanitarian situation in the first place, instead of heavy-handedly forcing Yugoslavia to accept a certain constitutional agreement and military privileges demanded by the NATO. Given the situation at that time, the ceasefire meant much more to normal civilians than the constitutional arrangement and military privileges demanded by the NATO, and the ceasefire is also a goal relatively easy to achieve: as discussed before, it was the ceasefire that the Serb delegation had nothing against. Nevertheless, because this goal was gratuitously bound with other unattainable goals, it became equally unattainable. Civilians of Kosovo could have expected a ceasefire; unfortunately, due to a certain constitutional arrangement and military privileges demanded by the NATO, this simple expectation was thwarted. From this perspective, this ultimatum should be condemned, as it could have met the most

[153]Krieger (2001), p. xxiv.

significant and imminent humanitarian demand but it failed in an inexplicable way. In other words, the ultimatum here become an obstacle to the humanitarian pursuit stressed in international law: including the constitutional arrangement and military privileges demanded by external actors in the ultimatum was both unjustified and counterproductive, so rejecting such an ultimatum cannot be a justification for launching military intervention, and such intervention has nothing to do with the humanitarian pursuit. To those who work hard at justifying military privileges demanded by the NATO, it is necessary to point out that military privileges can be justified when they are proved to be indispensable for the fulfillment of a humanitarian aim, as demonstrated in any UN peace-keeping operation. Obviously, military privileges demanded by the NATO do not fall into this category, given that such privileges actually blocked the ceasefire and the NATO has never convincingly explained why such military privileges were indispensable for the fulfillment of a humanitarian aim. External actors should never be allowed to pursue unjustified military privileges like these in the name of humanitarian intervention, because such external involvement can tarnish the nobleness of the humanitarian pursuit and transmute the humanitarian pursuit into a pretext for hegemony and power politics. In order to prevent the international order dominated by international law from being eroded by hegemony and power politics, unjustified elements such as military privileges should never be allowed to exist in an ultimatum issued by external actors, and it should be condemned rather than condoned when external actors issue such a counterproductive ultimatum.

In the third place, it is necessary to consider the issue whether the international security presence in Kosovo should be NATO-dominated. In the Security Council resolution 1244(1999) it was provided that "the international security presence with substantial North Atlantic Treaty Organization participation must be deployed under unified command and control and authorized to establish a safe environment for all people in Kosovo and to facilitate the safe return to their homes of all displaced persons and refugees".[154] It must be admitted that this Security Council authorization itself was problematic: was it really conducive to the settlement of the secessionist conflict when an undeniably biased external actor was mandated to perform a security-maintaining task? The destructive outcome of mandating biased external actor in secessionist conflicts has been witnessed in the case of Katanga discussed before: the pro-secessionist Belgium even assisted the secessionists under the cover of the UN mandate. Returning to the Kosovo case, through the bombing the NATO has demonstrated its pro-secessionist stance, so there is reason to worry that such pro-secessionist stance can affect the performance of the security-maintaining task. On this basis, it was no wonder that "by late-2000 more than 210,000 Serbs had fled the province; most of them left in the first six weeks of the NATO deployment".[155] It must be noted that their flight was not purely due to the subjective sense of insecurity but due to practical persecution: Kosovo Force led by the NATO in practice failed to

[154]S/RES/1244 (1999), Annex 2, para. 4.

[155]See Chap. 3, Note 88.

impede the violence committed by Kosovo secessionists against Serbs and other minorities. For instance, already in August 1999 Human Rights Watch has issued a report focusing on "the wave of arson and looting of Serb and Roma homes throughout Kosovo that has ensued and on the harassment and intimidation, including severe beatings, to which remaining Serbs and Roma have been subjected. Most seriously, there has been a spate of abductions and murders of Serbs since mid-June, including the massacre of fourteen Serb farmers on July 23."[156] Needless to say, the inability of the NATO to impede such violence committed by Kosovan secessionists against Serbs and other minorities can strengthen the speculation that the pro-secessionist NATO remained biased in performing the security-maintaining task mandated by the UN, since it did not "establish a safe environment for all people in Kosovo": to be more specific, the Kosovo Force led by the NATO established a safe environment for Kosovan secessionists but not for Kosovan Serbs and other minorities who were open to violence committed by Kosovan secessionists. In such circumstances, the raison d'être of the international security presence is inevitably open to question.

In view of the foregoing, it is certainly ill-advised for the UN to mandate the NATO to perform the security-maintaining task and equally ill-advised for the NATO to accept this mandate. It would have been better for the UN to mandate another external actor, which had not shown any preference for one conflicting party to perform the security-maintaining task; although mandating a biased external actor is not clearly prohibited, there are sufficient reasons to refrain from doing so, given the lessons learned in the case of Katanga. One should also realize when a biased external actor exhibits its partiality in performing the UN task, it is injuring the credibility of the UN as the external actor here acts on behalf of the UN. As the chief guardian of peace and security under international law, the UN Security Council is obliged to maintain its credibility, so it should not mandate a biased external actor which tends to undermine its credibility. It would also have been better for the NATO not to accept this mandate: given that the partiality of the NATO in the Kosovo crisis was quite evident, the inability of the NATO to impede violence committed by Kosovo secessionists against Serbs and other minorities would invariably be associated with a partiality for secessionists, although it was also possible that the NATO-led security presence was really unable to impede the atrocities committed by secessionists rather than had a partiality for secessionists. In order to get rid of the suspicion of being partial towards secessionists or avoid being accused due to its inability to impede violence committed by Kosovo secessionists against Serbs and other minorities, the NATO should not have accepted this mandate. Undeniably, to avoid giving the impression of being partial or unable is in the interest of the NATO: the bombing in Yugoslavia had contributed enough to a dreadful image, and the NATO should not have made it more dreadful by performing

---

[156] Human Rights Watch, Federal Republic of Yugoslavia: Abuses against Serbs and Roma in the New Kosovo, August 1999, Volume 11, No. 10 (D), https://www.hrw.org/reports/1999/kosov2/, last accessed on 15.06.2018.

the security-maintaining task. As an important regional organization which tends to play a crucial role in the maintenance of international peace and security according to Chapter VIII of the UN Charter, the NATO must care about its image: a partial or unable image will inevitably exert a negative influence on international cooperation between the NATO and other actors, which is aimed at maintaining international peace and security, and a lack of international cooperation usually renders conflicts more complex. This point can be discerned in the following case.

4.2.4 Crimea

The case of Crimea has several features: firstly, independence itself was not the end but a means of uniting with another state; secondly, independence was closely related to the coup d'état in the capital; thirdly, both the coup d'état and the ensuing independence have much to do with external involvement. Here the word coup d'état is only a factual description of a non-constitutional change of government and not concerned with any value judgment. To discuss the use of force in this case of secession, these features must be taken into account. Of course, it does not mean that these elements can decide the legality of the use of force under international law. In fact, the importance of considering these elements lies in avoiding the use of force. Needless to say, the avoidance of the use of force is much less discussed than the legality of the use of force under contemporary international law: compared with the latter, the former seems to be more of a political nature and less of a legal nature. Thus, it is quite understandable that the issue how to avoid the use of force is often left to international politics but not international law. Nevertheless, one must realize that in practice international politics and international law are inextricably interwoven with each other, especially when it comes to cases of dispute settlement. For instance, the UN Security Council is a political organ, but its resolutions have been treated as a part of international law; international political negotiations might lead to binding agreements, which signifies how closely related international politics and international law actually are. In the case of Crimea such entanglement is especially noteworthy because the ultimate solution to the secessionist conflict which was complicated by Russia's use of force seems dependent on political negotiations including all protagonists.[157]

Speaking of conflict settlement through political negotiations, one needs to focus on the hindrance to political negotiations: the case of Crimea has demonstrated the difficulty in having constructive negotiations after the escalation of conflicts, so the point here is preventing the conflict from being upgraded by the use of force, and in such circumstances, discussing the avoidance of the use of force is more meaningful than purely discussing the legality of the use of force, because the use of force which might be deemed legal from certain perspectives should also be avoided when it can

[157]Christakis (2015), p. 100.

upgrade a conflict and become the hindrance to conflict settlement. In order to avoid the use of force, it is necessary to discuss political mistakes made by the protagonists, which promote the use of force. At this stage one might still ask: do political mistakes which are detrimental to the avoidance of the use of force really have something to do with international law? Some hold the view that it is not a topic concerned with international law, and one reason is as long as a political mistake does not violate international law, it falls beyond the scope of international law.[158] To some extent, this view is impeccable. Nevertheless, if it is admitted that international law should play a pivotal role in settling conflicts and international law needs to be further developed, one should reconsider this view. After all, "international law aims for harmony and the regulation of disputes. It attempts to create a framework, no matter how rudimentary, which can act as a kind of shock-absorber clarifying and moderating claims and endeavouring to balance interests".[159] In this sense, when the rudimentary framework fails to achieve its aims, it is well-advised to improve the framework so as to achieve its aims. That is to say, when political mistakes which are detrimental to the avoidance of the use of force do not evidently violate international law, it is time to consider improving international law so as to deal with such issues, otherwise the role of international law in conflict settlement will invariably be limited and unsatisfying. Not every political mistake can be condoned by international law, particularly when this mistake is so serious that it hinders international law from achieving its aims.

It is also accurate to say that the evolution of international law has much to do with the translation of political issues into legal issues: the General Treaty for the Renunciation of War (the Kellogg-Briand Pact) was a typical case in point. The signatories of the Kellogg-Briand Pact "condemn recourse to war for the solution of international controversies, and renounce it, as an instrument of national policy in their relations with one another".[160] Clearly, the use of force used to be a political issue unregulated by positive international law; however, with the development of international law, particularly given the destructive effect of the use of force, it was gradually incorporated into the legal system. In the same vein, it is well-advised to combine the avoidance of the use of force with the further development of the international legal system, so political mistakes which promote the use of force should be regulated by an improved international legal system.

Therefore, the role of international law in the case of Crimea should not be limited to providing an answer to the question whether Russia's use of force could be justified on the basis of humanitarian intervention. Undeniably, it does not help settle the conflict by concluding that Russia's military intervention was illegal but legitimate: it was illegal because it did not receive prior approval from the United Nations Security Council, while the intervention was justified because all diplomatic avenues had been exhausted and because the intervention had the effect of liberating

158 Uerpmann-Wittzack (2015), p. 20.
159 Shaw (2008), p. 12.
160 Kellogg-Briand Pact 1928, Article 1.

the majority population of Crimea from a long period of oppression under Ukrainian rules. International law should play a more constructive role in settling such conflicts, which largely depends on avoiding or rectifying political mistakes which can be attributed to external actors. Perhaps it is the most thought-provoking lesson one can draw from the case of Crimea.

It is time to take a close look at political mistakes made by external actors. The Crimea crisis could be traced back to November 2013, when Yanukovych rejected a major economic deal he had been negotiating with the EU and decided to accept a $15 billion Russian counteroffer instead, which sparked antigovernment demonstrations and violence from both sides. Finally a coup d'état took place and Yanukovych was ousted. "Although the full extent of U.S. involvement has not yet come to light, it is clear that Washington backed the coup. Nuland and Republican Senator John McCain participated in antigovernment demonstrations, and Geoffrey Pyatt, the U.S. ambassador to Ukraine, proclaimed after Yanukovych's toppling that it was 'a day for the history books.' As a leaked telephone recording revealed, Nuland had advocated regime change and wanted the Ukrainian politician Arseniy Yatsenyuk to become prime minister in the new government, which he did."[161] The new government was pro-Western and anti-Russian to the core, which destroyed the fragile balance between the pro-Western and pro-Russian population within Ukraine, thus intensifying the self-determination conflict between them. The climax of the self-determination conflict was marked by the unilateral secession of Crimea and its immediate integration into Russia with the military support of Russia. The West imposed economic sanctions against Russia for annexing Crimea; nevertheless, the effect was not satisfactory: "history shows that countries will absorb enormous amounts of punishment in order to protect their core strategic interests. There is no reason to think Russia represents an exception to this rule."[162]

It must be admitted that general international law has provided some analytical tools for this issue. First one should look at the coup d'état backed by Washington. According to the principle of non-interference in internal affairs, Washington's backing of the coup d'état was suspected of being illegal; nevertheless, given that the right to self-determination was a right confirmed in international law and did not fully fall into internal affairs of a sovereign state, and the coup d'état launched by the pro-Western population could somewhat be associated with the exercise of the right to self-determination, it proved to be really difficult to assert that Washington's backing of the coup d'état definitely violated the principle of non-interference in internal affairs. In such circumstances, it can be said that general international law fails to address the external influence effectively, although the external influence contributes to the escalation of self-determination conflicts and threatens the aims of international law. Then one should look at the unilateral secession of Crimea and its immediate integration into Russia. The West focused on the violation of the non-use of force but largely ignored that the use of force was also associated with the

[161]Mearsheimer (2014).

[162]Ibid.

protection of the right to self-determination of the pro-Russian population: there is no denying that the pro-Western coup d'état violated the right to self-determination of the pro-Russian population. Obviously, such ignoring cannot be well-justified: in the case of Kosovo, the West had not ignored the right to self-determination of secessionists and had used force to protect it, just as Russia in Crimea. Of course, there is no annexation in the case of Kosovo; nevertheless, "how can it be ignored that Crimea is now annexed de facto by Russia and that this annexation, unlawful as it is, but achieved without bloodshed, was very probably what the majority of its population wanted?"[163] Once again, analytical tools provided by general international law did not work effectively.

In view of the foregoing, it is accurate to say that in the Crimea case both the West and Russia made the same mistake: they disregarded the detrimental effect of their involvement in the self-determination conflict within Ukraine, thus intensifying this conflict and rendering it out of control. It should be admitted that the West made the mistake in the first place: it should not have backed the coup d'état launched by the pro-Western population, which triggered the strong opposition of the pro-Russian population; respecting self-determination of the pro-Western population should not be the reason to injure self-determination of the pro-Russian population. One must realize that the pro-Russian self-determination has much to do with practical interests: it is said that in 2013 alone almost three million Ukrainians found such jobs as day laborers in Russia; according to some sources, in 2013 their earnings in Russia totaled over $20 billion, which is about 12% of Ukraine's GDP.[164] For this reason the pro-Russian population was unlikely to give in in the self-determination conflict. Moreover, their pursuit of pro-Russian self-determination is in the geopolitical interests of Russia and will invariably be supported by Russia. Nevertheless, this support becomes quite problematic when it overlooks self-determination of the other side: by militarily supporting the unilateral secession of Crimea, Russia actually disregarded the right to self-determination of those non-secessionists.

How can such mistake made by external actors be avoided or rectified? Clearly, the answer largely depends on properly exercising their external influence in settling self-determination conflicts: external actors who possess a particular influence on conflicting parties have to be aware of their influential power and exercise it in a constructive way. When external actors learn to respect conflicting claims based on the right to self-determination, avoiding or rectifying such mistakes will not be a problem. Moreover, external actors should work on enhancing mutual respect between conflicting parties, which requires a certain degree of cooperation between external actors themselves. Returning to the case of Crimea, it is clear that enhancing mutual respect between the pro-Western and pro-Russian population is somewhat dependent on a certain degree of cooperation between the West and Russia: given the close relations between the West and the pro-Western population, between

[163]See above Note 157.

[164]Address by President of the Russian Federation, March 18, 2014, http://en.kremlin.ru/events/president/news/20603, last accessed on 15.06.2018.

Russia and the pro-Russian population, confrontation between the West and Russia will invariably affect harmony between the pro-Western and pro-Russian population within Ukraine. In the same vein, given such close relations, if the West and Russia take a cooperative attitude towards this issue, their cooperation will also promote harmony between the pro-Western and pro-Russian population. Political negotiations, through which conflicts can be settled, are dependent on the cooperative attitude between all protagonists, so there is no reason to underestimate the detrimental effects caused by the lack of basic cooperation between powerful external actors such as the West and Russia.

Therefore, it is reasonable to conclude that avoiding or rectifying political mistakes made by external actors involved in secessionist conflicts requires a certain degree of cooperation between these external actors. It was the lack of basic cooperation between the West and Russia that pushed the self-determination conflict between the pro-Western and the pro-Russian population to the extreme: after the rejection of the EU offer and the acceptance of the Russian counteroffer, it was ill-advised for the West to respond excessively by backing the coup d'état launched by the pro-Western population, which in return destroyed the fragile balance between the pro-Western and the pro-Russian population and triggered the military support of Russia in the unilateral secession of Crimea. The West and Russia could actually have settled their problem in a much less drastic way: confrontation between the West and Russia caused by the offer and counteroffer could have been softened by diplomatic means without intensifying the self-determination conflict between the pro-Western and the pro-Russian population. Unfortunately, by backing the coup d'état the West demonstrated that it did not want to cooperate with Russia in seeking a less drastic solution. To be fair, the lack of cooperative attitude on the part of the West was not the whole reason for Russia's military support in the unilateral secession of Crimea. As mentioned before, given the role played by the West in the Kosovo case, Russia has a deep distrust of the West: "in the eyes of Russian leaders, EU expansion is a stalking horse for NATO expansion".[165] In addition, the use of force in Crimea can be seen as "a kind of revenge for the violation of international law that the US and EU committed in the Kosovo case".[166] Last but not least, "this is Geopolitics 101: great powers are always sensitive to potential threats near their home territory."[167] From the Russian perspective, "if the US thinks it reasonable to violate international legal rules when it serves its interests, why should Russia desist from ignoring international law when its fundamental interests are at stake?"[168] In short, the lack of basic cooperation between the West and Russia can be attributed to a series of reasons. To some extent, these reasons should not be deemed unrelated to international law, as according to international law "states have the duty to co-operate with one another, irrespective of the differences in their

[165]See above Note 161.

[166]Oeter (2015), p. 73.

[167]See above Note 161.

[168]See above Note 166.

political, economic and social systems, in the various spheres of international relations, in order to maintain international peace and security".[169] When certain reasons have impeded the necessary international cooperation aimed at maintaining international peace and security, it is necessary to consider improving international law to enable it to deal with such issue.

Given what has been discussed above, the key to the settlement of the Crimea crisis or similar issues is to prevent external actors from abusing their influential power over conflicting parties. Such external influence should be regulated by international law, abuse of which should no longer be taken solely as a political mistake, otherwise the aims of international law will be unaccomplished: the escalation of self-determination conflicts caused by external involvement does not only injure the right to self-determination but also pose a real threat to the maintenance of international peace and security. Unfortunately, to regulate an external influence is not easy: due to the close relation between the West and the pro-Western population, between Russia and pro-Russian population, the interference of the West in the internal affairs of Ukraine was closely related to self-determination of the pro-Western population, just as Russia's use of force was closely related to self-determination of the pro-Russian population. Thus, the principle of non-interference fails to regulate such external influence. With a view to regulating external influences, the principle of international cooperation should be highlighted here. For the sake of the maintenance of international peace and security, the self-determination conflict between the pro-Western and pro-Russian population should be settled in a peaceful manner, which necessitates a certain degree of cooperation between the West and Russia: when the West and Russia refuse basic cooperation with each other, it is difficult to expect their respective proxies in Ukraine to cooperate with each other. On this basis one can argue that the principle of international cooperation helps regulate external influences on secessionist conflicts.

What can international law do to promote international cooperation required by the settlement of secessionist conflicts? Obviously, it is a very complicated issue which will be thoroughly discussed in the following chapter. At the end of the case study, this point will not be discussed at length. Only one thing will be stressed here: when external actors are unable to cooperate with each other in an active way, they should at least manage passive cooperation. In the Crimea case, passive cooperation between the West and Russia means refraining from contributing to the escalation of the self-determination conflict between the pro-Western population and the pro-Russian population. Undeniably, had the West refrained from backing the coup d'état launched by the pro-Western population, Russia would have been less motivated to militarily support the unilateral secession of Crimea launched by the pro-Russian population. Had the West refused to back the coup d'état and Russia refused to support the unilateral secession, passive cooperation would have taken place between the West and Russia. Of course, passive cooperation is not as productive as active cooperation, but it is definitely better than nothing: requiring

[169] A/RES/25/2625, Annex, Principle 4, para. 1.

external actors to manage passive cooperation is to respect conflicting claims based on the right to self-determination, which is the key to effectively settling secessionist conflicts.

References

Annan K, Mousavizadeh N (2012) Interventions: a life in war and peace. The Penguin Press, pp 53–54

Brownlie I (1981) International law and the use of force by states. Oxford University Press, pp 272–275

Brownlie I, Apperley CJ (2000) Kosovo crisis inquiry: further memorandum on the international law aspects. Int Comp Law Q 49:910

Buchheit LC (1978) Secession: the legitimacy of self-determination. Yale University Press

Christakis T (2011) The ICJ Advisory Opinion on Kosovo: "Has International Law Something to Say about Secession?". Leiden J Int Law 24:80

Christakis T (2015) Self-determination, territorial integrity and *Fait Accompli* in the case of Crimea. ZaöRV 75:100

Clapham A (2006) Human rights obligations of non-state actors. Oxford University Press, p 50

Crawford TW (2001/2002) Pivotal deterrence and the Kosovo War: why the Holbrooke agreement failed. Polit Sci Q (Acad Polit Sci) 116:501

Evans G (2011) Responding to mass atrocity crimes: the responsibility to protect after Libya. Lecture at Chatham House, London, 6 October 2011, p 10. https://www.chathamhouse.org/publications/papers/view/178795. Last accessed 15 June 2018

Gray C (2010) The use of force and the international legal order. In: Evans MD (ed) International law, 3rd edn. Oxford University Press, p 622

Grigorian A (2006) Third-party intervention and escalation in Kosovo: "Does Moral Hazard Explain It?". In: Crawford TW, Kuperman AJ (eds) Gambling on humanitarian intervention: moral hazard, rebellion and civil war. Routledge, p 52

Grotius H (1964) De Jure Belli ac Pacis (trans: Kelsey FW), Book II, chapter 24. Oceana Publications Inc., New York, p 567

Henkin L (1999) That "S" word: sovereignty, and globalization, and human rights, et cetera. Fordham Law Rev 68:10

Janik R (2013) The responsibility to protect as an impetus for secessionist movements — on the necessity to re-think territorial integrity. In: Kettemann MC (ed) Grenzen im Völkerrecht. Jan Sramek Verlag

Jennings R, Watts A (eds) (1992) Oppenheim's international law, 9th edn. Pearson Education, Limited, p 440

Kasturi B, Mehra P (2001) Geo-politics of South Asian covert action: India's experience and need for action against Pakistan. Indian Defence Rev 16(2):24

Kingsbury B (1998) Sovereignty and inequality. Eur J Int Law 9:602

Krieger H (ed) (2001) The Kosovo conflict and international law: an analytical documentation 1974–99. Cambridge University Press, p xxiv

Kuperman AJ (2008) The moral hazard of humanitarian intervention: lessons from the Balkans. Int Stud Q 52

Kuperman AJ (2013) Humanitarian intervention. In: Goodhart M (ed) Human rights: politics and practice, 2nd edn. Oxford University Press, p 304

Lowe V, Tzanakopoulos A (2011) Humanitarian intervention. Max Planck Encyclopedia of Public International Law

Luban D (2011) War as punishment. Georgetown public law and legal theory research paper no. 11-71, p 36

Mackenzie L (1993) Peacekeeper: the road to Sarajevo. Douglas & McIntyre, p 159
Mearsheimer JJ (2014) Why the Ukraine crisis is the West's fault: the liberal delusions that provoked Putin. Foreign Affairs, September/October 2014 Issue, https://www.foreignaffairs.com/articles/russia-fsu/2014-08-18/why-ukraine-crisis-west-s-fault. Last accessed 15 June 2018
Nair R (1998) Confronting the violence committed by armed opposition groups. Yale Hum Rights Dev J 1:11
Oeter S (2015) The Kosovo case – an unfortunate precedent. ZaöRV 75:73
Pellet A (2013) Peaceful settlement of international disputes, para. 27. Max Planck Encyclopedia of Public International Law
Rose M (1998) Fighting for peace: Bosnia 1994. The Harvill Press, p 141
Schnabel A (2012) The responsibility to rebuild. In: Andy Knight W, Egerton F (eds) The Routledge handbook of the responsibility to protect. Routledge Chapman & Hall, p 57
Shaw MN (2008) International law, 6th edn. Cambridge University Press, p 12
Sisson R, Rose LE (1990) War and secession: Pakistan, India and the creation of Bangladesh. University of California Press
Uerpmann-Wittzack R (2015) Souveränität und Selbstbestimmung in der Ukraine-Krise: Ist Völkerrecht wichtig? Jahrbuch für Ostrecht 56:20
Verdirame G (2013) The law and strategy of humanitarian intervention. https://www.ejiltalk.org/the-law-and-strategy-of-humanitarian-intervention/. Last accessed 15 June 2018
Watkin K (2004) Controlling the use of force: a role for human rights norms in contemporary armed conflict. Am J Int Law 98:30
Weller M (2008) Settling self-determination conflicts: an introduction. In: Weller M, Metzger B (eds) Settling self-determination disputes: complex power-sharing in theory and practice. Martinus Nijhoff, p xi
Winkelmann I (2010) Responsibility to protect, para. 2. Max Planck Encyclopedia of Public International Law
Wippman D (2000) Pro-democratic intervention by invitation. In: Fox GH, Roth BR (eds) Democratic governance and international law. Cambridge University Press

[illegible] (2015) [illegible]

[illegible] (2015) [illegible]

[illegible] (2015) [illegible]

Chapter 5
Improving External Involvement in the Settlement of Secessionist Conflicts

As discussed in previous chapters, external involvement in secessionist conflicts is very common and in various forms: the most controversial one concerns the use of force, but one should not only focus on this point. As a matter of fact, external involvement also concerns many other different perspectives, which are closely connected with the effective settlement of secessionist conflicts but might not have gained sufficient attention. In this chapter these perspectives will be analyzed in terms of the current international legal system: improvement in external involvement is largely dependent on a more comprehensive understanding and more effective application of the current international legal system. It must be admitted that counterproductive or detrimental external involvement in the settlement of secessionist conflicts can generally be attributed to the problematic understanding and application of the current international legal system. When international law can be understood and applied more properly by external actors in secessionist conflicts, improved external involvement will become a matter of course.

Therefore, the following discussion will be structured in this way: based on the current international legal system and concrete practice by external actors, a number of actual issues concerning external involvement, which tend to hinder the effective settlement of secessionist conflicts, will be analyzed and external actors involved in secessionist conflicts will correspondingly be advised to play a more constructive role in conflict settlement.

5.1 Adopting a Comprehensive Approach in Dealing with Secessionist Conflicts

In order to render external involvement in secessionist conflicts really constructive, it is necessary to discern the inherent complexity of a secessionist conflict in the first place. That is to say, an external actor should have a clear picture of legal issues

J. Lu, *On State Secession from International Law Perspectives*,
https://doi.org/10.1007/978-3-319-97448-4_5

which are included in a secessionist conflict as any issue included should not be overlooked for the sake of conflict settlement. Thus, a comprehensive approach is invariably required: an external actor shall not attend to one issue and lose sight of another, and the nexus between legal issues included in a secessionist conflict must be taken into account, otherwise it will also be counterproductive to conflict settlement.

Legal issues included in a secessionist conflict should be understood from a multilevel point of view: some issues are deep-seated while others are on the surface. The trap hidden in a secessionist conflict lies in overlooking deep-seated legal issues and their nexus with legal issues on the surface. Needless to say, human rights protection is a legal issue on the surface of a secessionist conflict while conflicting self-determination over territorial interests is a deep-seated issue of a secessionist conflict. Addressing the issue concerning human rights protection cannot be isolated from settling conflicting self-determination over territorial interests: as discussed in previous chapters, if the self-determination conflict over territorial interests is not properly settled, it will invariably pose threat to human rights protection. Therefore, when external actors tend to protect human rights in disregard of conflicting self-determination over territorial interests, such kind of external involvement can hardly contribute to the effective settlement of secessionist conflicts. Worse yet, if the means taken by external actors to protect human rights actually hinders a fair solution to a self-determination conflict over territorial interests, the secessionist conflict can escalate due to this hindrance, so external actors actually do a disservice to human rights protection by escalating the conflict.

When it comes to the self-determination conflict over territorial interests, the main point here is to prevent its escalation and facilitate peaceful negotiation between secessionists and non-secessionists. Preventing escalation and facilitating peaceful negotiation are actually two sides of one coin: both are indispensable for the effective settlement of secessionist conflicts. As discussed before, if secessionist conflicts stay nonviolent, they will not give rise to severe human rights violations while the escalation of secessionist conflicts generally will involve much more violence which can lead to humanitarian crises. For this reason, the importance of preventing a conflict from escalating should be borne in mind by every external actor. As a matter of fact, failing to prevent the escalation of conflicts is more than a political mistake because it indirectly concerns the realization of a number of international legal principles: the escalation of a secessionist conflict will more often than not add an international color to the conflict, and in such circumstances the principle of non-interference in internal affairs will be affected; if a sovereign state feels that there is interference in its internal affairs, it will be reluctant to cooperate with external actors; if external actors interfere in disregard of the will of a sovereign state, sovereignty, in which non-secessionist self-determination is embodied, is suspected of being violated; if interference is in a military form which unfortunately causes additional human right violations, whether the use of force has been approved by the Security Council or not, such interference will be severely challenged from a legal point of view. Therefore, in order to avoid all these thorny legal issues, external actors shall spare no effort in preventing conflicts from escalating.

Nevertheless, one needs to realize that preventing the escalation of conflicts is a very complicated issue. In essence, it requires positive interplay between conflicting parties, between external actors and conflicting parties, and between external actors. Commonly seen negative interplay has been analyzed in previous chapters: by deliberately intensifying the conflict between them and non-secessionists in order to attract external intervention against non-secessionists, some secessionists maliciously exploit the enthusiasm of external actors for protecting human rights of secessionists, and such negative interplay can be more complicated given the geopolitical factors. Therefore, in order to prevent conflict escalation, an arrangement aimed at promoting positive interplay between different actors is undoubtedly required: given that such negative interplay is closely linked to the malicious exploitation of external involvement and geopolitical influence, this arrangement should focus on standardizing external involvement, which includes creating conflict-oriented guiding rules for external actors and concerting their individual actions in secessionist conflicts.

5.2 Standardizing External Involvement in Secessionist Conflicts

5.2.1 Balancing Conflicting Interests with the Help of External Involvement

When speaking of guiding rules of external involvement in secessionist conflicts, one can say that different external actors have different guiding rules for themselves, which largely depend on their understanding of secessionist conflicts. For those external actors who take a secessionist conflict solely as sovereign repression and resistance, guiding rules of external involvement are limited to human rights protection, more specifically, human rights protection of secessionists. For those who take a secessionist conflict mainly as a self-determination conflict over territorial interests between secessionists and non-secessionists, guiding rules of external involvement are more comprehensive: the balance of interests between conflicting parties occupies the foreground, and human rights protection is not ignored but taken in a broad sense including human rights of both conflicting parties. Needless to say, external actors of the former understanding are more likely to be exploited by secessionists and contribute to the escalation of secessionist conflicts, while external actors of the latter understanding are less likely to be exploited by secessionists and contribute to the escalation of the secessionist conflict. From this perspective, standardizing guiding rules of external involvement in secessionist conflicts is quite meaningful because the guiding rules of some external actors are evidently superior to the guiding rules of other external actors: to be more specific, the balance of interests between conflicting parties is superior to one-sided human rights protection, so the latter must be replaced by the former and humanitarian pursuit should be combined with the balance of conflicting interests.

In fact, such combination has already been required in UN instruments. A relevant one was mentioned in Chap. 4: General Assembly resolution 46/182, which was entitled Strengthening of the coordination of humanitarian emergency assistance of the United Nations, stressed that "humanitarian assistance must be provided in accordance with the principles of humanity, neutrality and impartiality. The sovereignty, territorial integrity and national unity of States must be fully respected in accordance with the Charter of the United Nations. In this context, humanitarian assistance should be provided with the consent of the affected country and in principle on the basis of an appeal by the affected country".[1] In this resolution, humanitarian pursuit and the balance of interests are somewhat connected with each other: respecting sovereignty, territorial integrity and national unity of States amounts to respecting sovereign interests of states, and respecting sovereign interests is essential to balancing conflicting interests, which should not be neglected by external actors in pursuing humanitarian values. When it comes to a secessionist conflict, respecting sovereign interests can be equated with respecting the interests of non-secessionists, and in this way, external actors help strike a balance of interests between secessionists and non-secessionists, which contributes to the equal protection of human rights of both sides and avoids conflicts between external actors and non-secessionists that are represented by a sovereign state. Therefore, the pursuit of humanitarian values by external actors in secessionist conflicts should be based on balancing conflicting interests between secessionists and non-secessionists, of which respecting sovereign interests is a necessary part.

Besides, it is also a good idea to standardize guiding rules of external involvement in secessionist conflicts through UN instruments. Up to now, contemporary international law has not provided relatively clear guidance on external involvement in secessionist conflicts in the post-colonial context. Therefore, standardizing guiding rules of external involvement in secessionist conflicts through UN instruments is of groundbreaking significance. With the guidance of UN instruments, the deep-seated legal issue included in secessionist conflicts, namely the self-determination conflict over territorial interests between secessionists and non-secessionists, is less likely to be neglected by external actors and external actors will learn to promote a balance of conflicting interests instead of solely focusing on protecting human rights of secessionists, which helps avoid malicious exploitation of external involvement and is conducive to preventing conflict escalation. Of course, it must be stressed that standardizing guiding rules of external involvement in secessionist conflicts through UN instruments means replacing one-sided human rights protection with the balance of conflicting interests, not the other way around. Otherwise the standardization through UN instruments would be not only meaningless but also detrimental: wrong guidance usually makes things worse.

[1]A/RES/46/182, Annex, I. Guiding Principles, paras. 2 and 3.

The importance of replacing one-sided human rights protection with the balance of conflicting interests is also embodied in the legal principle of international cooperation on conflict settlement. Obviously, effective international cooperation on conflict settlement is hardly possible when external actors focus solely on the human rights protection of one side, and as long as one conflicting party feels discriminated against by external actors, the conflicting party will be unwilling to cooperate with external actors. A secessionist conflict is no exception: if external actors solely focus on protecting human rights of secessionists and fail to care about human rights and territorial interests of non-secessionists, not only will effective cooperation between external actors and non-secessionists be unlikely, but also real confrontation between external actors and non-secessionists can be aroused when external actors choose to side with secessionists. In such circumstances, a secessionist conflict can escalate even without further malicious exploitation by secessionists of such biased external involvement. Therefore, it can be said that the balance of conflicting interests is the inherent requirement of the principle of international cooperation on conflict settlement, and because one-sided human rights protection is hardly in accordance with this international legal principle, it is once again proved that one-sided human rights protection cannot be the guiding rule of external involvement and needs to be replaced.

The failure of the Rambouillet peace conference has demonstrated that international cooperation on the settlement of a secessionist conflict must be established on the balance of conflicting interests of secessionists and non-secessionists: in the Rambouillet Kosovo Agreement such a balance simply did not exist. As pointed out by Jan Oberg, Director of the Transnational Foundation for Peace and Future Research, according to the Rambouillet Kosovo Agreement, "the self-governing Kosovo can influence Yugoslav politics while the authorities of FRY, the Federal Republic of Yugoslavia, are barred from influencing Kosovo's internal affairs... there shall be equal rights and equal access to employment in public services but [the Agreement] does not stipulate what that means for the 10–20 per cent of the people in the province who are not Albanians... FRY is prevented from prosecuting crimes related to the conflict and holds that past political and resistance activities shall not be a bar to holding office in Kosovo... the Chief of the OSCE/EU Implementation Mission, CIM, has the authority to issue binding directives to the Parties on all important matters he sees fit; like in Bosnia he can dismiss public security personnel and he can remove and appoint officials and curtail existing institutions – meaning he can overrule election results; there is no mention of FRY veto in any area... FRY shall give Kosovo an equitable share of benefits derived from international transactions while the economic resources and profits of the province shall be reallocated with 'the distribution of powers and responsibilities set forth in this agreement.' This hardly clarifies what to do with the province's considerable natural resources and industrial facilities... the civilian parts of the document lacks every reference to civilian peace-keeping, trust-building, civil society-based reconciliation, conflict-resolution training, support for NGOs, peace education or human rights training etc. So the chances that Albanians, Serbs and other citizens should begin to build trust and learn to live peacefully side by side during these three years is nil".[2] Diana Johnstone therefore worried about the human rights protection of the Serb minority in Kosovo: in the Rambouillet agreement "there was nothing to suggest any serious effort to prevent 'ethnic cleansing' of the Serb minority by the triumphant Albanian majority".[3] Unfortunately, her worry did become a reality: "in March 2000, Jiri Dienstbier, a former Czech Foreign Minister serving as a Special Rapporteur of the UN Commission on Human Rights, stated at the Commission that most of Kosovo was 'ethnically-cleansed of non-Albanians, divided, without any legal system, ruled by illegal structures of the Kosovo Liberation Army and very often by competing mafias'."[4] Thus, there is no denying that neglect of the interests of non-secessionists can render external involvement in secessionist conflicts counterproductive, even detrimental.

In view of the foregoing, balancing conflicting interests of secessionists and non-secessionists should no longer be ignored by external actors, otherwise external involvement can lead to terrible consequences which render international cooperation impossible and aggravate the situation of human rights. With a view to promoting international cooperation on conflict settlement and human rights protection, as required by international law, the balance of conflicting interests of secessionists and non-secessionists must be incorporated into the standardized guidance for external involvement in secessionist conflicts.

When speaking of the balance of conflicting interests, one should realize that in practice conflicting interests exist not only between secessionists and non-secessionists but also between external actors choosing to side with secessionists or non-secessionists. As discussed in previous chapters, the preference of external actors is much concerned with the geopolitical interests of them. When one external actor chooses to side with secessionists and another with non-secessionists, it indicates that these external actors have conflicting geopolitical interests. Although the status of geopolitical interests in the current international legal system is far from being clear, there is no denying that international cooperation on the settlement of secessionist conflicts also depends on the balance of conflicting geopolitical interests of external actors. Indeed, the lack of cooperation between external actors due to the imbalance of conflicting geopolitical interests can contribute significantly to the complication of those secessionist conflicts, rendering peaceful settlement less likely. For this reason, improving external involvement in secessionist conflicts also requires balancing conflicting interests between external actors.

Perhaps the Crimea case, or the Ukraine Crisis, is one of the most suitable cases to illustrate this point. As discussed in Chap. 4, the escalation of the self-determination conflict between the pro-Western population and the pro-Russian population in Ukraine, which has led to the independence of Crimea and its fusion with Russia,

---

[2]Oberg (1999).

[3]Johnstone (1999).

[4]Hannum (2011), Note 16.

is closely connected with the struggle for geopolitical interests between the West and Russia. Therefore, the reconciliation between the pro-Western population and the pro-Russian population in Ukraine seems unlikely to occur when the conflicting powerful external actors, namely the West and Russia, refuse to take a cooperative attitude to each other. Clearly, in such circumstances balancing conflicting interests between external actors becomes indispensable for the effective settlement of the conflict between internal parties: powerful external actors in pursuit of conflicting geopolitical interests should strive to achieve a certain degree of cooperation in the first place, and this will form the basis, on which the proxies of these external actors, namely internal conflicting parties, can settle their self-determination conflict. As wisely noted by Rosenau, "what happens abroad is inescapably a function of what happens within strife-ridden societies and, conversely, the dynamics of internal wars are conditioned, perhaps even sustained, by external events... the new weapons technology has forced the great powers to test each other's influence through involvement in the internal wars of small neutral nations."[5] This judgement deserves serious consideration when it comes to secessionist cases like the one in Crimea.

5.2.2 *Improving the Functioning of the UN in Conflict Settlement*

Needless to say, balancing conflicting interests should not only exist in theory and it should be put into practice. At such time, one needs to consider concerting the individual actions of internal and external actors: secessionists should be required to stop acting against human rights and territorial interests of non-secessionists; non-secessionists should be required to respect the democratic claims of secessionists; external actors should be required to promote peaceful settlement of secessionist conflicts instead of intensifying the tension between secessionists and non-secessionists. Undoubtedly, there should be a center for the concerting job. In the current international legal system, this center is the UN. Article 1(1) and (3) UN Charter provide the aims: "To maintain international peace and security, and to that end... To achieve international co-operation in solving international problems of an economic, social, cultural, or humanitarian character, and in promoting and encouraging respect for human rights and for fundamental freedoms for all without distinction as to race, sex, language, or religion"; Article 1(1) and (4) provide that the UN is to be a center for harmonizing the actions of nations for the maintenance of international peace and security. Therefore, the UN is obliged to concert individual actions of internal and external actors in secessionist conflicts, for the sake of peaceful settlement of conflicts.

In this sense, it can be said that the functioning of the UN constitutes the most important external involvement in secessionist conflicts. The kernel of improving

[5] Rosenau (1964), pp. 1 and 6.

external involvement in secessionist conflicts is improving the functioning of the UN: the UN shall strive to do a better job as a center for harmonizing individual actions of internal and external actors in secessionist conflicts. Clearly, it does not only require relevant UN organs to exercise its power in a rational manner but also effective cooperation between these UN organs. One should first look at which UN organs might be involved in the settlement of secessionist conflicts. Given the cases discussed before, the following UN organs are involved: General Assembly, Security Council, International Court of Justice, Secretariat and ad hoc organs intended for international territorial administration established under Security Council resolutions. It must be noted that the UN principal organs are not on an equal footing in fulfilling the task of settling secessionist conflicts in a cooperative manner with the aim of maintaining international peace and security: according to Article 12 of the UN Charter, the primary responsibility for the maintenance of international peace and security is placed on the Security Council, and therefore, the Security Council plays a leading role in promoting international cooperation in conflict settlement. The UN Secretary-General seemed to be quite active in some secessionist cases, such as Hammarskjöld in the Katanga case, but it should be noted that Security Council resolution 143 (1960) authorized the Secretary-General to take necessary steps to provide the Congolese government with military and technical assistance until the national security force might be able to fully meet their tasks, so the Secretary-General was still playing a supportive role alongside the Security Council. Similarly, when Secretary-General Annan appointed Martti Ahtisaari as his Special Envoy for the Future Status Process for Kosovo, this appointment was approved by the Security Council on 10 November 2005 and was effective as of that date.[6] Therefore, from an institutional perspective, the Security Council definitely deserves more attention in the discussion of concerting the individual actions of internal and external actors for the sake of peaceful settlement of secessionist conflicts.

5.2.2.1 More Rational Exercise of Power by the Security Council

When it comes to improving the functioning of the Security Council, the purposes and principles of the UN must be mentioned in the first place: Article 24(2) of the UN Charter provides that in discharging its duties the Security Council shall act in accordance with the purposes and principles of the United Nations. From this perspective, when Security Council resolutions are suspected of violating the purposes and principles of the UN, the legality of these resolutions is open to question as the Security Council fails to discharge its duties in the provided manner. Unfortunately, the compliance of the Security Council with the purposes and principles of the UN is not very satisfying. A typical case has been mentioned before: the Permanent Representative of Algeria expressed serious anxiety about the likely undermining effect of a decision made by the Security Council on state sovereignty

[6] United Nations Meetings Coverage & Press Releases, SG/A/955-BIO/3714.

in the name of humanitarian pursuit.[7] This anxiety is not legally groundless as the current international legal system does not provide any effective remedy for an injured party when the Security Council fails to act in accordance with the purposes and principles of the UN. In other words, it is nearly impossible to hold the Security Council responsible for its action or inaction that is suspected of violating the purposes and principles of the UN. This issue can be attributed to several reasons, and one of them is the underdevelopment of international legislation regarding the responsibility of international organizations. A set of draft articles on the responsibility of international organizations were adopted by the International Law Commission at its sixty-third session in 2011, and according to these articles, there is an internationally wrongful act of an international organization when conduct consisting of an action or omission is attributable to that organization under international law and constitutes a breach of an international obligation of that organization, and the international organization is obliged to make full reparation for injury caused by the internationally wrongful act.[8] However, it remains unclear how a breach of an international obligation can be confirmed. For instance, when an injured state claims that there is a breach of an international obligation, but the international organization denies, how can such a dispute be settled? To be more specific, only when the concrete international obligation of the international organization is confirmed can one start to discuss a breach of it. When there is not any institutional arrangement to confirm the existence of a concrete international obligation, it is too early to consider the breach of it and the relevant reparation.

Moreover, the immunity of the UN and its staff further complicates the confirmation of a breach of an international obligation of an international organization.[9] For this reason, even if the Security Council fails to act in accordance with the purposes and principles of the UN and causes injury, it will still be extremely difficult, if not impossible, for an injured party to acquire effective remedy, due to the privileges and immunities enjoyed by the UN. Nevertheless, it must be admitted that authority without accountability is detrimental to improvement in the functioning of the Security Council: the credibility of the Security Council and the trust relationship between the Security Council and the relevant party will certainly be undermined, if the Security Council need not be responsible for its decisions which seem to be incompatible with the purposes and principles of the UN and cause injury to a relevant party. Undoubtedly, states like Algeria will be less hesitant to support

[7]See Chap. 4, Note 38.

[8]UN Doc. A/66/10, p. 55, Art. 4 and p. 60, Art. 31.

[9]The ICJ's 1999 advisory opinion, Difference Relating to Immunity from Legal Process of a Special Rapporteur of the Commission on Human Rights, is a case in point. Malaysian companies deemed that comments a UN Special Rapporteur made during an interview with a magazine reporter constituted defamation and sued him before a national court. The ICJ held that the Special Rapporteur was immune from suit in national courts, and indicated that the UN could be required to bear responsibility for the damage arising from such acts according to section 29 of the Convention on the Privileges and Immunities of the United Nations. In fact this section also implied that the UN enjoys great autonomy in deciding the scope of its obligations.

the humanitarian pursuit advocated by the UN if the UN can pay more attention to the principle of state sovereignty when pursuing humanitarian aims. Similarly, when the Security Council concerts individual actions of internal and external actors for the settlement of secessionist conflicts in accordance with the purposes and principles of the United Nations, it will give rise to less distrust and resistance and thus a greater chance of success can be expected. That is to say, even in the absence of rigid legal regulations for the action or inaction taken by the Security Council, the Security Council shall consciously exercise its power in a rational manner on the basis of the purposes and principles of the UN, for the sake of functioning more effectively. When the powers possessed by the Security Council are not exercised in a rational manner, this will inevitably trigger distrust or resistance, which renders it unlikely for the Security Council to function effectively in the settlement of secessionist conflicts. More specifically, the irrational exercise of power by the Security Council will certainly affect the willingness of relevant actors to cooperate in the settlement of secessionist conflicts, and under such circumstances it becomes more difficult for the Security Council to concert individual actions of internal and external actors.

a. More Rationality in Making Decisions

Rendering the exercise of power by the Security Council more rational is definitely a very complicated theme. In general, it includes two aspects, namely making decisions and enforcing decisions, and they are closely connected with each other. When considering the issue of making decisions, one needs to pay special attention to the following problems: checks and balances between permanent members of the Security Council, the degree of reasonableness of the draft resolution to be voted, and the avoidance of ambiguous expressions. One can first look at checks and balances between permanent members of the Security Council. As mentioned above, the current international legal system fails to provide rigid legal regulations for the functioning of the Security Council, so self-restraint is particularly important for the Security Council. Closely related to the self-restraint of the Security Council is the significance of checks and balances between permanent members. Draft Security Council resolutions which are detrimental to the settlement of secessionist conflicts can only be vetoed by permanent members: when permanent members fail to exercise their veto powers despite realizing the detrimental effects embodied in draft Security Council resolutions, they contribute to the irrational exercise of power, because effective checks and balances between permanent members are missing, and in such circumstances the self-restraint of the Security Council cannot be expected. Therefore, when permanent members realize the detrimental effects embodied in draft Security Council resolutions, it is necessary for them to exercise their veto powers, which helps render the exercise of power by the Security Council more rational.

In order to understand this point, it is time to review the criticism made by Russia against the military intervention in Libya authorized by UN Security Council

Resolution 1973 (2011), and it is particularly noteworthy that the detrimental consequences were somewhat foreseen by Russia when it cast an abstention vote.[10] In fact, Russia is not the only permanent member which has foreseen the detrimental consequences of the Security Council resolution, as China, another permanent member, has also foreseen such consequences.[11] Both of them failed to exercise their veto powers to prevent the adoption of this problematic resolution, although they should have done to prevent other permanent members from making a huge mistake.[12] Preventing mistakes made by other permanent members helps increase the self-restraint of the Security Council, which is the key to rendering the exercise of power by the Security Council more rational, and it largely determines whether the Security Council can effectively concert individual actions of actors in conflict settlement. From this perspective, it is accurate to say that Russia and China need to do self-criticism: although they have realized the problem contained in the draft resolution and demonstrated their dissent, they have not performed their duty as permanent members in an adequate manner. They could have prevented the mistake and they were entitled to do so, but they still failed to do so. To some extent, the exercise of veto power can be regarded as an obligation, and when permanent members fail to fulfill this obligation, there will be no effective checks and balances between permanent members, which definitely lowers the rational degree of the exercise of power by the Security Council.

Of course, the reason behind the non-exercise of veto power should not be overlooked, and it is much concerned with the degree of reasonableness of the draft resolution to be voted. Needless to say, a certain degree of reasonableness was embodied in the draft resolution, and that is why Russia and China did not veto it.[13] However, this degree of reasonableness was not enough for the effective

[10]The Russian delegation pointed out: "the passion of some Council members for methods involving force prevailed. This is most unfortunate and regrettable. Responsibility for the inevitable humanitarian consequences of the excessive use of outside force in Libya will fall fair and square on the shoulders of those who might undertake such action. If this comes to pass, then not only the civilian population of Libya but also the cause of upholding peace and security throughout the entire region of North Africa and the Middle East will suffer. Such destabilizing developments must be avoided", see United Nations Security Council, Sixty-sixth year, 6498th meeting, 17 March 2011, S/PV.6498, p. 8.

[11]The representative of China pointed out: "China is always against the use of force in international relations. In the Security Council's consultations on resolution 1973 (2011), we and other Council members asked specific questions. However, regrettably, many of those questions failed to be clarified or answered. China has serious difficulty with parts of the resolution", see United Nations Security Council, Sixty-sixth year, 6498th meeting, 17 March 2011, S/PV.6498, p. 10.

[12]The US president Barack Obama in an interview even expressed that the worst mistake of his presidency was "failing to plan for the day after what I think was the right thing to do in intervening in Libya", see Malloy and Treyz (2016).

[13]The Russian delegation stated: "I underscore yet again that we are consistent and firm advocates of the protection of the civilian population. Guided by this basic principle as well as by the common humanitarian values that we share with both the sponsors and other Council members, Russia did not prevent the adoption of this resolution", see United Nations Security Council, Sixty-sixth year, 6498th meeting, 17 March 2011, S/PV. 6498, p. 8; the representative of China stated: "China is

settlement of the Libya issue but unfortunately, Russia and China somewhat contented themselves with the insufficient reasonableness. This problem is rather noteworthy because permanent members should react in a better way to this kind of draft resolutions which contain a certain degree of reasonableness but insufficient for conflict settlement. When permanent members simply content themselves with the insufficient reasonableness, the adoption of problematic draft resolutions which can lead to detrimental consequences cannot be avoided. Therefore, permanent members definitely need to pursue a high degree of reasonableness in dealing with practical issues, and this pursuit has to be reflected in the adoption of draft resolutions.

Admittedly, there is no clear standard with regard to the degree of reasonableness. High degree and low degree sometimes are not indisputably distinguishable. Nevertheless, this problem should not be exaggerated: when permanent members have already foreseen the detrimental consequences which can be caused by a Security Council resolution, it is clear that the reasonableness of the resolution is insufficient. The distinction between high and low degree of reasonableness becomes difficult mainly when the detrimental consequences to be caused by a Security Council resolution cannot be foreseen. In addition, when judging whether a Security Council resolution is sufficiently reasonable or not, one should focus on both the end to be pursued and the means being provided in it. A Security Council resolution is insufficiently reasonable not because the end being pursued is not reasonable but because the means being provided are problematic. Returning to UN Security Council Resolution 1973 (2011), it is clear that its aim, namely the protection of civilians, was reasonable, but the same cannot be said about the means being provided: "the resolution was however ambiguous on when force can be used. It is suggested that Resolution 1973 required a demonstrable risk of indiscriminate attack to civilians, per se necessity and jus ad bellum proportionality, the latter exceeding IHL's concept of proportionality because of the specificity of the resolution's aim".[14] When one only focuses on the end being pursued in the resolution and overlooks the means being provided, one is highly likely to make a wrong judgment on the degree of reasonableness embodied in draft Security Council resolutions.

In essence, this point can also be understood from the perspective discussed in Chap. 4, namely necessary condition and sufficient condition, or abstract legality and practical legality. Undoubtedly, that the end being pursued is reasonable is the necessary condition for a draft Security Council resolution to be reasonable, but a reasonable draft Security Council resolution requires more than a reasonable end as reasonable means count no less. A reasonable end can provide no more than abstract legality, and practical legality relies more on reasonable means. Improving the functioning of the Security Council is less related to a reasonable end as the end

gravely concerned by the continuing deterioration of the situation in Libya. We support the Security Council's adoption of appropriate and necessary action to stabilize the situation in Libya as soon as possible and to halt acts of violence against civilians", S/PV. 6498, p. 10.

[14]Lehmann (2012), p. 117.

being pursued by the Security Council has never been indisputably unreasonable. It is the means which are employed to pursue the end that need to be improved: in the absence of reasonable means, a reasonable end can hardly be achieved; for instance, it is unrealistic to expect a humanitarian end to be attained by means that cannot be deemed humanitarian. From this perspective, the expression that "all necessary means to protect civilians under threat of attack" contained in Security Council Resolution 1973 (2011) is questionable: the humanitarian end determined that the means which could be selected were rather limited and needed to be carefully devised. Given that the practical enforcement of Security Council Resolutions is generally through mandates, and mandates are more likely to get overstretched due to the combination of the ambiguity of resolutions and political considerations, one shall never underestimate the unreasonableness of practical means that are employed to pursue a reasonable end.

It is time to consider the third perspective regarding the decision-making of the Security Council, namely avoiding ambiguous expressions. Obviously, increasing the reasonableness of a draft Security Council resolution is much concerned with avoiding ambiguous expressions: the more unambiguous expressions are, the less open they are to political exploitation. This point is particularly meaningful when a Security Council decision is to be enforced through a mandate, because such a mandate as a legal device is currently still far from being mature: concrete regulations in this regard are still rather underdeveloped, and this underdevelopment is actually incompatible with the relatively frequent application of this device. This problem should be carefully considered, particularly when a mandate leads to a problematic outcome, because at such time the inadequacy of concrete regulations regarding mandates definitely becomes unbearable. The military action in Libya authorized by UN Security Council Resolution 1973 (2011) is a case in point: if the military action had not caused the disastrous consequences, the inadequacy of concrete regulations regarding mandates would have been less likely to be noticed, let alone be blamed; unfortunately, the military action caused the disastrous consequences and disclosed the inadequacy of concrete regulations regarding mandates. How can this problem be solved? One way is to add concrete regulations in the draft Security Council resolutions that authorize actions, as ambiguous expressions contained in mandates should be replaced by concrete regulations. In essence, this is also an issue of standardizing Security Council decisions.

The importance of standardizing Security Council decisions is based on practical needs. Security Council decisions, particularly resolutions, are of double nature, namely political decisions and international legal instruments. When one only focuses on the former nature, standardization seems rather unimportant or unnecessary. However, when one notices that Security Council resolutions are international legal instruments, standardization seems both important and necessary. As a matter of fact, Security Council resolutions are particularly powerful international legal instruments: "unlike any other international organization [the Security Council has] the power to rewrite or dispense with existing international law in particular situations, and possibly in more general terms... In effect the capacity to override other treaties and general international law amounts to a claim to formal legislative capacity".[15] In this sense, a higher degree of standardization is an inherent requirement. If Security Council resolutions lack the necessary standardization, applying Security Council resolutions as a part of international law in practice will be quite difficult: the deliberate ambiguity out of political considerations is hardly compatible with the requirement of legal certainty. Worse still, the deliberate ambiguity embodied in Security Council resolutions tends to complicate its interpretation by other UN organs, and it might even render the participation of other UN organs counterproductive in the settlement of conflicts, as will be discussed later.

b. More Rationality in Enforcing Decisions

More standardization and less ambiguity is meaningful for not only making decisions but also enforcing decisions. Undoubtedly, when a Security Council decision is rather ambiguous, its enforcement will certainly be affected in a negative manner, and many problems will be caused thereby. Just like Security Council Resolution 1973 (2011), the ambiguous expression "all necessary means to protect civilians under threat of attack" definitely contributed to the ill-advised enforcement of the resolution which triggered many serious doubts. Therefore, one can say that improving decision enforcement is highly dependent on better made decisions. However, from a more practical perspective, it is also unrealistic to expect that every decision made by the Security Council can fully avoid ambiguity: as noted by Wood, Security Council resolutions "are often drafted by non-lawyers, in haste, under considerable political pressure, and with a view to securing unanimity within the Council. This latter point is significant since it often leads to deliberate ambiguity and the addition of superfluous material (presumably thought at the time to be harmless)".[16] For this reason, it is necessary to consider improving decision enforcement in spite of less standardized and highly ambiguous decisions. This point becomes particularly important, when issues being addressed by the Security Council are untypical and the Security Council lacks mature experience in dealing with them, such as secessionist conflicts.

How can the enforcement of a Security Council decision be improved when the decision itself is rather ambiguously drafted? When it comes to a secessionist conflict, one thing is certain: the enforcement of a Security Council decision must help settle the conflict, so it is time to consider balancing conflicting interests in enforcing the Security Council decision. For instance, when a Security Council resolution regarding a secessionist conflict instructs that all necessary means should be taken to protect civilians under threat of attack, it should be understood that civilians of both conflicting parties under threat of attack shall be protected, and any selective protection, through which one conflicting party has not been treated fairly, represents problematic enforcement of this Security Council resolution. In the same

[15] Boyle and Chinkin (2007), p. 233.
[16] Wood (1998), p. 82.

vein, it is indisputable that threat of attack from both conflicting parties are opposed by the Security Council resolution, so biased opposition which condemned violence of one side and condoned that of the other side, is also bad enforcement of the Security Council resolution.

Good enforcement of Security Council decisions requires keeping the promise embodied in Security Council resolutions. In the first place, one needs to consider this question whether the Security Council is bound to keep its own promise. As the Security Council has the power to revoke its resolutions, there is such opinion that the Security Council is not bound to keep its own promise. Undeniably, the Security Council has this power, but it does not mean that exercising the power in this way is unproblematic. Whether the Security Council is bound to keep its own promise is a question not only about having the power or not but also about the rational exercise of power. Clearly, when the Security Council fails to keep its own promise, it definitely impairs the trust relationship between the Security Council and the recipient of the promise, and an international organization should realize that only when conflicting parties trust in the promise made by it will they consider cooperating with it, so keeping its own promise forms the basis for an international organization to effectively participate in the settlement of a secessionist conflict. When the promise made by the Security Council is no longer trustworthy, the basis for cooperation between the Security Council and a conflicting party is lost, and it renders any involvement of the Security Council in conflict settlement fruitless. Therefore, even if the Security Council had the power to break its promise, it would definitely be ill-advised for the Security Council to do so, given the detrimental effects on international cooperation.

This point can also be discussed from other perspectives, such as the effects of unilateral acts. In essence, a Security Council resolution is similar to a unilateral act instead of a treaty. Of course, it is not a typical unilateral act as a resolution is made by the Security Council rather than a state. From this perspective, the discussion on the effects of unilateral acts seems inapplicable here. Nevertheless, given the practical demand for more rationality in the exercise of power by the Security Council, particularly in terms of revocation, it is still meaningful to refer to the discussion on the effects of unilateral acts: what renders a unilateral act of a state more rational might also help increase the rationality of a Security Council resolution. In the Guiding Principles applicable to unilateral declarations of States capable of creating legal obligations (2006), the International Law Commission suggests that arbitrary revocations should not be permitted; "in assessing whether a revocation would be arbitrary, consideration should be given to: (i) Any specific terms of the declaration relating to revocation; (ii) The extent to which those to whom the obligations are owed have relied on such obligations; (iii) The extent to which there has been a fundamental change in the circumstances."[17] "The Commission has drawn up an open-ended list of criteria to be taken into consideration when determining whether

---

[17]UN Doc. A/61/10, p. 369.

or not a withdrawal is arbitrary".[18] Undeniably, if arbitrary revocations by states should not be permitted, there is no reason to believe that arbitrary revocations by the Security Council are unproblematic. As pointed out by the ICJ in the Nicaragua case, "estoppel may be inferred from the conduct, declarations and the like made by a State which not only clearly and consistently evinced acceptance by that State of a particular régime, but also had caused another State or States, in reliance on such conduct, detrimentally to change position or suffer some prejudice".[19] In the same vein, it is hard to conclude that the Security Council should be tolerated from the perspective of international law, when it breaks its promise and causes another state in reliance on its promise detrimentally to change position or suffer some prejudice.

It is particularly noteworthy that when the Security Council fails to respect its promise, one can suspect it of violating the principle of good faith. As mentioned above, according to Article 24(2) UN Charter, in discharging its duties the Security Council shall act in accordance with the purposes and principles of the United Nations. Article 2 has clearly stated that "the Organization and its Members, in pursuit of the Purposes stated in Article 1, shall act in accordance with the following Principles... All Members, in order to ensure to all of them the rights and benefits resulting from membership, shall fulfill in good faith the obligations assumed by them in accordance with the present Charter". When considering Article 24(2) and Article 2 in a combined style, one must admit that upholding the principle of good faith is closely connected with the rights and benefits of individual states: when the UN Security Council fails to discharge its duties in accordance with the principle of good faith, the rights and benefits of relevant states might not be fully ensured. To be more specific, the promise made by the Security Council in its resolution is generally related to the rights and benefits of an individual state or states, and when the Security Council fails to keep its promise, it can injure the rights and benefits of the relevant state or states. At such time, arguing that the Security Council has the power to revoke its resolutions is not convincing, and how the damage to the rights and benefits of the relevant state or states caused by the revocation can be redressed is an issue worth serious consideration. Simply arguing that the Security Council has the power to revoke its resolutions and ignoring the damage on the rights and benefits of the relevant state or states caused by the revocation will encourage irrational exercise of power. When the current international legal system is not in a position to offer a remedy for such damage, it is important to discourage such an irrational exercise of power, so the Security Council shall avoid breaking its own promise: when the Security Council keeps its promise, it is conducive to the observance of the principle of good faith and the ensurance of the rights and benefits of the relevant state or states.

---

[18] UN Doc. A/61/10, p. 380.

[19] Military and Paramilitary Activities in and against Nicaragua (Nicaragua v. United States of America), Jurisdiction of the Court and Admissibility of the Application, I.C.J. Reports 1984, p. 415, para. 51.

During the settlement of the Kosovo secessionist conflict, the Security Council was suspected of breaking its promise, given the following aspects. Firstly, according to Security Council resolution 1244(1999), sovereignty and territorial integrity of the Federal Republic of Yugoslavia should be carefully considered.[20] However, the Comprehensive Proposal for the Kosovo Status Settlement put forward by Martti Ahtisaari, who was the Special Envoy of the UN Secretary-General, definitely did not take full account of sovereignty and territorial integrity of the Federal Republic of Yugoslavia: it actually prevented Yugoslavia from resuming sovereign control over Kosovo. Needless to say, the work of the Special Envoy of the UN Secretary-General made up a part of the enforcement of the Security Council resolution, so it was certainly problematic for the Special Envoy to put forward a proposal which was incompatible with the requirement set in the previous Security Council resolution, ignoring the rights and benefits of non-secessionists represented by the sovereign state. In short, the right to self-determination over territorial interests of non-secessionists, which was respected in Security Council resolution 1244(1999), was disregarded by the Special Envoy in his proposal. Undeniably, a UN Special Envoy should not disregard the promise made by the UN Security Council and the rights and benefits of the party which used to trust in the Security Council. A proposal put forward by a UN Special Envoy who ignores the promise made by the UN Security Council should not be condoned, for the sake of optimizing the enforcement of the Security Council decision during the settlement of a secessionist conflict. A further discussion of the Ahtisaari plan is to be found later, in combination with the issue of mediation.

Secondly, Security Council resolution 1244(1999) expressly confirmed that "after the withdrawal, an agreed number of Yugoslav and Serb military and police personnel will be permitted to return to Kosovo to perform the functions in accordance with annex 2."[21] But in reality this promise was not honored: the Security Council did not create necessary conditions for the return of Yugoslav and Serb military and police personnel to Kosovo. Obviously, the return of Yugoslav and Serb military and police personnel to Kosovo could not be achieved unilaterally, since the Kosovo Force led by NATO was stationed there. If the Security Council did not create necessary conditions, like requiring the Kosovo Force to cooperate, such a return was out of the question. For this reason, the return clause should be taken as a promise made by the Security Council that it would provide the necessary assistance for this return based on the principle of good faith, and it was definitely reasonable for Yugoslavia to expect that the Security Council would help carry out the return of Yugoslav and Serb military and police personnel to Kosovo, as including the return clause in the resolution made no sense, if the Security Council did not help when the Kosovo Force led by the NATO refused to cooperate. Undeniably, the issue of inaction should not be neglected, for the sake of rendering the enforcement of a

[20] S/RES/1244 (1999), para. 8.

[21] S/RES/1244 (1999), para. 4.

Security Council decision more rational during the settlement of a secessionist conflict.

5.2.2.2 More Rational Exercise of Power by Other UN Organs

a. More Rational Exercise of Power to Issue Legally Non-Binding Instruments

Of course, not only the exercise of power by the Security Council needs to be more rational, the exercise of power by other UN organs also needs to be more rational. Unfortunately, the rational exercise of power by other UN organs is usually neglected: compared with the power possessed by the Security Council, powers of other UN organs seem quite obscure, given that Security Council resolutions are legally binding while General Assembly resolutions and other UN instruments are not. From this perspective, such neglect is quite understandable. Nevertheless, it must be admitted that being legally non-binding does not mean having no practical influence. As long as legally non-binding UN instruments have a practical influence, it is necessary to consider regulating the power possessed by UN organs to make these instruments because the practical influence can play a negative role in the settlement of conflicts or give rise to new conflicts. The conflict-causing aspect becomes more understandable, when one looks at the case concerning defamation due to comments a UN Special Rapporteur made during an interview with a magazine reporter, on which the ICJ delivered an Advisory Opinion in 1999[22]: Malaysian companies deemed that comments a UN Special Rapporteur made during an interview with a magazine reporter constituted defamation and sued him before a national court, and the ICJ held that the Special Rapporteur was immune from suit in national courts. Clearly, if comments made by a UN Special Rapporteur during an interview with magazine reporter could already cause a practical dispute, there is no reason to underestimate the practical influence of a UN instrument, despite being legally non-binding.

The Kosovo Advisory Opinion is a case in point. "A number of states – Oman, Niger, Côte d'Ivoire and Kuwait – invoked the Advisory Opinion as the basis for their decision to establish diplomatic relations. It is reasonable to assume that in other cases, too, the opportunity created by the Advisory Opinion facilitated recognition. Recognition is, in many ways, an indicator of the success or failure of any secessionist project."[23] Obviously, the Kosovo Advisory Opinion, despite being legally non-binding, could still tip the scale in favor of Kosovo secessionists and leave non-secessionists at a disadvantage, thus frustrating the balance of conflicting interests as the right to self-determination over territorial interests of non-secessionists has not been respected. Therefore, it can be said that a disservice

[22]Difference Relating to Immunity from Legal Process of a Special Rapporteur of the Commission on Human Rights, Advisory Opinion, I.C.J. Reports 1999, p. 62.

[23]Caplan and Wolff (2015), p. 320.

has been done to the settlement of the conflict thanks to the ICJ, a principal organ of the UN, although this outcome could have been avoided: as discussed above,[24] the ICJ could have interpreted international law in a well-advised way, which would not have tipped the scale in favor of Kosovo secessionists and leave non-secessionists at a disadvantage. Thus, it is evident that a legally non-binding UN instrument is still of practical influence, which necessitates regulating the power exercised by other UN organs. The practical influence of legally non-binding UN instruments also exists in negotiations between secessionists and non-secessionists: a legally non-binding instrument can be employed as a powerful argument in negotiations, thus influencing conflict settlement in a less direct manner.

Moreover, it should be noted that the influence of a non-binding UN instrument can be rather extensive, which might sound somewhat incredible but it is actually undeniable. One can notice the influence of the Kosovo Advisory Opinion on other secessionist conflicts. According to the then-president of Abkhazia, Sergei Bagapsh, "the decision of the International Court once more confirms the right of Abkhazia and [fellow breakaway Georgian region] South Ossetia to self-rule. And from a historical and legal point of view, Abkhazia and South Ossetia have much more right to independence than Kosovo".[25] Aitor Estaban, an MP from Spain's Basque nationalist PNV party, thought that the main consequence was that Spain cannot keep saying that the international rules don't allow for a split of the country for a new Basque independent country into the European Union, and that was good news for them.[26] According to Masis Mailyan, Chairman of the NKR (Nagorno-Karabakh Republic) Public Council for Foreign Policy and Security, "as a precedent, it is supposed to play an important role in the international recognition of the Nagorno-Karabakh Republic... The OSCE Minsk Group Co-Chairs should reject the obsolete methods they have so far applied to settle the Nagorno-Karabakh conflict and start drafting new proposals for the NKR in the context of present-day international legal norms".[27] The de facto Foreign Ministry of Transdniester region, which broke away from Moldova in a short but bloody war in the early 1990s, said in a statement on 27 July 2010 that the ICJ opinion was a "landmark" and "model" for other entities seeking independence.[28] To be fair, whether the pro-secessionist color in the Kosovo Advisory Opinion is indeed that strong, as understood by secessionists around the world, is still open to question: as discussed in Chap. 2, due to the narrow approach adopted by the ICJ, a right to secession is neither confirmed nor denied in the Kosovo Advisory Opinion, but it is indisputable that UN organs should refrain

[24]See Chap. 2, Sect. 2.4.3.

[25]Reaction in quotes: UN legal ruling on Kosovo, https://www.bbc.com/news/world-europe-10733837, last accessed on 15.06.2018.

[26]Ibid.

[27]ICJ verdict on Kosovo must be precedent for NKR's international recognition, https://news.am/eng/news/25826.html, last accessed on 15.06.2018.

[28]Transdniester Hails Court Ruling on Kosovo, https://www.rferl.org/a/Transdniester_Hails_Court_Ruling_On_Kosovo/2111867.html, last accessed on 15.06.2018.

from creating a pro-secessionist impression, for the sake of effective conflict settlement. This point proves to be more important when the UN organ is the ICJ, the judicial nature of which certainly requires an impartial image. Unfortunately, the ICJ created a pro-secessionist image for itself due to the Kosovo Advisory Opinion, although it could have avoided such an image by delivering a different advisory opinion.

In view of the foregoing, it is safe to conclude that one should not solely focus on the power exercised by the Security Council in the settlement of secessionist conflicts as effective settlement actually requires more than that: other UN organs, as long as their involvement has a practical influence on conflict settlement, shall be required to act in a more rational manner, and the power vested in them needs to be exercised in a more constructive way. Due to the authority of the UN, secessionists and non-secessionists are unable to ignore UN instruments related to their conflict: even a legally non-binding instrument can still influence the settlement of secessionist conflicts in a less direct and unexpected way. Therefore, the legally non-binding effect in the abstract sense is one thing, the practical influence in concrete circumstances is quite another. Overlooking this point is certainly unhelpful for the UN to play a constructive role in conflict settlement. As discussed above, the UN and its staff should remain impartial in secessionist conflicts, as required by the balance of conflicting interests, and a UN instrument should not tip the scale in favor of one conflicting party and undermine the necessary impartiality. Otherwise distrust can be aroused, thus affecting international cooperation. Worse still, the once in-doubt impartiality in the settlement of a secessionist conflict might cast a shadow on UN involvement in the settlement of other secessionist conflicts.

b. Improving Cooperation Between the Security Council and Other UN Organs

Given the secessionist cases discussed before, one can realize that during conflict settlement the cooperation between the Security Council and other UN organs has left much to be desired. If the cooperation had been better, the UN could have functioned better in the settlement of secessionist conflicts. For this reason, in order to improve the UN involvement in conflict settlement, the cooperation between the Security Council and other UN organs must be optimized. At such time, one needs to consider this issue: on which legal ground is this cooperation regulated?

According to Chapter VI, it is clear that the Security Council plays the leading role in the settlement of conflicts which are likely to endanger the maintenance of international peace and security. The General Assembly is also available for conflict settlement, but it has to respect the supervisory role of the Security Council in this regard, according to Article 12. According to Article 98, the Secretary-General shall perform the function entrusted to him by the Security Council. As for the legal relation between the Security Council and the ICJ, although the UN Charter does not directly provide that the ICJ has to respect the supervisory role of the Security Council in respect of conflict settlement, given that Security Council resolutions have been treated as a part of international law, it is not wrong to say that the ICJ also needs to respect the leading role played by the Security Council in conflict settlement. In addition to these principal UN organs, an ad hoc UN organ might also be involved in the settlement of secessionist conflicts, such as the United Nations Interim Administration Mission in Kosovo (UNMIK), which was established pursuant to paragraph 10 of Security Council resolution 1244 (1999). In view of the foregoing, it is safe to conclude that the cooperation between the Security Council and other UN organs is regulated by the UN Charter and relevant Security Council resolutions. For this reason, one can say that improving cooperation largely depends on regulations provided in relevant Security Council resolutions: the more definite regulations are, the more effective cooperation will be. In addition, more definite regulations provided in Security Council resolutions are also conducive to adjudication, when controversies occur.

In order to understand this point, it is time to review two cases concerning the unsatisfying cooperation between the Security Council and other UN organs. In the Katanga case, the unsatisfying cooperation was between the Security Council and the Secretary-General Hammarskjöld. Security Council resolution 143 (1960) authorized the Secretary-General to take necessary steps to provide the Congolese government with military and technical assistance until the national security force might be able to fully meet their tasks. Unfortunately, due to the severe disagreement between Hammarskjöld and the Congolese government, Hammarskjöld failed to accomplish this mission in a satisfying manner: the disagreement between Hammarskjöld and the Congolese government became so drastic that the Secretary-General even implied the UN participation in the Katanga crisis might be withdrawn.[29] Obviously, the severe disagreement between Hammarskjöld and the Congolese government directly led to the unsatisfying performance of the function entrusted to him by the Security Council, so it can be said that this disagreement undermined cooperation between the Security Council and the Secretary-General. For the sake of settling this issue, it is necessary to discern what contributed to the severe disagreement between Hammarskjöld and the Congolese government. Obviously, this was much concerned with Security Council resolution 143 (1960) which was open to distinct interpretations: from the perspective of the Congolese government, this resolution implied that the UN troops should help fight against secessionists in Katanga; nevertheless, the Secretary-General saw it in a different way and even deemed the inclusion of Belgian personnel into the UN task performers unproblematic,[30] which further enraged the Congolese government. Needless to say, if the resolution could have regulated the authorization more definitely, it would have certainly helped diminish the disagreement between the Congolese government and the Secretary-General, which would have been conducive to the accomplishment of the mission entrusted to the Secretary-General by the Security Council. More importantly, one must consider this issue: is it necessary for the

[29]United Nations Security Council Official Records, 887th Meeting, 21 August 1960, S/PV. 887, para. 8.

[30]Ibid. paras. 11, 70, 88.

Security Council to intervene when a Security Council resolution is so ambiguous that the performance of the Secretary-General is severely affected thereby? After all, the Security Council knows better than anyone else what the resolution actually means, and no interpretation of the resolution can be more convincing than the one provided by the Security Council itself. If the Security Council chooses to clarify ambiguities in its resolutions, it becomes easier for the Secretary-General to cooperate not only with the Security Council but also with relevant states, and the latter cooperation can promote the former.

In the Kosovo case, cooperation between the Security Council and the UNMIK was also unsatisfying: Security Council resolution 1244 (1999) demonstrated the respect for sovereignty and territorial integrity of the Federal Republic of Yugoslavia, but UNMIK failed to prevent the Kosovo declaration of independence. According to Judge Bennouna, it was an issue with regard to the functions and responsibility of the UNMIK, and he regretted that the ICJ failed to make real contribution to the clarification.[31] The opinion of Judge Bennouna is definitely reasonable; nevertheless, one should also realize that the Security Council is in a much better position than the ICJ to clarify the functions and responsibility of the UNMIK. After all, the UNMIK was established pursuant to paragraph 10 of Security Council resolution 1244 (1999), so the functions and responsibility of the UNMIK should be regulated by its establisher: the Security Council should have clarified the functions and responsibility of the UNMIK according to its will demonstrated in Security Council resolution 1244 (1999) and have prevented the UNMIK from acting in a way which did not seem to be in accordance with the Security Council resolution. Unfortunately, the Security Council failed to do so and thus the ICJ was required to clarify this issue, when the case brought before the ICJ needed such clarification. At such time, not only the issue of cooperation between the Security Council and the UNMIK, the main part of which was concerned with the functions and responsibility of the UNMIK, but also the cooperation between the Security Council and the ICJ deserves serious consideration. For instance, whether the ICJ should clarify the functions and responsibility of the UNMIK when the Security Council itself did not regulate this issue clearly is a very important question regarding the cooperation between the Security Council and the ICJ within the current international legal system. With a view to avoiding additional legal problems concerning cooperation between the Security Council and the ICJ, the Security Council should precisely regulate the functions and responsibility of ad hoc UN organs established pursuant to Security Council resolutions, otherwise it can also affect cooperation between the Security Council and the ICJ.

To conclude, in order to make other UN organs cooperate with the Security Council more effectively in the settlement of secessionist conflicts, more definite regulations regarding the cooperation provided in Security Council resolutions are required. When regulations are not sufficiently definite, other UN organs might fail

[31]Accordance with International Law of the Unilateral Declaration of Independence in Respect of Kosovo, Dissenting Opinion of Judge Bennouna, I.C.J. Reports 2010, p. 504, para. 22.

to interpret the meaning in an accurate manner, which can lead to the counterproductive exercise of power by other UN organs, frustrate the efforts made by the Security Council, complicate the conflict and give rise to additional thorny issues.

5.3 More Rational Exercise of Mediating Power in Conflict Settlement

5.3.1 Exercise of Mediating Power by External Actors

Much has been discussed from the perspective of external actors, and it is time to focus on a particularly important part of external involvement, that is mediation. In the first place, it is necessary to point out why mediation should be regarded as a particularly important part of external involvement in the settlement of secessionist conflicts. As discussed in Chap. 3, secessionist conflicts, in essence, are self-determination conflicts between secessionists and non-secessionists; as general international law cannot provide a complete solution but some abstract principal guidance, the settlement largely depends on special agreements reached between secessionists and non-secessionists regarding their conflicting rights to self-determination. How can such an agreement be reached? From the perspective of conflicting parties, the answer will be negotiation and from the perspective of external actors involved in secessionist conflicts, the answer will be mediation. It must be noted that there is no intention to make a strict distinction here between mediation, conciliation and good offices: as pointed out by Merrills, in practice "these distinctions tend to be blurred. In a given case it may therefore be difficult to draw the line between mediation and conciliation, or to say exactly when good offices ended and mediation began".[32] Mediation in a secessionist conflict is to persuade secessionists and non-secessionists to come together and to help reach an agreement between them. Effective mediation can contribute significantly to conflict settlement: as mentioned in Chap. 3, the settlement of the secessionist conflict between the Free Aceh Movement and the Indonesian Government owed much to the Helsinki Memorandum of Understanding, which was achieved through international mediation. Due to its contribution to the forming of lex specialis, it is reasonable to regard mediation as a particularly important part of external involvement in the settlement of secessionist conflicts.

Admittedly, the UN has already realized the importance of mediation, and a series of UN instruments can be found in this regard. At the outset of a mediation effort, the UN Department of Political Affairs provided an induction package composed of three key instruments: the Special Envoy Briefing Package, the United Nations Manual for Mediators: Advice from United Nations Representatives and Envoys, and the Mediation Start-up Guidelines; in addition to this induction package, generic

[32]Merrills (2010), p. 563.

guidance has been developed in areas including conflict-related sexual violence in ceasefire and peace agreements, natural resources, ceasefire negotiations and management and women's participation in conflict mediation; at the relevant points of a mediation effort, case-specific guidance is developed in response to requests from mediators: since 2008, the Mediation Support Unit and its standby team of experts have developed 63 technical papers in various areas.[33] Of course, these instruments are of a guiding instead of a binding character: when a mediator deviates from these guidelines, there will not be any legal consequence in a strict sense. Nevertheless, from the perspective of rendering the exercise of power more rational, such deviation deserves serious consideration, particularly when a mediator deviates from these guidelines and thus fails to make the situation better or makes it even more complicated: in such circumstances, it is necessary to reflect whether the mediator has abused its mediating power and what can be done to settle issues as such.

When speaking of the mediating power, one might question whether it is proper to regard it as a power, as mediators generally do not have the final say and they generally persuade conflicting parties to come together and agree on terms of settlement for themselves. However, it should be noted that power in practice means more than a final say: a mediator is still able to influence conflict settlement in other ways, even if it does not have the final say. As discussed in Chap. 3, in practice intervention can be hidden in proposals of mediation, when the proposal maker is too powerful to be ignored: powerful outsiders might choose to side with one party by offering a proposal of mediation in its favor. Of course, the disadvantaged party can reject this proposal, but it can do nothing to eliminate the influence of this proposal on the negotiation between it and the favored party. For instance, the favored party can employ this proposal as a powerful argument to refuse compromise on its own part and force the aggrieved party to give in in their negotiation. From this perspective, it is quite understandable that in the civil war the US warned Britain and France not to mediate in any way, for that would be regarded as virtual recognition of the secessionist entity and would invite war with the US.[34] The character of power becomes more evident when the assigned mediator is with a mandate approved by a powerful UN organ, as in such circumstances mediation is not a pure choice of conflicting parties. When a mediator, whose mandate is approved by the Security Council, deviates from UN guidelines on mediation and thus fails to make the situation better or makes it even more complicated, it runs definitely counter to the original intention of the mandate. In order to address such issue, one needs to reflect how the rational exercise of mediating power can be pursued.

In fact, those guiding instruments are standardizing mediation, which helps enhance the chances for success and minimize mediator error.[35] Needless to say,

---

[33]Report of the Secretary-General, Strengthening the role of mediation in the peaceful settlement of disputes, conflict prevention and resolution, A/66/811, pp. 10–11, paras. 36–38.

[34]See Chap. 3, Note 17.

[35]UN Doc. A/66/811, p. 31, para. 53.

different mediators will have different ways of exercising their mediating power, and the problem is that not every way can lead to a positive outcome. The standardization of mediation, in essence, is to sum up successful ways of exercising mediating power and to promote such successful experience. From this perspective, deviating from those guidelines is only justified when the mediator can do a better job in its own way, and the mediator should also offer convincing reasons to dispel relevant doubts. Otherwise it seems to suggest that mediators are allowed to act in a wrong way that lowers the chances for success. That is to say, although these UN instruments aiming to further standardize mediation are not legally binding, they should still be regarded as a part of the international legal framework intended for regulating external involvement in conflict settlement. A mediator should not deviate from these guidelines ad libitum simply because they are not legally binding, otherwise not only attempts made by the UN to further standardize mediation go in vain, the exercise of the mediating power will also prove to be irrational.

5.3.2 *Standardization for Increasing Rationality*

5.3.2.1 Following Legally Non-Binding UN Instruments

It must be realized that the further standardization of mediation and more rationality in exercising mediating power are closely associated with each other: generally speaking, a higher degree of standardization of mediation means a lower chance of the mediating power to be abused by mediators. Needless to say, the starting point of increasing rationality in exercising mediating power is to let mediators know how mediating power can be exercised in a rational manner: mediators need to know details about the successful experience of mediation in a systematic way. Satisfying this need requires the further standardization of mediation. Undeniably, it will be unfair to criticize mediators for the irrational exercise of mediating power if they are not clear about how mediating power can be exercised in a rational manner. Moreover, only when mediation becomes relatively standardized is it possible to judge whether the exercise of mediating power by mediators is rational or not. When the standard itself is absent, making such a judgement is unlikely. In this sense, it is safe to conclude that even if those guiding instruments regarding mediation cannot do much in preventing abuse of the mediating power, they still contribute significantly to the judgement on whether mediating power is exercised in a rational way.

The significance of those UN instruments regarding mediation becomes more understandable, when one considers mediation in the context of enforcing a Security Council decision. As mentioned before, there is no guarantee that every Security Council decision is drafted in a clear manner: since a Security Council decision including a mandate of mediation in a secessionist conflict could also be very general, the mediator might not get enough information on how to exercise its mediating power rationally from the decision. Obviously, something is required to fill this gap, and referring to those legally non-binding UN instruments regarding mediation is a good choice. For instance, the United Nations Manual for Mediators: Advice from United Nations Representatives and Envoys has shed much light on how mediating power can be effectively exercised in a detailed way: according to this manual, a mediator should listen to the conflicting parties to understand their interests, maintain impartiality, recognize and deal with actors behind the scenes, introduce international norms, standards and models to build agreements, find solutions that satisfy interests, eschew artificial deadlines…[36] It should be noted that these advices are concerned with not only the success or failure of mediation but also upholding the principles of the UN. For example, according to requirements of impartiality, "a mediator, especially a United Nations mediator, is typically mandated to uphold certain universal principles and values and may need to make them explicitly known to the parties"[37]; "UN mediators should be seen to apply these principles to all parties without favour, in order to earn their trust for the UN's role as an honest broker".[38] Obviously, if a mediator fails to apply these principles to all parties without favour and thus proves to be partial, not only the trust for the UN's role as an honest broker would be lost, upholding the principles of the UN is also in question.

The issue of deviating from the way of exercising mediating power suggested in those legally non-binding UN instruments actually deserves more attention from the perspective of international law. As discussed above, it is necessary for mediators deviating from those guiding instruments to offer a convincing explanation because of the likely drop in the chances for success, and the likely drop in the chances for success itself is closely related to the failure to uphold the principles of the UN. That is to say, deviating from those guiding instruments regarding mediation should be regarded as not only a strategic fault but also a principal mistake. Undeniably, it is ill-advised to confuse pure strategic faults and principal mistakes from the perspective of international law: pure strategic mistakes are not closely related to disregard for the principles of the UN, so it is hard to conclude that the existence of such mistakes proves that mediators have gone beyond their mandates approved by the Security Council, while principal mistakes which are closely related to disregard for the principles of the UN can prove that mediators have exceeded their mandates approved by the Security Council. Obviously, when the Security Council itself has to discharge its duties in accordance with the principles of the UN, it is not entitled to mandate a mediator to act in disregard of the principles of the UN, because "no Body can transfer to another more power than he has in himself".[39] Therefore, external actors that mediate in secessionist conflicts should not deviate from those legally

[36]The United Nations Manual for Mediators: Advice from United Nations Representatives and Envoys, published by The Programme in Peacemaking and Conflict Prevention of the United Nations Institute for Training and Research and The Mediation Support Unit of the United Nations Department of Political Affairs, 2010, pp. i–ii.

[37]UN Doc. A/66/811, p. 25, para. 27.

[38]The United Nations Manual for Mediators: Advice from United Nations Representatives and Envoys, 2010, p. 23.

[39]Locke (2012), Chapter 11 §135.

non-binding UN instruments ad libitum, because such deviation usually means disrespect for principles of the UN and no legal actor is allowed to do so in the current international legal system.

To conclude, upholding the principles of the UN requires mediators to follow legally non-binding UN instruments regarding mediation, and this requirement remains unchanged when mediators are mandated by the Security Council. Therefore, mediators in secessionist conflicts should not neglect legally non-binding requirements such as impartiality: neglecting this requirement can lead to disrespect for the principle of self-determination, as being partial to secessionists, such as satisfying their wish for exclusive territorial ownership, is disregarding the right to self-determination of non-secessionists over territorial interests. In addition to disrespect for principles of international law, such abuse of mediating power undermines the trust of conflicting parties in mediators, which might also affect the credibility of the UN when mediators are mandated by the UN. Given all these serious consequences, deviation from legally non-binding UN instruments regarding mediation should be condemned rather than condoned, and there should be corresponding measures against abuse of the mediating power. Otherwise mediation might not become positive external involvement in the settlement of secessionist conflicts.

5.3.2.2 Replacing Unsuitable Mediators

Unfortunately, despite progress made in the further standardization of mediation, rectifying abuse of the mediating power still proves to be unsatisfying. For instance, regarding the likely failure of a mediator to maintain impartiality in a secessionist conflict, UN instruments have actually not shed much light on an effective solution: it has been mentioned that mediators should "hand over to another mediator, or mediating entity, if they feel unable to maintain a balanced and impartial approach".[40] Obviously, such an arrangement cannot work well in practice: a mediator might act in an imbalanced and partial way but feel nothing about it, so it is ill-advised to rely on the subjective feeling of a mediator alone. A more practicable arrangement is required when a mediator is suspected of acting in an imbalanced and partial way. For example, an institution can be established to hear complaints made by conflicting parties against the mediator, in order to judge whether the mediator has maintained impartiality and acted within its mandate, and this judgement should play a decisive role in deciding whether the mediator should be replaced or not. That is to say, granting conflicting parties a procedural right to require replacing a mediator who is suspected of abusing its mediating power such as failing to be impartial can be a solution. Clearly, a procedural right to require replacing a mediator is more effective than the subjective feeling of a mediator in preventing abuse of mediating power. Such a procedural right becomes more

[40]UN Doc. A/66/811, p. 25, para. 28.

meaningful in the context of self-determination conflicts: abuse of mediating power tends to blur the demarcation between self-determination and other-determination, thus contributing to the complication of self-determination conflicts. It should be noted that the significance of mediation lies in its contribution to conflict settlement: in order to make mediation a positive contribution to conflict settlement instead of doing a disservice, procedural arrangements enabling a conflicting party feeling disadvantaged in the mediation to counter the undue influence exerted by an unsuitable mediator should be deemed indispensable. Whether the mediator is officially mandated by the UN or not will not affect the indispensability of such procedural arrangements.

In order to understand why the procedural right for conflicting parties to require replacing a mediator matters so much, it is necessary to review the disservice done by Holbrooke to the peaceful settlement of the Kosovo secessionist conflict. Despite being a mediator in the secessionist conflict, Holbrooke never bothered to conceal his partiality: in an interview made by the Financial Times he declared that "after the 1995 bombing, [Mr. Milosevic] knows that when I talk of NATO bombs, it is serious"[41]; while threatening non-secessionists by the use of force, Holbrooke was photographed meeting with a rebel in June 1998, which became a huge encouragement for secessionists: "I knew that since then, that USA, NATO, will put us in their hands", said the KLA fighter, Lirak Celaj.[42] In fact, Holbrooke was not alone: in the Kosovo case one can find a number of similar mediators neglecting impartiality and the need for a peaceful solution repeated in Security Council Resolutions. As mentioned in Chap. 4, one of the prominent American diplomats involved in the Rambouillet conference, Ambassador Christopher Hill, informed the Washington Post that the US representatives knew that there was a "zero point zero" chance that Serbs would agree to what they were offered at Rambouillet; another participant at Rambouillet even told the press off the record that "we intentionally set the bar too high for the Serbs to comply".[43] Dugi Gorani, who was an Albanian negotiator at Rambouillet, said that a foreign diplomat told him that the quota of five thousand deaths had to be passed to realize their secessionist pursuit.[44] Given the existence of such mediators in a secessionist conflict, mediation actually lowers the likelihood of a peaceful solution and such kind of mediation is undoubtedly a disservice.

Obviously, when unsuitable mediators can be replaced by suitable ones, mediation is more likely to be positive. If mediators in the Kosovo case had been as competent as those in the Aceh case, one could have expected a bright outcome. Thus, the replacement of mediators as a part of improving external involvement in the settlement of secessionist conflicts deserves serious consideration. Procedural arrangements are required, of which a procedural right for conflicting parties to require replacing unsuitable mediators is a crucial part, and an institution for hearing

[41]Financial Times, 8 Oct. 1998, p. 13.

[42]See Chap. 4, Note 91.

[43]See Chap. 4, Note 77.

[44]See Chap. 4, Note 91.

relevant complaints and making judgements should also be established. For many such procedural arrangements might sound somewhat exaggerated: is it a big fuss over mediation? In order to clarify this point, one must first recall the detrimental effects caused by unsuitable mediators. Clearly, unsuitable mediators, like those mentioned above, should not be allowed any more for reasons from different perspectives: they fail to contribute to the peaceful settlement of secessionist conflicts and even do a disservice; they fail to respect the right to self-determination of one conflicting party; they damage the image of a mediator and provoke distrust against mediation, which renders mediation unpopular in conflict settlement... In order to avoid all these problems, procedural arrangements regarding how to replace unsuitable mediators should be made, which helps prevent abuse of mediating power and restore the trust for mediation, thus contributing to the peaceful settlement of secessionist conflicts.

In the second place, one must realize that in practice the replacement of unsuitable mediators is certainly not easy, whether the mediator is mandated by the UN or not. When a mediator is mandated through a Security Council decision, its replacement generally involves the Security Council, and a conflicting party is unable to replace the mediator all by itself. In such circumstances, a procedural right for conflicting parties to require the replacement of unsuitable mediators becomes more necessary: a conflicting party needs to protect its own rights and interests, and the UN, particularly the Security Council, needs to correct its own mistakes. Of course, before correcting a mistake, it is necessary to confirm that this is really a mistake: the Security Council needs to confirm that the current mediator is indeed unsuitable then selects another one to replace this one. For this sake, an institution for hearing complaints against mediators and making judgements should be established, otherwise it will be impossible to know whether the mediator should be replaced when this one is regarded by a conflicting party as unsuitable but by the other party as suitable. When it comes to mediation which is not mandated by the UN, it is still not easy for a conflicting party to replace an unsuitable mediator mainly because the mediator can be too powerful to be rejected. Returning to the threatening words made by Holbrooke, it is clear that sometimes mediation is enforced on a conflicting party. The necessity of replacing an unsuitable mediator becomes more obvious when mediation itself is enforced: an enforced mediation undoubtedly indicates distrust of a conflicting party, and for this reason, it would be rather difficult, if not impossible, to disconnect enforced mediation from a disservice.

How can the issue of enforced mediation in practice be effectively addressed? It is time to review the responsibility to refrain discussed in Chap. 4 and combine this responsibility with concerting individual actions of external actors discussed in this chapter. Needless to say, according to what has been discussed regarding the responsibility to refrain, an external actor should endeavor to refrain from enforcing mediation on a conflicting party because enforced mediation generally contributes negatively to the settlement of secessionist conflicts, despite any (allegedly) good intention of a mediator. Of course, there is no guarantee that an external actor can always fulfill the responsibility to refrain, and enforced mediation is a case in point. Therefore, it is necessary to consider what should be done when mediation is forced by an external actor that disregards the responsibility to refrain. Clearly, when the external actor could realize its mistake and stop acting counterproductively in a secessionist conflict, the issue would be less troublesome. The difficult point here is to stop an unsuitable mediator who is enforcing mediation and unaware of his unsuitability, such as Holbrooke, who is capable of ruining mediation by blatantly demonstrating partiality.

It must be noted that mediation might be rejected by a conflicting party not because the conflicting party does not want to settle the issue through mediation, but mainly because the given mediator is not trustworthy. In other words, an unsuitable mediator can be a major obstacle to the peaceful settlement of conflicts, so replacing unsuitable mediators actually helps maintain international peace and security. Because the maintenance of international peace and security is the central mission of the UN, it is reasonable to expect the UN to play an active role in replacing unsuitable mediators, preventing them from doing a disservice in conflict settlement. As a matter of fact, preventing external actors from being unsuitable mediators in secessionist conflicts is also a part of concerting individual actions of external actors in secessionist conflicts. That is to say, even if an unsuitable mediator is not mandated by the UN, the UN still needs to contribute to the replacement of such a mediator. No other is in a better position to do it, given that the UN is empowered to be a center for harmonizing actions of actors for the maintenance of international peace and security in the current international legal system, while other legal actors are not explicitly empowered to do so and thus their attempts to replace unsuitable mediators might give rise to additional controversies. Therefore, it is not only reasonable but also practical for the UN to prevent unsuitable mediators from enforcing mediation and worsening secessionist conflicts.

To sum up, replacing unsuitable mediators is the key to the success of mediation in secessionist conflicts, and the UN can play an active role therein: for instance, there can be a procedural arrangement which allows a disadvantaged party in mediation to report this kind of issue to the UN, and the UN is to judge whether a mediator is really unsuitable in this case, in order to prevent the unsuitable mediator from further aggravating the situation. Abuse of mediating power such as enforced mediation can thus be avoided, which serves peaceful settlement of conflicts. As mentioned in Chap. 4, "when U.S. Ambassador Richard Holbrooke threatened NATO air strikes—compelling Serbian forces to cease fire and retreat—the rebels were able to regroup, reoccupy abandoned territory, and further escalate the war"[45]; if at that time Holbrooke had been prevented from doing such an unforgivable disservice, the UN could have saved itself much trouble, such as the endless debate caused by the unauthorized military intervention. One might argue that states that have appointed unsuitable mediators can become an obstacle to the replacement of them in the UN. Such argument is definitely reasonable but it cannot diminish the significance of the legal arrangement aimed at replacing unsuitable mediators: when mediators are wildly deemed unsuitable and states still reject the replacement of their

[45]See Chap. 4, Note 96.

unsuitable mediators, it becomes difficult for such states to blame the failure of peaceful settlement of conflicts on one of the conflicting parties. It is time to review the judgment that "if the international community acts early enough, the choice need not be a stark one between doing nothing or using force"[46] in the report Implementing the Responsibility to Protect of the UN Secretary-General. Obviously, with a view to preventing unsuitable mediators from further aggravating the situation, the international community should also replace such mediators early enough, and a legal arrangement regarding the replacement for unsuitable mediators serves such early actions.

5.3.3 Eschewing Artificial Deadlines

5.3.3.1 Setting Deadlines or Not

The time schedule of external actors working as mediators is an issue worth serious attention. External actors sometimes demonstrated a high degree of patience in dealing with secessionist conflicts, and the OSCE Minsk Group is a case in point: it is still making efforts to find a peaceful solution to the Nagorno-Karabakh conflict and conflicting parties are still required to negotiate on reaching a lasting and peaceful settlement to the Nagorno-Karabakh conflict.[47] In other cases external actors could be extremely impatient, despite the extreme intricacy of the secessionist conflict in question: the Kosovo case is a typical example, as an inexplicable impatience was demonstrated by external actors before and after the NATO military intervention in this case. One should first look at the Rambouillet Conference before the military intervention, "governments and media suddenly decided that the conflict had to be settled in two weeks . . . on terms laid down by the United States".[48] Then one should look at the Ahtisaari plan after the military intervention, in which such expression can be found: "after more than one year of direct talks, bilateral negotiations and expert consultations, it has become clear to me that the parties are not able to reach an agreement on Kosovo's future status... resolution of this fundamental issue is urgently needed. Almost eight years have passed since the Security Council adopted resolution 1244 (1999) and Kosovo's current state of limbo cannot continue".[49] Comparing these two cases, one cannot resist wondering why external actors can wait for a lasting and peaceful settlement of the Nagorno-Karabakh

[46]UN Doc. A/63/677, p. 9.

[47]Statement by the Co-Chairs of the OSCE Minsk Group in Munich on 17 February 2017, http://www.osce.org/mg/300591, last accessed on 15.06.2018.

[48]See above Note 3.

[49]Letter dated 26 March 2007 from the Secretary-General addressed to the President of the Security Council attaching the Report of the Special Envoy of the Secretary-General on Kosovo's future status, United Nations doc. S/2007/168, paras. 1 and 4.

conflict through negotiation for so many years but need a resolution of the Kosovo issue in an urgent manner.

Of course, Ahtisaari has explained the reason for this kind of urgency: "uncertainty over its future status has become a major obstacle to Kosovo's democratic development, accountability, economic recovery and inter-ethnic reconciliation. Such uncertainty only leads to further stagnation, polarizing its communities and resulting in social and political unrest. Pretending otherwise and denying or delaying resolution of Kosovo's status risks challenging not only its own stability but the peace and stability of the region as a whole".[50] The explanation is not convincing, because the case of Nagorno-Karabakh also perfectly fits this description: uncertainty over its future status has become a major obstacle to Nagorno-Karabakh's democratic development, accountability, economic recovery and inter-ethnic reconciliation; such uncertainty only leads to further stagnation, polarizing its communities and resulting in social and political unrest; pretending otherwise and denying or delaying resolution of Nagorno-Karabakh's status risks challenging not only its own stability but the peace and stability of the region as a whole. Clearly, the reason provided by Ahtisaari failed to explain why external actors can wait for a lasting and peaceful settlement of the Nagorno-Karabakh conflict through negotiation for so many years, but need a resolution of the Kosovo issue in an urgent manner. As a matter of fact, Ahtisaari has made a glaring error here: he confused two different things, namely an urgent resolution and an effective resolution; in order to eliminate uncertainty leading to further stagnation, polarizing communities and resulting in social and political unrest, an effective resolution rather than an urgent resolution is required. Obviously, there is no guarantee that an urgent resolution will be an effective one and it is also questionable whether an urgent resolution could be an effective one, given the extreme intricacy of a secessionist conflict.

Therefore, it is quite meaningful to consider what kind of time schedule is required for external actors involved in secessionist conflicts with a view to resolving such conflicts effectively. It should be noted that opinions diverge on this point. It seems that the OSCE Minsk Group has no intention to make a deadline for itself while the Special Envoy of the Secretary-General on Kosovo's future status preferred setting a deadline: according to Ahtisaari, the deadline should be around 1 year after direct talks, bilateral negotiations and expert consultations were commenced and 8 years after the Security Council adopted resolution 1244 (1999).[51] Although Ahtisaari himself failed to explain the necessity of and sufficient grounds for such a deadline, it might be understood from this perspective: indefinite negotiation seems unnecessary. Needless to say, this understanding is certainly reasonable; nevertheless, the assumption that indefinite negotiation seems unnecessary cannot explain why the deadline set by Ahtisaari, namely 1 year after direct talks, bilateral negotiations and expert consultations were commenced and 8 years after the Security Council adopted resolution 1244 (1999), is more suitable than another deadline, say,

[50]Ibid. para. 4.

[51]See above Note 49.

2 years after direct talks, bilateral negotiations and expert consultations were commenced and 9 years after the Security Council adopted resolution 1244 (1999). For this reason, the deadline set by Ahtisaari cannot be justified by the assumption that indefinite negotiation seems unnecessary, and it can be justified if Ahtisaari were able to offer convincing grounds why this deadline is more suitable than another one.

In view of the foregoing, is it correct to say that no deadline is better than deadlines set by external actors involved in secessionist conflicts with a view to resolving such conflicts effectively? Given eschewing artificial deadlines, which is mentioned in UN instruments dealing with mediation, the answer should be positive. According to the United Nations Manual for Mediators: Advice from United Nations Representatives and Envoys, "most mediators caution against setting deadlines. As one mediator puts it: 'Let the mediator beware of conjuring up deadlines not anchored in reality. Calls to settle by a given date 'or else' frequently put the mediator's credibility at risk and devalue the coin.'"[52] However, naturally-occurring deadlines, like those which are not in the power of the mediator or the parties to change, can be taken as exceptions: "one natural deadline occurred when Secretary-General Perez de Cuellar was leaving office at midnight on 31 December 1991. The full high command of the FMLN and President Cristiani were in New York with the Secretary-General and the UN mediator in last-ditch negotiations. After the Government of El Salvador consulted and was advised by the incoming Secretary-General-elect that they should finalize a deal under Perez de Cuellar, the parties finally reached agreement a little after midnight".[53] In the Report of the Secretary-General entitled *Strengthening the role of mediation in the peaceful settlement of disputes,* it is also stated that "a mediator needs to withstand external pressures and avoid unrealistic deadlines while also developing the support of partners for the mediation effort".[54]

5.3.3.2 Understanding the Importance of Eschewing Artificial Deadlines from Various Perspectives

a. Intricacy, Competency and Entitlement

The importance of eschewing artificial deadlines in improving external involvement in the settlement of secessionist conflicts can be considered from several perspectives. In the first place, the intricacy of a secessionist conflict is incompatible with a tight time schedule. As discussed above, a secessionist conflict concerns various international legal problems: self-determination conflicts over territorial interests, human rights protection, non-international armed conflicts, likely external

[52]The United Nations Manual for Mediators: Advice from United Nations Representatives and Envoys, 2010, p. 40.

[53]Ibid.

[54]UN Doc. A/66/811, p. 22, para. 13.

intervention driven by geopolitical interests or arising out of the ruse of self-inflicted injury employed by secessionists to gain international support for "victims"... In addition to legal problems usually there are other complex issues such as ethnic hostility, historic grievance, religious confrontation, cultural clash... Worse still, legal aspects and non-legal aspects of a secessionist conflict are intricately interwoven with each other. On this basis, it is definitely reasonable to believe that much patience is required for the effective settlement of a secessionist conflict. No one can deny that the pursuit of a quick settlement in general is meaningful; however, if the pursuit of quickness is established on the loss of effectiveness, quickness becomes meaningless: in such circumstances there is no real settlement, but only putative settlement. To be more specific, any subjective wish of external actors must correspond with reality: the extreme intricacy of a secessionist conflict remains unchanged when external actors decide to settle this issue within a tight time limit. The blind pursuit of quick work can be rather counterproductive, given that in this process an external actor is highly likely to ignore a key aspect of a secessionist conflict, which renders external involvement unlikely to be truly constructive: for instance, as discussed above, the Ahtisaari plan totally ignored the right to self-determination of non-secessionists over shared territorial interests. Therefore, one can say that external actors participating in secessionist conflicts should not be obsessed with quickness.

In the second place, it must be realized that the time needed for the settlement of a secessionist conflict is also closely related to the competency of external actors being involved. When external actors are very competent in persuading conflicting parties to reach an agreement through negotiation in the foreseeable future, less time is needed, while more time is needed when external actors are not so competent. From this perspective, if an external actor believes that its involvement cannot help bring about an agreement regarding conflict settlement in the foreseeable future, it needs to admit its incompetency and consider dealing with this issue, such as letting itself be replaced by another external actor. Clearly, when an external actor is unable to help bring about such an agreement, it does not mean that other external actors are equally incompetent, so it is well-advised to replace this one with another one. A similar point of view can also be found in the Report of the Secretary-General entitled *Strengthening the role of mediation in the peaceful settlement of disputes*: "mediators should handover to another mediator, or mediating entity, if they feel unable to maintain a balanced and impartial approach".[55] For this reason, when Ahtisaari felt that "the negotiations' potential to produce any mutually agreeable outcome on Kosovo's status is exhausted. No amount of additional talks, whatever the format, will overcome this impasse",[56] he should have informed the Secretary-General of this situation and let someone else to replace him. Obviously, the negotiations' potential to produce any mutually agreeable outcome on Kosovo's status in the foreseeable future might have been exhausted for Ahtisaari but not necessarily for

[55]Ibid. p. 25, para. 28.

[56]UN Doc. S/2007/168, para. 3.

others. It is rather inexplicable that Ahtisaari wanted to compensate for his incompetency with deadlines: logically speaking, when an external actor is quite sure that he is unable to persuade conflicting parties to reach an agreement through negotiation in the foreseeable future, deadlines should be the last thing he needs to think about; incompetency will not transform into competency because of deadlines. Undoubtedly, the pursuit of quickness by Ahtisaari cannot render his problematic plan, which served as guidelines of the Kosovo Declaration of Independence in 2008,[57] more acceptable in practice. In short, the pursuit of quickness by an external actor will in no way compensate for the incompetency of the external actor, and one needs to bear this point in mind when pursuing improvement in external involvement in the settlement of secessionist conflicts.

In the third place, the question whether an external actor is entitled to decide on a deadline deserves serious consideration. According to the Report of the Secretary-General entitled *Strengthening the role of mediation in the peaceful settlement of disputes,* "together with the mediator, the parties should establish ground rules at the outset of the process on the basis of which the following should be decided:... Deadlines: should deadlines be established or not? If so, who decides them — the mediator, the parties, the contributing countries?"[58] According to this statement, an external actor can decide the deadline when conflicting parties have decided that the external actor can do it. That is to say, when conflicting parties have not decided that the external actor participating in the settlement of their conflict can decide the deadline, the external actor cannot claim a right to decide it. Given the general principles of international law, particularly the principle of self-determination, the provision of this UN document is quite reasonable: a secessionist conflict concerns distribution of interests shared by conflicting parties and according to the principle of self-determination, conflicting parties definitely have the right to make any relevant decision, including the one regarding the procedural issue such as deadlines. Therefore, any decision regarding deadlines made by an external actor in disregard of self-determination of a conflicting party is problematic, and the aggrieved party will question whether its right to self-determination has been respected by the external actor. Some may argue that the negotiation between conflicting parties might seem endless, without the deadline set by the external actor. This argument is not wrong, but it does not explain why the right to self-determination of one conflicting party has to be ignored from the legal point of view. Perhaps one also needs to ask: is a seemingly endless negotiation really a problem? It seems that for the OSCE Minsk Group a seemingly endless negotiation is not a problem, and according to the United Nations Manual for Mediators: Advice from United Nations Representatives and Envoys, it is not a problem either while the artificial deadline is the problem.[59] No

[57]Ahtisaari plan is mentioned eight times in the Kosovo Declaration of Independence, the Kosovo Declaration of Independence, http://www.assembly-kosova.org/?cid=2,128,1635, last accessed on 15.06.2018.

[58]UN Doc. A/66/811, pp. 109–110.

[59]See above Note 52.

one will deny that it would be much better if the secessionist conflict can be effectively settled through a short-term negotiation, but there is no reason to say that it becomes a problem when the effective settlement of a secessionist conflict requires a long-term negotiation.

b. An Analysis of the Deadline Set in the Ahtisaari Plan

It is time to look back at the statement made by Ahtisaari regarding deadlines: "my mandate explicitly provides that I determine the pace and duration of the future status process on the basis of consultations with the Secretary-General, taking into account the cooperation of the parties and the situation on the ground... The time has come to resolve Kosovo's status. Upon careful consideration of Kosovo's recent history, the realities of Kosovo today and taking into account the negotiations with the parties, I have come to the conclusion that the only viable option for Kosovo is independence..."[60] One should pay attention to the right claimed by Ahtisaari to determine the deadline. It is a pity that the Special Envoy failed to cite the original text of the mandating document[61] with regard to his right to determine the pace and duration of the future status process: with the citation not only his claim would sound more convincing, it would also be easier to analyze whether the mandate itself was legally well-founded. As mentioned before, when Secretary-General Annan appointed Martti Ahtisaari as his Special Envoy for the Future Status Process for Kosovo, this appointment was approved by the Security Council on 10 November 2005 and was effective as of that date; therefore, it is safe to conclude that the Special Envoy was not entitled to do something that the Security Council itself is not entitled to do. The time has come to consider whether the Security Council itself is entitled to determine the deadline, namely the end of negotiation between conflicting parties, in disregard of the right to self-determination of one conflicting party. The answer lies in Article 24(2) of the UN Charter: it is clearly stated that in discharging its duties the Security Council shall act in accordance with the purposes and principles of the United Nations. From this perspective, it is hard to conclude that the Security Council is entitled to decide the end of negotiation between conflicting parties in disregard of the right to self-determination of one conflicting party. For this reason, it is certainly questionable when a Special Envoy claimed that he was entitled to do so. To be specific, when the Security Council was not entitled to decide the end of negotiation between Belgrade and Pristina in disregard of the right to self-determination of non-secessionists represented by the Belgrade authorities, Ahtisaari as a Special Envoy of the Secretary-General was not entitled to do it either on the basis of a mandate.

It seems meaningful to review Security Council resolution 1244 (1999), as Ahtisaari thought that the deadline was supposed to be around 8 years after the

[60]UN Doc. S/2007/168, paras. 3 and 5.

[61]The author also cannot find this document on the UN website.

Security Council had adopted this resolution.[62] Given the content of resolution 1244 (1999), it is certainly difficult to associate this resolution with the deadline set by Ahtisaari and according to this resolution, the principles of sovereignty and territorial integrity of the Federal Republic of Yugoslavia should be carefully considered,[63] which can be interpreted as respect demonstrated by the Security Council for the right to self-determination of non-secessionists: sovereignty and territorial integrity actually reflect the pursuit of non-secessionists in the secessionist conflict and from this perspective, it is correct to deduce that the decision to end negotiation with independence between secessionists and non-secessionists in disregard of the right to self-determination of non-secessionists is not in accordance with Security Council resolution 1244 (1999). Judge Koroma has pointed out in his dissenting opinion regarding the accordance with international law of the Kosovo Unilateral Declaration of Independence: "that resolution calls for a negotiated settlement, meaning the agreement of all the parties concerned with regard to the final status of Kosovo, which the authors of the declaration of independence have circumvented".[64] As a matter of fact, this judgement can also be applied to the Ahtisaari plan: Security Council resolution 1244 (1999) required an agreement between secessionists and non-secessionists with regard to the final status of Kosovo, which Ahtisaari has circumvented because he felt that "the negotiations' potential to produce any mutually agreeable outcome on Kosovo's status is exhausted... the only viable option for Kosovo is independence".[65] The circumvention by the authors of the declaration of independence is closely connected with the circumvention by Ahtisaari: the Ahtisaari plan, which perfectly satisfied the wish of secessionists to transform territorial co-ownership into exclusive ownership, has been mentioned eight times in the Kosovo Unilateral Declaration of Independence, so it is suitable to refer to the Ahtisaari plan, which was put forward in early 2007, as guidelines of and a catalyst for the Kosovo Declaration of Independence in 2008. To some extent, the deadline of negotiation marked the starting point of a new stage of the secessionist conflict because enforcing an end of negotiation between secessionists and non-secessionists in disregard of the right to self-determination of non-secessionists runs counter to the effective settlement of self-determination conflicts.

It seems that United Nations Representatives and Envoys see this issue less from the perspective of respecting the principle of self-determination and more from the perspective of the principle of good faith: setting deadlines is ill-advised as it "frequently put[s] the mediator's credibility at risk and devalue[s] the coin."[66] Undeniably, this point deserves no less attention given that it affects improvement

[62]See above Note 51.

[63]S/RES/1244 (1999), para. 8.

[64]Accordance with International Law of the Unilateral Declaration of Independence in Respect of Kosovo, Dissenting Opinion of Judge Koroma, I.C.J. Reports 2010, p. 470, para. 11.

[65]UN doc. S/2007/168, paras. 3 and 5.

[66]See above Note 52.

in external involvement in the settlement of secessionist conflicts and, meanwhile, one should note that respect for the right to self-determination and good faith are not isolated from each other. Needless to say, when an external actor fails to respect the right to self-determination of one conflicting party while participating in a secessionist conflict, it is inevitable for the disadvantaged party to distrust or refuse to cooperate with the external actor, and in such circumstances it is definitely unrealistic to expect external involvement to be valuable. For this reason, it is true to conclude that in this regard good faith is largely based on the respect for the right to self-determination: if an external actor fails to respect the right to self-determination, it also fails to observe the principle of good faith, the negative outcome of which can be worse than a devaluation of external involvement. Obviously, the raison d'être of external involvement in conflict settlement would become questionable if the external actor were not trusted by conflicting parties. In a strict sense, when the raison d'être of external involvement in secessionist conflicts is deemed questionable, one should consider excluding external involvement rather than improving it in settling secessionist conflicts.

The nexus between respect for the right to self-determination and good faith has been well demonstrated in the remark made by Christakis regarding the Kosovo Advisory Opinion: "which state would be foolish enough to accept arrangements that include loss of effective control? Will countries accept the guarantees of the UN Security Council or any other international organization promising respect of their territorial integrity in exchange for autonomy or provisional international administration arrangements knowing that 'the scope of the principle of territorial integrity is confined to the sphere of relations between States' and that this guarantee does not bind the separatist movement that can take advantage of the situation in order to declare independence and establish effective control?"[67] Non-secessionists in a self-determination conflict, which are represented by the central authorities, choose to co-operate with an external actor for the sake of conflict settlement mainly because they trust in the external actor: they believe that their right to self-determination over territorial interests can be respected by the external actor. External actors should not damage this trust. If an external actor damages this trust by disregarding the right to self-determination of non-secessionists over territorial interests, it can generally affect international cooperation in this regard: due to the distrust thereby caused, non-secessionists in secessionist conflicts will generally be more reluctant to co-operate with external actors that are likely to disregard the right to non-secessionist self-determination in a seemingly harmless way, such as setting a groundless deadline for negotiation in secessionist conflicts.

To be more specific, non-secessionists in the Kosovo case, which have been represented by the Belgrade authorities, chose to co-operate with the UN for the sake of conflict settlement mainly because they trusted in the UN: they believed that the UN would respect their right to self-determination over territorial interests, as provided in Security Council resolution 1244 (1999). The UN should not damage

[67] Christakis (2011), p. 86.

this trust and for this reason, the Special Envoy of the Secretary-General Ahtisaari was not allowed to damage this trust either. When the Ahtisaari plan damaged this trust by disregarding the right to self-determination of non-secessionists over territorial interests, it created more obstacles to conflict settlement: the Ahtisaari plan became the catalyst for the Kosovo Declaration of Independence and tensions were caused by such a declaration, and the ICJ was therefore involved and its interplay with other UN organs triggered much debate,[68] such as the functions and responsibility of the United Nations in respect of a territory placed under its administration[69]... In a strict sense, the Ahtisaari plan cannot reflect the official attitude of the UN as it was not approved by the Security Council.[70] Nevertheless, because Ahtisaari was the Special Envoy of the Secretary-General, the distrust caused by the Ahtisaari plan will certainly affect the credibility of the UN. As reminded by Christakis, other states on behalf of non-secessionists will not be foolish enough to ignore the lesson of Belgrade which falsely believed that the UN would respect their right to self-determination over territorial interests, as provided in Security Council resolution 1244 (1999), and chose to cooperate with the UN out of this trust: obviously, there is no reason for non-secessionists in other cases to take a similar risk. It seems quite easy for the UN to find a reason, whether convincing or not, to disregard the right to self-determination of non-secessionists over territorial interests: for example, a UN Special Envoy in other secessionist cases might follow the approach of Ahtisaari and declare that "after more than one year of direct talks, bilateral negotiations and expert consultations, it has become clear that the parties are not able to reach an agreement... the negotiations' potential to produce any mutually agreeable outcome is exhausted. No amount of additional talks, whatever the format, will overcome this impasse. Nevertheless, resolution of this fundamental issue is urgently needed... The time has come to resolve the future status... the only viable option is independence".[71] In order to avoid such risk,

---

[68]Accordance with International Law of the Unilateral Declaration of Independence in Respect of Kosovo, Declaration of Vice President Tomka, I.C.J. Reports 2010, pp. 455–456, para. 7; Accordance with International Law of the Unilateral Declaration of Independence in Respect of Kosovo, Dissenting Opinion of Judge Bennouna, I.C.J. Reports 2010, pp. 500–501, para. 3; Accordance with International Law of the Unilateral Declaration of Independence in Respect of Kosovo, Separate Opinion of Judge Keith, I.C.J. Reports 2010, pp. 483–484, para. 6.

[69]Accordance with International Law of the Unilateral Declaration of Independence in Respect of Kosovo, Dissenting Opinion of Judge Bennouna, I.C.J. Reports 2010, p. 504, para. 22.

[70]"Moscow had vowed to veto the two earlier drafts prepared by the US and European Union members based on the status proposals from Martti Ahtisaari, the UN envoy in the Kosovo dispute, which suggested a framework for statehood under EU-led supervision." Neil MacDonald, Russia rejects plan for Kosovo, Financial Times, 13 July 2007, https://www.ft.com/content/f3f09aae-30a0-11dc-9a81-0000779fd2ac, last accessed on 15.06.2018.

[71]This model declaration is fully based on the proposition of Ahtisaari, see Letter dated 26 March 2007 from the Secretary-General addressed to the President of the Security Council attaching the Report of the Special Envoy of the Secretary-General on Kosovo's future status, United Nations doc. S/2007/168, paras. 1–5.

non-secessionists in other cases have the impetus to refuse to cooperate with the UN in the first place: they certainly will learn something from the lesson of Belgrade.

To sum up, deadlines for negotiation between non-secessionists and secessionists set by external actors can give rise to various thorny issues hindering the effective settlement of secessionist conflicts. It is necessary for every external actor to bear in mind the importance of eschewing artificial deadlines to improvement in external involvement in the settlement of secessionist conflicts.

5.4 Reconsidering External Recognition Regarding Secessionist Conflicts

5.4.1 Recognizing the Significance of Non-Recognition

It must be noted that problems regarding external involvement exist not only in mediation but also in other aspects. Similarly, problems in other aspects also have much to do with disregard for the responsibility to refrain and the necessity of concerting individual actions of external actors. One should first look at the issue of state recognition which has been much discussed above. The point discussed here is the cloud of double standard cast over external involvement, due to the problematic recognition granted by external actors. As mentioned in Chap. 2, the European Community had adopted a Declaration on 16 December 1991 entitled 'Guidelines on the Recognition of New States in Eastern Europe and in the Soviet Union', and the Yugoslav Arbitration Commission had taken the view in Opinion No. 5 on 11 January 1992 that Croatia did not meet fully the conditions for recognition laid down in the Guidelines; nevertheless, the recognition of that state was still granted by the European Community and its member states (together with Austria and Switzerland) on 15 January 1992.[72] Such statement was found in a letter sent by Yugoslavia to the UN Secretary General in 1993: "The proclamation of new states in the territory of the former Yugoslavia has been welcomed by the international community as a kind of achievement in the exercise of the democratic right of nations to self-determination, whereas the Serb nation's invocation of the same right aimed at resolving its own political and legal status has been met with open opposition and the strongest condemnation. Thus, Serbs became a people who were denied the right to self-determination and continuation of life in their own state. They were accused of 'aggression' and 'occupation' of territories in which they had lived for centuries as the majority population. The world public welcomed the demolition of the Berlin Wall and the unification of the German people. Therefore, it is absurd that the same public supports the erection of another wall

[72]See Chap. 2, Note 114.

which divides an European people – Serbs".[73] In the parlance of international law, the main question embodied here is that the recognition of new states in the territory of the former Yugoslavia actually indicated kind of support for secessionist self-determination and opposition to non-secessionist self-determination, although it remains inexplicable why secessionist self-determination is superior to non-secessionist self-determination. The inexplicability becomes more obvious, given that the Serb Krajina was denied the right to secede from Croatia by the European Community[74]: one wonders why the European Community was unable to stay consistent with regard to the priority between secessionist self-determination and non-secessionist self-determination. If the humanitarian consideration plays a role in the inconsistency, one should notice that, just like the Serb military campaigns which resulted in much suffering on the Croatian side during the anti-secession struggle, "the Croatian military campaigns resulted in a mass exodus of over 150,000 Serbs from the areas captured by Croatian forces to Serbia and Bosnia and Herzegovina".[75]

Similar issues repeatedly occurred: as pointed out by Hannum, "it is difficult to find any morality or consistency in the continuing refusal of the Albanian majority in Kosovo to grant to some of its Serb minority population the same 'self-determination' that Kosovar Albanians claim… if the 'wishes of the people' are to be the basis of the state, then it is difficult to understand why the wishes of Kosovar Albanians to separate from Serbia deserve more support than the wishes of Serbs to separate from Kosovo".[76] Undoubtedly, external actors should avoid involving themselves in such a dilemma, otherwise external actors in secessionist conflicts will be suspected of exercising a double-standard. Non-recognition plays a key role in this regard: when external actors refuse to grant recognition to secessionists, non-secessionists have no reason to criticize external actors for ignoring non-secessionist self-determination, and sub-secessionists (secessionists who want to secede from a secessionist entity, like the Serb minority population in Croatia and Kosovo) also have no reason to advocate a similar right to secessionist self-determination. More importantly, non-recognition is conducive to forming new international law intended for regulating self-determination conflicts: as discussed in Chaps. 2 and 3, a secessionist conflict, in essence, is a self-determination conflict between secessionists and non-secessionists, so an effective settlement of such a conflict requires reaching a new balance of rights and duties between secessionists and non-secessionists, and this new balance is embodied in newly formed international law, namely the agreement achieved between conflicting parties, while granting recognition to

[73]Letter Dated 11 June 1993 from the Chargé d' affairs a.i. of the Permanent Mission of Yugoslavia to the United Nations Addressed to the Secretary-General, UN Doc. A/48/207—S/25936, 14 June 1993, p. 2.

[74]Conference on Yugoslavia, Arbitration Commission, Opinion No. 2, 31 International Legal Materials (1992), p. 1498.

[75]Radan (2011), p. 524.

[76]Hannum (2011), pp. 160–161.

secessionists is detrimental to forming a well-balanced agreement between secessionists and non-secessionists, as secessionists tend to expand their own interests at the cost of interests of the other side with the help of recognition. It is necessary to realize that if recognition takes place before a well-balanced agreement is achieved, the consequences can be rather disastrous.

The Bosnia case has demonstrated this point. When "the European Community's Badinter Panel ruled that Bosnia could qualify for international recognition as an independent state if its populace approved a referendum on secession from Yugoslavia... Bosnia's Serbs declared that they would not peacefully accept a declaration of independence of a unitary, centralized Bosnian state... Instead, the Serbs insisted that Bosnia be divided internally along ethnic lines prior to any secession. Izetbegovic initially agreed, in January 1992, to postpone a referendum on independence until such a constitutional reorganization could be negotiated. But he soon recanted. Belatedly, in February 1992, the European Community (EC) awoke to the danger that Bosnia's secession could lead to violence worse than in Croatia. So the EC sponsored negotiations among the republic's three main groups to divide Bosnia into ethnic cantons prior to secession... Bosnia's Muslim leaders participated in several rounds of these negotiations and agreed at least twice—in February and March 1992—to a framework for such cantonization. In both cases, however, they reneged within days. At the end of February 1992, Bosnia's Muslim-led government held the independence referendum, which was overwhelmingly approved by Muslim and Croat voters but boycotted by Serbs. In early March, the United States and the EC agreed that they would recognize Bosnia on April 6, even in the absence of cantonization. The decisions by Bosnia's Muslims to acquire arms, reject cantonization, and declare independence of a unitary republic—an armed secession from Yugoslavia—triggered a massive retaliation by Belgrade-supported Serb forces".[77]

Obviously, if at that time external actors had pressured Bosnia's Muslim-led government not to hold the independence referendum in the absence of cantonization and insisted that recognition would not be granted in case of independence without cantonization, a massive retaliation by Belgrade-supported Serb forces would have been less likely to be triggered, and the secessionist conflict would have been more likely to be settled by newly formed international law, namely an agreement on cantonization. Unfortunately, this possibility was destroyed by capricious secessionists who aimed to expand their own interests at the cost of interests of the other side. Recognition granted by external actors helps such secessionists destroy the possibility of settling secessionist conflicts though newly formed international law intended for balancing conflicting interests. Therefore, this kind of recognition should be regarded as detrimental external involvement in the settlement of secessionist conflicts and improving external involvement in conflict settlement requires settling such issue. Preventing such recognition is closely related

[77]Kuperman (2008), pp. 57–58.

to the function of the UN as a center for harmonizing the actions of nations for the maintenance of international peace and security.

More specifically, in order to prevent problematic recognition which might lead to an aggravation of secessionist conflicts which threaten international peace and security, the UN needs to play an active role: it is actually experienced in preventing problematic recognition. For instance, in the case of Southern Rhodesia, Security Council Resolution 216 (1965) required "all states not to recognize this illegal racist minority regime in Southern Rhodesia and to refrain from rendering any assistance to this illegal regime".[78] Similarly, Security Council Resolution 541 (1983) required "all states not to recognize any Cypriot State other than the Republic of Cyprus".[79] Likewise, the Resolution adopted by the General Assembly on 27 March 2014 required "all States, international organizations and specialized agencies not to recognize any alteration of the status of the Autonomous Republic of Crimea and the city of Sevastopol on the basis of the above-mentioned referendum and to refrain from any action or dealing that might be interpreted as recognizing any such altered status".[80] Given the above-mentioned experience, it is quite reasonable to expect the UN to play an active role in preventing problematic recognition. After all, national interest and perceived political advantage to the recognizing state obviously play an important role in granting recognition[81] and in such circumstances, it is hard to expect an external actor to disregard its own interest and perceived political advantage for the effective settlement of a secessionist conflict, so the UN needs to be active in preventing external actors from granting problematic recognition which can lead to the aggravation of secessionist conflicts.

It is time to consider the interplay between the UN and powerful individual external actors: on the one hand, the UN is able to restrain external actors participating in a secessionist conflict; on the other hand, powerful individual external actors, such as permanent members of the Security Council, are able to restrain the UN. Obviously, when a permanent member has granted recognition, a Security Council resolution aimed at preventing problematic recognition becomes out of the question. In this sense, one can conclude that powerful individual external actors, particularly permanent members of the Security Council, need to be more cautious about their involvement in secessionist conflicts. Problematic recognition granted by individual external actors might hinder collective action to prevent problematic recognition that can lead to the aggravation of secessionist conflicts, and in order to improve external involvement in secessionist conflicts, powerful individual external actors, particularly permanent members of the Security Council, must assume greater responsibility than other individual external actors, due to their practical influence. Although problematic recognition by ordinary external actors is also counterproductive to the settlement of secessionist conflicts, it is not as detrimental

[78] S/RES/216 (1965), para. 2.

[79] S/RES/541 (1983), para. 7.

[80] A/RES/68/262, para. 6.

[81] See Chap. 2, Note 107.

as problematic recognition by powerful individual external actors: the practical influence of problematic recognition by an ordinary external actor is likely to be ignored, but it is impossible to ignore the practical influence of problematic recognition by a powerful external actor and for this reason, powerful individual external actors, particularly permanent members of the Security Council, should be even more cautious in granting recognition.

This point can also be understood from the perspective of the responsibility to protect, in addition to the perspective of the responsibility to refrain. Indisputably, "gross and systematic violations of human rights that affect every precept of our common humanity",[82] in the parlance of the former UN Secretary-General Kofi Annan, is closely related to the aggravation of conflicts. For this reason, it is logic to conclude that fulfilling the responsibility to protect requires preventing the aggravation of conflicts, so any external involvement which is likely to aggravate the humanitarian situation is incompatible with the responsibility to protect. Problematic recognition by powerful individual external actors, particularly permanent members of the Security Council, is exceptionally noteworthy in this regard, because it can render collective attempts to prevent problematic recognition from aggravating conflicts impossible, which actually affects the prestige of the UN. It is time to review the remark made in the Report of the International Commission on Intervention and State Sovereignty in 2001: "If the Council – and the five permanent members in particular – fail to make the Council relevant to the critical issues of the day then they can only expect that the Council will diminish in significance, stature and authority".[83] Obviously, permanent members should refrain from doing something that diminishes the significance, stature and authority of the UN, so these powerful individual external actors should not grant problematic recognition as it can render the UN unable to prevent such recognition which will aggravate conflicts.

Therefore, it is accurate to conclude that non-recognition actually serves multifaceted ends. Firstly, non-recognition helps exclude double-standards. Non-recognition represents unbiased respect for self-determination which includes both secessionist and non-secessionist self-determination, which helps avoid criticism directed at external actors which take sides in secessionist conflicts by granting recognition. Although external actors which exercise a double-standard might not care about such criticism, there is no denying that they are well-advised to avoid being criticized for such involvement in secessionist conflicts. Secondly, non-recognition helps avoid the aggravation of conflicts, thus contributing to human rights protection. It is clear that recognition tends to make secessionists more reckless and thus force the authorities to take harsher anti-secessionists measures, so the aggravation of conflicts becomes inevitable and therefore severely affects human rights protection. Thirdly, non-recognition helps maintain the prestige of the UN, particularly given its role in fulfilling the responsibility to protect.

[82]UN Doc. A/54/2000, para. 217.

[83]The Responsibility to Protect: Report of the International Commission on Intervention and State Sovereignty, 2001, p. 51.

Problematic recognition granted by powerful individual external actors is certainly detrimental to a collective attempt to prevent such harmful external involvement in secessionist conflicts, which will diminish the UN in significance, stature and authority. When powerful individual external actors, particularly permanent members of the Security Council, learn the importance of non-recognition, they are also contributing to the significance, stature and authority of the UN in conflict settlement, which also bodes well for the responsibility to protect.

5.4.2 *Recognizing a Right Instead of a Wish*

Given the successful experience drawn from the case of Aceh, if external actors want to effectively fulfill the responsibility to protect, they need to do more than refrain from granting problematic recognition. External actors should also discourage secessionists from taking arms to pursue independence: at that time international actors made clear that the price of their involvement was secessionists' agreement to a peace deal that kept Aceh within Indonesia.[84] In essence this was the recognition of territorial interests of non-secessionists. As discussed in Chap. 3, the claim to independence made by secessionists is ill-grounded as they want to unilaterally alter co-ownership of the territory by declaring independence, but co-ownership of the territory cannot be altered in a unilateral way, given the violation of territorial interests of non-secessionists. The recognition of territorial interests of non-secessionists, or respect for non-secessionist self-determination is undoubtedly well-founded: as once pointed out by Lenin, "we fight against the privileges and violence of the oppressor nation, and do not in any way condone strivings for privileges on the part of the oppressed nation",[85] an external actor needs to do something to moderate repression of secessionists when such repression exists, but it is certainly wrong for an external actor to condone unilateral secession that infringes on territorial interests of non-secessionists, even if secessionists have been under repression. Moderating repression and condoning an infringement of territorial interests should not be confused, particularly given the detrimental effects: as repeatedly mentioned above, secessionists have learned to deliberately provoke excessive repression and exploited the exceptional circumstance caused thereby to infringe on territorial interests of non-secessionists with the help of external involvement. In other words, an external actor must distinguish between legal rights and pure wishes: human rights are legal rights but independence is merely a wish, so the pursuit of human rights should not be ignored but the same cannot be said about the pursuit of independence. International actors in the case of Aceh were aware of this distinction, so they clearly refused to back the wish of independence when they involved in the secessionist conflict.

---

[84]See Chap. 3, Note 92.

[85]See Chap. 3, Note 26.

Therefore, one can conclude that both avoiding recognition of independence and granting recognition of territorial interests of non-secessionists are crucial for improving external involvement in the settlement of secessionist conflicts. Avoiding recognition of independence means distinguishing a pure wish from legal rights: despite being scarcely discussed, an external actor participating in a secessionist conflict should be clear about which claim made by a conflicting party is based on a legal right and which claim is purely a wish. External involvement is well-founded when it is right-oriented, while external involvement is counterproductive or detrimental when it is wish-oriented, because in such circumstances the satisfaction of the legally groundless wish is usually in violation of a legal right of the other side. Clearly, the satisfaction of the legally groundless wish of secessionists to be independent violates the right to self-determination of non-secessionists over territorial interests, and thus it is certainly wrong for an external actor to satisfy the legally groundless wish of secessionists to be independent by granting recognition. In addition, as discussed in Chap. 3, the denial of the claim made by secessionists to unilaterally change ownership of the territory will not negatively affect the contribution made by an external actor to improve the protection of human rights of secessionists. Conversely, an external actor can make better contribution to improve the protection of human rights of secessionists by denying their claim to exclusive territorial ownership, because in such circumstances claims of both secessionists and non-secessionists can be reconciled: as pointed out before, territorial interests of non-secessionists and human rights protection of secessionists are not irreconcilable, and it is co-ownership of the territory claimed by non-secessionists and exclusive ownership claimed by secessionists that are irreconcilable. The success of external involvement in the case of Aceh has proved that it is definitely correct for external actors to ignore the legally groundless wish of secessionists and recognize self-determination of non-secessionists over territorial interests: thus a balance of interests between conflicting parties can be achieved with the help of external involvement. In other words, external actors manage to help protect human rights of secessionists and territorial interests of non-secessionists as co-owner in this way.

In fact, there had been a chance to settle the Kosovo issue in a similar way. As pointed out by Johnstone in 1998, "without the prospect of decisive outside intervention on their behalf, the ethnic Albanians of Kosovo might have tried to make use of the existing legal framework. They could, for instance, have voted to fill 42 of the 250 seats in the Serbian parliament with their representatives".[86] The EU had also attempted to settle the Kosovo issue within the borders of the Federal Republic of Yugoslavia (FRY): "during a visit by Milan Milutinović, Foreign Minister of the FRY, to Brussels in December 1996, Commissioner Hans van den Broek underlined that the normalization of relations between the Union and Belgrade cannot be dissociated from the Kosovo issue, and, in particular, from the possibility of opening a EU Information Office in the province. The Commissioner stressed that this initiative should not be interpreted as a wish on the part of the EU that Kosovo

[86]Johnstone (1998).

should become completely independent. He said that the Union believes that the province should regain a certain amount of autonomy, comparable to the situation prior to 1989."[87] Unfortunately, such attempt was "undermined by U.S. opposition and the growing Albanian militancy. Had the United States joined the European effort and credibly warned the rebels that it would not support violent provocation, a peaceful solution might have prevailed."[88]

Therefore, it is necessary to emphasize that powerful individual external actors shall be more conscious of discouraging secessionists from taking arms to pursue independence. For this sake, it is particularly meaningful for powerful individual external actors participating in a secessionist conflict to distinguish a wish and a right: if a powerful individual external actor chooses to satisfy the wish of secessionists in disregard of the legal right of non-secessionists, such kind of external involvement will destroy the balance of interests between secessionists and non-secessionists, which can worsen the secessionist conflict and thus endanger fundamental human rights and threaten international peace and security. In order to effectively fulfill the responsibility to protect, powerful individual external actors must avoid confusing a legally groundless wish to be independent made by secessionists and human rights protection required by secessionists, so they should discourage secessionists from taking arms to pursue independence. As demonstrated in the case of Aceh, international actors contributed to human rights protection, because they required secessionists to agree to a peace deal that kept Aceh within Indonesia rather than indulged their legally groundless wish to be independent, which actually was an infringement of the right to self-determination over territorial interests enjoyed by non-secessionists.

5.4.3 Recognizing Detrimental Effects Caused by Unilateral Secession

When discussing the relation between the responsibility to protect and unilateral secession, one must pay attention to the issue of ethnic cleansing. The prevention of ethnic cleansing is one major motive behind the responsibility to protect, and it is indisputable that ethnic cleansing constitutes gross and systematic violations of human rights. Therefore, it is necessary to consider the interrelation between ethnic cleansing and unilateral secession. When unilateral secession can lead to an outcome similar to ethnic cleansing, any external involvement that facilitates unilateral secession is incompatible with the responsibility to protect. One might wonder why unilateral secession can lead to an outcome similar to ethnic cleansing, and this is actually explicable through a number of cases. For instance, the statement made by the Parliamentary Assembly of the Council of Europe (CoE) with regard to

[87] Troebst (1998), p. 60.

[88] See Chap. 4, Note 96.

the conflict over the Nagorno-Karabakh region points out: "the military action, and the widespread ethnic hostilities which preceded it, led to large-scale ethnic expulsion and the creation of mono-ethnic areas which resemble the terrible concept of ethnic cleansing. The Assembly reaffirms that independence and secession of a regional territory from a state may only be achieved through a lawful and peaceful process based on democratic support by the inhabitants of such territory and not in the wake of an armed conflict leading to ethnic expulsion..."[89] When speaking of secession in the wake of an armed conflict leading to large-scale ethnic expulsion and the creation of mono-ethnic areas which resemble the terrible concept of ethnic cleansing, the Kosovo case immediately comes to mind: the de facto secession in the wake of the NATO military intervention has also led to large scale expulsion of Serbs[90] and facilitated the creation of purely Albanian areas,[91] which has been pursued by Albanian nationalists since the early 1980s.[92] Therefore, there is no denying that unilateral secession can lead to an outcome similar to ethnic cleansing.

For this reason, it is necessary to prevent external involvement from facilitating unilateral secession, in order to avoid an outcome similar to ethnic cleansing. Such an outcome inevitably dissociates external involvement from the responsibility to protect. For instance, the NATO military intervention might indeed have been driven by the responsibility to protect fundamental human rights, but given the outcome resembling the terrible concept of ethnic cleansing which is incompatible with human rights protection, it is really difficult, if not impossible, to associate the NATO military intervention with the responsibility to protect. To some extent, it is also necessary to reject such association: after all, when fulfilling the responsibility to protect can mean external involvement that facilitates unilateral secession leading to large-scale ethnic expulsion and the creation of mono-ethnic areas resembling the terrible concept of ethnic cleansing, it actually renders the responsibility to protect even more unpopular among states which are already alert to this concept. Therefore, one can argue that the fulfillment of the responsibility to protect requires external actors to prevent unilateral secession.

It is particularly noteworthy that external actors should not facilitate unilateral secession not only because it is incompatible with the responsibility to protect, but also because unilateral secession as a means cannot terminate secessionist conflicts: the pending situation caused by unilateral secession affects the maintenance of international peace and security. A unilateral declaration of independence made by

[89]The conflict over the Nagorno-Karabakh region dealt with by the OSCE Minsk Conference, Doc. 10364, 29 November 2004, https://assembly.coe.int/nw/xml/XRef/X2H-Xref-ViewHTML.asp?FileID=10733&lang=en, last accessed on 15.06.2018.

[90]See Chap. 3, Note 88.

[91]More relevant information see Johnstone (1999).

[92]"Serbs ... have reportedly been harassed by Albanians and have packed up and left the region. The exodus of Serbs is admittedly one of the main problems that the authorities have to contend with in Kosovo, an autonomous province of Yugoslavia inhabited largely by Albanians... The nationalists have a two-point platform... first to establish what they call an ethnically clean Albanian republic and then the merger with Albania to form a greater Albania." Howe (1982).

secessionists remains a destabilizing factor until non-secessionists accept it, and the secessionist conflict cannot be ultimately settled when there is no agreement between both sides. It is time to review the judgement made by Horowitz: "a secession or partition converts a domestic ethnic dispute into a more dangerous international one."[93] The unilateral secession of Kosovo has at best converted the conflict between secessionists and non-secessionists into a conflict between an alleged state called Kosovo and Serbia while nothing has been contributed to a better balance of interests between conflicting parties. No wonder 10 years after the unilateral declaration of independence, the real settlement of the Kosovo conflict is still out of sight. There is no reason to believe that a unilateral declaration of independence can make any positive contribution to a conflict as complicated as the one of Kosovo: as noted by Johnstone, "the conflict between ethnic Albanians and Serbs is a very old one, which can be traced back over three centuries. It is older than the Israeli-Palestinian or Northern Ireland conflicts, not to mention countless other ethnic conflicts in the world. The 'peace process' in such cases is expected to be long and delicate".[94] Because the peaceful settlement of such conflicts should be long and delicate, and unilateral secession as a means does not fit, external actors aiming to contribute to conflict settlement must do something to exclude unilateral secession which is counterproductive or detrimental to conflict settlement. As discussed above, unilateral secession can be facilitated by external involvement such as military intervention and problematic recognition, so external actors should consciously abstain from such kind of external involvement. Otherwise an external actor will contribute to a pending situation that affects the maintenance of international peace and security.

The case of Nagorno-Karabakh has also demonstrated that a peace process is indeed long and delicate: more than 20 years after the unilateral declaration of independence, the OSCE Minsk Group co-chaired by France, the Russian Federation, and the United States is still making efforts to find a peaceful solution to the Nagorno-Karabakh conflict. Meanwhile, the opinion that unilateral secession is not an optimal solution to secessionist conflicts has gained acceptance: in the report entitled *The conflict over the Nagorno-Karabakh region dealt with by the OSCE Minsk Conference,* the rapporteur mentioned the conclusion made by Andreas Gross, the Rapporteur of the CoE Parliamentary Resolution 1334 (2003), that "regional autonomy with a high degree of self-government may be a better solution than secession and independence".[95] Obviously, external actors in this case have realized that unilateral secession as a means cannot contribute positively to the settlement of the secessionist conflict. What deserves additional attention is that external actors in the case of Nagorno-Karabakh opposed unilateral secession through non-recognition of de facto secession. This point is particularly thought-provoking, given that there is much room for improvement in the response of external actors to de facto secession.

[93]See Chap. 1, Note 23.
[94]See above Note 3.
[95]See above Note 89.

5.5 Pursuing a More Reasonable Response to De Facto Secession

In the dissenting opinion of Judge Bennouna regarding the Kosovo case, it is stated that "while the Court cannot substitute itself for the Security Council in exercising its responsibilities, nor can it stand legal guarantor for a policy of fait accompli based simply on who can gain the upper hand."[96] Obviously, Judge Bennouna has already realized that the ICJ could make mistakes such as endorsing de facto secession. If external actors such as the ICJ cannot be immune from making mistakes of this kind, there is reason to worry that other external actors might also fail to respond reasonably to de facto secession. Therefore, discussing the response of external actors to de facto secession is certainly meaningful, with a view to improving external involvement in the settlement of secessionist conflicts: a more reasonable response to de facto secession, which can contribute positively to conflict settlement, is definitely worth pursuing, and one needs to consider why this response is more reasonable than that one from a legal point of view.

5.5.1 *Nullus Commodum Capere Potest De Injuria Sua Propria*

In general, responses of external actors to de facto secession fall into two categories: recognition and non-recognition. Judge Bennouna implied in his dissenting opinion that refusing to endorse de facto secession is well-advised for the ICJ. The OSCE Minsk Group has adopted a similar approach so there was non-recognition to de facto secession of Nagorno-Karabakh. Although the issue regarding recognition and non-recognition has already been much discussed above, a new perspective regarding this issue is to be revealed here with a view to rendering the external response to de facto secession more reasonable. In the first place, it should be noted that de facto secession is established on the infringement of the right to self-determination of non-secessionists over territorial interests. In this sense, one can conclude that de facto secession is created by wrongful acts of secessionists and any external involvement that contributes to the infringement of the right to self-determination of non-secessionists should also be deemed wrongful. In such circumstances, the well-known Latin maxim *nullus commodum capere potest de injuria sua propria*, which can be regarded as an aspect of the legal principle of good faith[97] enshrined in the UN Charter, deserves serious attention. According to this maxim, a legal actor cannot be allowed to derive any advantage from its own wrongful acts, so in cases of

[96]Accordance with International Law of the Unilateral Declaration of Independence in Respect of Kosovo, Dissenting Opinion of Judge Bennouna, I.C.J. Reports 2010, p. 505, para. 25.
[97]Cheng (1987), p. viii.

de facto secession which can be attributed to wrongful acts of secessionists and some external actors, one should consider preventing these wrong doers from profiting from the fait accompli. For this sake, non-recognition is required to prevent wrong doers from exploiting de facto secession deliberately created by themselves.

Restating this Latin maxim is of practical significance in settling secessionist conflicts as secessionists and external actors invariably intend to derive advantage from their own wrongful acts. The typical wrongful act of secessionists in this regard has been much discussed in Chaps. 3 and 4, namely actively provoking massive retaliation of the central government, "because they rely on thereby-triggered interventions as decisive help in overcoming the respective states' military, administrative, and financial superiority".[98] With the help of external intervention de facto secession is no more an unattainable goal for secessionists as demonstrated in the case of Kosovo and Nagorno-Karabakh. Undeniably, de facto secession has actually placed non-secessionists at a disadvantage: they have been deprived of their legal right to dispose of territorial interests shared with secessionists, and the deprivation gets more severe when de facto secession is recognized by external actors. Obviously, external recognition of the status quo arising out of wrongful acts of secessionists renders it more difficult for non-secessionists to restore their right to dispose of territorial interests and in such circumstances, secessionists can derive advantage from their own wrongful acts: they first deliberately create de facto secession in disregard of the right to self-determination of non-secessionists then profit from external recognition of the fait accompli to the detriment of the right of non-secessionists. If external actors refuse to recognize de facto secession, the situation for non-secessionists to restore their right to dispose of territorial interests will not be rendered that difficult and secessionists cannot profit so much from de facto secession deliberately created by themselves. From this perspective, non-recognition is certainly the more reasonable response of external actors to de facto secession both in theory and in practice.

Now one must consider the case that external actors intend to derive advantage from their own wrongful acts. This point should be understood in combination with geopolitical interests mainly discussed in Chap. 4. Undeniably, for the sake of geopolitical interests, an external actor can work actively in cooperation with secessionists to the detriment of the right to self-determination of non-secessionists over territorial interests. The decisive assistance offered by India to secessionists of East Pakistan is a case in point. "Pakistan's role in South Asia as a reasonably effective counter to India's status as the dominant power in the region would be seriously undermined, in part because the remnant Pakistan was likely to identify itself more with the Islamic states of Southwest Asia than with South Asia once East Pakistan had been lost."[99] The NATO intervention in support of Kosovo secessionists seems to be of a similar nature: according to Diana Johnstone, "the whole thrust of U.S. policy has been toward a violent conflict in Yugoslavia that would shatter

[98]See Chap. 1, Note 6.

[99]See Chap. 2, Note 125.

Serbia, the last bastion of old-fashioned independence in the Balkans, and bring NATO in as occupier and arbiter. The United States did not want to bring Yugoslavia into NATO, but NATO into Yugoslavia... a circle of strategic policy planners looking for the means to transform NATO from a West European defense alliance focused on containing the Soviet Union into the military arm of U.S. global hegemony, able to act anywhere in the world without regard to national sovereignty, the United Nations or international law".[100] Russia's use of force in Crimea can be interpreted in the same vein: "in the eyes of Russian leaders, EU expansion is a stalking horse for NATO expansion... this is Geopolitics 101: great powers are always sensitive to potential threats near their home territory."[101] The list can go on and on... Recognition granted by external actors is a part of cooperation with secessionists with a view to boosting their own geopolitical interests.

Given that legal actors cannot be allowed to derive any advantage from its own wrongful acts, there is no reason to indulge the pursuit of geopolitical interests of external actors at the expense of the right to self-determination of non-secessionists over territorial interests in secessionist conflicts. That is to say, when confronted with de facto secession created with the help of external actors that aim to boost their own geopolitical interests, other external actors need to demonstrate a dissenting attitude, such as non-recognition. Undeniably, when there is no such dissenting attitude, it somewhat amounts to kind of acquiescence to the pursuit of geopolitical interests of external actors at the expense of the right to self-determination of non-secessionists over territorial interests in secessionist conflicts. Worse still, it can provide incentives for other powerful external actors to take similar approach in pursuit of geopolitical interests. As noted by Oeter, the use of force by Russia in Crimea can be seen as "a kind of revenge for the violation of international law that the US and EU committed in the Kosovo case... if the US thinks it reasonable to violate international legal rules when it serves its interests, why should Russia desist from ignoring international law when its fundamental interests are at stake?"[102] Therefore, one can conclude that when a powerful external actor cannot be stopped from helping create de facto secession for pursuing its own geopolitical interests, at least a dissenting attitude towards such wrongful acts needs to be demonstrated: other external actors should refrain from granting recognition. This kind of non-recognition not only reflects respect for the right to self-determination of non-secessionists over territorial interests in secessionist conflicts, but also discourages external actors from pursuing geopolitical interests in this way. Otherwise it would help an external actor having assisted in secession profit from its own wrongful acts: when de facto secession gradually becomes de jure independence thanks to external recognition, the pursuit of geopolitical interests is consummated.

In view of the foregoing, the more reasonable response to de facto secession is non-recognition, in order to prevent wrong doers from further violating the right to

[100]See above Note 3.

[101]See Chap. 4, Note 161.

[102]See Chap. 4, Note 166.

self-determination of non-secessionists over territorial interests in secessionist conflicts. The well-known Latin maxim *nullus commodum capere potest de injuria sua propria*, as an aspect of the legal principle of good faith, should be applied here. When wrong doers can always profit from their wrongful acts, it is certainly unrealistic to expect that wrongful acts can be replaced by rightful ones, and in such circumstances it is meaningless to discuss any improvement in external involvement in the settlement of secessionist conflicts. Only when it becomes difficult for wrong doers to profit from their own wrongful acts does the replacement for wrongful acts seem likely, so this point is closely related to improvement in external involvement in the settlement of secessionist conflicts. To be more specific, if secessionists and external actors are less likely to profit as much as they have wished from de facto secession, they will be less motivated to create de facto secession through wrongful acts, and non-recognition is a means of reducing the advantage they wish to derive from de facto secession arising out of their wrongful acts.

5.5.2 Considering a Fair Distribution of Territorial Interests

It is noteworthy that non-recognition is meaningful not only because it is in accordance with the Latin maxim *nullus commodum capere potest de injuria sua propria*, but also because it is usually the best way an external actor can contribute to a fair distribution of territorial interests between secessionists and non-secessionists when confronting de facto secession. External recognition of de facto secession, particularly granted by powerful external actors, has a practical influence on the distribution of originally shared territorial interests of secessionists and non-secessionists. If this practical influence contributes to a fair distribution, it is certainly unproblematic. However, it has been proved that external actors actually lack the ability to distribute territorial interests between conflicting parties in a fair manner. As demonstrated in the case of Western Sahara, insuperable technical obstacles exist for external actors in search of definite evidence to confirm whether legal ties between inhabitants and territory are of a nature which can affect the application of the principle of self-determination. In the Western Sahara case Judge Petrén and Judge de Castro depicted these insuperable technical obstacles:

> It is true that each judge has had to struggle – as far as his knowledge of languages would allow – through the immense literature existing on the questions of African history to which reference was made, and has been able to inform his colleagues of the fruit of his reading. It is nevertheless striking that the Advisory Opinion should be based almost exclusively on the documents and arguments submitted by the interested States, which are accepted or dismissed in the light of an examination of the evidence adduced. One does not find here the margin of uncertainty in which an advisory opinion ought to leave the facts which have neither been proved nor disproved.[103]

[103] Western Sahara, Advisory Opinion, Separate Opinion of Judge Petrén, I.C.J. Reports 1975, p. 113.

> In any case, as regards the existence of those ties, the Court had nothing to go on, in my opinion, except vivid and touching descriptions of desert life – but no concrete facts about the beneficiary tribes or about the places subject to those ties which would fulfil the conditions required of evidence to be submitted to a court.[104]

If an external actor like the ICJ finds it extremely difficult to ascertain whether legal ties between inhabitants and territory are of a nature which can affect the application of the principle of self-determination, it is reasonable to conclude that other external actors tend to find themselves in the same difficulty when confronting secessionist conflicts. From this perspective, external recognition of de facto secession definitely requires reconsideration. One might argue that recognition of de facto secession does not need so much strenuous exploration as demonstrated in the case of Western Sahara: recognition here does not mean a recognition of the exclusive territorial interests based on the right to secessionist self-determination and it is only a recognition of a fact. Nevertheless, one needs to inquire: given that the recognition of de facto secession renders it more difficult for non-secessionists to restore their right to self-determination over territorial interests, is it justifiable to recognize a fact in disregard of the difficulty thereby caused for non-secessionists? Just like directly recognizing the exclusive territorial interests based on the right to secessionist self-determination, a simple recognition of de facto secession is also to the detriment of territorial interests of non-secessionists. As a matter of fact, although external actors having recognized de facto secession can argue that they have no intention of endorsing secessionist self-determination, it is undeniable that in practice there is no much difference between a recognition of de facto secession and an endorsement of secessionist self-determination: an endorsement of secessionist self-determination is flagrantly flouting non-secessionist self-determination, while recognition of de facto secession is flouting non-secessionist self-determination in a concealed manner. Therefore, with a view to respecting the right to self-determination of non-secessionists over territorial interests, recognition of de facto secession should not be granted by external actors, as such recognition actually disadvantages non-secessionists in secessionist conflicts.

At such time one needs to consider the ignorance about the fair distribution of territorial interests between secessionists and non-secessionists in combination with facilitating negotiation between them, in order to understand the importance of non-recognition in improving external involvement in the settlement of secessionist conflicts. As external actors know little about a fair distribution of territorial interests between secessionists and non-secessionists, for the sake of the settlement of a secessionist conflict, it is certainly well-advised for them to help create lex specialis addressing the issue of distribution. Facilitating negotiation between secessionists and non-secessionists is contributing to the creation of lex specialis: the agreement achieved between secessionists and non-secessionists and facilitated by external involvement can effectively fill the gap of general international law in respect of self-determination conflicts. As discussed in Chap. 2, recognition of de facto

[104]Western Sahara, Advisory Opinion, Separate Opinion of Judge de Castro, I.C.J. Reports 1975, p. 172.

secession is detrimental to the negotiation between secessionists and non-secessionists: if the negotiation is not closed, any recognition of independence will inevitably tip the scale in favor of the secessionist entity, which clearly prejudices the sovereign state on behalf of non-secessionists. To put it simply, the effective settlement of secessionist conflicts requires a fair distribution of territorial interests between secessionists and non-secessionists, but general international law cannot provide the required distribution and external actors know little about it, so lex specialis addressing the issue of distribution should be created in such circumstances, and external actors should contribute to the creation of lex specialis instead of doing a disservice, and therefore they should facilitate negotiation between secessionists and non-secessionists rather than grant recognition of de facto secession.

5.6 Considering the Influence of the Mass Media in Conflict Settlement

The influence of the mass media on the settlement of a secessionist conflict has been noticed by the Parliamentary Assembly of the Council of Europe in dealing with the case of Nagorno-Karabakh: "the Assembly condemns any expression of hatred portrayed in the media of Armenia and Azerbaijan. The Assembly calls on Armenia and Azerbaijan to foster reconciliation and to restore confidence and mutual understanding among their peoples through schools, universities and the media. Without such reconciliation, hatred and mistrust will prevent stability in the region and may lead to new violence. Any sustainable settlement must be preceded by and embedded in such a reconciliation process."[105] Undeniably, this insight should be applied to not only the case of Nagorno-Karabakh but also other secessionist conflicts in a broader sense: the mass media do not only influence reconciliation between conflicting parties but also external involvement in secessionist conflicts. For this reason, in order to improve external involvement in the settlement of secessionist conflicts, it becomes necessary to consider the issue how the mass media can influence external involvement in secessionist conflicts from the perspective of international law.

5.6.1 *The Distorted Media Coverage and the Ill-Informed Public*

"At the height of the First World War the Prime Minister, David Lloyd George, confided to C.P. Scott, editor of the Manchester Guardian: 'If people knew the truth,

[105]Council of Europe—Parliamentary Assembly Resolution 1416 (2005), para. 11.

the war would be stopped tomorrow. But they don't know and can't know.'"[106] Obviously, it was a sad story about the suppression of truth and the ill-informed public: because the public at that time was ill-informed, it failed to make the right decision. From this perspective, one can well understand why it is stated in Article 19(2) of the ICCPR that "everyone shall have the right to freedom of expression; this right shall include freedom to seek, receive and impart information and ideas of all kinds, regardless of frontiers, either orally, in writing or in print, in the form of art, or through any other media of his choice". In the settlement of secessionist conflicts, this point is no less important: the right decision is based on sufficient information, and sufficient information is largely dependent on the objective and fair media coverage at which the emphasis on freedom of expression is aimed. Unfortunately, the coverage of secessionist conflicts sometimes proves to be distorted, rendering the access to sufficient information quite difficult for the public: at such time people were supplied with the tailored truth rather than the original one. It did not only cast a shadow on the right to freedom of expression but also contribute negatively to conflict settlement.

A typical case is "the US Media's transformation of Kosovo's civil war into a one-sided ethnic holocaust"[107]: journalists followed the Secretary of State Albright in her description of the violence in Kosovo "as an anti-Albanian pogrom, rather than a civil war between security forces and rebel guerrillas".[108] Of course, journalists could argue that it was their way of exercising the right to freedom of expression; nevertheless, there is no denying that under such circumstances the right of the public to information was certainly at a discount: "eliminating one party from the description of each of these conflicts does not help readers to understand the situations in all their complexity; but it does help to simplify the conflict so that those without additional information will see that the side supported by Washington are the 'good guys', and the other side are the 'bad guys'."[109] Undoubtedly, when the people in the US were not well-informed about what was happening, they could not wisely decide what their country should do to settle this conflict. The coverage of what happened in Racak is a case in point: "CNN reported the story intensively but uncritically. It never mentioned that the Serb action was carried out with TV and OSCE observers invited and present, who along with a French journalist were in and around the villages for many hours, but said nothing about a massacre before the presentation of the corpses in a gully the following day. The account of the incident by the two Associated Press TV reporters who filmed the operation, cited in both Le Monde and Le Figaro, contradicted the conclusions of William Walker and the KLA, but was never picked up by CNN. CNN's one reporter who had the chance to see the bodies reported that they had been deliberately mutilated. But forensic tests by a Finnish investigating team as well as by Serb and Belorussian experts denied this

[106] Pilger (2000), p. 132.

[107] Ackerman and Naureckas (2000), p. 100.

[108] Ibid. p. 99.

[109] Ibid. p. 100.

and explained the damage as a result of animal bites (probably from packs of hungry stray dogs, numerous in Kosovo), contradictory evidence that went unreported by CNN".[110] Perhaps CNN thought it was their freedom to tailor the truth, but from the perspective of the right of the public to information, it is really hard to conclude that such freedom is in the spirit of the right to freedom of expression provided in Article 19 of the ICCPR. Worse still, given the words of Lloyd George mentioned above, it is reasonable to deduce that the US people might have promoted their country to play a real constructive role in the Kosovo conflict but unfortunately, they were deprived of the chance to do so because they had been ill-informed about the original truth.

The situation in the motherland of Lloyd George was not more optimistic. "What one media commentator dubbed 'the war of Simpson's voice' became an important sub-plot of coverage of the Kosovo conflict, after anonymous government sources rubbished the BBC's John Simpson for allegedly broadcasting 'pro-Serb' reports from Belgrade. In the House of Commons, in the heat of this war of words, Tory MP Edward Garnier asked Prime Minister Tony Blair publicly to repeat the allegations against Simpson which had been widely ascribed to the Prime Minister's official spokesman, Alastair Campbell. 'He's entitled to present what report he likes', Blair said of John Simpson in reply to Garnier, 'and we are perfectly entitled to say that these reports are provided under the guidance and instruction of the Serbs. That is the proper way to conduct a democracy.'"[111] Although Blair and his official spokesman might believe that democracy allows them to accuse journalists without providing corresponding evidence, there is no denying that this kind of action could not encourage journalists to express freely, and the public could hardly gain access to information which could be suspected of being "pro-Serb". To the satisfaction of the Prime Minister, most media organizations in Great Britain actively rejected leaving an impression of being pro-Serb, perhaps overly actively: "on 29 March [1999] the Daily Mail's front page reported, beneath a picture of Kosovo Albanian children in a lorry, headlined 'Flight from Genocide': 'Their terrified and bewildered faces evoke memories of the Holocaust'. On 1 April, the Daily Mirror ran a front-page picture of refugees with a mother and child picked out in black and white, *Schindler's List* Style. Under the headline '1939 or 1999?' it reported that 'Nazi style terror came to Kosovo yesterday in a horrific echo of the wartime Holocaust'."[112] Obviously, by nazifying the Serbs a media organization could certainly get rid of a pro-Serb image; the problem is that nazifying the Serbs was actually sowing hatred: if in the case of Nagorno-Karabakh sowing hatred was deemed counterproductive to conflict settlement, there was no reason to believe that sowing hatred could play a positive role in the settlement of the Kosovo conflict. Another inevitable problem of nazifying the Serbs is that it totally disregarded the fact that Serbs were longtime victims of violence caused by Kosovo secessionists who intended to establish what they call an ethnically clean Albanian republic and then merge with Albania to form a greater

---

[110]Ibid. p. 118.

[111]Hume (2000), p. 70.

[112]Ibid. p. 72.

Albania.[113] What the British people need regarding the Kosovo conflict is not hatred against one conflicting party but the truth, whether it sounds pro-Serb or not: in the parlance of John Simpson, "it's important that people should know about it when it happens, just as they should know when things are going well".[114] The British people were unlikely to prompt their country to make a positive contribution to conflict settlement, when reports suspected of being pro-Serb were deliberately avoided and the pattern for nazifying the Serbs became well-developed. To some extent, the British people at the end of the twentieth century suffered the same fate as their ancestors in the First World War: they don't know and can't know.

In Germany the situation was somewhat similar. According to Albrecht Reinhardt, head of the foreign section of Westdeutscher Rundfunk: "for us this time it is about the German government which has gone to the war willingly and convincingly. And in this situation the propaganda apparatus of the government attains a new quality. I have not known any Minister of Defense like Mr. Scharping, who went before the press with photos and requested us to describe exactly what he perceived therefrom. In interviews interposed questions were no more allowed. As if he must convince himself of what he said there."[115] Scharping definitely could form his own opinion about the Kosovo issue, but as the Minister of Defense requesting others to follow his opinions is something unrelated to Article 19 of the ICCPR. What the public need was not only the opinion of the Minister of Defense but also what really happened; when the public only knew the opinion of the Minister of Defense and thought it was what really happened, they could not make their own decision and were made to follow the decision of politicians without being aware of it. It is noteworthy that in response to problems existing in the coverage, the German Press Council, an independent agency which monitors compliance with professional standards, published a statement on 19 May 1999 restating the most basic concepts of war reporting[116]: journalists should not downplay or even glorify the war in their reports; journalist should not allow themselves to be exploited for interests of warring parties; euphemistic expressions like "collateral damage" or "ethnic cleansing" should be avoided, and the military language is not allowed to dominate the media language; journalists should keep distance from all sources of information; sources must be exactly recognizable, and when it is impossible, the difficulty of acquiring this information must be illustrated; background must be elaborately

[113]See above Note 92.

[114]Simpson (2008), p. 9.

[115]It is the translation of the author; the original text is: "Wir haben es diesmal mit einer deutschen Regierung zu tun, die willentlich und mit Überzeugung in diesen Krieg gegangen ist. Und in dieser Situation erreicht der Propaganda-Apparat der Regierung eine neue Qualität. Ich habe noch keinen Verteidigungsminister erlebt, der wie Herr Scharping mit Fotos vor die Presse gegangen ist und uns aufforderte, genau das zu beschreiben, was auch er daraus erkenne. Der in Interviews keine Zwischenfragen mehr zulassen will. Als müsse er sich selbst von dem überzeugen, was er da sagt.", Menschen Machen Medien, Heft 7/1999, https://mmm.verdi.de/beruf/wer-kritische-fragen-stellt-rechtfertigt-den-kriegsgegner-28529, last accessed on 15.06.2018.

[116]Deichmann (2000), p. 153.

displayed.[117] Undoubtedly, when these basic concepts are well observed, the public can have better access to the truth rather than emotions, particularly hatred. Unfortunately, given that the Press Council found it necessary to repeat these basic journalistic standards, it is not wrong to deduce that these standards were not well observed and the right of the public to information and their right to decide how to react, which were largely dependent on the information they received, were therefore severely affected.

In France a media person was also under pressure when he or she was considered as "being pro-Serb". "Régis Debray, who undertook to go see what was happening in Serbia, including Kosovo province, during the NATO bombing in May 1999. Debray reported that NATO bombs had struck civilian targets such as schools and factories; that Milosovic was an autocratic, manipulative leader without 'totalitarian' charisma, largely ignored by the population, and not the Hitlerian 'dictator' denounced by NATO; that Yugoslavia was a multiparty state without political prisoners and governed by a Constitution; that the Serbian exactions against Kosovo Albanians began with the NATO bombing and lasted three days; that ethnic Albanians had fled for a number of reasons, but that many had stayed behind or since returned; in short, that there was no 'genocide'; and that NATO was visibly not succeeding in destroying the Yugoslav army, which seemed to be in great shape... Debray wrote his main article as a 'letter of a traveler to the President of the Republic'. He warned President Jacques Chirac that the reality did not correspond to the official NATO version that Chirac himself was conveying."[118] Unlike Simpson in the UK, who was directly slandered by the Prime Minister, the thought policing here was conducted by other media elite. For example, Bernard-Henri Lévy's answering column declared: "once upon a time Mr Debray had courage and talent. He was one of our last great adventurers. But now I can only look on with astonishment and great sadness. This is the suicide of an intellectual. Farewell, Régis."[119] Libération, which favored the pro-war camp headed by the philosophers André Glucksmann and Pascal Bruckner, devoted its first six pages to a point-by-point rebuttal of Debray's letter, which culminated in the words: "Such rabid anti-Americanism can lead anywhere, including to concealed support for Slobodan Milosevic. Tough luck for the facts, and tough luck for 900,000 refugees".[120] As observed by Diana Johnstone, "what Debray stimulated was an uproar designed to ban dissent and close ranks around the official version", rather than a constructive debate about the war.[121] Undoubtedly, it deserves serious consideration whether this kind of media atmosphere is actually conducive to freedom to seek, receive and

---

[117]Presserat mahnt zu Sorgfalt bei Informationen und Quellen im Kosovo-Krieg, http://www.bdzv.de/nachrichten-und-service/branchennachrichten/artikel/detail/presserat_mahnt_zu_sorgfalt_bei_informationen_und_quellen_im_kosovo_krieg/, last accessed on 15.06.2018.

[118]Johnstone (2000), p. 148.

[119]Henley (1999).

[120]Ibid.

[121]See above Note 118.

impart information and ideas of all kinds, particularly whether the public can be well-informed despite this kind of thought policing.

It must be noted that the distorted media coverage can also influence international lawyers, particularly those holding significant positions. As discovered by Hannum, human rights violations committed by secessionists did not diminish human rights violations by the authorities, but "they illustrate the difficulties the Court would have faced if it had attempted to determine whether or not Kosovo met the criteria for self-determination or remedial secession referred to in para. 82 of the Advisory Opinion and alluded to by Judges Cançado Trindade, Simma, and Yusuf".[122] Although unilateral secessionist self-determination or remedial secession as a solution to secessionist conflicts has been denied in the discussion above, the discovery made by Hannum with regard to secessionist self-determination or remedial secession is still noteworthy: even if secessionist self-determination or remedial secession is not denied, it does not mean that human rights violations committed by secessionists in pursuit of secessionist self-determination or remedial secession can therefore be condoned or even justified. That is to say, even for international lawyers in support of secessionist self-determination or remedial secession, they should take human rights violations committed by secessionists into account when arguing secessionist self-determination or remedial secession. Therefore, they must be well-informed about human rights violations committed by secessionists in the first place. When the coverage of a civil war is transformed into a one-sided ethnic holocaust, being well-informed about human rights violations committed by secessionists is definitely not easy.

It is time to review the Separate Opinions of Judge Yusuf and Judge Cançado Trindade. According to Judge Yusuf, international law does not turn "a blind eye to the plight of such groups, particularly in those cases where the State not only denies them the exercise of their internal right of self-determination, but also subjects them to discrimination, persecution and egregious violations of human rights or humanitarian law. Under such exceptional circumstances, the right of peoples to self-determination may support a claim to separate statehood provided it meets the conditions prescribed by international law"[123]; similarly, Judge Cançado Trindade argued that "what has happened in Kosovo is that the victimized 'people' or 'population' has sought independence, in reaction against systematic and long-lasting terror and oppression, perpetrated in flagrant breach of the fundamental principle of equality and non-discrimination".[124] Obviously, the judgement of these two judges is largely based on the picture of one-sided ethnic oppression rather than a civil war between security forces and rebel guerrillas: there is reason to doubt whether Judge Yusuf would still consider a right to secessionist self-determination in exceptional circumstances, if he had been well-informed that such exceptional circumstances had been deliberately provoked by secessionists; similarly, one can

[122]See above Note 4.

[123]See Chap. 2, Note 12.

[124]See Chap. 2, Note 13.

also doubt whether Judge Cançado Trindade would still argue that what had happened in Kosovo was that the victimized "people" or "population" had sought independence in reaction against systematic and long-lasting terror and oppression, if he had been well-informed that the oppression "was a response to the Kosovo Liberation Army's first major military offensive in early 1998 – not a provocation which led to the KLA's uprising",[125] and "by the mid-1990s Kosovo's Albanians had re-established a degree of de facto autonomy".[126]

To conclude, the issue regarding the distorted media coverage and the ill-informed public definitely deserves serious consideration, not only because it concerns the realization of the right of the public to information, but also because it influences external involvement in the settlement of secessionist conflicts. In short, improving external involvement in the settlement of secessionist conflicts is largely dependent on that the people know the truth, the original one rather than the tailored and emotionalized one.

5.6.2 *Rendering the Public Well-Informed in Conflict Settlement*

In view of the foregoing, it is clear that something should be done to reverse the distorted media coverage, otherwise it would be really difficult, if not impossible, to render the public well-informed for the sake of conflict settlement. In order to achieve this end, efforts made by the media, by the authorities and by international organizations is required. For the sake of the right of the public to receive information, the media should not take the freedom of expression as a freedom to tailor the truth: a whole story containing different or even contradicting statements needs to be presented to the public, even if the whole story actually taking place does not follow the keynote set by politicians. For example, despite the keynote set by the Secretary of State Madeleine Albright that the Kosovo crisis was an anti-Albanian pogrom, the media should still present to the public the whole story of the civil war between security forces and rebel guerrillas, as the people have the right to know the original truth. Only when they know what is actually happening can they decide how to react, particularly when war becomes an option.

In addition, the report should let the people know rather than provoke hatred. deliberate and improper emotionalization should be avoided. Returning to the issue of nazifying Serbs, it actually contributed nothing to rendering the people well-informed about the civil war: as noted by writer Julia Gorin, "it's not that I believe Jews have the monopoly on suffering. But some comparisons to the Holocaust are beyond offensive--especially when they're used to manipulate public support for a war that is as absurd as it is unjust... I don't recall reading that Jews in the 1930s

[125] Ackerman and Naureckas (2000), p. 98.
[126] Clark (2000), pp. 70–121.

wanted to detach Berlin and keep it for themselves. In German towns where Jews might have been the majority, I never heard of them killing minority German citizens... it has been the KLA's open mission to break Kosovo away from Yugoslavia and make it part of Greater Albania, cleansing the area of its remaining Serbs in the process... both sides are long-time enemies who have taken part in ethnic hatred and violent conflict against each other. The Albanians are not being systematically annihilated, without provocation, because of who they are. The adversaries are much more the moral equivalents of each other than the Jews and the Nazis were."[127] One should not forget that any external involvement in a secessionist conflict is intended for the effective settlement of the conflict rather than the release of hatred, particularly when the hatred itself is ill-founded.

Moreover, it is also necessary to maintain a normal debate-type atmosphere within the circle of media, for the sake of the public. The public can certainly benefit much more when the media elite can hold a normal debate, compared with the case that they close ranks around the official version to ban dissent. For an intricate secessionist conflict which is of multi-dimension, a thorough debate is by no means dispensable: in the absence of a thorough debate, several dimensions of the issue will not be revealed and not be taken into consideration by external actors involved in conflict settlement. In short, wise external involvement in secessionist conflicts requires the public to be well-informed, which necessitates a thorough public debate. When media elite are eager to close ranks around the official version to ban dissent, a thorough public debate is unlikely to be provoked. Under such circumstances, the scenario described by Lloyd George would recur: the people don't know and can't know so they are not in a position to contribute to the peaceful settlement of conflicts.

Then one needs to look at the authorities. Undeniably, the authorities should cooperate with the media with a view to rendering the public well-informed. Therefore, publicly slandering a journalist because his report failed to follow the official keynote regarding a secessionist conflict, as the former British Prime Minister Tony Blair and his spokesman have done, is certainly questionable: in this way the public knows only the fact tailored according to the official keynote, as journalists are largely discouraged from reporting the fact not in accordance with the official keynote. To some extent, this kind of official discouragement is undermining the right of the public to receive information, lowering their ability to constructively contribute to conflict settlement. When the authorities believe the coverage of a secessionist conflict is far away from the official keynote, they should consider whether the keynote itself accords with the fact or not. Similarly, it is also questionable when a politician requests the media to follow exactly his or her interpretation of photos taken in a secessionist conflict and allows no inquiries, as the former German Minister of Defense Rudolf Scharping has done. It is hardly the cooperation between the media and the authorities as envisioned in the freedom of expression and hardly the way the right of the public to information can be realized. After all, any

[127] Gorin (1999).

interpretation is hardly free from subjectivity, and relevant inquires can help reduce the subjectivity. Realizing the right of the public to information requires reducing subjectivity.

Now the focus should be shifted onto international organizations. As mentioned before, in dealing with the case of Nagorno-Karabakh, the Parliamentary Assembly of the Council of Europe condemns any expression of hatred portrayed in the media of Armenia and Azerbaijan. Undoubtedly, it proves that how an international organization can help reverse the distorted media coverage for the sake of conflict settlement. On this basis, it is reasonable to envisage that the UN can play a similar role in settling secessionist conflicts. For example, the UN can choose to condemn any expression of nazifying one conflicting party in the media of some countries or, following the example of Germany, the UN can restate the professional journalistic standards and code of ethics, such as "respect for truth and for the right of the public to truth is the first duty of the journalist".[128] More importantly, the UN can show great concern for issues like journalistic reports that are gratuitously criticized or directly instructed by domestic politicians in respect of secessionist crises: this concern might become kind of international pressure for domestic politicians like Blair and Scharping, rendering them less active in hampering journalistic reports regarding secessionist crises. In short, the UN should perform proactively in order to render the people worldwide well-informed about the whole picture of an existing secessionist conflict: when they know the truth, military intervention will be stopped and peaceful settlement will be upheld, so in this sense, they are the decisive power for improving external involvement in the settlement of secessionist conflicts.

5.7 Conclusions

Improving external involvement in the settlement of secessionist conflicts begins with a change in the mentality of external actors. They must learn to understand the inherent complexity of a secessionist conflict and endeavor to address it in a comprehensive manner. Solely focusing on human rights protection and ignoring a fair distribution of territorial interests between secessionists and non-secessionists will not help settle secessionist conflicts; worse yet, such an approach can contribute to the escalation of conflicts, which further complicates the issue.

In order to prevent conflict escalation, an arrangement aimed at promoting positive interplay between different actors in secessionist conflicts is required. Thus it is quite meaningful to consider standardizing external involvement in secessionist conflicts. External involvement should invariably help balance conflicting interests, and it should be noted that in practice conflicting interests exist not only between secessionists and non-secessionists but also between external

[128] International Federation of Journalists Declaration of Principles on the Conduct of Journalists, Para. 1, http://www.ifj.org/about-ifj/ifj-code-of-principles/, last accessed on 15.06.2018.

actors choosing to side with secessionists or non-secessionists. Balancing conflicting interests requires concerting the individual actions of internal and external actors, as the UN is a center for harmonizing the actions of nations for the maintenance of international peace and security, so it is necessary to consider improving the functioning of the UN in conflict settlement, and the key to such improvement is rendering the exercise of power by the Security Council and by other UN Organs more rational.

Mediation as a particularly important part of external involvement deserves particular consideration. In order to prevent abuse of mediating power by external actors, mediation needs to be standardized, which requires external actors working as mediators in conflict settlement to follow legally non-binding UN instruments and replacing unsuitable mediators. Given the failure of Ahtisaari as the mediator in the Kosovo case, the importance of eschewing artificial deadlines should be borne in mind: mediators should never confuse an early resolution of the conflict with an effective resolution of the conflict, and any decision regarding deadlines made by a mediator in disregard of self-determination of a conflicting party is problematic.

External recognition is another form of external involvement which has great impact on the settlement of secessionist conflicts. The significance of non-recognition must be recognized, as problematic recognition might lead to an aggravation of secessionist conflicts which threatens international peace and security. In such circumstances both the right to self-determination and human rights are in grave peril, which makes the fulfillment of the responsibility to protect more difficult for the UN. External actors should not confuse the wish of secessionists with the right of them: the legally groundless wish of secessionists to be independent is incompatible with the right to self-determination over territorial interests enjoyed by non-secessionists. Detrimental effects caused by unilateral secession should also be recognized by external actors.

Pursuing a more reasonable response to de facto secession is also noteworthy. According to the Latin maxim *nullus commodum capere potest de injuria sua propria*, the more reasonable response to de facto secession is non-recognition, in order to prevent wrong doers from deriving advantage from their own wrongful acts and thus further violating the right to self-determination of non-secessionists over territorial interests in secessionist conflicts. Non-recognition is meaningful not only because it is in accordance with this Latin maxim which can be regarded as an aspect of the legal principle of good faith enshrined in the UN Charter, but also because it is usually the best way an external actor can contribute to a fair distribution of territorial interests between secessionists and non-secessionists when confronting de facto secession.

The influence of the mass media in conflict settlement should no longer be ignored. The distorted media coverage renders the public ill-informed, which not only violates the right of the public to information but also affects their ability to decide what should be done to settle this conflict. Improving external involvement in the settlement of secessionist conflicts largely depends on that the people know the truth, the original one rather than the tailored and emotionalized one. In order to render the public well-informed, an effort made by the media, by the authorities and by international organizations is required.

References

Ackerman S, Naureckas J (2000) Following Washington's Script: The United States Media and Kosovo. In: Hammond P, Herman ES (eds) Degraded capability: the media and the Kosovo crisis. Pluto Press

Boyle A, Chinkin C (2007) The making of international law. Oxford University Press, p 233

Caplan R, Wolff S (2015) Some implications of the advisory opinion for resolution of the Serbia-Kosovo conflict. In: Milanovic M, Wood M (eds) The law and politics of the Kosovo Advisory Opinion. Oxford University Press, p 320

Cheng B (1987) General principles of law as applied by International Courts and Tribunals. The Burlington Press Ltd., Cambridge, p viii

Christakis T (2011) The ICJ Advisory Opinion on Kosovo: "Has International Law Something to Say about Secession?". Leiden J Int Law 24:86

Clark H (2000) Civil resistance in Kosovo. Pluto Press, pp 70–121

Deichmann T (2000) From 'Never again War' to 'Never again Auschwitz': dilemmas of German Media Policy in the war against Yugoslavia. In: Hammond P, Herman ES (eds) Degraded capability: the media and the Kosovo crisis (trans: Abbott S). Pluto Press, p 153

Gorin J (1999) 'Never again'? This isn't exactly what we had in mind. Jewish World Review, 29 April 1999. http://www.jewishworldreview.com/0499/words1.asp. Last accessed 15 June 2018

Hannum H (2011) The Advisory Opinion on Kosovo: "An Opportunity Lost, or a Poisoned Chalice Refused?". Leiden J Int Law 24

Henley J (1999) Debray's betrayal provokes Régiside. The Guardian, Saturday, 15 May 1999. https://www.theguardian.com/world/1999/may/15/jonhenley. Last accessed 15 June 2018

Howe M (1982) Exodus of Serbians Stirs Province in Yugoslavia. New York Times, 12 July 1982. http://www.nytimes.com/1982/07/12/world/exodus-of-serbians-stirs-province-in-yugoslavia.html. Last accessed 15 June 2018

Hume M (2000) Nazifying the Serbs, from Bosnia to Kosovo. In: Hammond P, Herman ES (eds) Degraded capability: the media and the Kosovo crisis. Pluto Press, p 70

Johnstone D (1998) Notes on the Kosovo problem and the International Community, Dialogue 25. https://www.phdn.org/archives/www.ess.uwe.ac.uk/Kosovo/Kosovo-controversies2.html. Last accessed 15 June 2018

Johnstone D (1999) Hawks and Eagles: 'Greater NATO' Flies to the Aid of 'Greater Albania'. Covert Action Quarterly 67. http://emperors-clothes.com/articles/Johnstone/hawks.html#3. Last accessed 15 June 2018

Johnstone D (2000) The French Media and the Kosovo War. In: Hammond P, Herman ES (eds) Degraded capability: the media and the Kosovo crisis. Pluto Press, p 148

Kuperman AJ (2008) The moral hazard of humanitarian intervention: lessons from the Balkans. Int Stud Q 52:57–58

Lehmann JM (2012) All necessary means to protect civilians: what the intervention in Libya says about the relationship between the Jus in Bello and the Jus ad Bellum. J Confl Secur Law 17:117

Locke J (2012) The second treatise of government. Philipp Reclam jun, Stuttgart

Malloy A, Treyz C (2016) Obama admits worst mistake of his presidency. https://edition.cnn.com/2016/04/10/politics/obama-libya-biggest-mistake/. Last accessed 15 June 2018

Merrills J (2010) The means of dispute settlement. In: Evans MD (ed) International law, 3rd edn. Oxford University Press, p 563

Oberg J (1999) Read the Civilian Rambouillet Kosovo Agreement, 17 March 1999. https://yugoslavia-what-should-have-been-done.org/1999/03/17/read-the-civilian-rambouillet-kosovo-agreement/. Last accessed 15 June 2018
Pilger J (2000) Censorship by omission. In: Hammond P, Herman ES (eds) Degraded capability: the media and the Kosovo crisis. Pluto Press, p 132
Radan P (2011) The Serb Krajina: an unsuccessful secession from Croatia. In: Pavkovic A, Radan P (eds) The Ashgate research companion to secession. Ashgate Publishing Limited, p 524
Rosenau JN (1964) Introduction. In: Rosenau JN (ed) International aspects of civil strife. Princeton University Press, pp 1 and 6
Simpson J (2008) Strange places, questionable people. Pan Macmillan Ltd, p 9
Troebst S (1998) Conflict in Kosovo: failure of prevention? An analytical documentation, 1992–1998. ECMI working paper no. 1. European Centre for Minority Issues, Flensburg, p 60
Wood MC (1998) The interpretation of security council resolutions. Max Planck Yearb United Nations Law 2:82

The manufacturer's authorised representative in the EU is Springer Nature Customer Service Centre GmbH, Europaplatz 3, 69115 Heidelberg, Germany. If you have any concerns regarding our products, please contact ProductSafety@springernature.com

Printed and bound by CPI Group (UK) Ltd, Croydon, CR0 4YY
05/10/2026
02228140-0014